How to Prepare for the
GRE
BIOLOGY

Graduate Record
Examination in Biology

How to Prepare for the
GRE
BIOLOGY

Graduate Record
Examination in Biology
Fourth Edition

JOHN A. SNYDER, PH.D., AND C. LELAND RODGERS, PH.D.

Furman University
Greenville, South Carolina

BARRON'S

All inquiries should be addressed to:
Barron's Educational Series, Inc.
250 Wireless Boulevard
Hauppauge, New York 11788

Library of Congress Catalog Card No. 97-7743
International Standard Book No. 0-8120-9654-1

Library of Congress Cataloging-in-Publication Data

Snyder, John A., 1943–
    GRE biology : how to prepare for the graduate record
examination in biology / John A. Snyder and C. Leland
Rodgers. — 4th ed.
        p.   cm.
    Includes index.
    ISBN 0-8120-9654-1
    1. Biology—Examinations, questions, etc.   I. Rodgers,
C. Leland (Charles Leland), 1918–   . II. Title.
QH316.S64   1997
570'.76—dc21   97-7743
                                                                        CIP

PRINTED IN THE UNITED STATES OF AMERICA
987654321

Table of Contents

Part 1.   **Information About the Biology Subject Test**   1

Part 2.   **Tests in Biology**   13

        Sample Test 1   13
        Answer Key for Sample Test 1   47
        Answer Explanations for Sample Test 1   48

        Sample Test 2   63
        Answer Key for Sample Test 2   99
        Answer Explanations for Sample Test 2 100

        Sample Test 3 113
        Answer Key for Sample Test 3 149
        Answer Explanations for Sample Test 3 150

        Sample Test 4 163
        Answer Key for Sample Test 4 202
        Answer Explanations for Sample Test 4 203

Part 3.   **Review Aids** 219

        Glossary 279

PART 1

Information About the Biology Subject Test

Purposes of the Biology Subject Test

The primary purpose of the Biology Subject Test is to evaluate the accomplishments of biology majors. Both the student and the graduate school can use an individual's score as a basis for comparing his or her performance with the performances of a large number of other people at the same educational level. Such a comparison can be useful to ascertain a person's qualifications for pursuing certain types of advanced study and the probability of success in a particular course of study. It often serves also as a basis for preference in the granting of fellowships and other awards.

Although a minimum score for eligibility to graduate school has been set by many universities, that score is seldom if ever the sole criterion for acceptance. Rather, it is used in conjunction with scholastic records, recommendations, a personal interview, motivation, and/or evidence of improvement. Similarly, the examination score alone will not necessarily qualify a person to receive a fellowship.

The Biology Subject Test is also useful as evidence of strengths and weaknesses because the grade includes subscores for major subject-matter areas. Students may use the subscores to evaluate their own qualifications, or the graduate school may use them for counseling and placement.

Content of the Biology Subject Test

Presumably the test covers the content of undergraduate biology curricula. It changes constantly to keep pace with developments in science. At the same time, it includes a core of information that is considered basic to the field.

The questions are divisible into three categories representing different levels of organization. They are *cellular and molecular biology, organismal biology,* and *ecology and evolution,* each represented by approximately one third of the questions.

The cellular and molecular level covers the cell as a functional and structural unit, as well as its chemical composition. Obviously this category includes the atoms, molecules, macromolecules, and organelles that comprise the cell. A study of this level of organization of necessity involves energy transformations in photosynthetic and respiratory pathways plus the replication of cellular components and cells. Other related topics are Mendelian inheritance, molecular genetics, immunobiology, viral replication, and the cell cycle.

The organismal level deals with all aspects of the biology of individual organisms. Among the subjects covered are function, structure, growth, development, homeostatic mechanisms, animal behavior, diseases, aging, and the diversity of life (classification, features, life cycles). Emphasis is placed on vertebrate animals and seed plants.

The ecology and evolution level deals with the responses of groups of similar (interbreeding) organisms to genetic and environmental influences, relationships within communities and ecosystems, evolution and systematics, energy flow and cycling, community homeostasis, and human impact on the ecosystem.

Student Preparation for the Test

Because curricula in colleges differ so much and there is almost always some latitude in selecting courses in the major, each student has a highly individualized course of training. Furthermore, each reaches a certain level of competence in relation to his or her ability and dedication to achievement. Therefore each student approaches the examination uniquely trained.

In view of the broad coverage of subject matter and the unequal preparation of candidates, no biology student can expect to answer all of the questions on the test: Students may even fall short of achieving the goals they have set for themselves. Since so much is at stake, many students try to improve their chances by reviewing material not completely mastered and studying subjects to which they have had little or no exposure. One thing is certain—the more information you possess, the better you will do. Mastering the information included in this book is one way to increase your knowledge.

Of course, most of a student's preparation will have occurred in the form of taking appropriate courses in the biological and chemical sciences. Before taking the Biology Subject Test, one should review class notes and materials from broad-based undergraduate courses such as genetics, ecology, animal physiology, and plant physiology. Of particular value would be a systematic study of a large general biology textbook, such as is typically used in a two-semester introductory course for biology majors. A smaller book especially for general review has been written by the authors of the book you are now reading: *Biology* (in the College Review Series), published by Barron's Educational Series, Inc. It can be obtained in college bookstores or by writing Barron's at 250 Wireless Blvd., Hauppauge, NY 11788.

Whatever methods are used, it is essential to begin systematic review long before the Biology Subject Test is taken. Some would argue that the GRE General Test may not require intensive preparation since it does not deal with specific topics in great detail. However, the Biology Subject Test is quite specific and demands both detailed knowledge and skills in "thinking scientifically." Therefore, a good strategy would be to start through a general biology textbook several months before taking the test, dedicating some time almost every day to reviewing topics. As you reach each major topic, read the appropriate chapters in the general text, then go to whatever notes and study aids that you may have kept from a course in that topic.

The use of this GRE preparation book should not be saved until the last few days before the test. At least one of the four practice tests you will find here (in Part 2) should be taken early in the planned study period, to give an indication of the kinds of questions asked and the layout of the test. Be sure to read the comments and explanations that are part of the answer key at the end of each test. As you progress in your studies, use the review aids in Part 3. Save one practice test for a few days before taking the actual GRE, as a "warm-up" exercise.

When you have the Biology Subject Test in hand, you can do no more to prepare for it, but you should try to make the most of what you know. One ingredient contributing to maximum recall and application of information is confidence—or, at least, freedom from anxiety. Many students can attain a measure of calmness by remembering that they have a considerable amount of training, that no one can achieve perfection, and that success in life is not dependent on a single event such as the Biology Subject Test.

Sources of Additional Information

The Graduate Record Examinations, P.O. Box 6000, Princeton, NJ 08541-6000, will supply upon request a booklet entitled *GRE Biology Test.* It will be sent unsolicited, along with the admission ticket, to those who apply for the examination. Inquiries can be made by telephone to the Educational Testing Service: (609) 771-7670 (Princeton, NJ) or (510) 873-8100 (Oakland, CA). These calls must be made between 8:30 A.M. and 9:00 P.M. (local time) to Princeton or 8:15 A.M. and 4:30 P.M. (local time) to Oakland. ETS can also be contacted by e-mail, via the following address:

gre-info@ets.org

There is also a very useful World-wide Web (WWW) site maintained by the Educational Testing Service, just for information on the Graduate Record Examination. To reach these GRE pages, direct your Web browser to this address:

http://www.gre.org

Application forms and additional pertinent information about the Subject Tests and General Test are contained in the *GRE Information and Registration Bulletin,* available from most colleges' career planning offices and from the Educational Testing Service.

Nature of the Questions on the Test

Questions cover the broad content of undergraduate biology curricula and are divided among the cellular and molecular biology, organismal biology, and ecology and evolution components. Questions are designed to test the student's ability to apply information, interpret observations and data, and understand scientific methods. Some questions are based on graphs, diagrams, and experimental data. In short, the test is designed to measure the knowledge and skills that the examination committee considers most important for graduate study.

The test typically contains 200 questions of the multiple-choice type, each with five possible answers from which the student must select the most suitable one. The format of the questions, however, varies.

Some questions are straightforward and deal with a single item of information. Two possible variations in this type of question are as follows:

1. In which of the following pairs are the animals most closely related?   1. Ⓐ ● Ⓒ Ⓓ Ⓔ
   A. snake and fish
   B. frog and salamander
   C. bird and mammal
   D. nematode and annelid
   E. starfish and clam

2. The pyrimidine found in both DNA and RNA is   **2.** Ⓐ Ⓑ Ⓒ Ⓓ ●
    A. guanine
    B. thymine
    C. adenine
    D. uracil
    E. cytosine

Sometimes groups of questions are based on certain information given. For example, the next six questions are based on the drawing below:

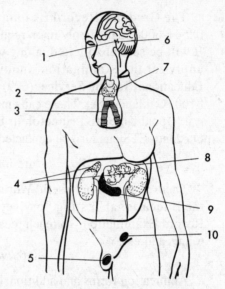

Locations of endocrine glands in the human.

1. This organ secretes both a hormone and enzymes.   **1.** Ⓐ Ⓑ Ⓒ ● Ⓔ
    A. 1
    B. 2
    C. 4
    D. 8
    E. 10

2. If this organ were removed, the metabolism of   **2.** Ⓐ Ⓑ Ⓒ ● Ⓔ
calcium and phosphorus would be drastically
upset.
    A. 1
    B. 3
    C. 4
    D. 7
    E. 9

3. There is a distinct homeostatic relationship   **3.** ● Ⓑ Ⓒ Ⓓ Ⓔ
between organs 4 and
    A. 1
    B. 3
    C. 6
    D. 7
    E. 8

4. Radioactive iodine is concentrated in gland   **4.** Ⓐ ● Ⓒ Ⓓ Ⓔ
   A. 1
   B. 2
   C. 5
   D. 6
   E. 10

5. The only gland directly influenced by the nervous   **5.** Ⓐ Ⓑ ● Ⓓ Ⓔ
system is
   A. 2
   B. 3
   C. 4
   D. 8
   E. 9

6. The only gland whose function is entirely hormonal   **6.** Ⓐ ● Ⓒ Ⓓ Ⓔ
is
   A. 5
   B. 7
   C. 8
   D. 9
   E. 10

In another type of question a group of five lettered headings (answers) are designated as A, B, C, D, and E. These are followed by several questions whose answers must be selected from the lettered headings. Any one of the lettered headings may be used more than once or not at all. The letter preceding the correct heading (answer) is then recorded on the answer sheet. A sample group of questions follows:

     A. bugs
     B. beetles
     C. flies
     D. aphids
     E. butterflies

1. have larvae called caterpillars   **1.** Ⓐ Ⓑ Ⓒ Ⓓ ●

2. have only two wings   **2.** Ⓐ Ⓑ ● Ⓓ Ⓔ

3. are the largest group of insects   **3.** Ⓐ ● Ⓒ Ⓓ Ⓔ

4. have chewing mouthparts   **4.** Ⓐ ● Ⓒ Ⓓ Ⓔ

5. are most closely related to cicadas   **5.** Ⓐ Ⓑ Ⓒ ● Ⓔ

Length of Test   The time allowed for the Biology Subject Test is 170 minutes. From reporting time to dismissal the testing period is about 3 hours, some of which is used for necessary preliminaries and for collecting materials when the test is finished. The three categories of subject matter—cellular and molecular biology, organismal biology, and ecology and evolution—are randomly scattered through the test. Typically, a test consists of 200 questions, but the number may vary slightly.

Taking the Test

Most examinees probably do better and save time by answering one question at a time instead of scanning the test first. Directions and questions should be read carefully. Since all questions are weighted equally, the easy ones should be answered first just in case time runs short. This is particularly important for the last portion of the test, which involves analysis of readings. Examinees should not spend an inordinate amount of time on a reading that is outside their area of expertise if there are other readings further on that will be easier for them. Rechecking questions is always advisable if time permits.

Before taking the test students should realize that some questions will be based on information to which they have never been exposed. They can leave some of the questions unanswered and still make a good score. The average score is based on correctly answering approximately half of the questions.

With respect to guessing, the examinee should keep in mind that a fraction of a point is deducted for each incorrect answer. It is probably unwise to guess if the subject matter is completely unknown, whereas it is probably advantageous if the material is somewhat familiar. Guessing is recommended when, by eliminating one or more answers, the student can arrive at what might be considered an "educated guess."

Understanding exactly how the score is calculated will show how much risk is involved in guessing. All correct answers count one point, unanswered questions count zero, and incorrect answers are deducted at the rate of a quarter of a point each. This evaluation is based on the fact that random guessing of five-choice questions results in one correct answer to four incorrect ones. Thus, if the examinee answers 120 questions correctly and 80 incorrectly, his or her raw score will be 120 minus 20, or 100. In general, if one or two of the five possible answers can be eliminated, it is advisable to guess among the remaining possibilities. *Caution:* The paper-based GRE General Test is *not* scored in the same way. For the General Test, there is no penalty for wrong answers; therefore no question should be left unanswered.

Who Prepares the Biology Test

The Educational Testing Service with the help of the American Institute of Biological Sciences, the Botanical Society of America, the Society for Integrative and Comparative Biology, and the Ecological Society of America, appoints a committee to plan and prepare the examination. The members represent different branches of biology, types of colleges, and geographical sections of the country. Their tenure is on a rotating basis, an arrangement that constantly brings in fresh ideas by new appointees and at the same time insures a continuity of policies.

In addition to determining the content and scope of the test, the committee of examiners writes questions. The examiners are assisted in this task by other subject matter specialists. Testing experts from the Educational Testing Service provide statistical information and expertise in the construction of tests. Before any question is approved, it is reviewed and, if necessary, revised to meet certain standards. Before the entire test is released for use, it must be approved by the committee.

Continuity and Uniformity of Tests

Although the Biology Subject Test is ever changing to incorporate new subject matter and to protect its security, the Educational Testing Service equates the different forms of the test by statistical procedures. This permits the comparability of test scores from different periods of time, so necessary to determine with accuracy the qualifications of students, the success of teaching, or the adequacy of a curriculum.

Scheduling of the Tests

Usually the General Test and Biology Subject Test are scheduled for the morning and afternoon of the same day for the convenience of students who have to take both of them. A student who is unwilling to take two tests consecutively can elect to take them on separate days. The reporting time for the General Test is usually 8:00 A.M.; for the Subject Test, 2:00 P.M. The first period ends at about 12:30 and the second at about 5:30.

Each year testing periods are scheduled on a nationwide basis. Recently, they have occurred in the months of November, December, and April. The Biology Subject Test is available in all of these periods. For the exact dates when tests are administered and the lead time necessary to meet all deadlines, such as admittance to a particular test and the report of grades to the proper place, a prospective candidate must consult the *GRE Information and Registration Bulletin* or a designated official in his or her college who advises on such matters.

The tests are given on Saturdays. If that day conflicts with the religious convictions of a candidate, he or she can arrange without any additional charge to take the test(s) on the Monday following, at the regular scheduled time.

You must take two things into consideration in selecting a test date: the advantage of waiting as long as possible to learn more biology, and the need to have scores ready at the proper time. To play it safe, you might want to take the test one scheduled period early to allow for any emergency that might arise.

Graduate school applications that include requests for fellowships or assistantships often have earlier dates for all supporting data, including GRE scores. The fall months of the senior undergraduate year are the latest you should wait to take the GRE if such financial aid is to be requested. Be sure to consult current graduate school catalogs for the exact deadlines.

Applying for the Test

To obtain tickets for tests, you must submit an official Registration Form for each test date. If the General and Biology Subject Tests are to be taken on the same day, only one form is used to register. Registration should be made in advance, not at the testing center. The Registration Form can be obtained from the Educational Testing Service or from college offices designated to handle testing or career planning.

Generally you should send the Registration Form about 5 weeks before the scheduled test in order to reserve a place and to avoid a penalty fee for late registration. A word of warning: deadlines established by the Educational Testing Service represent times of receipt in its office, not postmark dates. Early registration may be especially important if you wish to take the test in April, the last scheduled time of the academic year.

The completed Registration Form and the appropriate fee (check or money order) should be mailed to Educational Testing Service, P.O. Box 6004, Princeton, NJ 08541-6004.

Walk-in testing may be permitted at the testing center only if test materials and sufficient space are available. Since standby registration by this procedure is uncertain, students should not attempt it except in an emergency. It is much less likely that a specific unreserved Subject Test will be available than that an unreserved General Test will be available. If this method is attempted, the student should take a completed Registration Form to the test center. Test fees and an additional standby fee are payable at the test center. Arrive at the test center at least 15 minutes before the normal time.

If a student who has preregistered for a single test later decides to take a second one on the same day by walk-in, he or she may do so without additional charge provided that test materials and space are available. Instead of submitting a second Registration Form, he or she must use the registration number on the admission ticket to mark the answer sheet of the second test.

Places Where Tests are Administered

Numerous testing centers are located throughout the United States and in dozens of other countries. Centers in the United States are close enough so that candidates seldom have to travel more than 75 miles from home. Prospective candidates can find the nearest center by contacting the Educational Testing Service, or by consulting the *GRE Information and Registration Bulletin.*

Some of the testing centers administer tests on all of the nationwide testing dates, whereas others do not. Since some of them may add or delete testing dates, the current *GRE Information and Registration Bulletin* should be consulted.

The applicant for a particular test must indicate on the application blank the center of choice. The Educational Testing Service assigns the applicant to that center if at all possible.

Admission to Testing Center

For admission to the testing center an examinee must present an admission ticket from ETS and a means of identification. An identification document should contain your recent photograph and signature. Social security cards or credit cards are not acceptable because there is no way for the supervisor to know whether the person taking the test is the same person whose name is on the card.

Nobody (examinee or visitor) will be admitted to the examination room after the testing has started.

Regulations at Testing Centers

Examinees at all centers follow the same standard procedures and time schedules. The success of the testing process depends on cooperation with the supervisor and consideration for others. The supervisor has the authority to dismiss any person who engages in disruptive or irregular practices such as making noise, cheating, or failing to follow directions. The test of a person dismissed will not be graded.

For clarification of what is or is not permissible behavior, the supervisor should be consulted. Calculating is allowed if it is done only on the margins of the test booklets. Examinees wishing to leave the room must secure permission. Smoking, eating, or drinking is not permitted.

Bring: Ticket
Identification
Eraser
Three or four No. 2 (B or HB) pencils
Watch

Do not bring: Books
Rulers
Calculating devices or computers
Paper of any kind
Compasses
Beepers
Cellular phones
Radios
Watch alarms (with flashing lights or sounds)

Reporting Scores

Each examinee will receive a test score report unless he or she requests that the test not be scored. The scores are considered confidential and will not be sent to any place except those designated by the person taking the test. You can allow or forbid the sending of the score to your undergraduate institution by checking appropriate blanks on the Registration Form. In addition, you can indicate up to four other score recipients on the same form without paying an additional fee. Other recipients of scores can be designated at the time of registration or later by filling out a Request Form and paying a fee for each transcript.

Reports will be sent only to approved institutions of higher learning and to organizations granting fellowships. Most approved recipients are listed, along with identifying code numbers, in the *GRE Information and Registration Bulletin.* Once a request for a transcript is made, it cannot be canceled. The reports are mailed to all recipients 6 weeks after the testing date. The examinee can also obtain a test score by telephone, approximately 1 month after the test date, although other score recipients cannot use this service. There is a small additional fee for telephone reporting.

The reports are cumulative, giving all scores on file for the current year and the 5 previous years. To prevent a score from being recorded in the cumulative file, a request not to grade the test must be made to the test supervisor at the time of testing or be sent to and received by the Educational Testing Service within 7 days after the test. Graduate schools vary in their policies in regard to cumulative scores; some consider only the highest score, some use only the most recent score, some take an average of all scores.

Interpretation of Scores

Information on how to interpret scores is sent to each examinee with his or her score report. The score report includes two total score items, the *scaled score* and the *percentile.*

The raw score is obtained by subtracting a fraction of the wrong answers from the total of correct answers. It is then equated by statistical procedures to the scaled score so that the performance of students taking different forms of the test can be compared.

The percentile is the relative standing of an individual with respect to a specific group: that is, the percentage of examinees who made lower scaled scores. Because percentiles are percentage figures, they vary from 0 to 100.

In addition to a total scaled score and its percentile, a subscore will be reported for each of the three categories of biological knowledge. Subscores do not indicate a person's ability as reliably as the total score because each subscore is based upon fewer questions. Subscores do provide, however, some indication of where a person's relative strengths and weaknesses lie. Percentiles of the subscores are also given in the Score Interpretation Booklet that is sent with the score report.

The degree of reliance placed on the Biology Subject Test in relation to other methods of evaluation such as recommendations and the college transcript is variable. Also the relative values attached to the General Test and Biology Subject Test are not uniform. A specific graduate department may place more reliance on the General Test as a predictor of performance than on the Biology Subject Test.

A passing or failing grade is not established by the Educational Testing Service. A grade may be passing or failing according to standards set by the institution requiring the score. Some institutions refer to a *cut-off score,* meaning that they will not accept students scoring below that level. The cut-off score varies considerably from institution to institution, and many do not adhere to such strict guidelines.

How to Use the Sample Tests

Part 2 of this book consists of four sample tests similar to the GRE Biology Subject Test in style, content, and degree of difficulty. After each test is an answer key with explanations. The student should take each test under conditions simulating those of the actual Biology Subject Test. He or she may calculate a raw score for each test as described on page 6. It is impossible to determine whether the sample tests are of the *same* difficulty level as any *particular* GRE Biology Subject Test. However, if it is assumed that they are similar, a student may use the following table to make a rough estimate of the scaled score and percentile that would be calculated from the raw score:

Number of Correct Answers	Raw Score	Approximate Scaled Score	Approximate Percentile
152	140	880	99
116	95	700	75
98	72	610	50
80	50	550	25

Part 3 of this book is designed to strengthen a student's knowledge in areas of need, as diagnosed by his or her performance on one or more of the sample tests.

Answer Sheet for Sample Test 1

#		#		#		#	
1. Ⓐ Ⓑ Ⓒ Ⓓ Ⓔ		51. Ⓐ Ⓑ Ⓒ Ⓓ Ⓔ		101. Ⓐ Ⓑ Ⓒ Ⓓ Ⓔ		151. Ⓐ Ⓑ Ⓒ Ⓓ Ⓔ	
2. Ⓐ Ⓑ Ⓒ Ⓓ Ⓔ		52. Ⓐ Ⓑ Ⓒ Ⓓ Ⓔ		102. Ⓐ Ⓑ Ⓒ Ⓓ Ⓔ		152. Ⓐ Ⓑ Ⓒ Ⓓ Ⓔ	
3. Ⓐ Ⓑ Ⓒ Ⓓ Ⓔ		53. Ⓐ Ⓑ Ⓒ Ⓓ Ⓔ		103. Ⓐ Ⓑ Ⓒ Ⓓ Ⓔ		153. Ⓐ Ⓑ Ⓒ Ⓓ Ⓔ	
4. Ⓐ Ⓑ Ⓒ Ⓓ Ⓔ		54. Ⓐ Ⓑ Ⓒ Ⓓ Ⓔ		104. Ⓐ Ⓑ Ⓒ Ⓓ Ⓔ		154. Ⓐ Ⓑ Ⓒ Ⓓ Ⓔ	
5. Ⓐ Ⓑ Ⓒ Ⓓ Ⓔ		55. Ⓐ Ⓑ Ⓒ Ⓓ Ⓔ		105. Ⓐ Ⓑ Ⓒ Ⓓ Ⓔ		155. Ⓐ Ⓑ Ⓒ Ⓓ Ⓔ	
6. Ⓐ Ⓑ Ⓒ Ⓓ Ⓔ		56. Ⓐ Ⓑ Ⓒ Ⓓ Ⓔ		106. Ⓐ Ⓑ Ⓒ Ⓓ Ⓔ		156. Ⓐ Ⓑ Ⓒ Ⓓ Ⓔ	
7. Ⓐ Ⓑ Ⓒ Ⓓ Ⓔ		57. Ⓐ Ⓑ Ⓒ Ⓓ Ⓔ		107. Ⓐ Ⓑ Ⓒ Ⓓ Ⓔ		157. Ⓐ Ⓑ Ⓒ Ⓓ Ⓔ	
8. Ⓐ Ⓑ Ⓒ Ⓓ Ⓔ		58. Ⓐ Ⓑ Ⓒ Ⓓ Ⓔ		108. Ⓐ Ⓑ Ⓒ Ⓓ Ⓔ		158. Ⓐ Ⓑ Ⓒ Ⓓ Ⓔ	
9. Ⓐ Ⓑ Ⓒ Ⓓ Ⓔ		59. Ⓐ Ⓑ Ⓒ Ⓓ Ⓔ		109. Ⓐ Ⓑ Ⓒ Ⓓ Ⓔ		159. Ⓐ Ⓑ Ⓒ Ⓓ Ⓔ	
10. Ⓐ Ⓑ Ⓒ Ⓓ Ⓔ		60. Ⓐ Ⓑ Ⓒ Ⓓ Ⓔ		110. Ⓐ Ⓑ Ⓒ Ⓓ Ⓔ		160. Ⓐ Ⓑ Ⓒ Ⓓ Ⓔ	
11. Ⓐ Ⓑ Ⓒ Ⓓ Ⓔ		61. Ⓐ Ⓑ Ⓒ Ⓓ Ⓔ		111. Ⓐ Ⓑ Ⓒ Ⓓ Ⓔ		161. Ⓐ Ⓑ Ⓒ Ⓓ Ⓔ	
12. Ⓐ Ⓑ Ⓒ Ⓓ Ⓔ		62. Ⓐ Ⓑ Ⓒ Ⓓ Ⓔ		112. Ⓐ Ⓑ Ⓒ Ⓓ Ⓔ		162. Ⓐ Ⓑ Ⓒ Ⓓ Ⓔ	
13. Ⓐ Ⓑ Ⓒ Ⓓ Ⓔ		63. Ⓐ Ⓑ Ⓒ Ⓓ Ⓔ		113. Ⓐ Ⓑ Ⓒ Ⓓ Ⓔ		163. Ⓐ Ⓑ Ⓒ Ⓓ Ⓔ	
14. Ⓐ Ⓑ Ⓒ Ⓓ Ⓔ		64. Ⓐ Ⓑ Ⓒ Ⓓ Ⓔ		114. Ⓐ Ⓑ Ⓒ Ⓓ Ⓔ		164. Ⓐ Ⓑ Ⓒ Ⓓ Ⓔ	
15. Ⓐ Ⓑ Ⓒ Ⓓ Ⓔ		65. Ⓐ Ⓑ Ⓒ Ⓓ Ⓔ		115. Ⓐ Ⓑ Ⓒ Ⓓ Ⓔ		165. Ⓐ Ⓑ Ⓒ Ⓓ Ⓔ	
16. Ⓐ Ⓑ Ⓒ Ⓓ Ⓔ		66. Ⓐ Ⓑ Ⓒ Ⓓ Ⓔ		116. Ⓐ Ⓑ Ⓒ Ⓓ Ⓔ		166. Ⓐ Ⓑ Ⓒ Ⓓ Ⓔ	
17. Ⓐ Ⓑ Ⓒ Ⓓ Ⓔ		67. Ⓐ Ⓑ Ⓒ Ⓓ Ⓔ		117. Ⓐ Ⓑ Ⓒ Ⓓ Ⓔ		167. Ⓐ Ⓑ Ⓒ Ⓓ Ⓔ	
18. Ⓐ Ⓑ Ⓒ Ⓓ Ⓔ		68. Ⓐ Ⓑ Ⓒ Ⓓ Ⓔ		118. Ⓐ Ⓑ Ⓒ Ⓓ Ⓔ		168. Ⓐ Ⓑ Ⓒ Ⓓ Ⓔ	
19. Ⓐ Ⓑ Ⓒ Ⓓ Ⓔ		69. Ⓐ Ⓑ Ⓒ Ⓓ Ⓔ		119. Ⓐ Ⓑ Ⓒ Ⓓ Ⓔ		169. Ⓐ Ⓑ Ⓒ Ⓓ Ⓔ	
20. Ⓐ Ⓑ Ⓒ Ⓓ Ⓔ		70. Ⓐ Ⓑ Ⓒ Ⓓ Ⓔ		120. Ⓐ Ⓑ Ⓒ Ⓓ Ⓔ		170. Ⓐ Ⓑ Ⓒ Ⓓ Ⓔ	
21. Ⓐ Ⓑ Ⓒ Ⓓ Ⓔ		71. Ⓐ Ⓑ Ⓒ Ⓓ Ⓔ		121. Ⓐ Ⓑ Ⓒ Ⓓ Ⓔ		171. Ⓐ Ⓑ Ⓒ Ⓓ Ⓔ	
22. Ⓐ Ⓑ Ⓒ Ⓓ Ⓔ		72. Ⓐ Ⓑ Ⓒ Ⓓ Ⓔ		122. Ⓐ Ⓑ Ⓒ Ⓓ Ⓔ		172. Ⓐ Ⓑ Ⓒ Ⓓ Ⓔ	
23. Ⓐ Ⓑ Ⓒ Ⓓ Ⓔ		73. Ⓐ Ⓑ Ⓒ Ⓓ Ⓔ		123. Ⓐ Ⓑ Ⓒ Ⓓ Ⓔ		173. Ⓐ Ⓑ Ⓒ Ⓓ Ⓔ	
24. Ⓐ Ⓑ Ⓒ Ⓓ Ⓔ		74. Ⓐ Ⓑ Ⓒ Ⓓ Ⓔ		124. Ⓐ Ⓑ Ⓒ Ⓓ Ⓔ		174. Ⓐ Ⓑ Ⓒ Ⓓ Ⓔ	
25. Ⓐ Ⓑ Ⓒ Ⓓ Ⓔ		75. Ⓐ Ⓑ Ⓒ Ⓓ Ⓔ		125. Ⓐ Ⓑ Ⓒ Ⓓ Ⓔ		175. Ⓐ Ⓑ Ⓒ Ⓓ Ⓔ	
26. Ⓐ Ⓑ Ⓒ Ⓓ Ⓔ		76. Ⓐ Ⓑ Ⓒ Ⓓ Ⓔ		126. Ⓐ Ⓑ Ⓒ Ⓓ Ⓔ		176. Ⓐ Ⓑ Ⓒ Ⓓ Ⓔ	
27. Ⓐ Ⓑ Ⓒ Ⓓ Ⓔ		77. Ⓐ Ⓑ Ⓒ Ⓓ Ⓔ		127. Ⓐ Ⓑ Ⓒ Ⓓ Ⓔ		177. Ⓐ Ⓑ Ⓒ Ⓓ Ⓔ	
28. Ⓐ Ⓑ Ⓒ Ⓓ Ⓔ		78. Ⓐ Ⓑ Ⓒ Ⓓ Ⓔ		128. Ⓐ Ⓑ Ⓒ Ⓓ Ⓔ		178. Ⓐ Ⓑ Ⓒ Ⓓ Ⓔ	
29. Ⓐ Ⓑ Ⓒ Ⓓ Ⓔ		79. Ⓐ Ⓑ Ⓒ Ⓓ Ⓔ		129. Ⓐ Ⓑ Ⓒ Ⓓ Ⓔ		179. Ⓐ Ⓑ Ⓒ Ⓓ Ⓔ	
30. Ⓐ Ⓑ Ⓒ Ⓓ Ⓔ		80. Ⓐ Ⓑ Ⓒ Ⓓ Ⓔ		130. Ⓐ Ⓑ Ⓒ Ⓓ Ⓔ		180. Ⓐ Ⓑ Ⓒ Ⓓ Ⓔ	
31. Ⓐ Ⓑ Ⓒ Ⓓ Ⓔ		81. Ⓐ Ⓑ Ⓒ Ⓓ Ⓔ		131. Ⓐ Ⓑ Ⓒ Ⓓ Ⓔ		181. Ⓐ Ⓑ Ⓒ Ⓓ Ⓔ	
32. Ⓐ Ⓑ Ⓒ Ⓓ Ⓔ		82. Ⓐ Ⓑ Ⓒ Ⓓ Ⓔ		132. Ⓐ Ⓑ Ⓒ Ⓓ Ⓔ		182. Ⓐ Ⓑ Ⓒ Ⓓ Ⓔ	
33. Ⓐ Ⓑ Ⓒ Ⓓ Ⓔ		83. Ⓐ Ⓑ Ⓒ Ⓓ Ⓔ		133. Ⓐ Ⓑ Ⓒ Ⓓ Ⓔ		183. Ⓐ Ⓑ Ⓒ Ⓓ Ⓔ	
34. Ⓐ Ⓑ Ⓒ Ⓓ Ⓔ		84. Ⓐ Ⓑ Ⓒ Ⓓ Ⓔ		134. Ⓐ Ⓑ Ⓒ Ⓓ Ⓔ		184. Ⓐ Ⓑ Ⓒ Ⓓ Ⓔ	
35. Ⓐ Ⓑ Ⓒ Ⓓ Ⓔ		85. Ⓐ Ⓑ Ⓒ Ⓓ Ⓔ		135. Ⓐ Ⓑ Ⓒ Ⓓ Ⓔ		185. Ⓐ Ⓑ Ⓒ Ⓓ Ⓔ	
36. Ⓐ Ⓑ Ⓒ Ⓓ Ⓔ		86. Ⓐ Ⓑ Ⓒ Ⓓ Ⓔ		136. Ⓐ Ⓑ Ⓒ Ⓓ Ⓔ		186. Ⓐ Ⓑ Ⓒ Ⓓ Ⓔ	
37. Ⓐ Ⓑ Ⓒ Ⓓ Ⓔ		87. Ⓐ Ⓑ Ⓒ Ⓓ Ⓔ		137. Ⓐ Ⓑ Ⓒ Ⓓ Ⓔ		187. Ⓐ Ⓑ Ⓒ Ⓓ Ⓔ	
38. Ⓐ Ⓑ Ⓒ Ⓓ Ⓔ		88. Ⓐ Ⓑ Ⓒ Ⓓ Ⓔ		138. Ⓐ Ⓑ Ⓒ Ⓓ Ⓔ		188. Ⓐ Ⓑ Ⓒ Ⓓ Ⓔ	
39. Ⓐ Ⓑ Ⓒ Ⓓ Ⓔ		89. Ⓐ Ⓑ Ⓒ Ⓓ Ⓔ		139. Ⓐ Ⓑ Ⓒ Ⓓ Ⓔ		189. Ⓐ Ⓑ Ⓒ Ⓓ Ⓔ	
40. Ⓐ Ⓑ Ⓒ Ⓓ Ⓔ		90. Ⓐ Ⓑ Ⓒ Ⓓ Ⓔ		140. Ⓐ Ⓑ Ⓒ Ⓓ Ⓔ		190. Ⓐ Ⓑ Ⓒ Ⓓ Ⓔ	
41. Ⓐ Ⓑ Ⓒ Ⓓ Ⓔ		91. Ⓐ Ⓑ Ⓒ Ⓓ Ⓔ		141. Ⓐ Ⓑ Ⓒ Ⓓ Ⓔ		191. Ⓐ Ⓑ Ⓒ Ⓓ Ⓔ	
42. Ⓐ Ⓑ Ⓒ Ⓓ Ⓔ		92. Ⓐ Ⓑ Ⓒ Ⓓ Ⓔ		142. Ⓐ Ⓑ Ⓒ Ⓓ Ⓔ		192. Ⓐ Ⓑ Ⓒ Ⓓ Ⓔ	
43. Ⓐ Ⓑ Ⓒ Ⓓ Ⓔ		93. Ⓐ Ⓑ Ⓒ Ⓓ Ⓔ		143. Ⓐ Ⓑ Ⓒ Ⓓ Ⓔ		193. Ⓐ Ⓑ Ⓒ Ⓓ Ⓔ	
44. Ⓐ Ⓑ Ⓒ Ⓓ Ⓔ		94. Ⓐ Ⓑ Ⓒ Ⓓ Ⓔ		144. Ⓐ Ⓑ Ⓒ Ⓓ Ⓔ		194. Ⓐ Ⓑ Ⓒ Ⓓ Ⓔ	
45. Ⓐ Ⓑ Ⓒ Ⓓ Ⓔ		95. Ⓐ Ⓑ Ⓒ Ⓓ Ⓔ		145. Ⓐ Ⓑ Ⓒ Ⓓ Ⓔ		195. Ⓐ Ⓑ Ⓒ Ⓓ Ⓔ	
46. Ⓐ Ⓑ Ⓒ Ⓓ Ⓔ		96. Ⓐ Ⓑ Ⓒ Ⓓ Ⓔ		146. Ⓐ Ⓑ Ⓒ Ⓓ Ⓔ		196. Ⓐ Ⓑ Ⓒ Ⓓ Ⓔ	
47. Ⓐ Ⓑ Ⓒ Ⓓ Ⓔ		97. Ⓐ Ⓑ Ⓒ Ⓓ Ⓔ		147. Ⓐ Ⓑ Ⓒ Ⓓ Ⓔ		197. Ⓐ Ⓑ Ⓒ Ⓓ Ⓔ	
48. Ⓐ Ⓑ Ⓒ Ⓓ Ⓔ		98. Ⓐ Ⓑ Ⓒ Ⓓ Ⓔ		148. Ⓐ Ⓑ Ⓒ Ⓓ Ⓔ		198. Ⓐ Ⓑ Ⓒ Ⓓ Ⓔ	
49. Ⓐ Ⓑ Ⓒ Ⓓ Ⓔ		99. Ⓐ Ⓑ Ⓒ Ⓓ Ⓔ		149. Ⓐ Ⓑ Ⓒ Ⓓ Ⓔ		199. Ⓐ Ⓑ Ⓒ Ⓓ Ⓔ	
50. Ⓐ Ⓑ Ⓒ Ⓓ Ⓔ		100. Ⓐ Ⓑ Ⓒ Ⓓ Ⓔ		150. Ⓐ Ⓑ Ⓒ Ⓓ Ⓔ		200. Ⓐ Ⓑ Ⓒ Ⓓ Ⓔ	

PART 2

Tests in Biology

Sample Test 1

Directions for Taking Test: This sample test contains 200 questions or incomplete statements, and should be finished in 170 minutes. Each item has five possible answers or completions. Choose the best one, and blacken the corresponding letter on the answer sheet.

After finishing, you can determine your score by using the **Answer Key** at the end of this test. The **Answer Explanations** section should clarify the concepts involved in each question.

Questions 1–94
For each of the following questions or incomplete statements select the best answer or completion.

1. The primitive atmosphere of the Earth probably did NOT contain
   A. water
   B. methane
   C. ammonia
   D. oxygen
   E. hydrogen

2. Plasmolysis of plant cells occurs when
   A. the cell walls collapse
   B. turgor pressure increases
   C. protoplasm dies
   D. extracellular fluids are hypertonic to intracellular fluid
   E. microtubules are closed

3. Which of these is the most highly differentiated cell type?
   A. blastema cell
   B. blastomere
   C. erythrocyte
   D. neoblast
   E. zygote

4. Certain animal crosses regularly produce litters that are about 25% smaller than normal. A logical explanation is that this departure from normality results from
   A. sex-linked genes
   B. penetrance
   C. recessive lethal genes
   D. autopolyploidy
   E. chiasmatic interference

5. Plankton lives near the surface of the ocean. The primary reason is that deep oceanic areas are too
   A. cold
   B. dark
   C. dense
   D. unstable
   E. densely populated with primary consumers

6. The commercial growth of cereal crops is most closely associated with the
   A. chaparral biome
   B. middle-latitude grassland biome
   C. taiga biome
   D. savanna biome
   E. tundra biome

7. If all of the DNA contained in the nucleus of a typical human cell were stretched to full length and placed end to end, its length would be approximately
   A. 1 meter, composed of 46 separate pieces
   B. 1 meter, composed of thousands of separate pieces
   C. 1 micrometer, composed of a single piece
   D. 1 micrometer, composed of 46 separate pieces
   E. 1 micrometer, composed of thousands of separate pieces

8. Plants found in a desert biome are likely to
   A. be conifers
   B. be epiphytes
   C. occur in very high density
   D. demonstrate allelopathy
   E. produce flowers throughout the year

9. Which of these is an oxygen carrier in the blood of some invertebrate animals?
   A. chlorophyll
   B. cytochrome c
   C. hemocyanin
   D. NAD
   E. prothrombin

10. Sealing the stomata of leaves will slow or stop all processes EXCEPT
    A. respiration
    B. transpiration
    C. photosynthesis
    D. wilting
    E. guttation

11. Acquired Immune Deficiency Syndrome (AIDS) is caused by ineffective
    A. erythrocytes
    B. genes coding for antibody production
    C. T cells and macrophages
    D. platelets
    E. bacteria

12. The genotype of an individual showing a particular dominant trait can be determined by
    A. crossbreeding
    B. test-crossing
    C. inbreeding
    D. outbreeding
    E. looking at the individual

13. Which of these is a biome that is characteristic of the Mediterranean region?
    A. tundra
    B. tropical rain forest
    C. taiga
    D. desert
    E. chaparral

14. In the normal cell cycle the mitotic phase requiring the most time is
    A. anaphase
    B. leptonema
    C. metaphase
    D. prophase
    E. telophase

15. In the Hardy-Weinberg equation, with two alleles A and a, q2 represents the frequency of
    A. allele A
    B. allele a
    C. the Aa genotype
    D. the aa genotype
    E. the dominant phenotype

16. Which pigment is related to vitamin A?
    A. carotene
    B. xanthophyll
    C. anthocyanin
    D. chlorophyll
    E. tannin

17. F. W. Went's classic experiment with stumps of oat coleoptiles involved placing upon them blocks of agar saturated with a growth stimulator. The experiment demonstrated that
    A. the growth stimulator is diffusable and water soluble
    B. the stimulator is a fat-soluble substance
    C. growth is stimulated only when the light period exceeds the dark period
    D. bending is caused by a rapid increase in cell division on one side of the stem
    E. production of the stimulator depends on the presence of a high concentration of sugar

18. An antheridium is a plant organ that produces
   A. sperm cells
   B. spores
   C. eggs
   D. zoospores
   E. food

19. Which is a correct statement about photosynthesis?
   A. Oxygen generated from photosynthesis comes from carbon dioxide.
   B. Products of the light-dependent reaction of photosynthesis include ATP and NADPH.
   C. Oxygen is given off during the light independent reactions.
   D. The reactions causing the fixation of carbon dioxide require light.
   E. The color of light most used in photosynthesis is green.

20. In humans the major blood-type differences are determined by multiple alleles designated I^A, I^B and i. Alleles I^A and I^B are codominants, and i is recessive. Gene combinations $I^A I^A$ and $I^A i$ produce type A blood; $I^A I^B$ produces type AB blood; $I^B I^B$ and $I^B i$ produce type B blood; and ii produces type O blood. Suppose that one parent has type A blood, and the other has type B. Their first child has type O blood. What is the probability that their next child will have type AB blood?
   A. 0%
   B. 25%
   C. 50%
   D. 75%
   E. 100%

21. It is believed that carbon dioxide in the atmosphere keeps the Earth warmer by interfering with the reradiation of heat back into space. This phenomenon has come to be known as the
   A. heat trap
   B. Douglas theory of gaseous absorption
   C. principle of heat reflection
   D. carbon dioxide screen
   E. greenhouse effect

22. Which of the following environments is richest in free oxygen?
   A. warm fresh water
   B. cold fresh water
   C. salt water
   D. soil
   E. atmosphere

23. When ants follow the same route to a source of food, they are guided by
   A. visual tracking
   B. sun orientation
   C. landmark recognition
   D. pheromone marking
   E. frequency of body contacts

24. The greatest diversity of species occurs in
  A. tropical rain forests
  B. grasslands
  C. temperate broadleaf forests
  D. chaparrals
  E. savannas

25. Which of the following cellular substances or structures can be found in rabbits but NOT in *Escherichia coli*?
  A. enzymes
  B. genes
  C. ribosomes
  D. nuclear membranes
  E. semipermeable membranes

26. Which of these describes K-selected animals?
  A. reproduce early, have many offspring
  B. have short lifespan, many offspring
  C. reproduce only once in their lifetimes
  D. have few offspring, receive and give extended parental care
  E. have small body, long lifespan

27. If a freshwater protozoan did not have a contractile vacuole, it would NOT be able to
  A. breathe
  B. regulate water pressure
  C. excrete nitrogenous wastes
  D. move
  E. defend itself

28. Which of the following statements is INCORRECT?
  A. Mutations cannot occur in viruses.
  B. Unlike the Protista, viruses do not contain organelles such as mitochondria, nuclei, or plastids.
  C. Respiration does not occur within viruses.
  D. Viruses do not have independent means of propulsion.
  E. Viruses have genes for enzymes, but do not produce enzymes within themselves.

29. Of the various hormone or hormonelike substances that affect plants, which causes the ripening of fruit?
  A. indoleacetic acid
  B. kinetin
  C. gibberellin
  D. ethylene
  E. 2,4-D

30. The phenotype of an individual can best be determined by
    A. crossbreeding
    B. backcrossing
    C. inbreeding
    D. outbreeding
    E. observing the individual

31. Which of the following conclusions about evolutionary adaptations is based upon sound logic?
    A. Animals living in cold climates tend to have longer appendages than those living in warmer places.
    B. Pollen of wind-pollinated plants should be large so that it has buoyancy in the air.
    C. Since pollinating moths are most active at dusk and night, they depend heavily on bright-colored flowers to guide them to their target.
    D. On the basis of size, small mammals should have an advantage over larger ones in hot climates.
    E. Fish tend to be darker on their lower surfaces, which are more shaded from the light that comes from above.

32. The occurrence together of two or more morphologically distinct forms of a population is termed
    A. divergence
    B. hierarchical isolation
    C. morphogenesis
    D. polymorphism
    E. sympatric tolerance

33. A major difference between a climax community and any subclimax stage of succession is that the former
    A. has an increase in net productivity
    B. is composed of a smaller number of species
    C. has more biomass
    D. cannot reproduce itself
    E. has a photosynthesis-respiration ratio (P/R) greater than 1

34. Which of these is the lake zone supporting the greatest biomass?
    A. littoral
    B. deep floor
    C. oceanic
    D. neritic
    E. profundal

35. According to the British political economist Malthus,
    A. populations tend to outgrow the ability of their environments to support them
    B. human populations have a faster growth rate than other populations
    C. the human population growth potential decreases in inverse proportion to the population's growth
    D. all populations have the same growth rate
    E. population growth can be checked only by starvation

36. Genetic drift is a change in the gene pool caused by
  A. selection
  B. mutation
  C. migration
  D. hybridization
  E. chance

37. Down syndrome has been shown to have a direct relationship to the mother's
  A. parathyroid atrophy
  B. brain damage
  C. hypoglycemia
  D. age at conception
  E. vitamin K deficiency

38. Which of these describes a progressive change in allele frequencies occurring within a population over successive generations?
  A. natural selection
  B. macroevolution
  C. microevolution
  D. mutation
  E. punctuated equilibrium

39. The two strands of nucleotides that comprise the double helix of DNA are linked together by
  A. peptide bonds
  B. covalent bonds
  C. ionic bonds
  D. hydrogen bonds
  E. phosphate bonds

40. Which of these is most related to the concept of stabilizing selection?
  A. Human infants whose weight is near the population average are more likely to survive than those at weight extremes.
  B. There are more of the dark form of peppered moths in industry-darkened environments than in areas far from industrial pollution.
  C. Finch species on the Galápagos Islands occur with a number of distinctly different beak sizes and shapes.
  D. Some fish species whose populations are found only in deep caves do not have eyes.
  E. Both birds and insects have evolved wings that enable flying.

41. The glomerulus is a structure found in the
  A. lung
  B. kidney
  C. liver
  D. testis
  E. spleen

42. The punctuated equilibrium model of speciation is the main alternative
to the model known as
  A. gradualism
  B. cladistics
  C. disruptive selection
  D. sympatric speciation
  E. hybrid inviability

43. Which of these terms describes the environment at the bottom of an ocean?
  A. pelagic
  B. littoral
  C. benthic
  D. limnetic
  E. neritic

44. Which kingdom had NOT appeared on Earth by the end of the Cambrian
Period?
  A. Animalia
  B. Monera
  C. Protista
  D. Plantae
  E. Fungi

45. Mature plant cells originate from a tissue called
  A. parenchyma
  B. cortex
  C. meristem
  D. pericycle
  E. endodermis

46. Red tides that sometimes kill fish along a coastline are blooms of
  A. fungi
  B. bacteria
  C. krill
  D. dinoflagellates
  E. diatoms

47. Which of the following adjectives appropriately describes a particular
type of autotroph?
  A. herbivorous
  B. chemosynthetic
  C. saprozoic
  D. holozoic
  E. phagocytic

48. Mapping gene locations on a eukaryotic chromosome is possible because of
    A. episomal proliferation
    B. transduction
    C. giant chromosome formations
    D. template matching
    E. crossing-over of chromosomes

49. In ecological succession
    A. the climax is always a deciduous forest
    B. the pioneers are always xerophytes
    C. except for the climax, each stage alters the habitat to make it less suitable for itself
    D. the number of species decreases up to and including the climax
    E. net productivity remains constant throughout

50. Vertebrate predators would be expected to have
    A. front-field vision
    B. grinding teeth
    C. a long digestive tract
    D. the habit of sleeping lightly
    E. long legs

51. Which of these is NOT a density-dependent factor for the size of a population?
    A. the size of a predator population
    B. a large storm
    C. an infectious disease
    D. adult mortality within the population
    E. competition for resources

52. Which of these organelles is most closely associated with intracellular movement?
    A. endoplasmic reticulum
    B. Golgi apparatus
    C. lysosomes
    D. microfilaments
    E. mitochondria

53. Which of these is displaying a form of behavior most closely related to camouflage coloration?
    A. predators who wait in ambush
    B. predators who actively choose prey
    C. animals exhibiting character displacement
    D. animals exhibiting aposematism
    E. prey who escape predators by rapid locomotion

54. Impulses traveling through the nervous system are transmitted electrically in neurons and chemically across synapses. A well-known synaptic neuro-transmitter is the substance
A. angiotensin
B. acetylcholine
C. secretin
D. cholecystokinin
E. ecdysone

55. The temperature of endothermic animals may be increased by all of the following EXCEPT
A. panting
B. shivering
C. curling up
D. depositing fat in subcutaneous tissues
E. reducing peripheral circulation

56. In most mammals, where are eggs fertilized if a successful pregnancy is to occur?
A. vagina
B. uterus
C. lower portion of the oviduct
D. upper portion of the oviduct
E. ovary

57. If an organism that is heterozygous for two unlinked genes is bred with a homozygous recessive individual, the resulting genotype ratio is expected to be
A. 16:0
B. 9:3:3:1
C. 1:1:1:1
D. 3:1
E. 1:2:1

58. Of the following habitats, which has the lowest rate of productivity?
A. ocean
B. moist forest
C. moist grassland
D. cornfield
E. coral reef

59. Which of these describes a distasteful species whose shape and color pattern are similar to those of another species that is also distasteful to predators?
A. character displacement
B. Batesian mimicry
C. Müllerian mimicry
D. competitive exclusion
E. mutualism

60. In interrelationships among animals the greatest competition occurs between
   A. members of the same species
   B. males competing for a female
   C. members of two different species living in the same location
   D. predators and their prey
   E. members of young and old generations of the same species

61. The cellular assembling of amino acids in a particular sequence to construct a polypeptide is known as
   A. peptide linkage
   B. ordination
   C. codification
   D. translation
   E. transcription

62. Nitrogenous bases of DNA are normally paired as
   A. T-T
   B. A-A
   C. G-A
   D. C-C
   E. T-A

63. Which of the following is NOT a component of blood?
   A. monocyte
   B. lymphocyte
   C. erythrocyte
   D. granulocyte
   E. chondrocyte

64. The geologic period in which a large number of phyla appeared for the first time is the
   A. Cambrian
   B. Devonian
   C. Jurassic
   D. Pennsylvanian
   E. Silurian

65. The reproduction of a certain tree on the island of Mauritius may be dependent upon the ingestion and chemical modification of its seeds by the dodo bird. Since the dodo is now extinct, the tree seems destined for extinction also. Presumably, the dodo obtained nourishment by eating the fruit that contains the seed. This is therefore a case of
   A. coevolution
   B. commensalism
   C. Lamarckian adaptation
   D. preadaptation
   E. sympatric relationship

66. Which of the following is most likely to be common to plants that use C_4 photosynthesis?
    A. They are conifers.
    B. They do not use cyclic photophosphorylation.
    C. They originated in tropical zones.
    D. They tend to have slow photosynthesis rates in high-O_2 environments.
    E. They use a light-sensitive pigment other than chlorophyll.

67. In recombinant DNA technology, the first organisms used as hosts of artificially introduced DNA were
    A. chicken embryos
    B. fruit flies
    C. monkeys
    D. intestinal bacteria
    E. slime molds

68. One danger of using massive doses of antibiotics is that they
    A. cause emphysema
    B. destroy the intestinal flora
    C. accumulate in the bones
    D. block the absorption of water by cells
    E. crystallize in kidney tubules

69. Convergent evolution is illustrated by the
    A. rodent and dog
    B. starfish and fish
    C. fish and whale
    D. cactus and mistletoe
    E. bacterium and protozoan

70. All organisms that can share a gene pool are grouped together as a
    A. genus
    B. species
    C. phenotype
    D. community
    E. clone

71. If a species has been through a genetic bottleneck, it is likely to
    A. have little polymorphism
    B. show much genetic variability among its populations
    C. be on the list of endangered species
    D. be found only on a single island
    E. have a higher than average mutation rate

72. A plant molecule responsible for photoperiodism is
    A. florigen
    B. gibberellin
    C. oxytocin
    D. phytochrome
    E. thyroxin

73. Assume that the frequency of the recessive allele for sickle-cell anemia is currently 0.04 among African-Americans. If it is assumed that this population is in Hardy-Weinberg equilibrium, what is the likely frequency of African-Americans whose red blood cells demonstrate sickling in a normal environment?

A. 0.04
B. 0.0016
C. 0.08
D. 0.92
E. 0.20

74. In a partial chromosome region such as the one illustrated, the greatest amount of recombinations would be expected to occur between genes

A. *C* and *D*
B. *A* and *B*
C. *A* and *D*
D. *B* and *C*
E. *B* and *D*

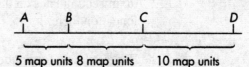

5 map units 8 map units 10 map units

75. How many different kinds of gametes can be produced by an organism with the genotype *AaBbCC*?

A. 1
B. 2
C. 4
D. 6
E. 8

76. If you were looking for a high rate of cell division in plants, you would find it in

A. phloem
B. xylem
C. cambium
D. pith
E. fibers

77. Cryptic coloration is illustrated by

A. monarch butterflies
B. flounders
C. blue crabs
D. coral snakes
E. redwing blackbirds

78. The behavioral form that is responsible for a dog's trying to bury a bone indoors although the animal has never been outside, where it could have this experience, is known as

A. fixed action pattern
B. imprinting
C. habituation
D. operant conditioning
E. insight

79. Sympatric speciation is most closely associated with
    A. geographic isolation
    B. convergent evolution
    C. hybrid inviability
    D. coevolution
    E. polyploid hybrids

80. Which of the following statements best explains why a green plant bends toward the light as it grows?
    A. Green plants need light to carry on photosynthesis.
    B. Light stimulates a more rapid growth of cells on the lighted side.
    C. Green plants seek light because they are phototropic.
    D. Cells divide faster on the shaded side.
    E. Auxin accumulates on the shaded side, causing greater cellular elongation there.

81. The Burgess Shale formation in Canada is most famous for illustrating
    A. early fossils of hominids
    B. continental drift
    C. the Cambrian explosion
    D. Lamarckian evolution
    E. genetic drift

82. Which came first, according to available fossil evidence?
    A. *Homo erectus*
    B. *Homo sapiens*
    C. *Australopithecus afarensis*
    D. *Homo habilis*
    E. *Australopithecus robustus*

83. The complex of 13 species of finches that Darwin studied in the Galápagos Islands is a good example of
    A. Batesian mimicry
    B. Müllerian mimicry
    C. competitive exclusion
    D. adaptive radiation
    E. convergent evolution

84. Which of these is NOT a compound with at least one ring?
    A. glucose
    B. cholesterol
    C. thymine
    D. insulin
    E. lactic acid

85. The term carrying capacity refers to the
   A. ability of an animal to store potential energy in the form of fat
   B. amount of seeds or spores that can be transported from one place to another by a specific animal
   C. total number of organisms that a particular place will support
   D. total number of genes transferable by a sperm cell to an egg
   E. maximum number of surviving individuals in a litter of placental animals

86. Most zinc fingers
   A. are shaped to bind ultimately with DNA
   B. regulate the intracellular degradation of zinc
   C. act to exclude zinc from roots of plants
   D. modulate the speed of mRNA translation
   E. are tools for inserting genes into defective cells as a therapy method

87. The young of some bird species will follow the first moving object, such as a person or a toy, they see and form a lasting attachment to it. This kind of behavior is known as
   A. habituation
   B. conditioning
   C. imprinting
   D. trial and error
   E. taxis

88. Which of these is most closely associated with microtubules?
   A. tubulin
   B. actin
   C. myosin
   D. pectin
   E. chromatin

89. Which of these could NOT be an isolating mechanism between species?
   A. infertility of offspring
   B. competition for resources
   C. mating behavior
   D. sperm-egg interaction
   E. time of mating season

90. A geneticist attempting to study the nucleotide sequence of a strand of DNA might use the class of enzymes called
   A. acetylcholine esterases
   B. cytochromes
   C. kinases
   D. proteases
   E. restriction endonucleases

91. Rejection of transplanted organs is most closely associated with
  A. monoclonal antibodies
  B. IgE
  C. MHC antigens
  D. secretin
  E. GABA

92. After pyruvate enters a mitochondrion, the first action upon the pyruvate converts it to
  A. an acetyl group attached to coenzyme A
  B. lactic acid
  C. citrate
  D. glucose
  E. oxaloacetate

93. Which statement is INCORRECT?
  A. Bacteria have circular chromosomes.
  B. Fungal cells have cell walls.
  C. Animal cells lack cell walls.
  D. Plant cells lack mitochondria.
  E. Prokaryotic cells lack nuclear membranes.

94. cDNA
  A. is made from mRNA, with the use of reverse transcriptase
  B. contains both introns and exons
  C. is triple-stranded
  D. is a hybrid of DNA from two or more species
  E. produces transgenic organisms

Questions 95–160
The next five questions (95–99) consist of a group of lettered isotopes and five numbered phrases. For each numbered phrase select the lettered isotope that is most accurately characterized by the phrase, and mark the answer accordingly. Any one of the lettered isotopes may be used one or more times or not at all.

  A. strontium-90
  B. nitrogen-15
  C. cesium-137
  D. iodine-131
  E. carbon-14

95. behaves physiologically like potassium

96. accumulates like calcium in bone tissue

97. is not radioactive

98. is used to date organic remains

99. concentrates in thyroid tissue

The next four questions (100–103) consist of a group of lettered names of scientists and numbered scientific achievements. For each numbered achievement select the lettered name(s) of the person(s) credited with making it, and mark the answer accordingly. Any one of the lettered names may be used one or more times or not at all.

> **A.** Hardy and Weinberg
> **B.** Watson and Crick
> **C.** Fleming
> **D.** Banting and Best
> **E.** van Leeuwenhoek

100. discovered blood corpuscles and bacteria

101. discovered the antibacterial action of penicillin

102. demonstrated gene frequency in a gene pool

103. built an accurate model of a double-stranded deoxyribonucleic acid

The next three questions (104–106) consist of a group of lettered phases in a cell cycle and numbered descriptions of phases. For each numbered description select the lettered phase that matches it, and mark the answer accordingly. Any one of the lettered phases may be used one or more times or not at all.

> **A.** anaphase
> **B.** interphase
> **C.** metaphase
> **D.** prophase
> **E.** telophase

104. Chromatids move toward poles of spindle.

105. This stage precedes metaphase.

106. Chromatids reach poles of spindle.

The next four questions (107–110) consist of a group of lettered animal phyla and numbered descriptive phrases. For each numbered phrase select the lettered phylum that matches it, and mark the answer accordingly. Any one of the lettered phyla may be used one or more times or not at all.

> **A.** Arthropoda
> **B.** Annelida
> **C.** Echinodermata
> **D.** Mollusca
> **E.** Platyhelminthes

107. includes barnacles

108. contains the largest number of living species

109. contains species that lack a coelom

110. includes the earthworms

The next four questions (111–114) consist of a group of lettered molecules and numbered descriptive phrases. For each numbered phrase select the lettered molecule that matches it, and mark the answer accordingly. Any one of the lettered molecules may be used one or more times or not at all.

> A. carbon dioxide
> B. ethanol
> C. glucose
> D. lactate
> E. ribose

111. is produced by fermentation in animal cells

112. is produced as a result of the Calvin cycle

113. is produced during the Krebs cycle

114. is the starting material for anaerobic glycolysis

The next five questions (115–119) consist of a group of lettered molecules and numbered descriptions. For each numbered description select the lettered molecule that matches it, and mark the answer accordingly. Any one of the lettered molecules may be used one or more times or not at all.

> A. chitin
> B. cholesterol
> C. collagen
> D. cyclic AMP
> E. phospholipid

115. is a polypeptide

116. is most closely related to nucleic acids

117. is most closely related to sex hormones

118. is most closely related to starch

119. is structurally related to adenosine triphosphate

The next three questions (120–122) consist of a group of lettered animal structures and numbered descriptions of these structures. For each numbered description select the lettered structure that matches it, and mark the answer accordingly. Any one of the lettered structures may be used one or more times or not at all.

> A. alveoli
> B. Malpighian tubules
> C. sphincters
> D. tracheoles
> E. villi

120. are functionally analogous to nephrons in function

121. serve for gas exchange in insects

122. provide large surface area for absorption of food in intestine

The next three questions (123–125) consist of a group of physiological or behavioral processes (lettered) and descriptions (numbered) of these processes. For each numbered description select the lettered process that matches it, and mark the answer accordingly. Any one of the lettered processes may be used one or more times or not at all.

    A. abscission
    B. gravitropism
    C. tension-cohesion
    D. cyclosis
    E. translocation

123. model for solvent movement against gravity in plants, alternative to root pressure theory

124. loss of leaves from deciduous trees

125. movement of solutes within a plant

The next five questions (126–130) consist of a group of lettered biomes and numbered descriptions of biomes. For each numbered description select the lettered biome that matches it, and mark the answer accordingly. Any one of the lettered biomes may be used one or more times or not at all.

    A. savanna
    B. temperate grassland
    C. taiga
    D. tropical rain forest
    E. tundra

126. Dominant trees tend to be cone bearers.

127. Few trees are present; hot and cold seasons alternate.

128. Few trees are present; it is hot year-round; wet and dry seasons alternate.

129. There are many tree species, forming dense canopy.

130. Winters are very cold; there are many trees but few species.

The next four questions (131–134) consist of a group of lettered ecological processes and numbered descriptions of processes. For each numbered description select the lettered process that matches it, and mark the answer accordingly. Any one of the lettered processes may be used one or more times or not at all.

A. biological magnification
B. eutrophication
C. interspecific competition
D. intraspecific competition
E. succession

131. This process is accelerated by the runoff of phosphorus into lakes.

132. As a result of this process animals at the top of the food chain are most affected by persistent chemicals.

133. This process often leads to a complex, stable ecosystem.

134. This process is produced by overlapping needs for a resource by two or more populations between which no gene flow occurs.

The next four questions (135–138) consist of a group of lettered neuronal activities and numbered physiological consequences of such activities. For each numbered consequence select the lettered activity that causes it, and mark the answer accordingly. Any one of the lettered activities may be used one or more times or not at all.

A. Permeability changes occur in adjacent membrane regions.
B. Exchanges of potassium and sodium occur simultaneously.
C. Potassium voltage-activated channels open.
D. Sodium voltage-activated channels open.
E. Sodium and potassium voltage-activated channels are closed.

135. The environment outside the membrane becomes progressively more positive with reference to the cytoplasm.

136. Positive ions flow into the cell by passive diffusion.

137. Nerve impulse is propagated along the axon.

138. Resting potential is maintained.

The next four questions (139–142) consist of a group of lettered plant types or parts and numbered descriptions. For each numbered description select the lettered plant type or part that matches it, and mark the answer accordingly. Any one of the lettered plant types or parts may be used one or more times or not at all.

A. cotyledon
B. endosperm
C. gametophyte
D. seed coat
E. sporophyte

139. embryonic leaf

140. most easily observed portion of a fern's life cycle

141. plant form that is diploid and produces haploid reproductive cells

142. tissue that nourishes the embryo

The next five questions (143–147) consist of a group of lettered processes of embryonic development in animals and numbered descriptive phrases. For each numbered phrase select the lettered process that matches it, and mark the answer accordingly. Any one of the lettered processes may be used one or more times or not at all.

A. cleavage
B. fertilization
C. gametogenesis
D. gastrulation
E. induction

143. chemically triggers differentiation

144. often results in formation of three layers of cells

145. programmed cell movements occur within embryo

146. rapid cell proliferation occurs by the process of meiosis

147. rapid cell proliferation occurs by the process of mitosis

The next three questions (148–150) consist of lettered groups of organisms and numbered descriptions of representative organisms. For each numbered description select the lettered group of which it is a part, and mark the answer accordingly. Any one of the lettered groups may be used one or more times or not at all.

    A. angiosperms
    B. bryophytes
    C. ferns
    D. fungi
    E. gymnosperms

148. plants that produce flowers

149. organisms of the kingdom Plantae, but not vascular plants

150. organisms NOT of the kingdom Plantae if the five-kingdom classification system is followed

The next four questions (151–154) consist of a group of lettered animal embryo regions and numbered adult parts that develop from these regions. For each numbered adult part select the lettered embryonic region that matches it, and mark the answer accordingly. Any one of the lettered embryonic regions may be used one or more times or not at all.

    A. archenteron
    B. coelom
    C. ectoderm
    D. endoderm
    E. mesoderm

151. an opening that becomes the cavity of the gut

152. the layer from which muscle is formed

153. the layer from which the brain is formed

154. the region that becomes the notochord

The next six questions (155–160) consist of a group of lettered terms from molecular genetics and numbered descriptions of such terms. For each numbered description select the lettered term that matches it, and mark the answer accordingly. Any one of the lettered terms may be used one or more times or not at all.

    A. codons
    B. histones
    C. introns
    D. messenger RNAs
    E. transposons

155. genetic elements that are capable of moving from one chromosome locus to another

156. proteins that are major components of eukaryotic chromosomes

157. regions of structural genes that are not translated into portions of polypeptides

158. products of transcription, containing complete codes for the amino acid sequences of proteins

159. three-base sequences of DNA or RNA

160. usually, chemical symbols for individual amino acids

The remaining questions (161–200) ask for analysis of experiments. For each set, read the descriptions and data carefully; also, study any diagrams, graphs, or tables that are given. Then answer the questions or complete the statements by choosing the best of the lettered alternatives and marking your answers accordingly.

Questions 161–165

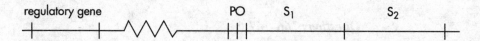

The diagram represents the arrangement of DNA sequences making up two portions of a bacterial chromosome. All of the labeled areas are components of a repressible system. S_1 and S_2 are a pair of structural genes coding for two enzymes that work together to produce an amino acid essential for protein synthesis. *P* symbolizes "promoter," and *O* symbolizes "operator."

161. What would be the likely result of a large deletion occurring in the regulatory gene?
   A. One of the structural genes would be transcribed, but the other would not.
   B. Nothing would change except that the regulatory gene's product would be different.
   C. The amino acid could no longer be produced.
   D. The amino acid would be continuously produced even if not needed.
   E. The operator region would no longer influence the promoter region.

162. What effect, if any, does the amino acid produced by the action of S_1 and S_2 have upon the gene system?
   A. As the end product, it has no effect.
   B. It acts as a corepressor.
   C. It acts as a repressor.
   D. It acts as an inducer.
   E. It stops the promoter's transcription.

163. Upon which region does a repressor have direct influence?

A. O

B. P

C. the regulatory gene

D. S_1

E. S_2

164. What would be the immediate effect of a mutation of the promoter region?

A. A portion of a messenger RNA molecule would be translated incorrectly.

B. DNA polymerase could not easily attach to the P region.

C. RNA polymerase could not easily attach to the P region.

D. The amino acid could not easily attach to the P region.

E. The repressor could not easily attach to the P region.

165. If it were necessary to change the diagram so that it represented an inducible system rather than a repressible system, what revision would have to be made?

A. The regulatory gene would have to be deleted.

B. The P and O regions would have to be interchanged.

C. The O region would have to be moved to fit between S_1 and S_2.

D. The regulatory gene would have to be moved to fit between O and S_1.

E. No change would be necessary in the diagram.

Questions 166–167

Fibronectin is a protein found on the surface of many embryonic cells. It is believed that fibronectin may act as a "pattern" for the shaping of embryonic muscle when the protein is supplied by cells other than the muscle-forming cells. To help test this view, an experiment was performed to determine whether an oriented fibronectin layer would influence the arrangement of myoblast cells (embryonic precursors to muscle) in a cell culture. A large drop of fibronectin solution was allowed to dry on a glass surface. Concentric rings of fibronectin formed on the plate. When chicken myoblast cells were spread over the surface, they quickly oriented themselves with their long axes parallel to the fibronectin rings.

166. What is the most important criticism of the experiment as outlined above?

A. An *in vitro* experiment does not tell much about the way the living organism works.

B. Conclusions to be drawn from the results contradict the hypothesis.

C. The experiment could lead to unforeseen dangers to human health.

D. Since the experiment involves embryos, it could lead to ethical problems if done with human cells.

E. There was not a control to determine whether materials other than fibronectin could also cause myoblast orientation.

167. What does the experiment demonstrate?
 A. Fibronectin is produced by myoblasts.
 B. Fibronectin orients embryonic muscle only under artificial conditions.
 C. Fibronectin is the most important factor in orienting embryonic muscle.
 D. Myoblasts always form concentric rings when cultured.
 E. Myoblasts can, under certain conditions, take orientation cues from underlying extracellular fibronectin.

Questions 168–171
The following graph illustrates an experiment in which two populations of the fruit fly *Drosophila* were raised in closed containers under identical conditions. Food and space were limiting factors in the containers.

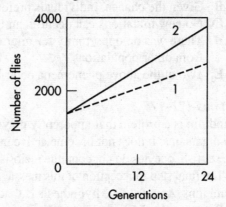

The population graphed as a broken line and labeled **1** was derived from a single inbred line. The population indicated by a solid line and labeled **2** was begun by crossing two different inbred strains. Electrophoresis of tissue proteins from each population at the beginning of the experiment indicated that the genetic variability of population 2 was about twice that of population 1.

168. What is the most that can be said about the populations from the data provided here?
 A. Both populations adapted to the conditions.
 B. If populations 1 and 2 had been allowed to interbreed, the resulting population would have done better than either 1 or 2.
 C. Neither population evolved.
 D. The population with more genetic variation adapted better to the conditions of the experiment.
 E. The population with more genetic variation would have done better under ANY conditions.

169. Why was electrophoresis used as a tool to determine genetic variability?
 A. It allows separation of genes for individual analysis.
 B. It can separate proteins in a complex mixture, making it possible to count the number of different ones present.
 C. It can be performed on every fly of the population without harming it.
 D. It is less expensive than the alternative method—cloning all of the flies' genes for individual analysis.
 E. It uses radioactive tracers and therefore is a very sensitive method for finding proteins in a tissue.

170. Although this aspect was not tested in the experiment described, population 2 probably
  A. eventually would have slowed its growth rate to match that of population 1
  B. had fewer visually observable abnormalities than population 1
  C. was closer to crashing to extinction soon after generation 24 than was population 1
  D. was less heterogeneous in generation 24 than in generation 1
  E. was more heterogeneous in generation 24 than in generation 1

171. Which of the following helps explain why inbreeding of population 1 led to lack of heterogeneity?
  A. Genetic drift had necessarily occurred.
  B. Given the chance, individuals prefer to mate with their own kind.
  C. No new mutations can occur in an inbred strain.
  D. There was no opportunity for migration of new genetic variations from other populations.
  E. Two of the above phenomena contributed to the loss of heterogeneity.

Questions 172–175
Calmodulin is a protein that apparently plays a fundamental regulatory role in many organisms. It does not become active until after it accepts the calcium ion. In the starfish, oocytes do not continue meiosis until they receive a hormonal message. The final step in reception of this message is dependent upon the presence of calcium ions. An attractive hypothesis is that calmodulin, if activated by a hormonally induced calcium ion population, may then activate the several enzymes that induce meiosis. To test this, starfish were injected with two chemicals known to inhibit the activities of calmodulin. The ability of the treated starfish to produce mature gametes was monitored, and the results are graphed below.

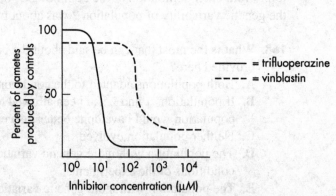

172. Which of these sequences is the one postulated for starfish gamete maturation control?
  A. calcium release → calmodulin activation → hormone production → enzymes activation → meiosis
  B. calcium release → hormone production → calmodulin activation → enzymes activation → meiosis
  C. calmodulin production → hormone production → calcium release → enzymes activation → meiosis
  D. enzymes activation → meiosis → calcium release → calmodulin activation → hormone production and release
  E. hormone arrival → calcium release → calmodulin activation → enzymes activation → meiosis

173. Which of the following is a correct statement about the experiment?
   A. At all doses vinblastin is a more effective meiosis inhibitor than trifluoperazine.
   B. At all doses trifluoperazine is a more effective meiosis inhibitor than vinblastin.
   C. At 10 micromolar concentration neither chemical is a meiosis inhibitor.
   D. At 100 micromolar concentration vinblastin is a more effective meiosis inhibitor than trifluoperazine.
   E. At 100 micromolar concentration trifluoperazine is a more effective meiosis inhibitor than vinblastin.

174. Which of these is a correct statement about the experiment?
   A. Because the two inhibitory chemicals did not give identical results, no conclusions can be drawn concerning the regulatory role of calmodulin.
   B. The experiment proved conclusively that calmodulin plays a controlling role in starfish meiosis.
   C. The experiment gave results opposite to those expected: calmodulin probably does not control starfish meiosis.
   D. The results were consistent with the hypothesis that calmodulin may play a controlling role in starfish meiosis.
   E. Since calmodulin was not used in the experiment, no conclusions can be drawn on its role in starfish meiosis.

175. Which of these would be the most logical experiment to perform next on this system in order to determine whether calmodulin is an important controller of starfish meiosis?
   A. Determine whether the starfish gonads contain calmodulin.
   B. Look for other calmodulin inhibitors to test in the same system.
   C. Remove calcium from the starfish gonads, and determine whether meiosis is thereby inhibited.
   D. Repeat the experiment with higher and lower doses of the two inhibitors.
   E. Try the same experiment with a different animal.

Questions 176–181
The following table shows the distribution of average weight in grams of seeds harvested from 1000 individual bean plants of the same species.

Average Weight (g)	Below 0.10	0.10–0.15	0.16–0.20	0.21–0.25	0.26–0.30	0.31–0.35	0.36–0.40	0.41–0.45	0.46–0.50	0.51–0.55	0.56–0.60	Above 0.60
Number of plants	15	22	40	62	140	210	200	152	70	50	25	14

176. What is the best genetic explanation for these data?
   A. A single gene existing as many alleles is responsible for the observed variation.
   B. All of the plants had the same genotype; the observed variation is an effect of the environment.
   C. Seed weight is inherited via several genes that add their individual effects.
   D. The small numbers of plants surveyed does not justify confidence about predicting the inheritance pattern.
   E. This is a case of pleiotropy.

177. What would be expected if a plant derived from the lightest seed were crossed with a plant derived from the heaviest seed?
  A. All of the seeds would be identical, falling at the average weight of all of the seeds shown in the table.
  B. Half of the seeds would be very light; the other half would be very heavy.
  C. The resulting seeds would fall into all of the 12 categories listed in the table above.
  D. The seeds would tend to be near the average weight of all of the seeds shown in the table, but would show some variation toward either extreme.
  E. The result would be totally unpredictable.

178. What would be expected if two plants were crossed, each of which had been derived from seeds that fell exactly at the average weight for the population shown in the table?
  A. Their seeds would fall at or very near the average weight of their parents.
  B. Their seeds would fall into two distinct categories, very light or very heavy.
  C. Their seeds would tend to duplicate the distribution of the table.
  D. There would be a 3:1 distribution of seed weights in the next generation, with the largest category being the weight of the parents.
  E. The result would be totally unpredictable.

179. This graph shows the distribution of the table:

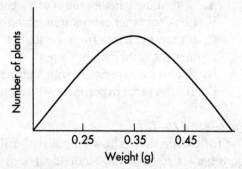

Approximately two thirds of the plants have average seed weights that fall in the range between 0.25 and 0.45 gram. Another way of expressing this is that 0.20 gram is
  A. one degree of freedom
  B. one standard deviation
  C. the chi-square value
  D. the mean deviation
  E. one standard error

180. In humans, a similar inheritance pattern is seen with
  A. adult height
  B. blood types
  C. cystic fibrosis
  D. hemoglobin abnormalities
  E. musical ability

181. In the inheritance mode illustrated by the table, what is the likely role of environmental factors such as rainfall, sunlight, and mineral availability?
  A. at least as potent as any individual genetic factor
  B. negligible
  C. overridingly important, subjugating all genetic factors
  D. totally unpredictable
  E. variable, depending on which end of the weight range is being examined

Questions 182–185
The table below shows data obtained from a study of how coyotes search prey. For each trial, a coyote was released into a large pen in which a rabbit had been placed. Some trials took place on moonless nights to effectively eliminate visual cues. In other trials, the rabbit was dead to eliminate auditory cues. In some trials, the coyote's nasal passages were chemically treated to deaden smell perception temporarily. Some trials involved various combinations of these three sensory deprivations. In all tests, the unit of measure was the duration of search (in seconds) before reaching the rabbit.

Condition	Average Duration (seconds)
1. All cues absent	150
2. Sight, smell, and hearing present	20
3. Sight present	50
4. Hearing present	200
5. Smell present	80
6. Sight and smell present	30
7. Sight and hearing present	40

182. Which of the three senses appears to be most important in locating prey?
  A. hearing
  B. sight
  C. smell
  D. All of them are equally important.
  E. This cannot be determined from the data.

183. From the data given above, which is the most accurate statement?
  A. Hearing is the sense relied upon least by a coyote during hunting, but it can serve as a backup if other senses fail.
  B. If deprived of all of the senses tested, a coyote would be unable to find food.
  C. Some other sense, not tested in these experiments, is probably just as important as any of the tested senses.
  D. The artificial conditions of the testing site make these results invalid.
  E. The color of the rabbit used in each test is an important factor in determining search duration.

184. Which of these would be the most important factor in determining whether these data are significant?
  A. the age of the rabbits used
  B. the journal in which they were presented
  C. the temperature during trials
  D. the physiological condition of the observer
  E. the number of separate trials of each category

185. Which of these would NOT have profoundly affected the results?
  A. the hunger state of the coyote
  B. the presence of coyote pheromones in the enclosure
  C. the shape of the enclosure
  D. the size of the rabbits
  E. the wind velocity and direction

Questions 186–189
Human inheritance patterns can be described by a diagram in which a circle indicates a female and a square represents a male. An open symbol indicates a "normal" appearance, and a filled symbol represents whichever "abnormal" condition is being studied. Look at the diagram below showing four generations.

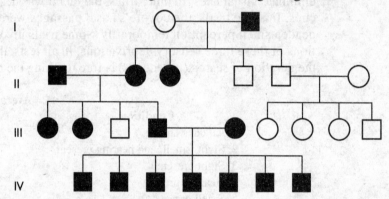

186. What is the best explanation for this inheritance pattern if the condition can be traced to a single gene?
  A. The allele for this condition is sex-linked and dominant.
  B. The allele for this condition is sex-linked and recessive.
  C. The allele for this condition is autosomal and dominant.
  D. The allele for this condition is autosomal and recessive.
  E. There is not enough evidence to determine unambiguously the mode of inheritance.

187. Which generation(s) provided evidence to rule out one or more inheritance possibilities?
  A. generation I
  B. generation II
  C. generation III
  D. generations I and II
  E. generations III and IV

188. Generation IV consists entirely of males. If an eighth child were born in this family, what is the probability that it would be a girl?
  A. 0
  B. .125
  C. .25
  D. .50
  E. 1.0

189. For this question only, assume that the mode of inheritance of the abnormal condition is through a sex-linked recessive allele, *b*. What are the genotypes of the parents that produce generation IV?

A. Father is *b* and mother is *bb*.
B. Father is *B* and mother is *BB*.
C. Father is *bb* and mother is *b*.
D. Father is *bb* and mother is *bb*.
E. Father is *Bb* and mother is *Bb*.

Questions 190–193

Blood clotting is a vital and complex process that requires the presence of several materials in their active form. If a blood platelet makes contact with collagen of a damaged blood vessel, and if a plasma protein called von Willebrand factor is present, the platelet initiates a series of biochemical reactions that leads to its release of ADP into the region of damage. ADP initiates the further accumulation of platelets, causing them to aggregate with each other in the damaged area to form a plug over the wound. Serotonin, a central nervous system neurotransmitter, is also released from the platelets. It causes nearby blood vessels to constrict, thereby limiting further bleeding. Meanwhile prothrombin, a plasma protein, is converted to thrombin by a "tissue factor" released from the damaged vessel wall. This reaction also involves calcium ions and other plasma materials. Thrombin, in turn, acts upon another plasma protein, fibrinogen, to convert it to fibrin. Thrombin has a second function, to stimulate further platelet aggregation and secretion of ADP and serotonin. The fibrin produced from fibrinogen is a tough, stringlike material that adheres to the plug of aggregated platelets, strengthening it and enmeshing erythrocytes to complete the clot.

190. Which of the following is a correct statement?
A. Damaged tissue releases a material that becomes part of the clot.
B. Platelets act both to stimulate clot formation and to become part of the clot.
C. The central nervous system releases one of the materials that act to form a clot.
D. Thrombin and fibrin combine to become a fibrous mesh that entraps red blood cells.
E. All of the above statements are correct.

191. Aspirin interferes with the biochemical reactions that lead to secretion of ADP by platelets. The IMMEDIATE effect of treating platelets with aspirin would be
A. lack of fibrin production
B. lower concentration of von Willebrand factor
C. production of "thin" blood that will not clot easily
D. reduced aggregation of platelets
E. slower conversion of prothrombin to thrombin

192. Hemophilia is a disease in which a plasma protein needed for the conversion of prothrombin to thrombin is lacking. However, an alternative pathway exists to produce reduced amounts of thrombin with help solely from tissue factor. It would be expected, therefore, that a hemophiliac would be able to

A. produce the fibrin portion of a clot, but not the platelet portion

B. produce no clots at all

C. produce the platelet portion of a clot, but not the fibrin portion

D. quickly produce small clots, but not large ones

E. release serotonin from platelets, but not ADP

193. Atherosclerosis is a deposition of fatty materials and endothelial cells within a blood vessel. Sometimes an atherosclerotic vessel triggers formation of a clot. Based only on what you have read here, which of these is a logical explanation for this inappropriate clot formation?

A. Endothelial cells attract the white blood cells that initiate clot formation.

B. Erythrocytes attach to atherosclerotic areas; their presence attracts platelets that initiate clotting.

C. Fatty deposits cause a localized reduction in the concentration of von Willebrand factor; this in turn initiates clot formation.

D. If the turbulent blood flow causes damage to the endothelial cells, collagen is exposed and the clotting mechanism is activated.

E. Reduced blood flow through the constricted vessels is enough to trigger clotting.

Questions 194–197

The pores of bird egg shells are essential for maintenance of gas exchange between the developing embryo and the atmosphere. The two graphs shown below present some data from a comparative study of pore sizes in the eggs of many species. In Graph 1, "Pore length" is the average length of an air passageway through the shell from outside to inside. In Graph 2, "Pore area" is the estimated cross-sectional area of the egg shell that actually consists of openings (pores) rather than shell.

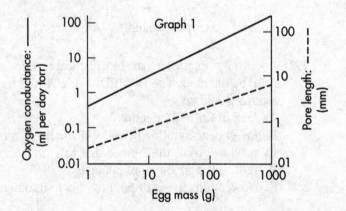

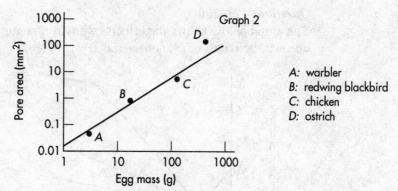

194. Which of these is the most accurate statement about the data in Graph 2?
  A. Pore area bears no predictable relationship to egg mass.
  B. Pore area is directly proportional to egg mass.
  C. Pore area is inversely proportional to egg mass.
  D. Pore area is directly proportional to the logarithm of egg mass.
  E. Pore area is inversely proportional to the logarithm of egg mass.

195. Which of these is the most accurate statement about the relationship between changes in oxygen conductance with changes in pore length?
  A. As egg mass increases, these two change at the same rate.
  B. As egg mass increases, these two do the opposite: one increases, the other decreases.
  C. As egg mass increases, oxygen conductance increases at a faster rate than does pore length.
  D. As egg mass increases, oxygen conductance increases at a slower rate than does pore length.
  E. These two changes cannot be directly compared.

196. From data presented in the graphs, which of these is the most accurate statement about ostrich eggs?
  A. Although their pore area is disproportionately high, its relationship to egg mass is not significantly different from that of other birds.
  B. Their pore lengths are at the upper range of lengths that have been measured.
  C. They do not conduct as much oxygen per gram of egg mass as do the eggs of other birds.
  D. They do not obey Fick's law of diffusion.
  E. They seem to operate under entirely different principles of oxygen conductance than do other eggs.

197. Why is pore length considered to be an important factor in this study?
  A. It is a measure of shell thickness, which determines the degree of protection afforded by the shell.
  B. It is easy to measure.
  C. It was the only factor that showed an increase similar to the increase of oxygen conductance as egg mass increased.
  D. The longer the passageway through which gases must pass, the slower will be the rate of exchange between the embryo and the atmosphere.
  E. Transport of materials through a semipermeable membrane depends particularly upon the shape of the membrane's pores.

Questions 198–200

The graph below shows the effects of environmental oxygen upon three biochemical activities of cyanobacteria.

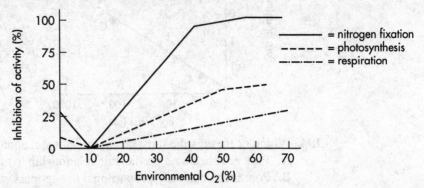

198. What does this graph show about the effect of oxygen upon ALL THREE processes?
A. Nitrogen fixation is least affected by a total lack of oxygen.
B. No generalization can be made, because each of the three processes responds in an entirely different way.
C. The processes all do better at higher oxygen levels.
D. The processes all do better at 10% oxygen than at 50% oxygen.
E. The processes all do worse at 10% oxygen than at 30% oxygen.

199. The Earth presently has an atmosphere of which about 20% is molecular oxygen. What relationship does this fact have to the information presented in the graph?
A. Cyanobacteria do better under current atmospheric conditions than they would have in early Earth history when there was less free oxygen.
B. Cyanobacteria do not seem to be adapted perfectly to present Earth conditions.
C. Since cyanobacteria are prokaryotic, their performance in a 20% oxygen environment is probably explained by their chromosomal arrangement.
D. The evolutionary history of cyanobacteria probably involves a common ancestry with oxygen-requiring eukaryotes.
E. There is no connection between the current Earth value for oxygen and the graph values, since the latter were derived under controlled conditions in a laboratory.

200. Which of these statements would seem to be a logical hypothesis, based on the data of the graph?
A. All prokaryotes evolved in an atmosphere that included 10% molecular oxygen.
B. Cyanobacteria would enjoy the greatest ATP availability at oxygen levels over 40%.
C. Nitrogen fixation is completely inhibited in all environments in which the oxygen level is above 60%.
D. Nitrogen fixation is inhibited by all levels of oxygen because it occurs only in root nodules, which are below ground level.
E. Some prokaryotes evolved in an atmosphere that included 10% molecular oxygen.

Answer Key for Sample Test 1

Use this key to obtain a score for Test 1. Then use the answer explanations on the following pages to gain a better understanding of the concepts needed to answer all questions correctly.

1. D	41. B	81. C	121. D	161. D
2. D	42. A	82. C	122. E	162. B
3. C	43. C	83. D	123. C	163. A
4. C	44. D	84. E	124. A	164. C
5. B	45. C	85. C	125. E	165. E
6. B	46. D	86. A	126. C	166. E
7. A	47. B	87. C	127. B	167. E
8. D	48. E	88. A	128. A	168. D
9. C	49. C	89. B	129. D	169. B
10. E	50. A	90. E	130. C	170. D
11. C	51. B	91. C	131. B	171. D
12. B	52. D	92. A	132. A	172. E
13. E	53. A	93. D	133. E	173. E
14. D	54. B	94. A	134. C	174. D
15. D	55. A	95. C	135. C	175. A
16. A	56. D	96. A	136. D	176. C
17. A	57. C	97. B	137. A	177. D
18. A	58. A	98. E	138. E	178. C
19. B	59. C	99. D	139. A	179. B
20. B	60. B	100. E	140. E	180. A
21. E	61. D	101. C	141. E	181. A
22. E	62. E	102. A	142. B	182. B
23. D	63. E	103. B	143. E	183. A
24. A	64. A	104. A	144. D	184. E
25. D	65. A	105. D	145. D	185. D
26. D	66. C	106. E	146. C	186. E
27. B	67. D	107. A	147. A	187. C
28. A	68. B	108. A	148. A	188. D
29. D	69. C	109. E	149. B	189. A
30. E	70. B	110. B	150. D	190. B
31. D	71. A	111. D	151. A	191. D
32. D	72. D	112. C	152. E	192. D
33. C	73. B	113. A	153. C	193. D
34. A	74. C	114. C	154. E	194. B
35. A	75. C	115. C	155. E	195. C
36. E	76. C	116. D	156. B	196. A
37. D	77. B	117. B	157. C	197. D
38. C	78. A	118. A	158. D	198. D
39. D	79. E	119. D	159. A	199. B
40. A	80. E	120. B	160. A	200. E

Answer Explanations for Sample Test 1

1. **(D)** According to Oparin, the primitive atmosphere consisted of a mixture of all of the items listed except oxygen. Later work by Stanley L. Miller resulted in the identification of a variety of organic compounds, including amino acids, from such a mixture.

2. **(D)** Plasmolysis is the shrinking of protoplasm due to the loss of water. Water diffuses into and out of cells, but the net movement is from places of higher concentration to places of lower concentration. If the solution surrounding a cell is hypertonic (containing more solute), it is so diluted by the solute that the solution contains less water than the cell; therefore, the net movement of water will be out of the cell, causing the plant cell to plasmolyze. This effect will also be produced by drinking seawater, salting a ham, or overfertilizing plants.

3. **(C)** Erythrocytes (red blood cells) are produced by mitosis of cells in bone marrow. Before they are released into circulation, they have become differentiated "bags" of hemoglobin and a few enzymes. Blastema cells and neoblasts are undifferentiated animal cells that participate in the regeneration of body parts. Zygotes and blastomeres are undifferentiated cells of early embryos.

4. **(C)** If the genotypes of both parents are *Bb*, the gene combinations in the offspring will be *BB*, *Bb*, and *bb* (see diamond).

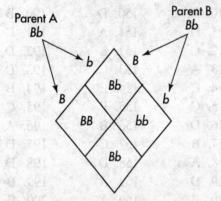

If *b* is recessive and lethal, the genotype *bb* will die. In the case suggested, death occurred early in development, in the embryonic stage, since there is no visible evidence of it. Of course the effects of a lethal gene might occur instead in a fetal or postnatal stage. You can see from the genotypes in the diamond that the probability of gening the lethal gene combination *bb* is 25%.

5. **(B)** Phytoplankton consist largely of chlorophyll-containing algae that require light to carry on photosynthesis. Naturally they cannot survive in the absence of light, and light of sufficient intensity to drive photosynthesis does not penetrate deeply in water. Planktonic animals (zooplankton) are also concentrated near the surface because they are primary consumers of the algae.

6. **(B)** The cereal-producing crops are grass species, well suited to temperate grassland biomes.

7. **(A)** A typical human cell contains the diploid number of chromosomes, 46. Although it is difficult to prove, most geneticists agree that each chromosome is a single length of DNA. Astonishingly, the DNA of chromosomes is so compacted that it would stretch about 1 meter if all 46 chromosomes' worth was laid end to end. Coiling and supercoiling squeeze this DNA into a nucleus about 5 mμ in diameter.

8. **(D)** Allelopathy is the production and release, by a plant, of chemicals that inhibit the establishment of competing plants nearby. The result is a uniform spacing of plants, which is advantageous in a harsh climate with little available water.

9. **(C)** Hemocyanin is the oxygen-carrying pigment in the blood of horseshoe crabs (in phylum Arthropoda, class Merostomata) and in some molluscs and crustaceans.

10. **(E)** Respiration, transpiration, and photosynthesis are effected by exchanges of gases through the stomata. Wilting results when the loss of water by transpiration exceeds the amount absorbed. All of these processes would be retarded or stopped if the stomata of leaves were sealed. Guttation is the loss of water in

drops from special structures called hydathodes, which are usually located on the tips and margins of leaves. It occurs when absorption of water exceeds its loss by transpiration or use. Actually, sealing the stomata stops transpiration and increases guttation.

11. **(C)** AIDS symptoms can be traced to the destruction of helper T cells. The result is an inability to ward off infections or to recognize and destroy cancer cells.

12. **(B)** In test-crossing, an individual showing the dominant trait (*AA* or *Aa*) is crossed with one that is homozygous recessive (*aa*) to determine whether the genotype of the individual showing the dominant trait is homozygous (*AA*) or heterozygous (*Aa*). If *AA* is crossed with *aa*, all offspring will be *Aa* and have the dominant trait. This result indicates that only *A*'s come from the parent showing the dominant trait, and hence that its genotype must be *AA*. If *Aa* is crossed with *aa*, half of the offspring will be *aa* and have the recessive trait. This result indicates that one of the *a*'s had to come from the parent showing the dominant trait, and hence its genotype would be *Aa*.

13. **(E)** Chaparral is characterized by mild and rainy winters followed by very dry summers. These conditions, and the plants that thrive in them, are found around the Mediterranean Sea and in California, South Africa, Chile, and western Australia.

14. **(D)** Prophase usually requires more time than all of the other phases of mitosis combined, about 60% of the total. The time when the cell is not dividing, called interphase, is a preparatory period when DNA is duplicated. This period, though part of a cell cycle, is not regarded as a phase of mitosis. Even in cells that divide repeatedly, interphase requires a great deal more time than all of the phases of mitosis.

15. **(D)** The Hardy-Weinberg equation is $p^2 + 2pq + q^2 = 1$. The p^2 predicts the frequency of genotype *AA*; $2pq$ predicts *Aa*; and q^2 predicts *aa*.

16. **(A)** Carotene is a yellow-to-red hydrocarbon produced by many plants. It is present in foods such as yellow and green vegetables and the animal products butter, egg yolks, and liver. Carotene is converted to vitamin A in the liver.

17. **(A)** Went cut off the tips of oat coleoptiles and placed them on agar. After a short time he removed the coleoptiles and put little blocks of the agar on decapitated plants, which responded to light as if the coleoptiles had not been removed (without coleoptiles the plants would not respond to light). Clearly the coleoptiles produced a substance that diffused into the agar, and then from the agar to the growing tissues of the stem.

18. **(A)** An antheridium (pl., antheridia) produces sperm cells. In plants that have antheridia, these organs are unicellular in most plants below the level of bryophytes and multicellular in bryophytes and higher plants. The antheridial wall is a single cell in lower plants and a multicellular jacket (called a sterile jacket) in higher plants. Of course antheridia vary considerably in shape and size in the various plants that have these organs.

19. **(B)** During the light-dependent phase of photosynthesis, when light is trapped by chlorophyll molecules, light energy is converted into electrical energy. In turn, the electrical energy is converted into chemical energy and stored in the bonds of NADPH and ATP.

20. **(B)** Probability is based on possible gene combinations, not on what happened the last time. However, in the case given, knowing the genotype of the firstborn helps in determining the genotype of the parents. Since the firstborn has type O blood, its genotype must be *ii*, indicating that each parent had to contribute one *i* by its gamete. The genotype of the parent with type A blood would then have to be $I^A i$, and that of the parent with type B blood would have to be $I^B i$. All possible gametes and genotypes that the parents can produce are shown in the diagram that follows:

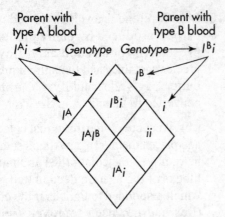

Parent with
type A blood

Parent with
type B blood

$I^A i$ ⟵ Genotype Genotype ⟶ $I^B i$

You can see from the genotypes in the diamond that these parents can produce children with four blood types and that the possibility is 25% for each type. The combination on the left corner of the diamond would result in type AB blood.

21. **(E)** Glass is transparent to light rays but not to heat rays. Sunlight enters a greenhouse and raises the temperature of objects such as soil and pots, which then emit heat rays that are trapped because they cannot escape through the glass. It is thought that carbon dioxide in the atmosphere may act like the glass of a greenhouse, interfering with reradiation of heat back into space. Many scientists believe that the quantity of carbon dioxide in the atmosphere is increasing because of accelerated burning of fossil fuels. Some fear that enough heat may be trapped near the earth's surface to change the weather drastically and melt the polar ice caps, thereby overfilling the present oceanic basins. However, a large reservoir of carbon dioxide is dissolved in the oceans, much more than in the atmosphere. No doubt the oceans will continue to absorb and hold some of the additional carbon dioxide resulting from combustion.

22. **(E)** The atmosphere is 21% oxygen. The oxygen content of the soil varies greatly but is much less than that of the air. Much oxygen is consumed by soil organisms (including bacteria and the roots of higher plants), decreasing the amount of oxygen available to the point where many organisms die for lack of it. The same is true in aquatic habitats where the amount of oxygen is one twentieth to one fortieth of that in the air. Oxygen diffuses into water slowly. That is the reason for agitating water to increase the absorption of oxygen (the movement increases the surface area in contact with air). Temperature is an important factor in the oxygen-holding capacity of water; more can be held at colder temperatures.

23. **(D)** Ants leave chemical trails by secreting a pheromone. Pheromones are defined as chemical secretions that influence the behavior or development of other members of the same species. Besides their use for trail marking, pheromones are used for member recognition and sexual attraction.

24. **(A)** Tropical rain forests support the majority of all species in the world.

25. **(D)** *Escherichia coli* is a bacterium, and hence a prokaryote. Rabbits are, of course, eukaryotes. Eukaryotes have nuclear material surrounded by a well-defined nuclear membrane, whereas prokaryotes have the nucleus unenclosed. Many other eukaryotic organelles have membranes as well.

26. **(D)** The K strategy for successful reproduction is to provide extended care for a small number of offspring. The alternative r strategy is to invest energy in large numbers rather than parental care.

27. **(B)** In freshwater environments the percentage of water within protozoa is less than on the outside. Consequently the net diffusion of water (osmosis) is into the organisms. Excess water must, however, be eliminated, or the organisms will swell and probably burst. Excess water accumulates in the contractile vacuoles, which periodically contract, expelling the water to the outside.

28. **(A)** The constant appearance of new strains of influenza virus is ample evidence of mutation within a viral genome.

29. **(D)** Ethylene is a naturally occurring substance that promotes ripening of

fruits. It causes color changes, softening of the tissues, and usually an increase in sugar content. These changes make fruits more attractive and palatable to animals that use them for food and incidentally disperse their seeds. Anybody can ripen fruits on a small scale by enclosing them in a plastic bag with ripe apples or bananas, which generate ethylene.

30. **(E)** By definition, phenotype generally means expressed hereditary characteristics, many of which, such as size and color, are visible. Certain physiological characteristics, for example, resistance to disease, or internal morphological characteristics, such as circulatory anomalies, may not be readily observed, although they are of hereditary origin. However, if caused by genes, the characteristic— visible or not—is a phenotype.

31. **(D)** Animals in hot climates may get too hot, especially since they also generate heat from internal metabolic processes. The smaller the size of a body, the greater is its surface area in proportion to its mass. An animal with a larger surface area in contact with the environment can dissipate metabolic heat faster than an animal with a smaller surface area. Animals in colder climates may need to conserve heat and would therefore be favored by having larger bodies with relatively small surface areas.

32. **(D)** Polymorphism is the occurrence of several distinct forms of a species. It may involve morphological differences (such as color or shape) or differences at the physiological or biochemical levels. Examples of polymorphism are the dark and light color forms of the peppered moth (subjects of a classic study involving industrial melanism) and the gray and black forms of the gray squirrel. Each form of the species may have a survival advantage at different seasons or in different locations. However, it is to the species' evolutionary advantage to maintain polymorphism even if there is no immediate advantage in having multiple forms.

33. **(C)** Climax communities are characterized ordinarily by being self-perpetuating and having species diversity, maximum biomass, complex food chains, and a low photosynthesis-respiration (P/R) ratio that approximates 1.

34. **(A)** The littoral zone is the shallow region of the lake, nearest the shoreline. It supports the greatest plant growth because light penetrates it; this plant growth, in turn, supports a large animal population.

35. **(A)** This principle noted by Malthus became a fundamental part of Darwin's concept of evolution and an important consideration of population biologists. Almost without exception, populations increase beyond the carrying capacity of the places where they live. Thus individuals in a population must compete for limited resources, and as a consequence many individuals die, often because they are weaker competitors.

36. **(E)** Genetic drift is a change in the gene frequencies of small breeding populations. The change is due to the chance assortment of genes in meiosis and fertilization or to random loss of individuals. When a change occurs in a small population, the percentage change is greater than if the change occurs in a large population.

37. **(D)** Down syndrome is caused by the presence of an extra 21st chromosome, which is either separate or attached to another chromosome. The incidence of Down syndrome increases with the mother's age at conception, particularly after the age of 35.

38. **(C)** Since the change in allele frequencies is progressive (not random), it is not mutation. Also, since it is occurring within a population (therefore, within a single species), it is not macroevolution. Natural selection is a process by which the change could occur, but it is not the change itself. *Punctuated equilibrium* is a term describing relatively sudden change that would not be likely to continue progressively.

39. **(D)** Hydrogen bonds are weak bonds that link hydrogen atoms to other atoms, usu-

ally oxygen or nitrogen. Each nucleotide pair is linked by two or three hydrogen bonds to either oxygen or nitrogen.

40. **(A)** Stabilizing selection is the form of natural selection in which the intermediate phenotype is favored. It is probably the form that is occurring in most populations most of the time.

41. **(B)** The glomerulus is a cluster of capillaries that deposits filtrate from the bloodstream into Bowman's capsule, which surrounds it. The glomerulus is a part of the nephron, the functional unit of the kidney.

42. **(A)** The gradualist model of speciation posits a slow, rather constant accumulation of changes until a new species has evolved. Punctuated equilibrium, an alternative view, proposes that rapid bursts of relatively radical change follow long periods of very little change.

43. **(C)** The benthic region, by definition, forms the bottom of an ocean. The organisms dwelling there comprise the benthos.

44. **(D)** The fossil record indicates that members of the plant kingdom first appeared about 460 million years ago, 45 million years after the close of the Cambrian Period.

45. **(C)** Meristematic tissues differentiate into mature tissues. They may be classified as apical or cambial. Apical meristem is located at the tips of roots and stems, where it produces primary tissues that lengthen them. Cambial meristem is of two types, vascular and cork. Vascular cambium, located between the wood and bark, produces secondary xylem and phloem that increase the plant's girth; cork cambium produces cork that replaces epidermis in older roots and stems.

46. **(D)** Blooms are rapid increases in populations that are obvious to the eye. Some species of dinoflagellates make the ocean water red by their abundance. They are harmless to crustaceans and molluscs that eat them but are toxic to vertebrates that then eat the crustaceans and molluscs. When blooms are unusually large, countless fish are usually killed.

47. **(B)** Autotrophs are organisms that manufacture their own food. Most of them do this by photosynthesis, but some bacteria, such as nitrifying ones, are chemosynthetic, using the energy of chemical reactions (instead of light) to synthesize foods.

48. **(E)** If genes are linked together on the same chromosome, they should normally remain together when transmitted to offspring. For example, if the genotype of two parents is *AaBb* and the genes *AB* are on one chromosome and *ab* are on the other, there should be only two phenotypes. If the genes are on separate chrornosomes, there should be four phenotypes. However, because of crossing-over, or exchange of parts between chromosomes, cases occur in which genes linked on the same chromosome produce four phenotypes instead of the expected two. The study of linkage and crossing-over has resulted in genetic maps of chromosomes.

49. **(C)** Succession is a series of community changes related to habitat changes that precede the development of a climax community. The climax is relatively stable since it is shaped by long-persisting climatic conditions. The successional stages are temporary because habitat conditions change from extreme to intermediate.

50. **(A)** Animals with front-field vision have eyes that focus simultaneously on the same objects ahead. As a result their vision is stereoscopic, that is, three-dimensional, with the ability to judge depth. Such animals have good perception of distance, which makes it easier for them to capture prey.

51. **(B)** A density-dependent factor is one whose effect increases as the population density increases. Random weather events, causing unpredictable damage to populations, are considered density-independent.

52. **(D)** Microfilaments are fibers that run through a cell's cytoplasm. Composed of

actin or an actin-like protein, they can cause movement of attached structures by rapid self-assembly and dis-assembly.

53. **(A)** Obviously, a predator who combines the behavior of lying in wait with a body color that blends in with the environment is likely to be successful.

54. **(B)** Acetylcholine is one of the best known of the synaptic neurotransmitters. It is secreted in the craniosacral portion of the autonomic nervous system, probably in the central nervous system, and at junctions with skeletal muscle.

55. **(A)** Panting lowers the body temperature by evaporating water that absorbs heat. Panting is especially useful in reducing the body temperature of animals, such as dogs, that do not sweat.

56. **(D)** If a pregnancy is to ensue, the mammalian egg should be fertilized in the one-third of the oviduct nearest the ovary. If fertilization occurs elsewhere, the timing of embryo development and uterine wall preparation will be improper, and implantation in the wall will fail.

57. **(C)** The heterozygote is *AaBb*, and the homozygous recessive is *aabb*. When crossed, the possible combinations are as shown in the rectangular sections of the diagram.

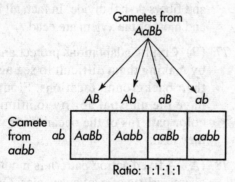

Gametes from
AaBb

AB   Ab   aB   ab

Gamete
from   ab | *AaBb* | *Aabb* | *aaBb* | *aabb*
aabb

Ratio: 1:1:1:1

58. **(A)** Some people mistakenly think that the ocean is an unlimited reservoir of food. It is actually very unproductive when compared to forest land. The most productive parts of the ocean are in regions of upwelling and along the fringes of continents. Approximately half of the world's fish harvest is taken from about 1% of the oceans.

59. **(C)** Müllerian mimicry is described by this example. If one of the species were tasty to predators, it would be practicing Batesian mimicry.

60. **(B)** Members of the same species compete with one another more than with members of another species because intraspecies needs are the same. Within a species the greatest intensity of competition occurs between males competing for a female. Usually the period of intense sexual activity in male mammals occurs at specific seasons and is called rutting.

61. **(D)** Translation is the process described in the question. It occurs when tRNA, with its attached amino acid, finds its place on the mRNA strand, thus bringing the proper amino acid into a position where it can be bonded (by peptide linkage).

62. **(E)** The four nucleotide bases can be paired as A-T (or T-A) and C-G (or G-C).

63. **(E)** The suffix *-cyte* to all of the words means "cell." The first four listed are blood cells; the last is a cartilage cell.

64. **(A)** The rocks formed in Precambrian times (earlier than about 600 million years before the present) contain far fewer fossils than those of the Cambrian and later periods, both in absolute numbers and in numbers of phyla represented.

65. **(A)** Coevolution is the process whereby two species gradually adapt to each other's presence until each becomes somewhat dependent upon the other's characteristics. Commensalism, on the other hand, is a symbiotic relationship in which one species derives clear benefit and the other neither benefits nor is harmed.

66. **(C)** These plants are grouped together because they share certain anatomical features and perform photosynthesis in a unique way that involves production of a four-carbon intermediate rather than the usual three-carbon molecule of the Calvin cycle. Comprising over 100 genera, they

have a common biogeographical history, originating in tropical regions. They can carry out photosynthesis in a high-O_2, low-CO_2 environment such as occurs in hot weather when leaf stomata close to retain water. Corn is a good example of a C_4 plant.

67. **(D)** *Escherichia coli,* a common inhabitant of the human intestinal tract, was the first organism used to clone genetic information that had been inserted via plasmids.

68. **(B)** Intestinal bacteria serve several useful purposes, such as digestion of food, synthesis of vitamins, and regulation of fecal consistency. In humans, bacteria may comprise 25 to 50% of the bulk of feces. Obviously damage is done when antibiotics kill these bacteria.

69. **(C)** Convergent evolution is the development of similar adaptive characteristics by organisms with dissimilar origins. Fish and whales, though in different vertebrate classes (whales are mammals), have similar body shapes that facilitate their movements in water.

70. **(B)** A gene pool consists of all of the genes in a population, and a population, in the broad sense, is all of the individuals that comprise a species. Generally speaking, individuals of the same species can interbreed, thereby sharing genes with one another.

71. **(A)** When a large population is rapidly reduced to a much smaller size, the survivors are said to have gone through a genetic bottleneck. Since there are few survivors, the population that arises from them is likely to be less variable (less polymorphic) than the original population.

72. **(D)** Photoperiodism is the phenomenon exhibited by plants when they change under the influence of daytime length. Spring flowering of fruit trees is such a response. A light-sensitive pigment, phytochrome, may be the material whose response to daylight triggers such changes.

73. **(B)** The Hardy-Weinberg equation for a two-allele gene is $p^2 + 2pq + q^2 = 1$, where the recessive allele's frequency is symbolized by q. The frequency of the homozygous recessive sickle-cell anemia genotype is equal to $q^2 = (0.04)^2 = 0.0016$.

74. **(C)** The distance between B and D is 18 map units. The distances between C and D, A and B, and A and C are less. The largest distance, between A and D, is 23 units. A greater distance indicates that more recombination events have been observed between the two reference points. Map unit distances determined by recombination frequency are approximately equivalent to actual physical distances along the chromosome.

75. **(C)** The kinds of gametes that can be produced by an organism with the genotype $AaBbCC$ are as follows: ABC, AbC, aBC, and abC.

76. **(C)** Plant cells divide in specific locations known as meristems. One such location is cambium. Vascular cambium, located between the xylem and phloem of roots and stems, adds annual rings of xylem (from which the age of the plant can be determined) and secondary phloem in the inner bark. Cork cambium, located in the bark, produces cork on the outside and other cells on the inside. Mature cells such as phloem, pith, xylem, and fibers do not divide. In fact, all fibers and most of the xylem are dead.

77. **(B)** Cryptic adaptations protect animals by making them difficult to see against their background locations. Flounders have the unusual ability to mimic the color patterns of the ocean floor where they rest.

78. **(A)** A fixed action pattern is innate and characteristic of a given species. Often it is expressed at birth or hatching, but it may occur later. Other examples than the one mentioned in the question are the tern's orientation of a fish head to facilitate its swallowing and the dog's turning around several times before lying down. Perhaps the latter is a lingering behavioral

pattern used by dogs' ancestors to check the surroundings for safety before going to sleep.

79. **(E)** Some plant species are particularly adept at producing hybrids that are viable. Examination of the chromosomes of the new species reveals chromosomes of both of the original species. Of course, the original two species had to be living together; thus, this is sympatric speciation.

80. **(E)** Auxin, under the influence of light, migrates to the shady side of a growing tip. Elongation of cells is greater on the shady side because of this increase in auxin concentration. The growth takes place in two phases, cell multiplication and cell elongation. The latter occurs because auxin makes cell walls soften, allowing them to stretch as water is absorbed and pressure increases.

81. **(C)** The amazing radiation of life that occurred during the Cambrian Period is clearly shown by the fossils of the Burgess Shale formation.

82. **(C)** Members of genus *Australopithecus* are the earliest known hominids and appear to have preceded *Homo* by about 0.5 million years. *A. robustus* is in the fossil record about 1.5 million years after *A. afarensis* first appears and was probably contemporary with members of genus *Homo*.

83. **(D)** Adaptive radiation is the evolution of specialized types of organisms from a relatively unspecialized type. Darwin found 13 species of finches in the Galápagos Islands, each having evolved adaptations fitting it for specific feeding habits. The most obvious differences are in beak size and shape.

84. **(E)** Lactic acid is a three-carbon molecule, unable to twist into a ring formation. Each of the other compounds listed in the question has at least one ringed portion.

85. **(C)** Carrying capacity is an ecological term for the size of a population that can be adequately supported in a particular location, for example, the number of people who can live on the Earth or in a particular country, the number of eagles that can survive in Alaska, or the number of plum trees in a thicket. Carrying capacity is determined by fluctuations in biotic (competition, etc.) and abiotic (space, etc.) factors.

86. **(A)** Usually, zinc fingers are proteins that fold into proper shape (fingerlike) to match the grooves along a DNA molecule. When fitted properly, a zinc-finger protein changes the "on-off" status of a gene. Some zinc-finger proteins attach to specific regions of other proteins, rather than to DNA.

87. **(C)** Imprinting is an especially strong response in hatchling ducks, geese, turkeys, swans, and chickens. The behavioral attachment to objects other than their mothers occurs only within a short period of time after hatching, sometimes in less than 1 day. Konrad Lorenz is responsible for much research on imprinting.

88. **(A)** A microtubule is assembled from repeating units of the protein tubulin.

89. **(B)** Competition for resources, such as food or oxygen, occurs among organisms of the same species as well as between species. All of the other choices are well-known isolating mechanisms that can prevent members of different species from successfully reproducing.

90. **(E)** Restriction endonucleases cleave the bonds between specific nucleotides of a nucleic acid. Biochemists can easily determine the nucleotide sequences of the short strands that are produced by treatment with these enzymes.

91. **(C)** The major histocompatibility (MHC) antigens are surface proteins that can be recognized as foreign if they are significantly different from those of the transplant recipient's body tissues. If this occurs, an attack on the foreign tissue is begun by T cells.

92. **(A)** Acetate, a two-carbon molecule, is formed when CO_2 is lost from pyruvate.

The acetate is attached to coenzyme A (CoA), which takes it to the first reactions within the Krebs (citric acid) cycle.

93. **(D)** While animal cells lack chloroplasts, the converse idea that plant cells lack mitochondria is false. Where else would plants fully metabolize the glucose that they make in photosynthesis?

94. **(A)** Complementary (or copy) DNA (cDNA) is artificially produced by causing the enzyme reverse transcriptase to act upon cytoplasmic messenger RNA from a eukaryotic cell. Since this mRNA has already been processed within the cell nucleus, its introns have been removed.

95. **(C)** Cesium-137 is a member of the alkali group of elements, and its physiological actions are similar to those of potassium.

96. **(A)** Strontium-90 is a product of uranium fission and is dangerous because it is deposited, as is calcium, in bones. It accumulates in plants and is passed on to animals that eat them.

97. **(B)** Nitrogen-15 is a heavy isotope of nitrogen, containing one more neutron than normal. It does not emit high-energy particles and so is not radioactive. Compounds containing nitrogen-15 are distinguishable from their normal counterparts by their greater density. The two forms are separable in an ultracentrifuge.

98. **(E)** Carbon-14, with a half-life of 5760 years, is incorporated into organic products and is used to date organic remains.

99. **(D)** Iodine is in the thyroxin molecule, which is produced by the thyroid gland. The isotope iodine-131, which is radioactive, will substitute for the stable form of the element and concentrate in the gland.

100. **(E)** Although he did not invent the microscope, A. van Leeuwenhoek (1632–1723) refined the instrument and used it to discover and describe many cell types and structures.

101. **(C)** Alexander Fleming discovered the antibacterial action of penicillin when he saw that the mold *Penicillium* on a culture plate destroyed the bacteria around it. Fleming a bacteriologist at the University of London, reported the discovery in 1929.

102. **(A)** Hardy and Weinberg showed that, when mating is purely at random and there is no survival advantage of one allele over another, the percentages of the dominant and recessive genes in a population tend to stay the same.

103. **(B)** Working in England, James Watson and Francis Crick used X-ray diffraction data and other information to conclude that DNA can exist as a double helix with the two polynucleotide strands hydrogen-bonded at their nitrogenous bases.

104. **(A)** After chromosomes assemble at the equator of the spindle in metaphase, the two chromosome halves (chromatids) separate and move to the poles, apparently pulled by fibers attached at positions called kinetochores. The cell is in anaphase when the daughter chromosomes are going to the poles.

105. **(D)** The chronological sequence of mitotic stages is as follows: prophase—metaphase—anaphase—telophase.

106. **(E)** In telophase the chromatids are at the poles of the spindle; the cell completes its division; and two new nuclei are formed. Once division is completed, the two new cells are in interphase, during which time DNA is reduplicated.

107. **(A)** Although a barnacle's shell might lead one to conclude that it is a member of the Mollusca, its jointed appendages place it within phylum Arthropoda.

108. **(A)** Insects make phylum Arthropoda the most diverse phylum. The number of identified insect species is over one million.

109. **(E)** Even though they possess three distinct layers of tissue (ectoderm, mesoderm, and endoderm), as do all of the others on the list, the flatworms lack any significant cavity within the mesoderm.

110. **(B)** Phylum Annelida includes class Oligochaeta (earthworms).

111. **(D)** Lactate, or lactic acid, is the product of glycolysis under anaerobic conditions in most organisms. If a cell lacks molecular oxygen, it feeds pyruvic acid and reduced NAD to the fermentation reaction.

112. **(C)** Melvin Calvin won a Nobel Prize in 1961 for his work in elucidating the mechanism by which many plants convert 3-carbon molecules to glucose by the addition of CO_2 and hydrogen, using the energy of the light-dependent reactions of photosynthesis. The Calvin cycle is a set of light-independent reactions occurring with or without light if "light reactions" have previously supplied sufficient energy stored in bonds of compounds.

113. **(A)** The Krebs cycle, also known as the citric acid cycle or the tricarboxylic acid cycle, accepts 2-carbon molecules and yields 1-carbon molecules, CO_2. In the course of this activity bonds are broken and their energy is captured as bonds of ATP. Sir Hans Krebs received a Nobel Prize in recognition of his work on this nearly universal mechanism for transfer of energy to readily usable form in a cell that is operating aerobically.

114. **(C)** The word *glycolysis* means "splitting of glucose." This is the first series of reactions that a cell runs if it is to obtain energy by tearing apart glucose. It occurs whether or not O_2 is present, but its products are used differently, according to which of these conditions is in effect.

115. **(C)** Collagen is a protein of connective tissue. All proteins are polypeptides, although some proteins also include portions made of other material (like heme groups of hemoglobin).

116. **(D)** The letters AMP signify adenosine monophosphate. This is a nucleotide, being composed of a nitrogenous base (adenine), a 5-carbon sugar (ribose), and a phosphate group. Ribonucleic acids (RNA) are polymers of similar nucleotides. Cyclic AMP is an important intracellular messenger.

117. **(B)** The steroid cholesterol is a molecule that can be converted to other steroids, including sex hormones. Cholesterol is a major component of cell membranes.

118. **(A)** Both starch and chitin are polysaccharides. Chitin is used by many invertebrates as tough skeletal material.

119. **(D)** Adenosine triphosphate (ATP) is, like AMP, a nucleotide, but it has two additional phosphates. It is an energy-carrying molecule.

120. **(B)** Named for the famous Italian anatomist Marcello Malpighi, these tubes receive nitrogenous wastes from an insect's coelom and transfer them to the intestinal tract. A vertebrate animal's nephrons (the functional units of the kidney) also process nitrogenous wastes.

121. **(D)** Tracheoles are tiny tubes at the end of larger tubes called tracheae. Continuous with the exoskeleton, tracheoles contain atmospheric oxygen, which diffuses into nearby cells.

122. **(E)** A cross-sectional view of a vertebrate animal's intestine reveals the presence of many fingerlike projections into the lumen (opening) of the tract. These villi enhance absorption by presenting a large surface area to contact digested food molecules.

123. **(C)** The tension-cohesion model of upward water movement in a vascular plant involves two forces. Tension is applied from leaf surfaces, where water molecules evaporate into the atmosphere. Each such molecule exerts a pulling force on other attached molecules, bringing them up to the leaf surface. This attachment to other water molecules, by hydrogen bonding, is called cohesion. An unbroken chain of molecules is thus pulled upward. A third factor causes pushing from below, a phenomenon called root pressure.

124. **(A)** Abscission is the development of a layer of cells at the base of a leaf, flower, or fruit. The result is to make the petiole weaken, eventually leading to a break. Abscission is under hormonal control.

125. **(E)** The products of photosynthesis, dissolved in water, may be redistributed in the process called translocation. This occurs principally in phloem.

126. **(C)** The northern coniferous forests (taiga) include occasional deciduous trees, but annual plants are sparse.

127. **(B)** Both savanna and temperate grassland are characterized by a paucity of trees, but savanna is an area of relatively constant temperature.

128. **(A)** See answer 127, above.

129. **(D)** Tropical rain-forest trees grow densely in their well-watered environment. To compete for sunlight, they tend to become quite tall, with their leafy canopies near the tops.

130. **(C)** Needle-leafed evergreens of the taiga are well adapted for shedding snow before enough can accumulate to break branches. Much of Canada, Siberia, and Scandinavia is covered by taiga.

131. **(B)** Phosphorus, needed by organisms to make nucleotides, is the major limiting resource for green plants in lakes. If this element is supplied in abundance to a lake via the runoff of agricultural fertilizer placed on nearby fields, an algal bloom may be expected. This increase of organic material is termed eutrophication.

132. **(A)** A stable, fat-soluble chemical that tends to accumulate in low concentrations within simple organisms at the bottom of a food chain will be passed intact to animals that eat these organisms. Passage of the chemical will continue up the food chain; and since each animal in the chain eats many of its prey species, the concentration per animal of the persistent chemical will increase. Therefore, animals at the top of a food chain are most likely to contain an unhealthy concentration of the chemical.

133. **(E)** When fresh rock or soil is exposed in a particular biome, only certain plant species will be able to colonize there. These species eventually tend to change the area in such a way that they cannot compete with other incoming species. Thus, a predictable succession of species ensues. This displacement occurs several times in a predictable manner until certain species reach maturity and cannot be easily displaced. This stable climax condition often involves a large number of animal and plant species with complex interactions, all depending upon the ecosystem influenced by the larger plants that contribute most to characterizing the region.

134. **(C)** If two populations occupy the same territory but do not exchange genetic information by sexual reproduction, they are of different species. The result may be interspecific competition for certain resources.

135. **(C)** Just after sodium ions rush into a neuron as a result of the opening of the voltage-activated sodium channels, positively charged potassium ions leave the neuron. This transfer leads to an increase of positive charge on the outside of the membrane.

136. **(D)** Much sodium (a positively charged ion) is held outside the cell until stimulation causes the voltage-activated sodium channels to open, and sodium enters by diffusion.

137. **(A)** When the events of an action potential occur in a particular portion of the neuronal membrane, these changes stimulate adjacent membrane, causing its sodium and potassium channels to open. Thus, an action potential propagates a copy of itself. When repeated many times, the effect is of an action potential "flowing" along the elongated neuron.

138. **(E)** The sodium-potassium active transport mechanism ensures that more positive ions will be held outside the membrane than are present within the cytoplasm, but only if the voltage-activated sodium and potassium channels are closed. The net effect is the maintenance of a small but significant potential difference (voltage) across the membrane.

139. **(A)** The cotyledons lie within a plant seed. As the seedling lifts out of the soil, the cotyledons often rise also.

140. **(E)** The diploid sporophytic stage of a fern is the familiar form of the plant, having large leaves. The far less conspicuous form in a fern's life cycle is the haploid gametophyte, which rarely exceeds 5 millimeters in its longest dimension.

141. **(E)** For any plant having alternation of generations between diploid and haploid, the diploid form may be called a sporophyte. It produces haploid spores by meiosis.

142. **(B)** Endosperm is specialized tissue within a seed. It is adjacent to the embryo and holds stored food.

143. **(E)** An inducer is a chemical produced in one group of embryonic cells that, upon diffusion to another group, triggers the differentiation of the latter.

144. **(D)** The single layer of cells of the blastula stage becomes a double or triple thickness of cells by the programmed movements of gastrulation.

145. **(D)** See answer 144, above.

146. **(C)** Gametes are haploid sex cells produced by the process of meiosis.

147. **(A)** The process of producing the hollow ball called a blastula involves many asexual divisions (cleavages) of cells by mitosis.

148. **(A)** Flowers, which are highly modified stems and leaves, are found only in angiosperms.

149. **(B)** The bryophytes, including mosses, do not contain tubes for internal transport. This lack limits their independence from an aquatic environment.

150. **(D)** Kingdom Fungi, according to the five-kingdom system first proposed by R. H. Whittaker, includes parasitic multicellular organisms with cell walls that are chemically unlike those of plants.

151. **(A)** The archenteron forms as a result of gastrulation movements and is an opening that remains as the gut.

152. **(E)** Mesoderm can become a wide variety of materials, including muscle, bone, connective tissue, and blood.

153. **(C)** The brain is an anterior expansion of the neural tube, which is formed by an insinking of ectoderm along the embryo's middorsal line.

154. **(E)** The part of mesoderm that becomes the notochord is the archenteron roof, but the term *archenteron* refers to an open space, not the cellular material that forms its boundary.

155. **(E)** A number of genes are capable of moving from one site to another among the chromosomes. Transposons are DNA segments that carry these genes and also have insertion sequences enabling the carried genes to be inserted into the new chromosomal locations.

156. **(B)** Occurring in multiple forms, histones are basic proteins that easily attach to nucleic acids. Their general effect is to inhibit the transcription of genes to which they reversibly bind.

157. **(C)** Some genes of eukaryotic cells have sequences that appear in the primary RNA transcript, but are cut out of mRNA before it leaves the nucleus. These introns contain information that is absent in the mature protein that results.

158. **(D)** Any RNA may be said to be transcribed as it is being produced under the direction of DNA. Messenger RNA is the type of RNA that carries instructions on the primary sequencing of a polypeptide.

159. **(A)** Sets of three nitrogenous bases (codons) are the smallest units that can provide enough symbols for the 20 amino acids commonly found in proteins.

160. **(A)** The shapes of the nitrogenous bases comprising a codon are critical in determining which transfer RNA molecules sit side by side on a ribosome. Since each tRNA carries a specific amino acid, the codons act indirectly to determine which amino acids will have the opportunity to bond as neighbors in a polypeptide chain.

161. **(D)** The product of the regulatory gene is a protein called a repressor. If the repressor is incorrectly produced, it can-

not attach to the operator. The result of an open operator region is that all contiguous structural genes may be transcribed. Since the two structural genes in the illustrated region are catalysts for reactions to make an amino acid, this product would accumulate in the cell.

162. **(B)** Since the system is repressible, the end product of the structural genes can act as a corepressor. It does so by attaching to the repressor, thereby forming an aggregate shaped correctly to interact with the operator region.

163. **(A)** If a repressor is shaped correctly, it reversibly attaches to the operator (*O*) region. The effect is to hinder the interaction of RNA polymerase with the nearest structural gene, thus preventing transcription.

164. **(C)** For RNA polymerase, the recognition site along a bacterial chromosome is the promoter (*P*) region. A mutation of the region could interfere with attachment of the RNA polymerase.

165. **(E)** An inducible system, in which an outside agent stimulates genes S_1 and S_2 to begin transcription, can be described by the same diagram as is used for a repressible system. The major difference is that the inducer modifies the product of the regulatory gene to become active (in an inducible system), and the corepressor makes the product of the regulatory gene inactive (in a repressible system).

166. **(E)** One might object that some other, yet undiscovered, material could perform the same function of pattern determination for overlying myoblasts.

167. **(E)** Although the experiment is too narrow to demonstrate that fibronectin is the pattern determinant *in vivo,* it does show that fibronectin can orient myoblasts in the artificial situation described here.

168. **(D)** Not only did both groups become adapted to the environment (as shown by the fact that both increased in numbers although they were limited in food and space), but also the one with more genetic variation did better than the other. It would be pure conjecture, however, to say that this would occur in ANY environment, or that interbreeding would lead to better organisms for this environment.

169. **(B)** Electrophoresis is a powerful tool to separate small quantities of macromolecules that differ in size and/or charge. The description of the experiment indicates that the macromolecules being studied were proteins, which are the products of genes.

170. **(D)** Any closed population with the relatively small number of individuals used in this experiment tends to lose some genes in successive generations either by accidents or by natural selection. This loss is sometimes counteracted by the phenomenon of balanced polymorphism.

171. **(D)** Inbreeding is the controlled mating of closely related organisms, such as brother-sister matings.

172. **(E)** The first activity in the proposed sequence is release of calcium, which is induced by the appearance of a hormone from elsewhere.

173. **(E)** At 100 micromolar concentration, trifluoperazine inhibited about 90% of the gametes and vinblastin inhibited only about 10%.

174. **(D)** Although the results support the hypothesis that calmodulin plays a role in gamete maturation, it is possible that the inhibitors were acting on some material in addition to calmodulin, or that the inhibitors acted directly upon the oocytes. Further study would be necessary.

175. **(A)** The results outlined here are consistent with the hypothesis that calmodulin is present in the starfish, but it would be necessary to isolate the material from the gonads before any further refinement of the hypothesis could be attempted.

176. **(C)** If these results were graphed (see question 179), the resulting bell-shaped curve would point to multiple-factor (multifactor) inheritance.

177. **(D)** It may safely be assumed that one of the two extremes is homozygous dominant for as many genes as are operating, and that the other extreme is homozygous recessive. A cross between these extremes produces organisms that have identical genotypes, heterozygous for each gene. However, a characteristic of multiple-factor inheritance is that the phenotypes are determined by both genotypes and environmental factors. Therefore, some variation about the mean values would be expected.

178. **(C)** Since the likelihood is high that such parents would be heterozygous for all of the contributing genes, each could produce a large variety of gametes and every category of phenotype could be expected in the next generation.

179. **(B)** A standard deviation is defined as the range (centered about the mean) that includes 68% of the measured individuals. One standard error (standard deviation of the mean) is also 68% of a set of values, but the values in that case are all mean values of different populations, rather than individuals.

180. **(A)** Adult height is determined partially by the additive effects of several genes (the exact number is unknown) and partially by nutrition, an environmental factor. Musical ability may have much, some, or little genetic basis; an inheritance pattern has not been determined. None of the other choices involves multiple-factor inheritance.

181. **(A)** This environmental-factor effect is characteristic of most multiple-factor cases, since each of the several involved genes makes a relatively small contribution.

182. **(B)** The coyotes hunted more efficiently when only sight was available than when any other single sense was available.

183. **(A)** Coyotes with hearing as their only sense took significantly longer to find prey than others with only a single sense.

184. **(E)** Whether an observer was tired would perhaps affect the timing accuracy, but the more important factor is whether a sufficiently large number of trials was run. In a study of complex behavior, any single trial may give quite different results from any other, but averaging a large number of trials run under identical conditions will validate any apparent trends.

185. **(D)** In a large enclosure, even doubling the size of the target would not make the search task significantly easier.

186. **(E)** From the evidence of this pedigree, the mode of inheritance could be either sex-linked dominant or autosomal dominant.

187. **(C)** Generation III's results rule out either sex-linked recessive or autosomal recessive inheritance. Neither is possible because such a mode would not allow two affected individuals (therefore having only the recessive allele) to produce any normal children. As the pedigree shows, affected parents of generation II did produce one normal child (a male) in generation III.

188. **(D)** Unless cytological evidence is provided, it must be assumed that the seven males of generation IV were produced by a father who could just have easily produced a girl by providing an X-bearing sperm cell. Since normal meiosis leads to production of equal numbers of X-bearing and Y-bearing sperm, the probability of a girl developing from each fertilized egg is .5, regardless of the number of each sex already in the family.

189. **(A)** The evidence of seven affected children without a normal sibling leads one to suspect that neither parent could provide the normal allele. If sex linkage is assumed, the father, carrying only one X chromosome, upon which the gene is carried, would have a single *b* allele. The genotype of the mother, with two X's, would be *bb*. Just as with answer 188, above, it cannot be ruled out that the eighth child would be normal simply because the first seven were affected. The appearance of any normal child in generation IV would require reassessment of the parents' genotypic analysis.

190. **(B)** Platelets release ADP, which attracts other platelets. All accumulated platelets become part of the clot.

191. **(D)** As stated in answer 190, above, ADP causes further aggregation of platelets. Therefore, decreased secretion of ADP due to aspirin interference would reduce platelet aggregation.

192. **(D)** A hemophilia victim could produce a platelet plug. In addition, he could reinforce this plug with some fibrin made by the reduced amounts of thrombin from the alternative pathway.

193. **(D)** The trigger to clotting is damage to tissue such that platelets can make contact with collagen, a fibrous protein not normally present on the surface of the blood vessel walls. If atherosclerotic plaques include cells with exposed collagen, the platelets will react just as if there were a break in the vessel wall.

194. **(B)** Both axes of Graph 2 are scaled logarithmically. Since the line is straight and pore area also increases as egg mass increases, the relationship is direct.

195. **(C)** The slope of the oxygen conductance curve (solid line on Graph 1) is greater than the slope of pore length (dashed line on Graph 1) when both are plotted against egg mass. Therefore, oxygen conductance increases at a faster rate.

196. **(A)** The pore-area value of ostrich eggs, when compared with egg mass, is somewhat higher than the values for the other plotted eggs, but not enough different to require a new theory. Fick's law, mentioned in choice (D), states that diffusion rate is directly proportional to the cross-sectional area available for the movement. No evidence is presented here that would contradict this fundamental assumption.

197. **(D)** The longer the passageway, the greater will be the time needed for a molecule to traverse it. Also, a longer passageway affords more opportunity for friction with side walls, with oxygen molecules slowing or even reversing direction after colliding with wall structures.

198. **(D)** The vertical axis of the graph shows inhibition of activity, not activity itself. Therefore, all three processes are at highest level in a 10% oxygen environment.

199. **(B)** The facts of the graph—that cyanobacteria in normal atmosphere do not operate any of these vital pathways at their theoretical maximum rates—indicate that their biochemical operations are still geared for Earth conditions that probably occurred billions of years ago.

200. **(E)** Cyanobacteria are prokaryotic organisms. Other prokaryotes may also have maximum metabolic rates in 10% oxygen atmosphere, but the graph does not give this information. Of course, one could not be sure that cyanobacteria evolved in a 10% oxygen environment; many more data would be necessary to make a more positive statement.

Answer Sheet for Sample Test 2

1. Ⓐ Ⓑ Ⓒ Ⓓ Ⓔ 51. Ⓐ Ⓑ Ⓒ Ⓓ Ⓔ 101. Ⓐ Ⓑ Ⓒ Ⓓ Ⓔ 151. Ⓐ Ⓑ Ⓒ Ⓓ Ⓔ
2. Ⓐ Ⓑ Ⓒ Ⓓ Ⓔ 52. Ⓐ Ⓑ Ⓒ Ⓓ Ⓔ 102. Ⓐ Ⓑ Ⓒ Ⓓ Ⓔ 152. Ⓐ Ⓑ Ⓒ Ⓓ Ⓔ
3. Ⓐ Ⓑ Ⓒ Ⓓ Ⓔ 53. Ⓐ Ⓑ Ⓒ Ⓓ Ⓔ 103. Ⓐ Ⓑ Ⓒ Ⓓ Ⓔ 153. Ⓐ Ⓑ Ⓒ Ⓓ Ⓔ
4. Ⓐ Ⓑ Ⓒ Ⓓ Ⓔ 54. Ⓐ Ⓑ Ⓒ Ⓓ Ⓔ 104. Ⓐ Ⓑ Ⓒ Ⓓ Ⓔ 154. Ⓐ Ⓑ Ⓒ Ⓓ Ⓔ
5. Ⓐ Ⓑ Ⓒ Ⓓ Ⓔ 55. Ⓐ Ⓑ Ⓒ Ⓓ Ⓔ 105. Ⓐ Ⓑ Ⓒ Ⓓ Ⓔ 155. Ⓐ Ⓑ Ⓒ Ⓓ Ⓔ
6. Ⓐ Ⓑ Ⓒ Ⓓ Ⓔ 56. Ⓐ Ⓑ Ⓒ Ⓓ Ⓔ 106. Ⓐ Ⓑ Ⓒ Ⓓ Ⓔ 156. Ⓐ Ⓑ Ⓒ Ⓓ Ⓔ
7. Ⓐ Ⓑ Ⓒ Ⓓ Ⓔ 57. Ⓐ Ⓑ Ⓒ Ⓓ Ⓔ 107. Ⓐ Ⓑ Ⓒ Ⓓ Ⓔ 157. Ⓐ Ⓑ Ⓒ Ⓓ Ⓔ
8. Ⓐ Ⓑ Ⓒ Ⓓ Ⓔ 58. Ⓐ Ⓑ Ⓒ Ⓓ Ⓔ 108. Ⓐ Ⓑ Ⓒ Ⓓ Ⓔ 158. Ⓐ Ⓑ Ⓒ Ⓓ Ⓔ
9. Ⓐ Ⓑ Ⓒ Ⓓ Ⓔ 59. Ⓐ Ⓑ Ⓒ Ⓓ Ⓔ 109. Ⓐ Ⓑ Ⓒ Ⓓ Ⓔ 159. Ⓐ Ⓑ Ⓒ Ⓓ Ⓔ
10. Ⓐ Ⓑ Ⓒ Ⓓ Ⓔ 60. Ⓐ Ⓑ Ⓒ Ⓓ Ⓔ 110. Ⓐ Ⓑ Ⓒ Ⓓ Ⓔ 160. Ⓐ Ⓑ Ⓒ Ⓓ Ⓔ
11. Ⓐ Ⓑ Ⓒ Ⓓ Ⓔ 61. Ⓐ Ⓑ Ⓒ Ⓓ Ⓔ 111. Ⓐ Ⓑ Ⓒ Ⓓ Ⓔ 161. Ⓐ Ⓑ Ⓒ Ⓓ Ⓔ
12. Ⓐ Ⓑ Ⓒ Ⓓ Ⓔ 62. Ⓐ Ⓑ Ⓒ Ⓓ Ⓔ 112. Ⓐ Ⓑ Ⓒ Ⓓ Ⓔ 162. Ⓐ Ⓑ Ⓒ Ⓓ Ⓔ
13. Ⓐ Ⓑ Ⓒ Ⓓ Ⓔ 63. Ⓐ Ⓑ Ⓒ Ⓓ Ⓔ 113. Ⓐ Ⓑ Ⓒ Ⓓ Ⓔ 163. Ⓐ Ⓑ Ⓒ Ⓓ Ⓔ
14. Ⓐ Ⓑ Ⓒ Ⓓ Ⓔ 64. Ⓐ Ⓑ Ⓒ Ⓓ Ⓔ 114. Ⓐ Ⓑ Ⓒ Ⓓ Ⓔ 164. Ⓐ Ⓑ Ⓒ Ⓓ Ⓔ
15. Ⓐ Ⓑ Ⓒ Ⓓ Ⓔ 65. Ⓐ Ⓑ Ⓒ Ⓓ Ⓔ 115. Ⓐ Ⓑ Ⓒ Ⓓ Ⓔ 165. Ⓐ Ⓑ Ⓒ Ⓓ Ⓔ
16. Ⓐ Ⓑ Ⓒ Ⓓ Ⓔ 66. Ⓐ Ⓑ Ⓒ Ⓓ Ⓔ 116. Ⓐ Ⓑ Ⓒ Ⓓ Ⓔ 166. Ⓐ Ⓑ Ⓒ Ⓓ Ⓔ
17. Ⓐ Ⓑ Ⓒ Ⓓ Ⓔ 67. Ⓐ Ⓑ Ⓒ Ⓓ Ⓔ 117. Ⓐ Ⓑ Ⓒ Ⓓ Ⓔ 167. Ⓐ Ⓑ Ⓒ Ⓓ Ⓔ
18. Ⓐ Ⓑ Ⓒ Ⓓ Ⓔ 68. Ⓐ Ⓑ Ⓒ Ⓓ Ⓔ 118. Ⓐ Ⓑ Ⓒ Ⓓ Ⓔ 168. Ⓐ Ⓑ Ⓒ Ⓓ Ⓔ
19. Ⓐ Ⓑ Ⓒ Ⓓ Ⓔ 69. Ⓐ Ⓑ Ⓒ Ⓓ Ⓔ 119. Ⓐ Ⓑ Ⓒ Ⓓ Ⓔ 169. Ⓐ Ⓑ Ⓒ Ⓓ Ⓔ
20. Ⓐ Ⓑ Ⓒ Ⓓ Ⓔ 70. Ⓐ Ⓑ Ⓒ Ⓓ Ⓔ 120. Ⓐ Ⓑ Ⓒ Ⓓ Ⓔ 170. Ⓐ Ⓑ Ⓒ Ⓓ Ⓔ
21. Ⓐ Ⓑ Ⓒ Ⓓ Ⓔ 71. Ⓐ Ⓑ Ⓒ Ⓓ Ⓔ 121. Ⓐ Ⓑ Ⓒ Ⓓ Ⓔ 171. Ⓐ Ⓑ Ⓒ Ⓓ Ⓔ
22. Ⓐ Ⓑ Ⓒ Ⓓ Ⓔ 72. Ⓐ Ⓑ Ⓒ Ⓓ Ⓔ 122. Ⓐ Ⓑ Ⓒ Ⓓ Ⓔ 172. Ⓐ Ⓑ Ⓒ Ⓓ Ⓔ
23. Ⓐ Ⓑ Ⓒ Ⓓ Ⓔ 73. Ⓐ Ⓑ Ⓒ Ⓓ Ⓔ 123. Ⓐ Ⓑ Ⓒ Ⓓ Ⓔ 173. Ⓐ Ⓑ Ⓒ Ⓓ Ⓔ
24. Ⓐ Ⓑ Ⓒ Ⓓ Ⓔ 74. Ⓐ Ⓑ Ⓒ Ⓓ Ⓔ 124. Ⓐ Ⓑ Ⓒ Ⓓ Ⓔ 174. Ⓐ Ⓑ Ⓒ Ⓓ Ⓔ
25. Ⓐ Ⓑ Ⓒ Ⓓ Ⓔ 75. Ⓐ Ⓑ Ⓒ Ⓓ Ⓔ 125. Ⓐ Ⓑ Ⓒ Ⓓ Ⓔ 175. Ⓐ Ⓑ Ⓒ Ⓓ Ⓔ
26. Ⓐ Ⓑ Ⓒ Ⓓ Ⓔ 76. Ⓐ Ⓑ Ⓒ Ⓓ Ⓔ 126. Ⓐ Ⓑ Ⓒ Ⓓ Ⓔ 176. Ⓐ Ⓑ Ⓒ Ⓓ Ⓔ
27. Ⓐ Ⓑ Ⓒ Ⓓ Ⓔ 77. Ⓐ Ⓑ Ⓒ Ⓓ Ⓔ 127. Ⓐ Ⓑ Ⓒ Ⓓ Ⓔ 177. Ⓐ Ⓑ Ⓒ Ⓓ Ⓔ
28. Ⓐ Ⓑ Ⓒ Ⓓ Ⓔ 78. Ⓐ Ⓑ Ⓒ Ⓓ Ⓔ 128. Ⓐ Ⓑ Ⓒ Ⓓ Ⓔ 178. Ⓐ Ⓑ Ⓒ Ⓓ Ⓔ
29. Ⓐ Ⓑ Ⓒ Ⓓ Ⓔ 79. Ⓐ Ⓑ Ⓒ Ⓓ Ⓔ 129. Ⓐ Ⓑ Ⓒ Ⓓ Ⓔ 179. Ⓐ Ⓑ Ⓒ Ⓓ Ⓔ
30. Ⓐ Ⓑ Ⓒ Ⓓ Ⓔ 80. Ⓐ Ⓑ Ⓒ Ⓓ Ⓔ 130. Ⓐ Ⓑ Ⓒ Ⓓ Ⓔ 180. Ⓐ Ⓑ Ⓒ Ⓓ Ⓔ
31. Ⓐ Ⓑ Ⓒ Ⓓ Ⓔ 81. Ⓐ Ⓑ Ⓒ Ⓓ Ⓔ 131. Ⓐ Ⓑ Ⓒ Ⓓ Ⓔ 181. Ⓐ Ⓑ Ⓒ Ⓓ Ⓔ
32. Ⓐ Ⓑ Ⓒ Ⓓ Ⓔ 82. Ⓐ Ⓑ Ⓒ Ⓓ Ⓔ 132. Ⓐ Ⓑ Ⓒ Ⓓ Ⓔ 182. Ⓐ Ⓑ Ⓒ Ⓓ Ⓔ
33. Ⓐ Ⓑ Ⓒ Ⓓ Ⓔ 83. Ⓐ Ⓑ Ⓒ Ⓓ Ⓔ 133. Ⓐ Ⓑ Ⓒ Ⓓ Ⓔ 183. Ⓐ Ⓑ Ⓒ Ⓓ Ⓔ
34. Ⓐ Ⓑ Ⓒ Ⓓ Ⓔ 84. Ⓐ Ⓑ Ⓒ Ⓓ Ⓔ 134. Ⓐ Ⓑ Ⓒ Ⓓ Ⓔ 184. Ⓐ Ⓑ Ⓒ Ⓓ Ⓔ
35. Ⓐ Ⓑ Ⓒ Ⓓ Ⓔ 85. Ⓐ Ⓑ Ⓒ Ⓓ Ⓔ 135. Ⓐ Ⓑ Ⓒ Ⓓ Ⓔ 185. Ⓐ Ⓑ Ⓒ Ⓓ Ⓔ
36. Ⓐ Ⓑ Ⓒ Ⓓ Ⓔ 86. Ⓐ Ⓑ Ⓒ Ⓓ Ⓔ 136. Ⓐ Ⓑ Ⓒ Ⓓ Ⓔ 186. Ⓐ Ⓑ Ⓒ Ⓓ Ⓔ
37. Ⓐ Ⓑ Ⓒ Ⓓ Ⓔ 87. Ⓐ Ⓑ Ⓒ Ⓓ Ⓔ 137. Ⓐ Ⓑ Ⓒ Ⓓ Ⓔ 187. Ⓐ Ⓑ Ⓒ Ⓓ Ⓔ
38. Ⓐ Ⓑ Ⓒ Ⓓ Ⓔ 88. Ⓐ Ⓑ Ⓒ Ⓓ Ⓔ 138. Ⓐ Ⓑ Ⓒ Ⓓ Ⓔ 188. Ⓐ Ⓑ Ⓒ Ⓓ Ⓔ
39. Ⓐ Ⓑ Ⓒ Ⓓ Ⓔ 89. Ⓐ Ⓑ Ⓒ Ⓓ Ⓔ 139. Ⓐ Ⓑ Ⓒ Ⓓ Ⓔ 189. Ⓐ Ⓑ Ⓒ Ⓓ Ⓔ
40. Ⓐ Ⓑ Ⓒ Ⓓ Ⓔ 90. Ⓐ Ⓑ Ⓒ Ⓓ Ⓔ 140. Ⓐ Ⓑ Ⓒ Ⓓ Ⓔ 190. Ⓐ Ⓑ Ⓒ Ⓓ Ⓔ
41. Ⓐ Ⓑ Ⓒ Ⓓ Ⓔ 91. Ⓐ Ⓑ Ⓒ Ⓓ Ⓔ 141. Ⓐ Ⓑ Ⓒ Ⓓ Ⓔ 191. Ⓐ Ⓑ Ⓒ Ⓓ Ⓔ
42. Ⓐ Ⓑ Ⓒ Ⓓ Ⓔ 92. Ⓐ Ⓑ Ⓒ Ⓓ Ⓔ 142. Ⓐ Ⓑ Ⓒ Ⓓ Ⓔ 192. Ⓐ Ⓑ Ⓒ Ⓓ Ⓔ
43. Ⓐ Ⓑ Ⓒ Ⓓ Ⓔ 93. Ⓐ Ⓑ Ⓒ Ⓓ Ⓔ 143. Ⓐ Ⓑ Ⓒ Ⓓ Ⓔ 193. Ⓐ Ⓑ Ⓒ Ⓓ Ⓔ
44. Ⓐ Ⓑ Ⓒ Ⓓ Ⓔ 94. Ⓐ Ⓑ Ⓒ Ⓓ Ⓔ 144. Ⓐ Ⓑ Ⓒ Ⓓ Ⓔ 194. Ⓐ Ⓑ Ⓒ Ⓓ Ⓔ
45. Ⓐ Ⓑ Ⓒ Ⓓ Ⓔ 95. Ⓐ Ⓑ Ⓒ Ⓓ Ⓔ 145. Ⓐ Ⓑ Ⓒ Ⓓ Ⓔ 195. Ⓐ Ⓑ Ⓒ Ⓓ Ⓔ
46. Ⓐ Ⓑ Ⓒ Ⓓ Ⓔ 96. Ⓐ Ⓑ Ⓒ Ⓓ Ⓔ 146. Ⓐ Ⓑ Ⓒ Ⓓ Ⓔ 196. Ⓐ Ⓑ Ⓒ Ⓓ Ⓔ
47. Ⓐ Ⓑ Ⓒ Ⓓ Ⓔ 97. Ⓐ Ⓑ Ⓒ Ⓓ Ⓔ 147. Ⓐ Ⓑ Ⓒ Ⓓ Ⓔ 197. Ⓐ Ⓑ Ⓒ Ⓓ Ⓔ
48. Ⓐ Ⓑ Ⓒ Ⓓ Ⓔ 98. Ⓐ Ⓑ Ⓒ Ⓓ Ⓔ 148. Ⓐ Ⓑ Ⓒ Ⓓ Ⓔ 198. Ⓐ Ⓑ Ⓒ Ⓓ Ⓔ
49. Ⓐ Ⓑ Ⓒ Ⓓ Ⓔ 99. Ⓐ Ⓑ Ⓒ Ⓓ Ⓔ 149. Ⓐ Ⓑ Ⓒ Ⓓ Ⓔ 199. Ⓐ Ⓑ Ⓒ Ⓓ Ⓔ
50. Ⓐ Ⓑ Ⓒ Ⓓ Ⓔ 100. Ⓐ Ⓑ Ⓒ Ⓓ Ⓔ 150. Ⓐ Ⓑ Ⓒ Ⓓ Ⓔ 200. Ⓐ Ⓑ Ⓒ Ⓓ Ⓔ

Tests in Biology

Directions for Taking Test: This sample test contains 200 questions or incomplete statements, and should be finished in 170 minutes. Each item has five possible answers or completions. Choose the best one, and blacken the corresponding letter on the answer sheet.

After finishing, you can determine your score by using the **Answer Key** at the end of this test. The **Answer Explanations** section should clarify the concepts involved in each question.

Questions 1–83
For each of the following questions or incomplete statements select the best answer or completion.

1. Glycogen belongs in the category of molecules known as
    A. amino acid
    B. monosaccharide
    C. polysaccharide
    D. fat
    E. protein

2. The middle lamella is a part of
    A. cell walls
    B. book gills
    C. skin
    D. Haversian systems
    E. membranes

3. Barnacles are most closely related to
    A. clams
    B. sea urchins
    C. crayfishes
    D. insects
    E. brachiopods

4. Myotomes of embryos give rise to
   A. endocrine glands
   B. reproductive organs
   C. the central nervous system
   D. the notochord
   E. muscles

5. Which of the following sequences is INCORRECT?
   A. cell — tissue — organ
   B. blastula — morula — gastrula
   C. individual — population — community
   D. green plants — herbivores — carnivores
   E. gametes — zygote — embryo

6. Assume that the rate of increase in a population is constant. The actual number of organisms in this population
   A. also remains constant
   B. becomes smaller because there are more deaths than births
   C. accelerates because there is a constant increase in the number of parents
   D. increases, but only by the same number each month
   E. increases, but only until the number of parents drops to zero

7. Angiosperms differ from gymnosperms in having
   A. fruits
   B. cotyledons
   C. megagametophytes
   D. broad leaves
   E. tracheids in xylem

Questions 8 and 9 refer to this equation:

$$\frac{dN}{dt} = rN\left(\frac{K-N}{K}\right)$$

8. The population growth curve described by this equation is
   A. a straight line
   B. a J-shaped line
   C. an S-shaped line
   D. an erratically changing line
   E. a line that eventually drops to zero

9. The equation can be used to determine a value for K, which is
   A. the population's carrying capacity
   B. the population's initial size
   C. the number of predators acting upon the population
   D. the mortality rate of the population
   E. the sum of density-independent factors

10. The Watson-Crick hypothesis is an explanation of
    A. nitrogen fixation
    B. fat synthesis
    C. DNA structure
    D. energy bonding
    E. genetic drift

11. Of the following answers, which correctly explains why plants die when overfertilized?
    A. Overfertilization causes flocculation of soil colloids
    B. Overfertilization damages walls of delicate root hairs
    C. Overfertilization upsets soil environment by poisoning soil bacteria
    D. Overfertilization causes dehydration of plants
    E. Overfertilization blocks absorption of nitrogenous ions

12. Lakes left undisturbed for a long time develop distinct marginal zones. Which of these is the correct sequence of plant growth from deep water to shallow margin?
    A. rooted plants to floating plants
    B. emergent plants to floating plants
    C. rooted plants with floating leaves to emergent plants
    D. emergent plants to rooted plants with floating leaves
    E. floating plants to emergent plants

13. Organic compounds having carbon, hydrogen, and oxygen in the proportion of CH_2O are
    A. carbohydrates
    B. lipids
    C. proteins
    D. carbonates
    E. nucleic acids

14. Hypofunctioning of the thyroid gland will cause
    A. a subnormal metabolic rate
    B. a rapid drop in the calcium content of blood
    C. sexual precocity
    D. enlargement of bones
    E. rapid heartbeat and nervousness

15. Allopolyploidy is a significant factor in the speciation of
    A. flowering plants
    B. archaebacteria
    C. mammals
    D. birds
    E. Protista

16. In the binomial system, the name of an organism is composed of the
    A. phylum and class
    B. order
    C. genus and species
    D. species
    E. species and variety

17. Which of these human conditions demonstrates the phenomenon of heterozygote advantage?
    A. Down syndrome
    B. Turner syndrome
    C. hemophilia
    D. AIDS
    E. sickle-cell anemia

18. What group of animals is totally marine?
    A. sponges
    B. flatworms
    C. cnidaria
    D. molluscs
    E. echinoderms

19. Which of these best describes the principle of competitive exclusion?
    A. When two species occupy the same niche, competition is excluded.
    B. No two species can occupy the same niche indefinitely.
    C. If two species occupy the same niche, both will become extinct.
    D. Two species occupying the same niche will cooperate in sharing resources.
    E. When two species occupy the same niche, both will eventually be forced to leave that niche.

20. Which of these is the best-matched pair?
    A. autoimmunity—AIDS
    B. hybridoma cells—monoclonal antibody
    C. cytotoxic T cells—antibody release
    D. natural killer cells—allergy
    E. thymus tissue—plasma cells

21. The growth of pollen tubes to ovules illustrates
    A. thigmotropism
    B. chemotropism
    C. hydrotropism
    D. geotropism
    E. phototropism

22. The umbilical cord contains
    A. arteries and vein
    B. allantois and yolk sac
    C. arteries, vein, and allantois
    D. arteries, vein, and yolk sac
    E. arteries, vein, allantois, and yolk sac

23. The process by which genetic material is transferred from one bacterium to another by a virus is
    A. recombination
    B. translocation
    C. transduction
    D. contamination
    E. inoculation

24. The *AaBbccDd* genotype will produce what proportion of *aaBBccDd* individuals when self-crossed?
    A. 1/64
    B. 1/32
    C. 1/16
    D. 3/9
    E. 3/32

25. Lotic best describes the environment of a(n)
    A. freshwater stream
    B. freshwater lake
    C. swamp
    D. saltwater lake
    E. ocean

26. The practice of subjecting seeds to low temperatures for a period of time in order to break dormancy is called
    A. thermolysis
    B. winterizing
    C. acclimatization
    D. vernalization
    E. desensitization

27. In the ocean, where the following organisms live together, which has the LEAST biomass?
    A. phytoplankton
    B. zooplankton
    C. herring
    D. harbor seal
    E. killer whale

28. The hormone influencing the conversion of glycogen to glucose, enrichment of blood supply to muscles, and stimulation of heart muscles is produced by the
    A. thyroid
    B. adrenal
    C. pituitary
    D. parathyroid
    E. pancreas

29. Which organisms are NOT heterotrophic?
A. dogs
B. *Escherichia coli*
C. mushrooms
D. conifers
E. tapeworms

30. To which division do ferns belong?
A. Chlorophyta
B. Phaeophyta
C. Eumycophyta
D. Bryophyta
E. Pterophyta

31. DNA analysis indicates that the nearest living relatives of humans are
A. chimpanzees
B. gorillas
C. *Homo erectus*
D. lemurs
E. orangutans

32. Which of the following is derived primarily from ectoderm in vertebrate animals?
A. brain
B. liver
C. bone
D. blood
E. muscle

33. Green plants carry out cellular respiration
A. only when photosynthesis ceases
B. when the rate of photosynthesis is high enough to produce enough oxygen
C. only when photosynthesis is in progress
D. at all times
E. only when stomates are open

34. The part of the human brain having control over intelligence and personality is the
A. cerebrum
B. cerebellum
C. pons
D. thalamus
E. medulla oblongata

35. Which of the following is NOT an aneuploid?
A. monoploid
B. $2n - 1$
C. trisomic
D. $4n + 2$
E. monosomic

36. Because of its unusual adaptation, Venus' fly-trap is best described as
    A. herbivorous
    B. carnivorous
    C. insectivorous
    D. omnivorous
    E. parasitic

37. Lacteals are
    A. ducts in the mammary gland
    B. tear glands
    C. lymph vessels
    D. lac-secreting glands of a scale insect
    E. latex-secreting tubes in plants

38. Hardy-Weinberg equilibrium may be in effect for a population where
    A. mutations are occurring
    B. migration to and from the population is frequent
    C. selection is not operating upon alleles
    D. matings between parents and offspring are common
    E. the population size is very small

39. Gibberellins affect plants by
    A. stimulating growth
    B. retarding growth
    C. causing leaf fall
    D. ripening fruits
    E. setting fruits without seed formation

40. What is the best interpretation of the structure of skeletal muscles?
    A. acelluar
    B. cellular and uninucleate
    C. cellular and multinucleate
    D. coenocytic
    E. anastomosing and fibrous

41. Lawn grasses ordinarily suffer little damage when cut because
    A. there are no apical meristems
    B. grass leaves quickly regenerate lost parts
    C. shorter plants can transport water and minerals better
    D. cutting increases rate of growth
    E. leaves grow from their bases

42. Which of the following is a name at the class level of taxonomic categories?
    A. Animalia
    B. Chordata
    C. *Homo*
    D. Mammalia
    E. Primates

43. Sex cells in ferns are produced by the
A. frond
B. prothallus
C. rhizome
D. embryo sac
E. pollen

44. What field of biology might be especially concerned with the problems of biologically degradable products?
A. taxonomy
B. ecology
C. paleontology
D. histology
E. dendrology

45. The chemical functional group —NH$_2$ is part of the molecule called
A. ethanol
B. glucose
C. glycerol
D. lactic acid
E. urea

46. Feminine qualities are maintained by the hormone
A. glucagon
B. parathormone
C. testosterone
D. renin
E. estrogen

47. In mitosis, chromosomes move to the poles of the spindle during
A. interphase
B. prophase
C. metaphase
D. anaphase
E. telophase

48. If organisms are classified in kingdom Monera, they
A. are uninucleate
B. lack definite nuclei
C. all are unicellular
D. have coenocytic bodies
E. all have sexual reproduction

49. Contractile vacuoles in protozoa are most important
A. to store food
B. for excretion
C. to eliminate excess water
D. for jet propulsion
E. to circulate cytoplasm

50. The oxygen given off during photosynthesis comes from
   A. CO_2
   B. H_2O
   C. $C_6H_{12}O_6$
   D. $C_3H_6O_3$
   E. $NaNO_3$

51. Deoxygenated blood is transported in the
   A. aorta
   B. pulmonary artery
   C. pulmonary vein
   D. hepatic artery
   E. carotid artery

52. Materials enter cells against a concentration gradient because of
   A. active transport
   B. passive absorption
   C. turgor pressure
   D. diffusion pressure deficit
   E. membrane selectivity

53. The fusion of two gametes ordinarily produces a cell that is
   A. haploid
   B. diploid
   C. triploid
   D. tetraploid
   E. pentaploid

54. The primary advantage of sexual over asexual reproduction is
   A. improvement in the chances of reproduction
   B. involvement of two parents in the care of the young
   C. ability to reproduce in all types of environments
   D. introduction of variations in the offspring
   E. acceleration of the reproductive process

55. Which of the following is NOT derived from mesoderm?
   A. thyroid gland
   B. bone
   C. blood
   D. kidney
   E. muscle

56. Suppose a pure red-flowered four-o'clock is crossed with a pure white-flowered four-o'clock. The red allele and the white allele are each incompletely dominant, producing a pink flower. Members of the F_2 generation will be
   A. all red
   B. all pink
   C. all white
   D. one-half red, one-half white
   E. one-fourth red, one-half pink, one-fourth white

57. Convergent evolution is illustrated by
  A. clover and the mimosa tree
  B. flies and mosquitos
  C. snakes and turtles
  D. cats and bats
  E. fish and whales

58. The role played by any kind of organism with respect to other organisms with which it is associated is that organism's
  A. niche
  B. habitat
  C. ecotone
  D. ecosystem
  E. environment

59. Bits of wood, cloth, grain, etc., found in cliff dwellings of the American West might be dated with
  A. ^{131}I
  B. ^{40}K
  C. ^{238}U
  D. ^{14}C
  E. ^{60}Co

60. Green moss growing on the bark of a tree is best described as a(n)
  A. parasite
  B. epiphyte
  C. saprophyte
  D. mimic
  E. mutualist

61. Sympatric populations CANNOT be isolated by
  A. behavioral barriers
  B. geographical barriers
  C. seasonal barriers
  D. habitat barriers
  E. structural (anatomical) barriers

62. The basic unit of nucleic acids is a
  A. nucleotide
  B. pentose sugar
  C. phosphate group
  D. purine
  E. pyrimidine

63. In what shape of cell is there the smallest external membrane surface in relation to volume?
  A. spherical
  B. spindle-shaped
  C. columnar
  D. fibrous
  E. flat

64. Distinction between a short-day and a long-day plant is based on
    A. time of flowering
    B. season of planting
    C. season of harvesting
    D. rate of growth
    E. size of plants

65. Sucrose is digested to
    A. glucose
    B. fructose
    C. glucose and fructose
    D. galactose
    E. maltose

66. Which of these is a version of endoplasmic reticulum, found only in muscle cells?
    A. actin fibers
    B. Golgi complex
    C. intercalated disks
    D. sarcoplasmic reticulum
    E. T tubules

67. The pairing of homologous chromosomes in meiosis is known as
    A. syngamy
    B. synapsis
    C. synapse
    D. synergy
    E. syngenesis

68. The penetration of the egg by the sperm in humans occurs
    A. before ovulation
    B. after the first meiotic division
    C. after the second meiotic division
    D. after implantation
    E. during early cleavage

69. Which of these is a generalized adaptation as opposed to a specialized adaptation?
    A. human foot
    B. horse's hoof
    C. bird's wing
    D. elephant's trunk
    E. human brain

70. The reason that humans cannot drink seawater is that the
    A. water content is less than the water content of cells
    B. salt content is less than the salt content of cells
    C. body is unaccustomed to certain salts in seawater
    D. unpalatable taste induces vomiting
    E. delicate acid-base equilibrium of the body is upset

71. A person who underwent removal of a submaxillary gland would subsequently
   A. be unable to regulate calcium and phosphorus in the blood
   B. have a depressed rate of metabolism
   C. become obese
   D. be irritable and sleepless
   E. not be affected seriously

72. The best procedure to separate two proteins that are very similar in molecular weight but differ in net charge is
   A. dialysis
   B. electrophoresis
   C. gel exclusion chromatography
   D. spectrophotometry
   E. ultracentrifugation

73. Photorespiration is an inefficient form of light-independent photosynthesis caused by very
   A. low chlorophyll level
   B. low light level
   C. low environmental temperature
   D. high ATP level
   E. high oxygen level

74. Which cellular structure is NOT membranous?
   A. endoplasmic reticulum
   B. mitochondrion
   C. chloroplast
   D. chromosome
   E. Golgi complex

75. Color changes in such animals as the chameleon result from changes in
   A. melanin
   B. cytochromes
   C. phytochromes
   D. chromoplasts
   E. chromatophores

76. All of the following are true about oncogenes EXCEPT
   A. at least some oncogenes carry codes for building proteins
   B. oncogenes are related to the initiation of cancer
   C. oncogenes never have normal functions in cells
   D. oncogenes may be present in cells without transforming them to the cancerous condition
   E. some cancer-causing viruses can carry oncogenes

77. The diploid number of chromosomes in humans is
A. 23
B. 24
C. 46
D. 47
E. 48

78. The blastodisc of a chicken embryo is equivalent to the
A. egg nucleus
B. zygote
C. morula
D. blastula
E. gastrula

79. In which of the following are the structures homologous?
A. eye of squid and eye of human
B. arm of human and wing of bat
C. gill of fish and lung of dog
D. leaf of moss and frond of fern
E. rumen of cow and appendix of rabbit

80. Views on the origin of species most similar to Darwin's were held by
A. DeVries
B. Wallace
C. Lysenko
D. Lamarck
E. Lyell

81. In which of the following do the structures NOT have a direct anatomical connection with each other?
A. urinary bladder and urethra
B. lung and coronary artery
C. gallbladder and bile duct
D. metatarsals and phalanges
E. epididymis and vas deferens

82. The body of a sensory neuron involved in a simple reflex is located in the
A. dorsal root ganglion
B. gray matter of the spinal cord
C. white matter of the spinal cord
D. brain
E. effector organ

83. There is a tendency among mammals living in the tundra and northern coniferous forests to have shorter limbs, tails, and ears than their counterparts in temperate and tropical biomes. The reason may be that
A. random, neutral mutations have occurred
B. a smaller surface area causes reduction of body heat loss
C. snow cannot cling as easily to shortened extremities
D. these differences help the animals avoid interspecific mating
E. longer structures are more noticeable to predators

Questions 84–158

The next four questions (84–87) are based on the five lettered graphs below. Any one of the graphs may depict the answer to one or more questions or none at all. The *y*-axis of each graph represents numbers (quantity); the *x*-axis, some other variable such as time or size.

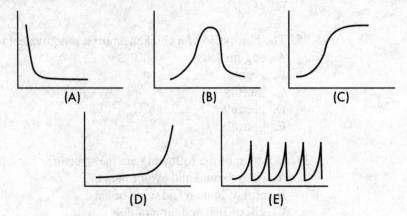

84. Which graph indicates the typical growth of a population?

85. Which graph represents human mortality rates at different ages?

86. Which graph represents the weights of 1000 individuals?

87. Which graph represents the mortality of fish?

The next seven questions (88–94) consist of five lettered ecological terms and seven numbered descriptive phrases. For each numbered phrase select the lettered heading that is most accurately characterized by the phrase, and mark the answer accordingly. Any one of the headings may be used one or more times or not at all.

A. ecosystem
B. biome
C. community
D. population
E. individual

88. is characterized by a predominant life-form

89. will be altered most by a mutation

90. consists of a self-sustaining group of organisms and their physical environment

91. contains organisms all of which are capable of interbreeding

92. is composed of animals or plants but not both

93. may be a balanced aquarium

94. may be a desert

The next four questions (95–98) consist of five lettered properties of water and numbered implications of these properties for life on Earth. For each numbered implication select the lettered property that is most closely associated with it, and mark the answer accordingly. Any one of the lettered properties may be used one or more times or not at all.

> A. good solvent
> B. high heat of vaporization
> C. high heat capacity
> D. high surface tension
> E. relatively less density in solid state

95. A niche for some animals exists at the interface between a pond and the atmosphere.

96. Organisms in temperate lakes live through the winter.

97. People and dogs stay cool in the midday sun.

98. Ecosystems near large bodies of water are more uniform through the seasons than would otherwise be expected.

The next four questions (99–102) consist of a group of lettered molecule types and numbered descriptions. For each numbered description select the lettered molecule type that matches it, and mark the answer accordingly. Any one of the lettered molecule types may be used one or more times or not at all.

> A. enzyme
> B. prosthetic group
> C. structural protein
> D. substrate
> E. vitamin

99. has an active site that might be changed by allosteric inhibition

100. is the molecule that is changed by a catalyzed reaction

101. is a material, not formed of amino acids, that becomes attached to a protein, thereby changing the protein in a fundamental way to allow it to perform normally

102. is an organic molecule necessary for normal cellular activity, but not synthesized by the organism that needs it

The next six questions (103–108) consist of a group of lettered names and numbered scientific accomplishments. For each numbered accomplishment select the lettered name of the person responsible for it, and mark the answer accordingly. Any one of the lettered names may be used one or more times or not at all.

> A. Crick
> B. Golgi
> C. Koch
> D. Pasteur
> E. Schleiden

103. presented the theory that all living organisms are composed of cells

104. described the membranous organelle that produces secretory vesicles

105. worked on DNA structure and genetic code

106. devised a series of steps that determines whether a particular microorganism causes a particular disease

107. was the first to link bacteria with disease

108. disproved the common belief of his day in the spontaneous generation of life

The next three questions (109–111) consist of a group of lettered parts or accessories of a microscope and numbered descriptive phrases. For each numbered phrase select the lettered part or accessory that matches it, and mark the answer accordingly. Any one of the lettered parts may be used one or more times or not at all.

> A. condenser
> B. field micrometer
> C. illuminator
> D. diaphragm
> E. objective

109. is a set of magnifying lenses placed beneath the stage

110. in an electron microscope, is replaced by an electron emitter

111. is of primary importance in determining resolving power

The next four questions (112–115) consist of a group of lettered vertebrate intestinal tract regions and accessories and numbered descriptive phrases. For each numbered phrase select the lettered region or accessory that matches it, and mark the answer accordingly. Any one of the lettered regions or accessories may be used one or more times or not at all.

    A. colon
    B. gallbladder
    C. gizzard
    D. small intestine
    E. stomach

112. in birds, serves the function of teeth

113. in terrestrial animals, is the chief area of water reabsorption

114. in humans, is the principal site of digestion

115. in humans, is the temporary storage area for a fat emulsifier

The next four questions (116–119) consist of a group of lettered cell components and numbered descriptive phrases. For each numbered phrase select the lettered structure with which it is most closely associated, and mark the answer accordingly. Any one of the lettered structures may be used one or more times or not at all.

    A. endoplasmic reticulum
    B. messenger RNA
    C. ribosomal protein
    D. ribosomal RNA
    E. transfer RNA

116. captures specific amino acid, brings it to protein synthesis site

117. is transcribed, then becomes part of a ribosome

118. includes a complete set of instructions for the primary amino acid sequence of a polypeptide

119. is the only component in the list that is directly made by translation

The next three questions (120–122) consist of a group of lettered probability values (1.0 = 100%) and numbered genetics problems. For each numbered problem select the correct lettered value, and mark the answer accordingly. Any one of the lettered values may be used one or more times or not at all.

    A. 0
    B. .125
    C. .25
    D. .50
    E. 1.0

120. In humans, cleft ("dimpled") chin is traceable to the action of a single dominant autosomal allele. If a cleft-chinned man who is homozygous marries a woman without cleft chin, what is the probability that their first son will have the cleft?

121. Tay-Sachs disease is inherited via a single recessive allele. If two heterozygotes have a child, what is the probability that the child will also be a heterozygote?

122. If a heterozygote for both cleft chin and Tay-Sachs disease marries another person of the same genotype, what is the probability that their first child will be heterozygous for Tay-Sachs and will NOT have a cleft chin? (Assume that the two genes are not on the same chromosome.)

The next four questions (123–126) consist of a group of lettered cell structures and numbered descriptions. For each numbered description select the lettered cell structures that match it, and mark the answer accordingly. Any one of the lettered cell structures may be used one or more times or not at all.

A. chloroplasts
B. microfilaments
C. microtubules
D. lysosomes
E. mitochondria

123. Functional portions are thylakoids.

124. The structures can form basal bodies if arranged properly.

125. The structures are membranous vesicles.

126. The structures are contained within cilia.

The next six questions (127–132) consist of a group of lettered molecules that are important in the control of plant functions and numbered descriptions or examples of such molecules. For each numbered description or example select the lettered molecule that matches it, and mark the answer accordingly. Any one of the lettered molecules may be used one or more times or not at all.

A. auxin
B. cytokinin
C. gibberellin
D. ethylene
E. phytochrome

127. is capable of bringing to full size plants that are genetic dwarfs

128. is related to control of photoperiodism

129. initiates fruit ripening

130. induces mitosis

131. is linked to phototropism

132. is the class of compounds that includes indoleacetic acid

The next five questions (133–137) consist of a group of lettered concepts and numbered descriptions. For each numbered description select the lettered concept that matches it, and mark the answer accordingly. Any one of the lettered concepts may be used one or more times or not at all.

> **A.** clonal selection
> **B.** competitive exclusion
> **C.** sliding filament model
> **D.** model of evolution by inheritance of acquired characteristics
> **E.** hypothesis of spontaneous generation of life

133. a model attempting to explain the formation of antibodies

134. an accurate view of skeletal muscle contraction

135. the hypothesis that if two species occupy one niche, only one will survive

136. an alternative to natural selection

137. a view of what may have happened at least once in the Earth's history, but does not occur now

The next six questions (138–143) consist of a group of lettered men of science and numbered descriptions of their work. For each numbered description select the lettered scientist with which it belongs, and mark the answer accordingly. Any one of the lettered names may be used one or more times or not at all.

> **A.** Chargaff
> **B.** Darwin
> **C.** Lorenz
> **D.** Morgan
> **E.** Oparin

138. did his most important work before 1900

139. worked on chemical theories of the origin of life

140. showed the ecological importance of earthworms and the importance of the coleoptile for phototropism

141. was the first to recognize imprinting

142. examined sex linkage in fruit flies

143. found the first hint of specific base-pairing in nucleic acids

The next six questions (144–149) consist of a group of lettered molecules important in genetics and numbered descriptions of these molecules. For each numbered description select the lettered molecule that matches it, and mark the answer accordingly. Any one of the lettered molecules may be used one or more times or not at all.

    A. amino acyl tRNA synthetase
    B. anticodon
    C. DNA polymerase
    D. thymine
    E. uracil

144. is a nitrogenous base not normally part of DNA

145. is important in linking amino acids to specific tRNA molecules

146. is important in linking tRNA molecules to specific regions of mRNA

147. is important in linking nucleotides together with covalent bonds

148. forms hydrogen bonds with adenine of DNA during transcription

149. forms hydrogen bonds with adenine during DNA replication

The next four questions (150–153) consist of a group of lettered brain regions and numbered descriptions of the regions. For each numbered description select the appropriate lettered region, and mark the answers accordingly. Any one of the lettered regions may be used one or more times or not at all.

    A. cerebellum
    B. cerebral cortex
    C. hypothalamus
    D. olfactory lobes
    E. medulla oblongata

150. in mammals, tends to preempt control of functions from other regions of the brain

151. maintains balance and muscular coordination

152. is the brain region nearest the spinal cord

153. can control glandular functions via its release of hormones

The next five questions (154–158) consist of a group of lettered models or phenomena and numbered descriptions of them. For each numbered description select the lettered model or phenomenon that matches it, and mark the answer accordingly. Any one of the lettered models or phenomena may be used one or more times or not at all.

A. adaptive radiation
B. Cambrian explosion
C. continental drift
D. balanced polymorphism
E. symbiosis model of eukaryotes

154. explains some floral and faunal distributions across oceans

155. describes a sudden increase in types and numbers of fossils in certain geologic strata

156. is related to possession of DNA by mitochondria and plastids

157. is a theory of speciation by natural selection

158. is linked to the observation that a population with genetic variability adapts better to environmental change than does a homogeneous population

The remaining questions ask for analysis of experiments. For each set, read the descriptions and data carefully; then answer the questions or complete the statements by choosing among the lettered alternatives and marking your answers accordingly.

Questions 159–164
In the fruit fly *Drosophila,* kidney-shaped eyes occur only in homozygous recessive individuals. The gene controlling eye shape is autosomal. A population was sampled and found to be composed of 100 kidney-eyed individuals and 300 normal-eyed individuals.

159. Assume that the population is in equilibrium. Which of these equations would be most appropriate for determining the number of heterozygotes in the population?
   A. $(p + q)^2 = 1$
   B. $(p + q + r)^2 = 1$
   C. $p + q = 1$
   D. $s = 1 - W$
   E. none of them: simply count the heterozygotes by observation of the individuals

160. If the population is assumed to be in equilibrium, what is the expected number of homozygous dominant individuals?
A. 100
B. 125
C. 200
D. 300
E. 400

161. If the number of homozygous dominant individuals were determined by actual count and found to be lower than predicted, what might be a good hypothesis to explain this variance from the expected?
A. A mistake was made in the census.
B. Some homozygous dominant individuals had become heterozygous.
C. The fitness value (W) for homozygous individuals is higher than predicted.
D. The population is too large to expect equilibrium.
E. There is selection against the phenotype of the homozygous dominant individuals.

162. If the homozygous dominant individuals have the same phenotype as heterozygotes, how could one determine the actual number of the former in the population?
A. Cross each normal-eyed individual with a kidney-eyed organism.
B. It would be impossible to determine the actual number.
C. Keep accurate records of the phenotypes of each individual's parents.
D. Since the proper equation always gives the exact number of each genotype, rely upon this calculated value.
E. Using a microscope, analyze the configuration of each organism's salivary gland chromosomes.

163. A pair of men, working in the first decade of the twentieth century, derived the rules used to predict the composition of a population in equilibrium. One of them was:
A. H. Spemann
B. M. Lyon
C. M. Meselson
D. T. Dobzhansky
E. W. Weinberg

164. What does the term *in equilibrium* mean when describing a population?
A. For each individual that has a forward mutation, a backward mutation of the same gene will occur in another individual.
B. Over a period of time, some individuals migrate out of the population, but they are replaced by an equal number migrating into the population from elsewhere.
C. Selection for one gene is negated by selection against another gene.
D. The birth rate equals the death rate.
E. The gene pool of the population remains unchanged from one generation to the next.

Questions 165–168

Organisms of a group of bacteria, the halobacteria, contain a purple material in their cell membranes. An absorbance spectrum of this fraction is shown in the graph.

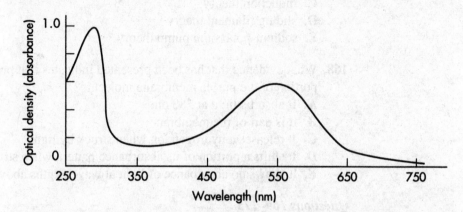

When workers attempted to isolate the purple membrane material by breaking up the membrane with detergent, the material retained the 280-nanometer absorption peak but lost the 550-nanometer peak. The material no longer appeared to be purple. Further work indicated that the molecule is rhodopsin, a prominent compound of the animal retina, whose changes in response to light are closely linked to vision. The intact purple membrane is reversibly bleached by visible light, just as is isolated rhodopsin. During bleaching, the bacterial material releases a proton. This, in a complex way, leads to the production of ATP within the cell.

165. Light whose wavelength is 550 nanometers is perceived by humans as yellow-green. Light at 280 nanometers is in the ultraviolet region. Which statement is correct about the purple membrane material?
   A. The material appears purple because it absorbs no light at 750 nm.
   B. It is the 280-nm portion of its absorbance spectrum that makes the material appear purple to us.
   C. It is the 550-nm portion of its spectrum that makes the material appear purple to us.
   D. The purple color is unrelated to the absorbance spectrum of the material, since colors are a product of brain analysis.
   E. The purple color is a result of interaction between the absorbance peak at 280 nm and that at 550 nm.

166. Which of the following is the most logical statement about the fact that rhodopsin is found in both halobacteria and human eyes?
   A. It demonstrates that both organisms were created simultaneously.
   B. It indicates an error of contamination in one or the other.
   C. It is an example of little-related organisms using similar genetic instructions to perform different functions.
   D. It is a clear-cut example of convergent evolution.
   E. It shows that these two organisms are more closely related than previously suspected.

167. Relating the pumping of protons across a cell membrane to the production of ATP is a feature of a theory proposed for many organisms, called the
   A. chemiosmotic theory
   B. Davson-Danielli theory
   C. induction theory
   D. sliding filament theory
   E. sodium-potassium pump theory

168. What evidence that has been presented indicates that protein comprises a portion of the purple membrane molecule?
   A. It absorbs light at 280 nm.
   B. It is part of the membrane.
   C. It releases a hydrogen ion when struck by light.
   D. It shifts a portion of its absorbance pattern when struck by light.
   E. It shows no absorbance of light at wavelengths above 750 nm.

Questions 169–175
During fertilization in sea urchins thousands of sperm cells may touch the egg, but only one will be accepted to contribute its chromosomes. Two barriers to polyspermy occur. The first happens within a few seconds of the first sperm contact and involves a flow of sodium ions into the egg, leading to a voltage change across the membrane.

The slower block to polyspermy begins 25–35 seconds after sperm contact and requires about 30 seconds to become complete. Approximately 15,000 vesicles stored just below the egg surface burst open. These vesicles, called cortical granules, contain an enzyme that changes the egg surface so that sperm cells bound to it fall away. A second granule enzyme promotes the release of a separate membrane over the plasma membrane of the egg. This outer membrane, called the vitelline membrane, rises off the egg surface. Colloids released from cortical granules move into the space created by the rise of this membrane. They attract water, swelling this area into a protective jellylike region around the egg that repels late-arriving sperm cells.

A trigger to the cortical granule reaction is the release of calcium ions from intracellular depots. Demonstration of the importance of these ions comes from the use of drugs called ionophores, which make cell membranes selectively permeable to calcium. When sea urchin eggs are treated with an ionophore, in the absence of sperm, they go through the normal sequence of fertilization reactions, including both cortical granule changes and mitosis to produce blastomeres.

Later activities, including synthesis of DNA and proteins, occur as a result of a rise in egg pH caused by loss of protons to the environment. This proton loss is linked to uptake of sodium from the environment. Treatment of eggs with amiloride, a drug that blocks sodium transfer across membranes, leads to loss of egg activation upon sperm contact.

169. What is the role of sodium in the early block to polyspermy?
   A. It causes a voltage change across the egg membrane that somehow affects sperm touching the membrane.
   B. It initiates cortical granule changes.
   C. It is linked to a change of intracellular pH.
   D. It enters cortical granules and is stored there.
   E. It produces a drug, amiloride, that acts on sperm.

170. Which of these is NOT an accurate description of cortical granules?
   A. Their bursting open leads to formation of a thick watery layer over the egg membrane.
   B. They are formed in response to contact by a sperm.
   C. They contain an enzyme that can cause release of unsuccessful sperm cells from the egg membrane.
   D. They do not change their structure until after the fast block to polyspermy has occurred.
   E. They help to separate the vitelline membrane from the plasma membrane shortly after fertilization.

171. Which of the following is a correct statement?
   A. Calcium is stored in cortical granules before fertilization.
   B. Calcium can initiate both cortical granule changes and later embryonic activities.
   C. It is likely that the sperm cell triggers egg response by providing calcium to the egg.
   D. The link between calcium and embryonic events is demonstrated by experiments involving the drug amiloride.
   E. The release of calcium within an egg leads to colloid production.

172. Which of these experiments shows the role of sodium in the activation of DNA and protein synthesis?
   A. amiloride treatment of fertilized eggs
   B. ionophore treatment of fertilized eggs
   C. ionophore treatment of unfertilized eggs
   D. measurement of voltage across the egg membrane
   E. treatment of cortical granules with sodium

173. What would be a likely consequence of polyspermy?
   A. a hybrid that would be a new species
   B. abnormal distribution of chromosomes during each mitotic event
   C. an animal that would be hermaphroditic
   D. normal embryonic mechanisms
   E. response of more than the normal number of cortical granules

174. Which of the following is the most valid statement?
   A. Since the sea urchin has already provided so many answers to questions about fertilization and early embryology, its future value to workers is limited.
   B. Since most animals erect barriers to polyspermy, the research described above may be a useful model for further work with other species.
   C. This research may be invalid because of the extensive use of artificial conditions, such as addition of synthetic drugs.
   D. The research on sea urchin development shows how early embryology of all animals is triggered.
   E. This research may have limited value for workers with other animals, since most animals do not normally produce as many sperm cells as do sea urchins.

175. Choose the correct statement.
  A. Amiloride is an ionophore.
  B. An ionophore triggers fertilization events only indirectly, by its action on plasma membranes.
  C. Cortical granules release their enzyme when they are touched by ionophores.
  D. Ionophores are normally released by sperm cells during fertilization.
  E. Ionophores mimic sperm action by providing genetic information to the egg.

Questions 176–180

Hemoglobin and myoglobin are proteins that share structural and functional features. Both are capable of reversibly accepting molecular oxygen (O_2). Both do this through the use of a nonprotein portion called heme. A myoglobin molecule has one heme group, capable of holding a single O_2; a hemoglobin has four hemes, each capable of holding an O_2. Myoglobin is found in muscle; hemoglobin is carried within red blood cells. The graph shows the ability of each protein to carry O_2 (be "saturated with oxygen") in a variety of environments that differ by their oxygen content. Both curves are for proteins isolated from adult humans.

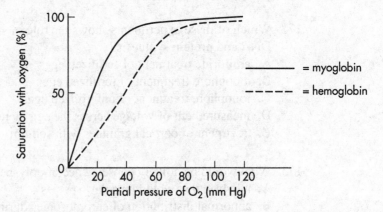

176. Which of the following is a correct statement?
  A. At 60 mm of environmental oxygen pressure, a given quantity of myoglobin carries twice as much oxygen as does the same quantity of hemoglobin.
  B. At 100 mm of environmental oxygen pressure, neither protein carries enough oxygen to be of value to an organism.
  C. Hemoglobin can release oxygen when it is in an environment with little oxygen, but myoglobin cannot.
  D. Hemoglobin releases oxygen more readily in a high-oxygen environment than does myoglobin.
  E. Myoglobin accepts oxygen more readily in a low-oxygen environment than does hemoglobin.

177. The shape of the curve described by hemoglobin shows the most resemblance to the curve describing
   A. the change in free energy of a system during a period in which an enzyme-mediated reaction is occurring
   B. the change in blood pressure as blood circulates around the body, beginning at the capillaries
   C. the growth of a population of bacteria within a confined area
   D. the growth of a population of bacteria with no constraints of resources or space
   E. the relationship between reaction velocity and substrate concentration during an enzyme-mediated reaction

178. Which statement best describes the relationship between hemoglobin and myoglobin?
   A. If hemoglobin were in muscle and myoglobin in red blood cells, the efficient transport of oxygen from lungs to muscle would not be adversely affected.
   B. If oxygen is not needed by a muscle at a particular time, myoglobin will release it back to hemoglobin to be carried elsewhere.
   C. Their structural similarities indicate that hemoglobin and myoglobin are made under the direction of the same gene.
   D. They compete for the same function; animals would do better to have only one or the other.
   E. They cooperate in transporting oxygen to muscles; as hemoglobin releases oxygen to the oxygen-poor muscles, myoglobin can accept it and hold it until needed.

179. Certain marine worms that live in the thick mud of the ocean floor have a variety of hemoglobin whose oxygen saturation curve looks more like that of myoglobin in the graph. Which statement is correct about these worms?
   A. The similarity of their hemoglobin curve to that of human myoglobin is purely coincidental, since the two organisms are not taxonomically similar.
   B. The shape of the hemoglobin curve is not important; all that matters is that hemoglobin be able to both accept and release oxygen.
   C. They are at a disadvantage since their hemoglobin holds oxygen more tightly than ours.
   D. They are ideally fitted to their environment since their hemoglobin can "load up" with oxygen even in the low-oxygen environment of mud.
   E. This similarity is good evidence that at least some human genes have been passed almost unchanged from ancient ancestors.

180. When hemoglobin of a variety of mammals is tested, the mammals' oxygen saturation curves vary considerably. In general, very large mammals produce curves resembling the one for human myoglobin, while very small mammals produce curves that are shifted to the right of the human hemoglobin curve. What is the most likely explanation for this?

A. Large mammals are more insulated by fat, so they do not lose oxygen as easily.

B. Large mammals have large lungs, so the hemoglobin does not have to carry as much oxygen.

C. Small mammals are likely to have a higher internal temperature, which tends to cause oxygen to bind to hemoglobin more tightly.

D. Small mammals tend to hide from danger rather than to fight; therefore, they do not need to transport as much oxygen to muscles during periods of stress.

E. Small mammals use oxygen faster, and need to unload oxygen more readily to metabolizing tissues.

Questions 181–185

In birds, karyotype analysis shows that males have two Z sex chromosomes, which are analogous to the X chromosome of humans or *Drosophila*. A cell of females contains one Z and one W, the latter being analogous to the human Y chromosome. Feather color of canaries is a characteristic wherein the allele for green (*C*) is dominant over the allele for cinnamon (*c*). Thirty green males whose mothers were cinnamon-colored were individually mated to 30 cinnamon virgin females. The offspring resulting from these matings were as follows:

Phenotype	Number
Green males	13
Green females	16
Cinnamon males	17
Cinnamon females	14

181. Which of these most accurately describes the chromosomes of a female canary?

A. XX
B. XY
C. ZZ
D. ZY
E. ZW

182. The gene for feather color is best described as

A. autosomal

B. either sex-linked or autosomal: cannot be determined from the data

C. sex-linked, on the Z chromosome

D. sex-linked, on the W chromosome

E. difficult to analyze, since none of the four categories exactly matched in size any of the others

183. All of the green birds had black eyes; all of the cinnamon birds had red eyes. Which of the following best describes this phenomenon?
  A. dihybrid cross: one gene sex-linked, the other autosomal
  B. multiple alleles
  C. multifactor (multiple-factor) inheritance
  D. pleiotropy
  E. position effect

184. If hypothetical gene A (or its allele, a) is a sex-linked gene, and if a canary is heterozygous for this gene,
  A. a translocation must have occurred
  B. the bird could be either male or female, depending on which chromosome carries the dominant allele
  C. the bird must be female
  D. the bird must be male
  E. the bird must be aneuploid

185. To more accurately determine the mode of inheritance of the feather color gene, which of these tests should be performed?
  A. Cross some of the green males of the table with green females of the same generation.
  B. Cross some of the cinnamon males of the table with cinnamon females of the same generation.
  C. Cross some of the green males of the table with any females.
  D. Cross some of the green females of the table with any males.
  E. Repeat the described cross with larger numbers of parents.

Questions 186–189

Cytochrome c is a protein found almost universally among organisms. The complete amino acid sequence is available for this protein from many species of bacteria and algae. When compared, some regions of the protein are nearly identical from species to species, whereas other regions show considerable variation. Table 1 illustrates these variations for selected regions.

Table 1

Region	Number of Amino Acids Present	Number of Amino Acids Identical*
A	20	8
B	15	9
C	21	5
D	15	5

From five species of bacteria of a single genus.

Table 2 compares those amino acids of the bacteria that are identical for all five species with the amino acids at the same positions of cytochrome c from the tuna fish, a eukaryotic organism.

Table 2

Region	Number of Positions Identical in All Bacteria	Number of Positions Identical in Tuna and All Bacteria
A	8	5
B	9	3
C	5	1
D	5	0

186. Which of these statements is supported by the data?
    A. Even though amino acid sequences are somewhat different from species to species, their genes for cytochrome *c* are probably identical.
    B. Mutation within the gene for cytochrome *c* appears to have occurred significantly more times in some regions than in others.
    C. Mutation within the gene for cytochrome *c* appears to have been totally random.
    D. The mutations within the cytochrome *c* gene that have been retained appear to have been significantly more numerous in some regions than in others.
    E. The mutations within the cytochrome *c* gene that have been retained appear to be totally random.

187. Which region of the protein in the tuna is the LEAST like the corresponding region in bacteria?
    A. *A*
    B. *B*
    C. *C*
    D. *D*
    E. This cannot be determined from the data.

188. Which region of the protein is most alike among the bacterial species examined?
    A. *A*
    B. *B*
    C. *C*
    D. *D*
    E. This cannot be determined from the data.

189. What is the most biologically sensible explanation for the relationship between bacterial and tuna cytochrome *c*?

A. Amino acid sequencing studies are not valuable for determining or confirming evolutionary relationships; the data indicate more heterogeneity among closely related bacteria than between bacteria and fish.

B. Although the proteins of the bacteria and tuna have diverged, as have many of their structures, the two organisms still use cytochromes in quite similar ways; this fact is reflected by the similarity of the amino acid sequences in certain essential regions of the molecule.

C. Natural selection operates on the whole organism, not its component parts; therefore, amino acid sequence studies say nothing about evolutionary relationships among organisms.

D. The huge period of time since these organisms diverged from a common ancestor is reflected in the presence of many differences in amino acid sequences, scattered randomly through the protein.

E. The two organism types compared here have developed entirely different ways of using cytochromes, as demonstrated by their diversity in regions *C* and *D*.

Questions 190–192

The following three questions are based on the work of Engelmann, who devised a classic experiment in which he exposed an aquatic green algal filament to a minute spectrum of colors. He put the filament in a water medium containing bacteria that were known to be attracted to oxygen. After a period of time the bacteria congregated in spectral zones approximately as indicated in the sketch.

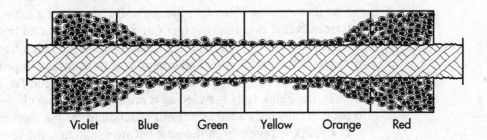

| Violet | Blue | Green | Yellow | Orange | Red |

190. The distribution of bacteria indicates that these organisms

A. are especially repelled by green light

B. can be attracted by either high oxygen concentration or particular wavelengths of light

C. are more active under violet and red light

D. congregate where photosynthesis is most active

E. congregate where carbon dioxide is generated by the alga

191. Which of the following statements is true?
  A. The behavior of the bacteria shows that they are autotrophs.
  B. All anaerobic bacteria will congregate in the same zones as the species used in the experiment.
  C. If the alga were kept in the dark, the bacteria would soon be uniformly dispersed.
  D. Viruses would be expected to behave like the bacteria because their oxygen and light needs are the same.
  E. If the alga were removed, the bacteria would soon die.

192. Which of these experiments would be most useful in the further clarification of this behavior of bacteria?
  A. Move the entire experiment to an area that includes a pure-nitrogen atmosphere.
  B. Use a different species of alga.
  C. Use a narrower range of wavelengths.
  D. Use a more precise device to split light into its component wavelengths.
  E. Use the same physical apparatus but treat the alga with an inhibitor of Photochemical System II.

Questions 193–196

The interaction between mother and chick of a species of gull determines the mother's feeding behavior. When she returns to the nest after having swallowed a small fish, she points her red bill downward and swings it from side to side. A hungry chick will respond by pecking at her bill in a particular fashion. The response of the mother is to regurgitate the fish into the nest. The chick will peck at her bill only when it is hungry. Observation shows that a chick pecks at the mother's bill on the day of hatching, but its aim is poor; it misses on two-thirds of its attempts. Within 2 days the chick can hit its target on 75% of its attempts. By appropriate experiments, it was determined that this improvement of accuracy is related to the amount of "visual experience"; that is, the amount of time the chick has used its eyes to observe the world. A second component of accuracy improvement is the accumulation of experience at pecking. If a chick is too far away from the mother, the chick falls forward as it misses. If it is too close when it starts to peck, it falls backward as a result of rebound off the mother's bill.

If a chick is taken from the nest before it hatches and then is presented with an accurate model of an adult female, it goes through the same pecking development as it would have in the nest. If such a chick is presented with a variety of models that differ in some features of shape and color from a real adult female gull, it has been found that the head is the most important feature in eliciting pecking, and the bill is the most important area of the head. An older chick is less likely to peck at any variant model than is a newly hatched chick. Chicks at any age respond best to a red-bill model that is placed vertically and moved back and forth horizontally.

193. Which of these is an example of learning?
    A. the chick's improvement in aim at the mother's bill
    B. the chick's recognition that the mother's bill should be pecked
    C. the greater likelihood that pecking will occur if the chick is hungry
    D. the chick's recognition that the mother's bill is red
    E. the mother's regurgitation of food

194. Which of these is instinctive?
    A. the chick's improvement in aim at the mother's bill
    B. the chick's recognition that the mother's bill should be pecked
    C. the greater ability of an older chick to refrain from pecking at an inaccurate model
    D. the chick's memory of the mother's bill being red
    E. the chick's visual perception of the shape of the mother's head and bill

195. What is the most significant statement that can be made about these observations?
    A. Only the instinctive portion of this behavior can be accurately assessed, since learning is more complex.
    B. The observations show that this behavior is instinctive with a component of learning.
    C. The observations are invalid because one cannot distinguish instinctive behavior from learned behavior.
    D. The observations show that a chick communicates with its mother by a language that consists of pecking out a variety of messages upon her bill.
    E. The observations show that the food-eliciting response is much simpler than it would appear upon first observation.

196. What would be an "appropriate experiment" to determine that pecking accuracy is related to the amount of visual experience the chick has?
    A. Alternately place a chick in dark and light during testing.
    B. Change the color of the model's bill during testing.
    C. Keep chicks in the dark for various amounts of time from hatching until testing.
    D. Move the model's bill at different rates during testing.
    E. Permanently blind a newly hatched chick.

Questions 197–200

The following graph shows the population growth curves of two similar species of organisms that were grown both separately and mixed together. The beginning populations were the same size, and the abiotic conditions were identical. Assume that the food supply was a limiting factor.

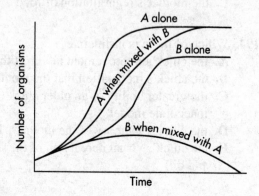

197. The typical growth curve exhibited by many populations is represented here by
   A. species *A* growing alone
   B. species *A* when mixed with species *B*
   C. species *B* growing alone
   D. species *B* when mixed with species *A*
   E. both species *A* growing alone and species *B* growing alone

198. When species *A* and species *B* are grown together,
   A. species *A* is benefited by the presence of species *B*
   B. species *A* is handicapped by the presence of species *B*
   C. both species *A* and species *B* are benefited
   D. both species *A* and species *B* are handicapped
   E. the results are atypical for competing organisms

199. These experiments illustrate what has become known as
   A. Hardy's law
   B. competitive tension
   C. population divergence
   D. Gause's principle
   E. incomplete dominance

200. The experiments confirm that
   A. species *A* and species *B* have different food requirements
   B. when two species compete, they quickly learn to cooperate with each other
   C. when two species compete, only one is benefited
   D. when two species compete for the same resource, only one species survives
   E. growth curves *A* and *B* would be identical if both species had been of the same size

Answer Key for Sample Test 2

Use this key to obtain a score for Test 2. Then use the answer explanations on the following pages to gain a better understanding of the concepts needed to answer all questions correctly.

1. C	41. E	81. B	121. D	161. E
2. A	42. D	82. A	122. B	162. A
3. C	43. B	83. B	123. A	163. E
4. E	44. B	84. C	124. C	164. E
5. B	45. E	85. D	125. D	165. C
6. C	46. E	86. B	126. C	166. C
7. A	47. D	87. A	127. C	167. A
8. C	48. B	88. B	128. E	168. A
9. A	49. C	89. E	129. D	169. A
10. C	50. B	90. A	130. B	170. B
11. D	51. B	91. D	131. A	171. B
12. E	52. A	92. D	132. A	172. A
13. A	53. B	93. A	133. A	173. B
14. A	54. D	94. B	134. C	174. B
15. A	55. A	95. D	135. B	175. B
16. C	56. E	96. E	136. D	176. E
17. E	57. E	97. B	137. E	177. C
18. E	58. A	98. C	138. B	178. E
19. B	59. D	99. A	139. E	179. D
20. B	60. B	100. D	140. B	180. E
21. B	61. B	101. B	141. C	181. E
22. E	62. A	102. E	142. D	182. B
23. C	63. A	103. E	143. A	183. D
24. B	64. A	104. B	144. E	184. D
25. A	65. C	105. A	145. A	185. A
26. D	66. D	106. C	146. B	186. B
27. E	67. B	107. D	147. C	187. D
28. B	68. B	108. D	148. E	188. B
29. D	69. A	109. A	149. D	189. B
30. E	70. A	110. C	150. B	190. B
31. A	71. E	111. E	151. A	191. C
32. A	72. B	112. C	152. E	192. E
33. D	73. E	113. D	153. C	193. A
34. A	74. D	114. D	154. C	194. B
35. A	75. E	115. B	155. B	195. B
36. B	76. C	116. E	156. E	196. C
37. C	77. C	117. D	157. A	197. E
38. C	78. D	118. B	158. D	198. D
39. A	79. B	119. C	159. A	199. D
40. C	80. B	120. E	160. A	200. D

Answer Explanations for Sample Test 2

1. **(C)** Glycogen is a polysaccharide (carbohydrate) composed of many linked glucoses, commonly stored in the liver and muscles.

2. **(A)** The middle lamella is a layer that binds adjacent cell walls together; it is a layer shared by adjacent cells.

3. **(C)** Both barnacles and crayfish are crustaceans, gill-breathing arthropods.

4. **(E)** Myotomes lie between the dermatome and sclerotome (all derived from somites). They are segmentally arranged and give rise to all of the skeletal musculature except that found in the head and neck region.

5. **(B)** All sequences represent levels of increasing complexity or direction. The sequence in choice (B) should be morula—blastula—gastrula, stages in the early development of an embryo.

6. **(C)** This is exponential growth. It occurs in any system where the produced units are themselves able to (re)produce.

7. **(A)** Angiosperms have seeds enclosed in fruits, whereas gymnosperms have naked (unenclosed) seeds. While most angiosperms have broad leaves and gymnosperm-narrow leaves, there are many exceptions.

8. **(C)** The equation describes a sigmoid (or S-shaped) curve: slow growth initially, then rapid (exponential) growth, finally no growth (but also no decrease). The last phase represents the theoretical carrying capacity of the population.

9. **(A)** The term K represents the carrying capacity, that is, the number of individuals in the population when it reaches its maximum size. The population should be able to maintain this number indefinitely.

10. **(C)** DNA occurs in two strands, parallel to each other and twisted.

11. **(D)** In effect, the soluble salts in fertilizer dilute the water of the soil. If it is diluted enough, the plant will contain more water than the soil surrounding its roots. Since the movement of water by osmosis is in proportion to the quantity of water on each side of a membrane, the net movement will be out of the plant, thus dehydrating it.

12. **(E)** The complete sequence of zones is as follows: floating plants—rooted but submerged plants—rooted plants with floating leaves—emergent plants.

13. **(A)** Examples of carbohydrates are glucose, $C_6H_{12}O_6$, and fructose, $C_6H_{12}O_6$. Compound sugars such as sucrose, $C_{12}H_{22}O_{11}$, have the same proportions less one molecule of water.

14. **(A)** A hypofunctioning thyroid gland does not produce enough thyroxin to keep the oxidative energy-releasing reactions of the body at a normal level. In adults, a hypofunctioning thyroid causes such symptoms as goiter, physical lethargy, obesity, loss of hair, slower heartbeat, and mental dullness.

15. **(A)** Perhaps because their sex is not heavily dependent on chromosome numbers, flowering plants can relatively often produce viable hybrids when the gametes of two species are united. Sometimes such a hybrid, containing chromosomes of both parent species, is able to mate but only with another such hybrid. By definition, these hybrids, known as allopolyploids, constitute a separate, new species.

16. **(C)** Linnaeus first devised the binomial system whereby any organism can be identified by its genus and species names.

17. **(E)** People who are heterozygous for the recessive sickling allele do not usually have symptoms of sickle-cell anemia, but their red blood cells are inhospitable to any malaria parasite that tries to inhabit them. Thus, in any region of the world where malaria is a hazard, being heterozygous for this gene has some advantage and the otherwise deleterious sickling allele will be kept in rather high frequency.

18. **(E)** The phylum Echinodermata includes starfishes, sea urchins, and other animals that are all aquatic but never in fresh water.

19. **(B)** This is a conclusion reached by Gause from his classical work with *Paramecium* species. In almost all situations studied, there is competition between species attempting to share the same niche. As a result, one of the species dwindles in number, sometimes to extinction.

20. **(B)** A hybridoma cell is formed by fusion of a cancer cell with an antibody-producing cell. Thus, its descendants have the ability to reproduce indefinitely in culture (making a clone) and the ability to produce antibody of only one sort (monoclonal antibody). Cytotoxic T cells directly attack antigens after gaining competence by residing in the thymus. Plasma cells (B cells) release antibody and are not dependent upon residence in the thymus. Antibody of plasma cells, if of the IgE variety, can induce allergic reactions. The function of natural killer cells is most closely linked to defense against cancer cells and destruction of cells harboring viruses.

21. **(B)** The tube unfailingly grows to the position of the egg, following a chemical gradient.

22. **(E)** At birth the umbilical cord is about 2 ft. long and 3/4 in. in diameter. It contains the allantois, yolk sac, two arteries, and one vein, all held together with a loose connective tissue. The allantois, a rudimentary organ in mammals, outpockets into the umbilical cord from the posterior part of the primitive digestive tract. The yolk sac outpockets from the ventral part of the primitive digestive tract. Like the allantois, it is rudimentary.

23. **(C)** Chromosome fragments of the host bacterium may become enclosed by new viral sheaths that form during viral multiplication. A virus containing such a fragment introduces it, along with its own genetic material, into the bacterium it enters. This form of bacterial gene transfer is called transduction.

24. **(B)** The genotype *AaBbccDd* can produce the gene combinations *ABcD, ABcd, AbcD, Abcd, aBcD, abcD,* and *abcd*. The easy way to calculate the chance that the offspring will be *aaBBccDD* is to determine the chance of each gene combination occurring individually and then multiply all of them together. The chance of being *aa* is 1/4 (25%), *BB* is 1/4 (25%), *cc* is 1/1 (100%), and *Dd* is 1/2 (50%). Therefore, $1/4 \times 1/4 \times 1/1 \times 1/2 = 1/32$.

25. **(A)** *Lotic* means "of streams" (flowing water); *lentic* means "of lakes" (standing water).

26. **(D)** Vernalization is the preconditioning of seeds, seedlings, or mature plants to induce physiological events such as breaking of dormancy and flowering. The preconditioning usually involves subjection to low temperatures for a certain period of time. It is often used to precondition winter wheat so that it can be planted during spring in regions where winters are too severe for fall planting and suitable spring varieties are not available.

27. **(E)** In the order listed, the organisms represent successive trophic levels of the food pyramid. Being at the top of the pyramid, the killer whale has much less biomass than any of the others. There is about a 90% loss from one level to the next.

28. **(B)** Epinephrine (adrenaline) is produced by the medulla of the adrenal and provides quick energy for defense or flight.

29. **(D)** A heterotroph gains energy-storing organic molecules from outside itself; it cannot make them. Conifers, the cone-bearing gymnosperm plants, are auto-trophic since they can perform photosynthesis.

30. **(E)** The word *fern* means "feather (or "wing") plant," perhaps referring to the feathery appearance of fern fronds.

31. **(A)** Humans share about 95% of their genes with chimpanzees. Of those shared genes, many (such as those for hemoglobin) are identical in both species. *Homo erectus* is extinct.

32. **(A)** In vertebrates the central nervous system is derived from a dorsal groove in the ectoderm. The sides of the groove eventually fuse over the top to form a tube that lies beneath the outer wall. The anterior portion of that tube enlarges and develops into the brain.

33. **(D)** Presumably, all living organisms must continually respire to sustain life.

34. **(A)** The cerebrum is proportionally very large in humans. It does not regulate automatic body functions such as those that continue during sleep.

35. **(A)** An aneuploid organism has an irregular number of a particular chromosome (not an irregular number of whole sets). Monoploids, diploids, triploids, etc., cannot be considered aneuploid because they contain only whole sets of chromosomes. A trisomic is $2n + 1$, and a monosomic is $2n - 1$.

36. **(B)** Plants such as Venus' fly-trap that capture and utilize animals for food have been incorrectly referred to as insectivorous. Since they capture any animal of appropriate size that chances to fall into their traps, they should be described as carnivorous or flesh-eating.

37. **(C)** Lacteals are minute lymph vessels that absorb finely emulsified fats from the intestinal cavity and transport them to the thoracic duct.

38. **(C)** If a population is in Hardy-Weinberg equilibrium, the frequency of its alleles is remaining constant. Of the choices given, only (C) tends to keep allele frequencies unchanging.

39. **(A)** Originally isolated from a fungal parasite of rice, gibberellins have now been found in higher plants. When applied to plants, they cause a dramatic increase in size.

40. **(C)** Each fiber of skeletal muscle is a single large cell with many nuclei. This cell was formed in the embryo by the fusion of many smaller cells, called myoblasts.

41. **(E)** Because the growth region is at the base of the leaf, cropping the tips of lawn grasses destroys only mature tissues, which are replaced from below.

42. **(D)** Proceeding from the largest (most inclusive), the scheme of taxonomic levels is kingdom, phylum (called division for plants and fungi), class, order, family, genus, species. Humans are of kingdom Animalia, phylum Chordata, class Mammalia, order Primates, genus *Homo,* species *sapiens.*

43. **(B)** Sex cells are produced by gametophytes, and the gametophytes of ferns are known as prothalli (sing., prothallus).

44. **(B)** This is an environmental problem, and ecology deals with organismal-environmental relationships.

45. **(E)** Urea, the principal nitrogenous waste molecule of vertebrate animals, includes two amino ($-NH_2$) groups.

46. **(E)** Hormones secreted by the ovary are estrogen and progesterone, the former being especially important in causing the development of the female secondary sexual characteristics.

47. **(D)** While chromosomes are moving to the poles, the cell is in anaphase; when chromosomes reach the poles, the cell is in telophase.

48. **(B)** Besides having no definite nuclei, monerans lack mitochondria, plastids, endoplasmic reticulum, Golgi bodies, and lysosomes.

49. **(C)** Contractile vacuoles regularly expel excess water that diffuses into the protozoa. If it were not eliminated, the organisms would burst.

50. **(B)** During the light-dependent phase of photosynthesis, water is split into hydrogen and oxygen. The hydrogen later combines with carbon dioxide and water in the synthesis of food.

51. **(B)** Deoxygenated blood is pumped by the heart through the pulmonary artery to the lungs, where it is again oxygenated.

52. **(A)** Active transport depends on something more than molecular movement, which is all that is required for passive absorption. The process requires an expenditure of energy, since molecules entering a cell against a concentration gradient move from an area of low to an area of high concentration.

53. **(B)** Diploid cells have two sets of chromosomes, one set from each parent.

54. **(D)** In asexual reproduction there is only one parent, and the offspring has the same genes as the parent. In sexual reproduction two parents with individual differences pool their genes in producing a third individual, which will be different from either parent. The results may or may not be an improvement. Presumably, however, superior individuals are more likely to survive.

55. **(A)** Secretory cells of the thyroid are derived from endoderm.

56. **(E)** F_1 individuals will all be *Rr*, or pink. See the illustration for how the F_2 is formed.

57. **(E)** Though belonging to different taxonomic groups, fish and whales have forms that are similar, an adaptation to the environment where both live. The resemblance is superficial, however, as indicated by such fundamental differences as the manner in which they breathe—gill breathing by fish and lung breathing by whales.

58. **(A)** A niche is not a location. It is a mode of life, including all of the organism's relationships. It has sometimes been likened to the profession of a person.

59. **(D)** The process is called radiocarbon dating. Carbon-14 is a radioactive isotope used to date organic items such as those mentioned. The process is reasonably accurate up to 25,000 years.

60. **(B)** The moss gives nothing to and takes nothing away from the plant to which it is attached. Such an epiphyte is maintaining a commensal relationship with the tree.

61. **(B)** By definition, the term *sympatric* means "having the same geographic range."

62. **(A)** The nucleotide is a molecule composed of a pentose sugar to which is attached a phosphate group and a nitrogenous base (purine or pyrimidine).

63. **(A)** Since a spherical cell has a larger volume in relation to its outer boundary, it is especially suited for the storage of food.

64. **(A)** The time of flowering of many plants is keyed to the lengths of darkness and light to which they are exposed. Short-day plants bloom in the spring and fall; long-day plants, in the summer.

65. **(C)** Sucrose is a disaccharide sugar that is digested to the monosaccharides glucose and fructose.

66. **(D)** As cells differentiate to become skeletal muscle cells, their smooth endoplasmic reticulum takes on the proper configuration to function as sarcoplasmic reticulum. As such, this set of membranous bags controls the distribution of calcium, which is necessary for muscle contraction.

67. **(B)** The word *synapsis* is often confused with *synapse,* which is the gap over which an impulse travels between two neurons (or between neuron and muscle or other organ).

68. **(B)** After the first meiotic division the sperm enters the secondary oocyte (ordinarily called the egg), usually while the

latter is in the Fallopian tube (oviduct). The so-called egg is not really an egg until all polar bodies form.

69. **(A)** Unspecialized limbs terminate in five digits. Any divergence from that pattern, which is present in the early embryo, is specialization. The human foot retains the five-digit pattern in the adult. The elephant's trunk is certainly a specialized adaptation of the nose, just as the human brain is an extreme development of a brain.

70. **(A)** Seawater with a salinity of 3.5% is hypertonic to body tissues, meaning that it contains less water (and more solute molecules) than the tissues. A 0.85% solution of sodium chloride or a 5% solution of glucose is approximately isotonic to human cells. Since isotonic solutions have the same concentration of osmotically active particles as the cells, there is no net movement of water into and out of them. Seawater would have fewer water molecules than the tissues, so the net movement of water would be from the tissues to the seawater in the digestive tract.

71. **(E)** A submaxillary gland is but one of several salivary glands that serve primarily to lubricate food for easy swallowing.

72. **(B)** Electrophoresis produces differential migrations of molecules according to their net charges. Dialysis, ultracentrifugation, and gel exclusion chromatography all effect separations based on size and shape but not charge. Spectrophotometry can analyze molecular characteristics but is not a separation method.

73. **(E)** When a plant is abnormally hot or dry during daylight, it closes many of its stomata but continues some photosynthesis, leading to buildup of the waste product oxygen. Excess oxygen can then begin to replace carbon dioxide in the Calvin cycle. The photorespiration reactions that follow are very inefficient since neither ATP nor carbohydrate is produced.

74. **(D)** The chromosome is composed of DNA and proteins. In shape, the chromosome is cordlike. It is not membrane-bound.

75. **(E)** The chromatophores are specialized pigment cells that have irregular shapes and branching processes. In shape, they resemble some amoebas. There are different types containing different pigments. The stimulus to change color comes through the eyes and causes nervous and hormonal changes that regulate the chromatophores.

76. **(C)** Many different cancer-causing genes have been found. These oncogenes either are modified from normal genes (protooncogenes) or are normal genes whose product should be made only in specific parts of the life cycle (such as in embryonic stages). If such genes make an abnormal product or make a normal embryonic product in postembryonic times, the result can be a cancerous cell.

77. **(C)** Any variation from 46 produces abnormal results. At one time biologists thought the normal number was 48.

78. **(D)** The blastodisc does not develop into a hollow ball of equal cells because the presence of a great deal of yolk causes the embryo to be very asymmetrical. In either case, this stage immediately precedes the formation of germ layers.

79. **(B)** Homologous structures have the same embryological origin regardless of how different they appear as a result of later modification. Humans and bats are both mammals, and their arms and wings are forelimbs specialized for specific needs.

80. **(B)** While Alfred Russel Wallace was in Malaya, he sent Darwin a paper on the subject of evolution asking him to forward the paper to Lyell, a famous geologist of that day. To the surprise of Darwin, Wallace's views were strikingly similar to his own. At first Darwin was ready to grant priority for the idea to Wallace, but another scientist arranged to have a joint presentation of their papers in which they expressed their views on the subject of natural selection.

81. **(B)** In all the other choices the structures are connected directly to each other

and function together. The lung is a part of the respiratory system, whereas the coronary artery is a part of the circulatory system.

82. **(A)** The dendrite of a sensory neuron is connected with peripheral areas, and its axon synapses with another neuron in the spinal cord. The cell body, from which dendrite and axon extend, is located in the dorsal root ganglion.

83. **(B)** Just as in a home or an automobile radiator, heat loss in an organism is directly related to the size of the exposed surface area.

84. **(C)** A typical growth curve is sigmoid and resembles the letter S. Growth starts slowly, with few individuals. The population then enters a phase of logarithmic increase. When one or more environmental resources becomes scarce, the curve levels.

85. **(D)** In humans the death rate sharply increases in old age.

86. **(B)** When a variable characteristic such as weight in a large population is plotted, the graph is usually bell-shaped.

87. **(A)** Unlike humans, most fish die when they are very young.

88. **(B)** Biomes are communities having large geographical dimensions where relatively uniform climatic conditions prevail. The characteristic life form of the dominant vegetation is of course related to the climate conditions: for example, deciduous forest to areas where there are distinct growing and dormant seasons, and grassland to locations where precipitation is too low to support trees.

89. **(E)** A mutation is a single event occurring in a single cell of a single organism. Therefore, it affects that individual immediately and most profoundly.

90. **(A)** By definition, an ecosystem is a more or less self-contained community of organisms together with the environment in which it lives.

91. **(D)** A population is all of the individuals of a species or all members of the same species in a particular location. Being so closely related, they can interbreed.

92. **(D)** The first three choices involve a mixture of plants and animals. A population consists of only one species.

93. **(A)** As long as a system is self-sustaining, it is an ecosystem no matter what its size.

94. **(B)** A desert is a biome characterized by rather evenly and widely spaced plants. The plants are similar in having adaptations to conserve water, a necessary prerequisite to survival in extremely dry environments.

95. **(D)** Because the hydrogen bonds between the molecules of water increase its surface tension, water resists pressure from the legs of insects. Therefore, they can walk across its surface.

96. **(E)** As water freezes, its individual molecules spread apart. Ice therefore is less dense than liquid water and floats, allowing life to continue in ponds and streams.

97. **(B)** The sweating of humans and the panting of dogs constitute cooling mechanisms that result from the fact that water takes up an unusually large amount of energy (heat) as it evaporates.

98. **(C)** Large lakes act as reservoirs of heat during summer, slowly losing the heat to the atmosphere in winter.

99. **(A)** The term *active site* refers to the portion of an enzyme that makes contact with a substrate. A change in this region's shape by attachment of some other material elsewhere on the enzyme will inhibit enzymatic activity.

100. **(D)** By definition, a substrate is a molecule that is changed in a reaction catalyzed by an enzyme.

101. **(B)** Some proteins are inactive until a nonprotein group is added. An example is hemoglobin, whose prosthetic groups are iron-containing heme.

102. **(E)** This is a definition of a vitamin.

103. **(E)** M. Schleiden, in 1838, stated that all plants are composed of cells. T. Schwann made a similar statement about animals in the next year.

104. **(B)** The organelle is called the Golgi body or apparatus in Golgi's honor.

105. **(A)** Francis Crick shared a Nobel Prize with James Watson and Maurice Wilkins for their work on the structure of DNA. He also studied the mechanism of the translation process, whereby the message of the gene is "read" to produce a polypeptide.

106. **(C)** R. Koch's protocol for proving the bacterial basis for tuberculosis has been extended for use with any living disease-causing agent.

107. **(D)** Louis Pasteur showed that a ravaging disease in silkworms was caused by a bacterium, shortly before Koch did the same with sheep anthrax and human tuberculosis.

108. **(D)** Pasteur devised an elegant test that demonstrated the continued sterility of a broth as long as it was sealed away from contact with airborne bacteria, thus disproving the belief that life could be generated spontaneously.

109. **(A)** Condenser lenses beneath the stage focus light on the object to be viewed.

110. **(C)** A light microscope's illuminator provides light; the equivalent in an electron microscope is the electron emitter, which sends a beam of electrons toward the object to be viewed. The advantage of using electrons is that their shorter wavelength dramatically improves resolution.

111. **(E)** Resolving power increases directly with the index of refraction of the lenses within the objective, and inversely with the wavelength of energy striking the material to be viewed. An indirect expression of the index of refraction is the numerical aperture value displayed on each objective of a microscope.

112. **(C)** A bird's gizzard contains swallowed sand, stones, and other objects that grind food before it reaches the intestinal tract.

113. **(D)** Although the colon (large intestine) performs some water reabsorption, most of this activity occurs in the small intestine. Of course, water reabsorption is a vital function for animals living on land.

114. **(E)** Most enzymatic breakdown of food occurs in the small intestine. Although digestive enzymes may be swept into the colon and remain active there, in humans the small intestine is the major site of digestion.

115. **(B)** The gallbladder, a bag on the liver's surface, collects and stores bile. The principal components of bile are bile salts that break down large globules of fat in the intestine. Bile is delivered to the intestine by a small tube, the bile duct.

116. **(E)** The point of attachment between tRNA and its matching amino acid is on the end of the tRNA, which consists of three nucleotides symbolized as CCA.

117. **(D)** The word *transcription* describes the process whereby RNA is synthesized under the direction of DNA.

118. **(B)** The only RNA whose structure includes a sequence of codons that specify amino acid sequence is messenger RNA.

119. **(C)** Translation is the process of building a protein (such as ribosomal protein) or a portion of a protein. Endoplasmic reticulum, being a membranous material, contains both protein and phospholipid. Only the former is directly made by translation.

120. **(E)** Let *C* symbolize the allele for cleft chin, and *c* symbolize the allele for lack of the cleft feature. If the man is cleft-chinned, he must have the *C* allele. If he is homozygous, his genotype is *CC*. His wife, lacking the feature, must be *cc*. All of their children must therefore have one allele from each parent and be *Cc*. Since *C* is dominant, a *Cc* individual will have the cleft.

121. **(D)** Let *T* symbolize the allele for normal, and *t* symbolize the allele for Tay-Sachs disease. Each parent, being heterozygous, has the genotype *Tt*. For each mating, the possible outcomes are diagrammed as follows:

Genotypes of
each parent

Alleles in gametes
(on margin
of diamond)

Genotypes in
body cells of
offspring
(inside diamond)

Genotype of F$_2$
(inside diamond)

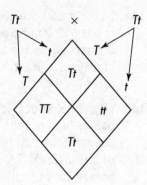

Cross between two heterozygotes for Tay-Sachs disease: Since two of every four offspring are expected to be *Tt*, the probability of any child being *Tt* (heterozygous) is 1/2, or .50.

122. **(B)** If the two genes are unlinked, this mating is the classical dihybrid cross first performed by Mendel. The analysis is as follows:

Genotypes of
parents

Genotype of F$_2$
(inside diamond)

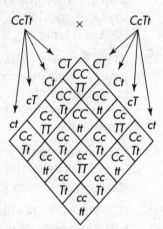

Cross between two double heterozygotes: The genotype we are seeking is *ccTt*. It occurs in two of the 16 boxes, indicating a 2/16 or .125 probability at each mating. If the two genes had been linked (on the same chromosome), they would not have assorted independently and the constitution of the next generation would be unpredictable, depending on the frequency of crossing-over between the genes.

123. **(A)** Thylakoids are membranous, flattened bags within chloroplasts. The light-dependent reactions of photosynthesis occur here.

124. **(C)** A basal body is a centriolelike object at the base of each flagellum or cilium. Like centrioles, a basal body is composed of microtubules in nine groups, forming a hollow cylinder.

125. **(D)** Lysosomes are small membranous bags containing digestive enzymes.

126. **(C)** A cross section of a cilium reveals an intricate pattern of microtubules, with nine pairs arranged concentrically around two individual central ones.

127. **(C)** Genetic dwarfs grow to normal size when treated with gibberellin.

128. **(E)** Photoperiodism, the response of a plant to changes in the 24-hour light-dark cycle, is mediated by a pigment called phytochrome. It changes its form when struck by light, then influences the plant's functions while in the altered state.

129. **(D)** Fruit growers use ethylene to ripen fruits that were picked while green.

130. **(B)** Working with auxin, cytokinin causes rapid production of new cells. Plant cells isolated in culture undergo mitosis when treated with cytokinin alone.

131. **(A)** Fritz Went, in 1926, discovered the hormonal nature of a plant's bending toward light. The class of compounds that can induce the response is auxins.

132. **(A)** While not the only auxin, IAA is the most common naturally produced auxin.

133. **(A)** The clonal selection model is an alternative to the instruction model; both are concerned with the method by which a newly introduced antigen elicits copious production of a specifically reacting antibody. The clonal selection model states that the body contains tiny groups of cells, each group capable of producing a different type of antibody. Contact with an antigen causes rapid mitosis of the appropriate cell type to form a large clone of productive cells.

134. **(C)** The image of actin filaments sliding over myosin filaments during contraction of skeletal muscle was first devised by H. E. Huxley and others in the mid-1950s.

135. **(B)** The competitive exclusion principle, also known as Gause's principle, states that, if two or more species of organism with overlapping ranges compete for some portion of the ecosystem, one will eventually gain in numbers and the other(s) will decline.

136. **(D)** Lamarck and others proposed a mechanism for evolution that involves the transfer from parent to offspring of structural or functional characteristics that are acquired by the parent during its lifetime.

137. **(E)** The spontaneous generation hypothesis involves the formation of an organism solely from nonliving materials. Biochemists believe that present conditions on Earth do not permit spontaneous generation, but that primitive conditions may have been conducive to this series of events.

138. **(B)** Charles Darwin culminated 20 years of study with his landmark book *On the Origin of Species* in 1859. He died in 1882.

139. **(E)** A. I. Oparin, a Russian biochemist, wrote persuasively on the origins of living organisms from nonliving materials in a primitive Earth setting.

140. **(B)** Darwin spent several years studying the way earthworms condition soil for optimal plant growth. With his son, he was the first to investigate the bending of plant stems toward light.

141. **(C)** Konrad Lorenz, an outstanding student of behavior, has contributed to our understanding of the type of learning (imprinting) shown by hatchling birds when they follow the first moving object they see.

142. **(D)** T. H. Morgan used white-eyed fruit flies as models to elucidate the inheritance of genes located on the sex chromosome.

143. **(A)** An important clue used by Watson and Crick in formulating the structure of DNA was Chargaff's data showing that the total number of DNA adenines equals the number of thymines. The same holds true for the cytosine-guanine pair.

144. **(E)** Uracil is found only in RNA.

145. **(A)** For each amino acid, there is a specific enzyme (amino acyl tRNA synthetase) that recognizes the correct tRNA for it and catalyzes the attachment of one to the other.

146. **(B)** The specific base-pairing that occurs between the three bases of a messenger RNA's codon and the three bases of a transfer RNA's anticodon is a temporary but crucial linkage during protein synthesis.

147. **(C)** DNA polymerase catalyzes the formation of polynucleotide DNA.

148. **(E)** Transcription is the process of forming RNA. According to the rules of base-pairing, adenine can temporarily hydrogen-bond with thymine or uracil, but only uracil can be incorporated into RNA.

149. **(D)** Thymine, whose atoms are arranged properly to hydrogen-bond with certain atoms of adenine, is incorporated into DNA as it replicates.

150. **(B)** The mammalian cerebral cortex controls many other brain regions, taking responsibility for functions that these other regions control in nonmammalian vertebrates.

151. **(A)** Damage to the cerebellum results in loss of ability to make proper muscular responses to sensory input.

152. **(E)** The medulla oblongata is the most posterior region of the brain and merges imperceptibly with the spinal cord.

153. **(C)** The ventral outgrowth of the hypothalamus is the posterior pituitary, which produces hormones that travel the short distance to the anterior pituitary. The latter responds by releasing its own hormones, which have profound influence over several other glands of the body.

154. **(C)** It has been shown that the continents are slowly moving apart. Extrapolation suggests that some of them were once connected, thus explaining the presence of closely related organisms on continents now separated by oceans.

155. **(B)** Rocks formed during the Cambrian Period (nearly 600 million years ago) contain many more fossils, including all of the phyla presently known, than do earlier rocks.

156. **(E)** Many cell biologists believe that mitochondria and plastids were once free-living prokaryotes and that their presence in modern cells originated as a symbiotic relationship. The presence of genetic material in these organelles tends to lend credence to the theory.

157. **(A)** Adaptive radiation is evolution of two or more specialized species from a single less specialized species. Each of the resulting species is adapted to fit a particular niche. Natural selection is the most powerful means of achieving such change.

158. **(D)** Mechanisms exist which tend to ensure that more than one allele of a gene will remain represented in a population from generation to generation. This balanced polymorphism enables a population to be more likely to respond successfully to environmental changes because it includes some individuals whose phenotypes are a good match for new conditions.

159. **(A)** Expansion of $(p + q)^2 = 1$ gives three expressions that correspond to the three possible genotypes when a two-allele system is under scrutiny.

160. **(A)** Expansion of the equation yields $p^2 + 2pq + q^2 = 1$. If p is the frequency of the dominant allele and q is the frequency of the recessive allele, $p + q = 1$. The value for q is derived by taking the square root of q^2, which represents the frequency of the homozygous recessive individuals. Since one fourth of the population is homozygous recessive, $q^2 = 0.25$ and $q = 0.5$. The value for p must be 0.5 also, since $p = 1 - q$. The term in the expansion that represents the expected frequency of homozygous dominant individuals is p^2. Therefore, this value is $(0.5)^2 = 0.25$. In a total population of 400, this would be 100 individuals.

161. **(E)** Natural selection is a potent force that will upset the equilibrium and render the mathematical prediction invalid. Among other forces capable of this effect are genetic drift in a small population, mutation, and migration.

162. **(A)** A testcross will produce offspring whose phenotypic ratios will show whether the parent with the dominant phenotype is homozygous or heterozygous. If homozygous dominant, all offspring will have the dominant phenotype; if heterozygous, only one half of them will be of this appearance.

163. **(E)** G. H. Hardy and W. Weinberg, working independently in 1908, derived the mathematical expression for genotype frequencies in a population.

164. **(E)** Equilibrium is attainment of a genetic steady state, manifesting an unchanged gene pool, regardless of the nature of the forces operating within the population.

165. **(C)** The graph shows much absorbance at around 550 nm, meaning that yellow-green light enters the membrane but does not leave it. Light in the 350–450 nm range does leave the membrane and is available to strike our eyes. We perceive these wavelengths as violet. The range above 650 nm, also not absorbed, is perceived as red.

166. **(C)** Another striking example is the presence of leghemoglobin, very similar in structure to vertebrate animals' hemoglobin, in certain plants. Fossils of bacteria far predate those of vertebrate animals.

167. **(A)** The chemiosmotic mode of oxidative phosphorylation was proposed by P. Mitchell, who received a Nobel Prize in 1978 for this work. According to the model, the mitochondrial membrane pumps out hydrogen ions and then allows them to reenter the mitochondrion by diffusion at specific sites. The energy of their inward flow is used to produce the high-energy phosphate bond of ATP.

168. **(A)** The 280-nm peak of the graph is evidence of absorption by two aromatic amino acids, tryptophan and tyrosine, found in nearly every protein. This distinctive absorption peak is a good indicator of a protein portion in the purified purple membrane molecule.

169. **(A)** The same effect can be mimicked by voltage change imposed by other means than sodium flow.

170. **(B)** The cortical granules are already in place just under the egg membrane well before sperm contact. Under normal conditions, the sperm-egg contact initiates (indirectly) granule bursting, not forming.

171. **(B)** Evidence for this function of calcium is provided by observation of both cortical granule bursting and mitosis upon treatment of an unfertilized egg with ionophores, which increase the intracellular calcium concentration.

172. **(A)** Amiloride makes the egg membrane impermeable to sodium and also blocks normal postfertilization events, including mitosis.

173. **(B)** Polyspermy leads to a greater than diploid number of chromosomes in the cell. If the zygote continues to develop, distribution problems during cell reproduction can result.

174. **(B)** Although the embryology of sea urchins certainly differs in some ways from that of other animals, it continues to be a valuable model system. Because sea urchin fertilization occurs in open water rather than in the body of the female, it is currently better understood than vertebrate fertilization. Recent *in vitro* fertilization work with humans, however, is rapidly changing this situation.

175. **(B)** The passage states that ionophores are drugs that mimic a component of sperm action by causing the release of calcium from depots in the egg. Ionophores are not present during natural fertilization.

176. **(E)** Look, for example, at the percentage saturation of both molecules when in a 20-mm O_2 environment. Myoglobin is carrying about 60% as much O_2 as it could in a maximum-O_2 environment, whereas hemoglobin is carrying only about 20%.

177. **(C)** Any population is likely to start growing slowly, then accelerate to maximum growth. If it meets some environmental limitation, such as amount of available space, its growth rate drops to zero and the population size remains constant. The population therefore describes the same S-shaped curve as the hemoglobin curve shown here.

178. **(E)** Because of the different behaviors of the proteins in low-oxygen areas, such as actively metabolizing muscles, a release-acceptance sequence will occur in the proper direction. If the two proteins were reversed in position, myoglobin would efficiently pick up O_2 at the lungs, but would fail to release a useful amount near the muscles. The O_2 that was released would not be picked up efficiently by hemoglobin if the latter were in muscles.

179. **(D)** Although worms are not closely related to humans, some of our cells have an O_2 environment similar to that of these marine worms: they both need to have O_2-accepting molecules that work in an area low in O_2.

180. **(E)** Small mammals have a high surface area-to-volume ratio, which leads to much loss of energy as heat radiation. To maintain optimal internal temperature, small mammals must run their metabolic processes at a high rate. Thus, they need hemoglobin that will release a large percentage of its O_2 at a given low-O_2 area.

181. **(E)** The chromosome makeup of the canaries is clearly stated in the passage.

182. **(B)** Although the offspring do not fall exactly into 1:1:1:1 ratio for feather color, they approximate this and give a reasonable clue to the inheritance pattern. If the gene is sex-linked, it may be assumed that it is located on the Z chromosome and that the cross would be as follows:

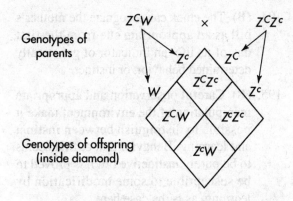

Genotypes of parents

Genotypes of offspring (inside diamond)

Cross involving sex-linkage: Predicted phenotypes of these offspring, in a 1:1:1:1 ratio, would be green males, cinnamon males, green females, and cinnamon females.

Here is the same cross if the gene was autosomal:

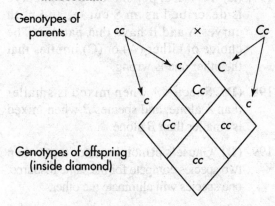

Genotypes of parents

Genotypes of offspring (inside diamond)

Cross involving autosomal gene: The phenotypes of these offspring would be cinnamon or green in a 1:1 ratio. Each category would include males and females in a 1:1 ratio, so the same 1:1:1:1 ratio would occur as is predicted for sex-linkage.

183. **(D)** A pleiotropic gene is one that expresses itself in more than one phenotypic characteristic.

184. **(D)** A sex-linked gene is almost always carried on only one of the two different sex chromosomes. A heterozygote is an organism with two alleles of a gene in each of its cells. Since only male canaries have two copies of the same sex chromosome, they alone could be heterozygous.

185. **(A)** If the mode of inheritance is sex-linkage, all males of such a cross should be green. If an autosomal gene is involved, one-fourth of the males should be cinnamon.

If sex-linked:

Genotypes of parents

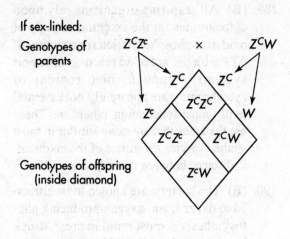

Genotypes of offspring (inside diamond)

If autosomal:

Genotypes of parents

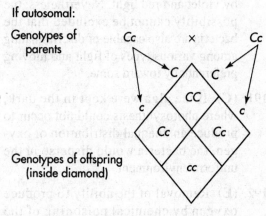

Genotypes of offspring (inside diamond)

Here, each block represents the genotype of males and females, so some *cc* males (cinnamon) would be expected.

186. **(B)** Examination of Table 1 shows that regions with the same number of amino acids have significantly different numbers of those that are identical in all five species. For instance, regions *B* and *D* both have 15 amino acids, but *B* is identical at 9 of its sites while *D* is identical at only 5 of its sites.

187. **(D)** From Table 2, region *D* of tuna has no amino acids in identical positions with all five bacterial species. In each other region, at least one position has the same amino acid in all reported species.

188. **(B)** Both Table 1 and Table 2 indicate that region *B* has 9 of its 15 positions occupied by the same amino acid in all bacteria. None of the other regions has as much as this 60% correspondence.

189. **(B)** All respiring organisms rely upon cytochromes for the essential activity of oxidative phosphorylation (production of ATP with the aid of an electron transport system). Although some regions of cytochrome *c* are apparently not essential to its proper functioning, others are. These are the areas that are quite similar in most studied species regardless of the taxonomic distance between these species.

190. **(B)** The bacteria are known to be attracted to oxygen, and oxygen-producing photosynthesis is most rapid in areas struck by violet and red light. Nevertheless, the possibility cannot be excluded that the bacteria are also capable of discriminating among various types of fight and moving preferentially toward some.

191. **(C)** If the alga were kept in the dark, where photosynthesis could not occur to produce an unequal distribution of oxygen, the bacteria would disperse in the uniform environment.

192. **(E)** Removal of the ability to produce oxygen by chemical poisoning of the bacteria's Photochemical System II, the portion of the photosynthesis apparatus that splits water to produce O_2, would help to determine whether the bacteria are attracted by both O_2 and light.

193. **(A)** Although developmental maturation of an instinctive behavior cannot be ruled out, gradual improvement in an activity as it is repeated is usually indicative of learning.

194. **(B)** The chick can recognize the mother's bill as an appropriate cue from the first day of its life, an indicator of genetically determined behavior, or instinct.

195. **(B)** Careful observation and appropriate manipulation of the environment make it possible to distinguish between instinct and learning. Behavior that at first seems to be purely instinctive often is proved to be susceptible to some modification by learning, as is the case here.

196. **(C)** The best way to test the role of vision in pecking accuracy would be to alter the total time the chicks have to use their vision before they reach adulthood.

197. **(E)** A typical population-growth curve is described as an S curve, and both curves A and B have that pattern. The choice of either (A) or (C) implies that the other one is wrong.

198. **(D)** Species *A* when mixed is smaller than *A* alone, and species *B* when mixed is smaller than *B* alone.

199. **(D)** Gause's principle states that, when two species compete for the same resource, one species will eliminate the other.

200. **(D)** In the graph the population curves for the mixed cultures are the second and fourth from the top. At first, population *A* plus *B* is smaller than *A* alone; however, it is increasing at the expense of *B*. Almost from the beginning, population B plus *A* is less than population *B* alone, and it steadily decreases until extinction.

Answer Sheet for Sample Test 3

1. Ⓐ Ⓑ Ⓒ Ⓓ Ⓔ
2. Ⓐ Ⓑ Ⓒ Ⓓ Ⓔ
3. Ⓐ Ⓑ Ⓒ Ⓓ Ⓔ
4. Ⓐ Ⓑ Ⓒ Ⓓ Ⓔ
5. Ⓐ Ⓑ Ⓒ Ⓓ Ⓔ
6. Ⓐ Ⓑ Ⓒ Ⓓ Ⓔ
7. Ⓐ Ⓑ Ⓒ Ⓓ Ⓔ
8. Ⓐ Ⓑ Ⓒ Ⓓ Ⓔ
9. Ⓐ Ⓑ Ⓒ Ⓓ Ⓔ
10. Ⓐ Ⓑ Ⓒ Ⓓ Ⓔ
11. Ⓐ Ⓑ Ⓒ Ⓓ Ⓔ
12. Ⓐ Ⓑ Ⓒ Ⓓ Ⓔ
13. Ⓐ Ⓑ Ⓒ Ⓓ Ⓔ
14. Ⓐ Ⓑ Ⓒ Ⓓ Ⓔ
15. Ⓐ Ⓑ Ⓒ Ⓓ Ⓔ
16. Ⓐ Ⓑ Ⓒ Ⓓ Ⓔ
17. Ⓐ Ⓑ Ⓒ Ⓓ Ⓔ
18. Ⓐ Ⓑ Ⓒ Ⓓ Ⓔ
19. Ⓐ Ⓑ Ⓒ Ⓓ Ⓔ
20. Ⓐ Ⓑ Ⓒ Ⓓ Ⓔ
21. Ⓐ Ⓑ Ⓒ Ⓓ Ⓔ
22. Ⓐ Ⓑ Ⓒ Ⓓ Ⓔ
23. Ⓐ Ⓑ Ⓒ Ⓓ Ⓔ
24. Ⓐ Ⓑ Ⓒ Ⓓ Ⓔ
25. Ⓐ Ⓑ Ⓒ Ⓓ Ⓔ
26. Ⓐ Ⓑ Ⓒ Ⓓ Ⓔ
27. Ⓐ Ⓑ Ⓒ Ⓓ Ⓔ
28. Ⓐ Ⓑ Ⓒ Ⓓ Ⓔ
29. Ⓐ Ⓑ Ⓒ Ⓓ Ⓔ
30. Ⓐ Ⓑ Ⓒ Ⓓ Ⓔ
31. Ⓐ Ⓑ Ⓒ Ⓓ Ⓔ
32. Ⓐ Ⓑ Ⓒ Ⓓ Ⓔ
33. Ⓐ Ⓑ Ⓒ Ⓓ Ⓔ
34. Ⓐ Ⓑ Ⓒ Ⓓ Ⓔ
35. Ⓐ Ⓑ Ⓒ Ⓓ Ⓔ
36. Ⓐ Ⓑ Ⓒ Ⓓ Ⓔ
37. Ⓐ Ⓑ Ⓒ Ⓓ Ⓔ
38. Ⓐ Ⓑ Ⓒ Ⓓ Ⓔ
39. Ⓐ Ⓑ Ⓒ Ⓓ Ⓔ
40. Ⓐ Ⓑ Ⓒ Ⓓ Ⓔ
41. Ⓐ Ⓑ Ⓒ Ⓓ Ⓔ
42. Ⓐ Ⓑ Ⓒ Ⓓ Ⓔ
43. Ⓐ Ⓑ Ⓒ Ⓓ Ⓔ
44. Ⓐ Ⓑ Ⓒ Ⓓ Ⓔ
45. Ⓐ Ⓑ Ⓒ Ⓓ Ⓔ
46. Ⓐ Ⓑ Ⓒ Ⓓ Ⓔ
47. Ⓐ Ⓑ Ⓒ Ⓓ Ⓔ
48. Ⓐ Ⓑ Ⓒ Ⓓ Ⓔ
49. Ⓐ Ⓑ Ⓒ Ⓓ Ⓔ
50. Ⓐ Ⓑ Ⓒ Ⓓ Ⓔ

51. Ⓐ Ⓑ Ⓒ Ⓓ Ⓔ
52. Ⓐ Ⓑ Ⓒ Ⓓ Ⓔ
53. Ⓐ Ⓑ Ⓒ Ⓓ Ⓔ
54. Ⓐ Ⓑ Ⓒ Ⓓ Ⓔ
55. Ⓐ Ⓑ Ⓒ Ⓓ Ⓔ
56. Ⓐ Ⓑ Ⓒ Ⓓ Ⓔ
57. Ⓐ Ⓑ Ⓒ Ⓓ Ⓔ
58. Ⓐ Ⓑ Ⓒ Ⓓ Ⓔ
59. Ⓐ Ⓑ Ⓒ Ⓓ Ⓔ
60. Ⓐ Ⓑ Ⓒ Ⓓ Ⓔ
61. Ⓐ Ⓑ Ⓒ Ⓓ Ⓔ
62. Ⓐ Ⓑ Ⓒ Ⓓ Ⓔ
63. Ⓐ Ⓑ Ⓒ Ⓓ Ⓔ
64. Ⓐ Ⓑ Ⓒ Ⓓ Ⓔ
65. Ⓐ Ⓑ Ⓒ Ⓓ Ⓔ
66. Ⓐ Ⓑ Ⓒ Ⓓ Ⓔ
67. Ⓐ Ⓑ Ⓒ Ⓓ Ⓔ
68. Ⓐ Ⓑ Ⓒ Ⓓ Ⓔ
69. Ⓐ Ⓑ Ⓒ Ⓓ Ⓔ
70. Ⓐ Ⓑ Ⓒ Ⓓ Ⓔ
71. Ⓐ Ⓑ Ⓒ Ⓓ Ⓔ
72. Ⓐ Ⓑ Ⓒ Ⓓ Ⓔ
73. Ⓐ Ⓑ Ⓒ Ⓓ Ⓔ
74. Ⓐ Ⓑ Ⓒ Ⓓ Ⓔ
75. Ⓐ Ⓑ Ⓒ Ⓓ Ⓔ
76. Ⓐ Ⓑ Ⓒ Ⓓ Ⓔ
77. Ⓐ Ⓑ Ⓒ Ⓓ Ⓔ
78. Ⓐ Ⓑ Ⓒ Ⓓ Ⓔ
79. Ⓐ Ⓑ Ⓒ Ⓓ Ⓔ
80. Ⓐ Ⓑ Ⓒ Ⓓ Ⓔ
81. Ⓐ Ⓑ Ⓒ Ⓓ Ⓔ
82. Ⓐ Ⓑ Ⓒ Ⓓ Ⓔ
83. Ⓐ Ⓑ Ⓒ Ⓓ Ⓔ
84. Ⓐ Ⓑ Ⓒ Ⓓ Ⓔ
85. Ⓐ Ⓑ Ⓒ Ⓓ Ⓔ
86. Ⓐ Ⓑ Ⓒ Ⓓ Ⓔ
87. Ⓐ Ⓑ Ⓒ Ⓓ Ⓔ
88. Ⓐ Ⓑ Ⓒ Ⓓ Ⓔ
89. Ⓐ Ⓑ Ⓒ Ⓓ Ⓔ
90. Ⓐ Ⓑ Ⓒ Ⓓ Ⓔ
91. Ⓐ Ⓑ Ⓒ Ⓓ Ⓔ
92. Ⓐ Ⓑ Ⓒ Ⓓ Ⓔ
93. Ⓐ Ⓑ Ⓒ Ⓓ Ⓔ
94. Ⓐ Ⓑ Ⓒ Ⓓ Ⓔ
95. Ⓐ Ⓑ Ⓒ Ⓓ Ⓔ
96. Ⓐ Ⓑ Ⓒ Ⓓ Ⓔ
97. Ⓐ Ⓑ Ⓒ Ⓓ Ⓔ
98. Ⓐ Ⓑ Ⓒ Ⓓ Ⓔ
99. Ⓐ Ⓑ Ⓒ Ⓓ Ⓔ
100. Ⓐ Ⓑ Ⓒ Ⓓ Ⓔ

101. Ⓐ Ⓑ Ⓒ Ⓓ Ⓔ
102. Ⓐ Ⓑ Ⓒ Ⓓ Ⓔ
103. Ⓐ Ⓑ Ⓒ Ⓓ Ⓔ
104. Ⓐ Ⓑ Ⓒ Ⓓ Ⓔ
105. Ⓐ Ⓑ Ⓒ Ⓓ Ⓔ
106. Ⓐ Ⓑ Ⓒ Ⓓ Ⓔ
107. Ⓐ Ⓑ Ⓒ Ⓓ Ⓔ
108. Ⓐ Ⓑ Ⓒ Ⓓ Ⓔ
109. Ⓐ Ⓑ Ⓒ Ⓓ Ⓔ
110. Ⓐ Ⓑ Ⓒ Ⓓ Ⓔ
111. Ⓐ Ⓑ Ⓒ Ⓓ Ⓔ
112. Ⓐ Ⓑ Ⓒ Ⓓ Ⓔ
113. Ⓐ Ⓑ Ⓒ Ⓓ Ⓔ
114. Ⓐ Ⓑ Ⓒ Ⓓ Ⓔ
115. Ⓐ Ⓑ Ⓒ Ⓓ Ⓔ
116. Ⓐ Ⓑ Ⓒ Ⓓ Ⓔ
117. Ⓐ Ⓑ Ⓒ Ⓓ Ⓔ
118. Ⓐ Ⓑ Ⓒ Ⓓ Ⓔ
119. Ⓐ Ⓑ Ⓒ Ⓓ Ⓔ
120. Ⓐ Ⓑ Ⓒ Ⓓ Ⓔ
121. Ⓐ Ⓑ Ⓒ Ⓓ Ⓔ
122. Ⓐ Ⓑ Ⓒ Ⓓ Ⓔ
123. Ⓐ Ⓑ Ⓒ Ⓓ Ⓔ
124. Ⓐ Ⓑ Ⓒ Ⓓ Ⓔ
125. Ⓐ Ⓑ Ⓒ Ⓓ Ⓔ
126. Ⓐ Ⓑ Ⓒ Ⓓ Ⓔ
127. Ⓐ Ⓑ Ⓒ Ⓓ Ⓔ
128. Ⓐ Ⓑ Ⓒ Ⓓ Ⓔ
129. Ⓐ Ⓑ Ⓒ Ⓓ Ⓔ
130. Ⓐ Ⓑ Ⓒ Ⓓ Ⓔ
131. Ⓐ Ⓑ Ⓒ Ⓓ Ⓔ
132. Ⓐ Ⓑ Ⓒ Ⓓ Ⓔ
133. Ⓐ Ⓑ Ⓒ Ⓓ Ⓔ
134. Ⓐ Ⓑ Ⓒ Ⓓ Ⓔ
135. Ⓐ Ⓑ Ⓒ Ⓓ Ⓔ
136. Ⓐ Ⓑ Ⓒ Ⓓ Ⓔ
137. Ⓐ Ⓑ Ⓒ Ⓓ Ⓔ
138. Ⓐ Ⓑ Ⓒ Ⓓ Ⓔ
139. Ⓐ Ⓑ Ⓒ Ⓓ Ⓔ
140. Ⓐ Ⓑ Ⓒ Ⓓ Ⓔ
141. Ⓐ Ⓑ Ⓒ Ⓓ Ⓔ
142. Ⓐ Ⓑ Ⓒ Ⓓ Ⓔ
143. Ⓐ Ⓑ Ⓒ Ⓓ Ⓔ
144. Ⓐ Ⓑ Ⓒ Ⓓ Ⓔ
145. Ⓐ Ⓑ Ⓒ Ⓓ Ⓔ
146. Ⓐ Ⓑ Ⓒ Ⓓ Ⓔ
147. Ⓐ Ⓑ Ⓒ Ⓓ Ⓔ
148. Ⓐ Ⓑ Ⓒ Ⓓ Ⓔ
149. Ⓐ Ⓑ Ⓒ Ⓓ Ⓔ
150. Ⓐ Ⓑ Ⓒ Ⓓ Ⓔ

151. Ⓐ Ⓑ Ⓒ Ⓓ Ⓔ
152. Ⓐ Ⓑ Ⓒ Ⓓ Ⓔ
153. Ⓐ Ⓑ Ⓒ Ⓓ Ⓔ
154. Ⓐ Ⓑ Ⓒ Ⓓ Ⓔ
155. Ⓐ Ⓑ Ⓒ Ⓓ Ⓔ
156. Ⓐ Ⓑ Ⓒ Ⓓ Ⓔ
157. Ⓐ Ⓑ Ⓒ Ⓓ Ⓔ
158. Ⓐ Ⓑ Ⓒ Ⓓ Ⓔ
159. Ⓐ Ⓑ Ⓒ Ⓓ Ⓔ
160. Ⓐ Ⓑ Ⓒ Ⓓ Ⓔ
161. Ⓐ Ⓑ Ⓒ Ⓓ Ⓔ
162. Ⓐ Ⓑ Ⓒ Ⓓ Ⓔ
163. Ⓐ Ⓑ Ⓒ Ⓓ Ⓔ
164. Ⓐ Ⓑ Ⓒ Ⓓ Ⓔ
165. Ⓐ Ⓑ Ⓒ Ⓓ Ⓔ
166. Ⓐ Ⓑ Ⓒ Ⓓ Ⓔ
167. Ⓐ Ⓑ Ⓒ Ⓓ Ⓔ
168. Ⓐ Ⓑ Ⓒ Ⓓ Ⓔ
169. Ⓐ Ⓑ Ⓒ Ⓓ Ⓔ
170. Ⓐ Ⓑ Ⓒ Ⓓ Ⓔ
171. Ⓐ Ⓑ Ⓒ Ⓓ Ⓔ
172. Ⓐ Ⓑ Ⓒ Ⓓ Ⓔ
173. Ⓐ Ⓑ Ⓒ Ⓓ Ⓔ
174. Ⓐ Ⓑ Ⓒ Ⓓ Ⓔ
175. Ⓐ Ⓑ Ⓒ Ⓓ Ⓔ
176. Ⓐ Ⓑ Ⓒ Ⓓ Ⓔ
177. Ⓐ Ⓑ Ⓒ Ⓓ Ⓔ
178. Ⓐ Ⓑ Ⓒ Ⓓ Ⓔ
179. Ⓐ Ⓑ Ⓒ Ⓓ Ⓔ
180. Ⓐ Ⓑ Ⓒ Ⓓ Ⓔ
181. Ⓐ Ⓑ Ⓒ Ⓓ Ⓔ
182. Ⓐ Ⓑ Ⓒ Ⓓ Ⓔ
183. Ⓐ Ⓑ Ⓒ Ⓓ Ⓔ
184. Ⓐ Ⓑ Ⓒ Ⓓ Ⓔ
185. Ⓐ Ⓑ Ⓒ Ⓓ Ⓔ
186. Ⓐ Ⓑ Ⓒ Ⓓ Ⓔ
187. Ⓐ Ⓑ Ⓒ Ⓓ Ⓔ
188. Ⓐ Ⓑ Ⓒ Ⓓ Ⓔ
189. Ⓐ Ⓑ Ⓒ Ⓓ Ⓔ
190. Ⓐ Ⓑ Ⓒ Ⓓ Ⓔ
191. Ⓐ Ⓑ Ⓒ Ⓓ Ⓔ
192. Ⓐ Ⓑ Ⓒ Ⓓ Ⓔ
193. Ⓐ Ⓑ Ⓒ Ⓓ Ⓔ
194. Ⓐ Ⓑ Ⓒ Ⓓ Ⓔ
195. Ⓐ Ⓑ Ⓒ Ⓓ Ⓔ
196. Ⓐ Ⓑ Ⓒ Ⓓ Ⓔ
197. Ⓐ Ⓑ Ⓒ Ⓓ Ⓔ
198. Ⓐ Ⓑ Ⓒ Ⓓ Ⓔ
199. Ⓐ Ⓑ Ⓒ Ⓓ Ⓔ
200. Ⓐ Ⓑ Ⓒ Ⓓ Ⓔ

Test in Biology

Sample Test 3

Directions for Taking Test: This sample test contains 200 questions or incomplete statements, and should be finished in 170 minutes. Each item has five possible answers or completions. Choose the best one, and blacken the corresponding letter on the answer sheet.

After finishing, you can determine your score by using the **Answer Key** at the end of this test. The **Answer Explanations** section should clarify the concepts involved in each question.

Questions 1–86

For each of the following questions or incomplete statements there are five suggested answers or completions. Select the best choice.

1. In mature mammals, cells are very actively dividing in the
   A. muscles
   B. brain
   C. liver
   D. bone marrow
   E. kidney

2. Which answer is the most accurate description of transpiration in plants?
   A. necessary for lifting water to leaves
   B. necessary for cooling plant
   C. mechanism for eliminating waste
   D. harmful, with no benefit
   E. potentially harmful, but unavoidable

3. Choose the correct statement about homeotic genes.
   A. They are found only in *Drosophila*.
   B. Their most profound effects are during the embryonic development period.
   C. They are oncogenes.
   D. They are most closely associated with the determination of sexual preference.
   E. They are always sex-linked.

4. What is the most likely consequence of a frameshift mutation in a structural gene?
   A. no change in the produced polypeptide
   B. no polypeptide produced
   C. polypeptide produced, with an entirely new amino acid sequence beyond the mutation point
   D. several random amino substitutions scattered over the produced polypeptide
   E. new amino acid sequences in several polypeptides

5. Crossing-over is a familiar term for
   A. hybridization
   B. migration across difficult geographical barriers
   C. interchange of sections of chromatids
   D. diffusion from one side of a membrane to the other
   E. pollination involving separate flowers, male and female

6. Gene amplification
   A. is a way for a cell to produce an unusually large number of mRNA copies
   B. involves a lengthening of a gene
   C. is the addition of spacer regions between the several structural genes of an operon
   D. is a causative factor in human oncogenesis
   E. is a method of making genes visible during electron microscopy

7. Water remaining in the soil after a plant has permanently wilted is
   A. groundwater
   B. hygroscopic water
   C. capillary water
   D. gravitational water
   E. field capacity

8. A sex-influenced human trait is controlled by a gene
   A. on the X chromosome
   B. on the Y chromosome
   C. whose mode of expression depends on the sex of the person
   D. that is expressed only in one of the sexes
   E. that is present only in sex cells

9. Natural systems of classification are based on
   A. body form
   B. environmental adaptations
   C. kinship
   D. community associations
   E. food relationships

10. Tying a paper bag over the silks of an ear of corn would immediately interfere with
    A. growth of the entire plant
    B. germination
    C. pollination
    D. ovulation
    E. translocation

11. DNA is known to be duplicated in
    A. interphase
    B. prophase
    C. metaphase
    D. anaphase
    E. telophase

12. The pit organ of a pit viper is a
    A. thermal detector
    B. balancing organ
    C. scent gland
    D. seminal vesicle
    E. vestigial ear

13. What is chromatin?
    A. the DNA of a chromosome
    B. the DNA of a chromosome and the RNA and proteins associated with the DNA
    C. the portion of a chromosome's DNA that is part of functioning genes
    D. the portion of a chromosome that is not actively producing RNA
    E. the portion of a chromosome that comprises the centriole

14. Which cavity is found in adult insects?
    A. atrium
    B. archenteron
    C. pseudocoel
    D. hemocoel
    E. blastocoel

15. Organisms using carbon dioxide as the only carbon source are termed
    A. autotrophic
    B. heterotrophic
    C. autoecious
    D. deliquescent
    E. haustorial

16. The immediate source of energy for muscular contraction is
    A. ADP
    B. ATP
    C. actomyosin
    D. glycogen
    E. sucrose

17. Generally gametes are derived by reduction division of cells that are
A. haploid
B. diploid
C. triploid
D. tetraploid
E. pentaploid

18. It has been observed that the number of North and Central American bird species steadily increases from the Arctic region to the tropic region. This is an example of
A. a tropism
B. a food chain
C. biome diversity
D. adaptive radiation
E. a cline

19. Suppose that flower color is determined by a single pair of genes and that the case represents incomplete dominance. The genotype resulting from a cross between a homozygous red (*RR*) and a homozygous white (*rr*) will be
A. red
B. white
C. *RR*
D. *Rr*
E. *rr*

20. The natural flora of Australia is particularly distinct from those of other continents because
A. most of Australia is a desert
B. Australia is the only continent totally within the Southern Hemisphere
C. Australia has been separated from other continental masses for a comparatively longer period of time
D. Australia is smaller than other continents
E. Australia is the youngest continent

21. The best example of secondary succession is the consecutive changes from
A. bare rock to mat of lichens and mosses
B. mat of lichens and mosses to forest
C. lake to bog
D. bog to forest
E. abandoned field to forest

22. Benthic organisms CANNOT live in the
A. littoral zone
B. bathyal zone
C. profundal zone
D. abyssal zone
E. pelagic zone

23. Which of these is an example of biological magnification?
    A. Carbon dioxide released by industrial burning accumulates in the atmosphere.
    B. There are many more producers in an ecosystem than there are secondary consumers.
    C. A low concentration of a pesticide in lakes and streams leads to its high concentration in fish-eating birds.
    D. The male peacock has evolved a spectacularly enlarged tail.
    E. The human small intestine has many villi, each of which extends many microvilli into the lumen.

24. Which of these is an example of eutrophication?
    A. Runoff of agricultural fertilizer causes a huge increase of algae in a lake.
    B. DDT accumulates in eagles.
    C. The Calvin cycle is inhibited by excess oxygen in leaves.
    D. Two phylogenetically distant species evolve similar structures.
    E. Two species compete for the same niche and one of them is driven to extinction.

25. Which of these is NOT a defense against herbivory?
    A. induced increase in production of alkaloids or tannins
    B. production of trichomes
    C. production of thorns or spines
    D. production of chemicals that mimic insect hormones
    E. increased rate of photosynthesis

26. Plant cells in the process of mitosis are found in the
    A. root cap
    B. meristem
    C. region of elongation
    D. primary phloem
    E. primary xylem

27. Mycorrhizae grow best in
    A. water
    B. soil
    C. snails
    D. bacteria
    E. fruits

28. Bacteriophages are
    A. gram-positive bacteria
    B. gram-negative bacteria
    C. viruses
    D. rickettsiae
    E. actinomycetes

29. Which of these is always a characteristic of any r-selected species?
   A. It has coevolved with another species.
   B. It has a genetically controlled tendency toward extended care of offspring.
   C. It demonstrates gradualistic evolution.
   D. Its individuals require little time to reach reproductive maturity and then have many offspring.
   E. It came into existence by sympatric speciation.

30. Light energy used in photosynthesis is first captured by
   A. chlorophyll
   B. water
   C. carbon dioxide
   D. PGA
   E. ATP

31. Fibrinogen and prothrombin, both necessary for the clotting of blood, are located in
   A. erythrocytes
   B. granulocytes
   C. lymphocytes
   D. platelets
   E. plasma

32. Chemiosmosis occurs in both mitochondria and
   A. chloroplasts
   B. Golgi complexes
   C. microtubules
   D. nucleoli
   E. nucleosomes

33. A small population of birds became separated from a large population and was kept isolated for several generations. Subsequent examination of both populations showed that they differed significantly in the frequency of alleles for several genes. This difference is best explained as an example of
   A. genetic drift
   B. natural selection
   C. rapid mutation
   D. polymorphism
   E. hybrid vigor

34. Children of a color-blind mother and a normal father would be
   A. females normal; males color-blind
   B. females normal, but carriers; males color-blind
   C. females color-blind; males color-blind
   D. females color-blind; males normal
   E. females normal, but carriers; males normal

35. A climax community is recognizable because it is
   A. highly productive
   B. composed of trees
   C. uniform in composition
   D. not replaced by another community
   E. dying out

36. Organisms descending from a common ancestor by asexual propagation belong to the same
   A. cline
   B. clone
   C. placebo
   D. syndrome
   E. pride

37. Which characteristic appeared earliest in the evolutionary history of monkeys?
   A. vertebrae
   B. hair
   C. jaws
   D. lungs
   E. social behavior

38. The clitellum of the earthworm is useful in
   A. excretion
   B. reproduction
   C. locomotion
   D. respiration
   E. circulation

39. Which of the following pigments is important in hydrogen transfer (electron transport)?
   A. phycoerythrin
   B. hemocyanin
   C. carmine
   D. safranine
   E. cytochrome

40. Which term is used in embryology for the change of position of cells as they move over the surface of a growing embryo?
   A. epiboly
   B. integration
   C. invagination
   D. evagination
   E. aggregation

41. Alternate forms of a gene at the same locus are called
  A. homologues
  B. alleles
  C. gametes
  D. difactors
  E. associates

42. Which of these is INCORRECT?
  A. Humans coexisted with saber-toothed tigers.
  B. Mammals coexisted with dinosaurs.
  C. Land animals preceded land plants.
  D. Reptiles evolved after amphibians.
  E. Ferns evolved before angiosperms.

43. The approximate number of amino acids from which all proteins are constructed is
  A. 8
  B. 12
  C. 16
  D. 20
  E. 64

44. The unit most useful for measuring the diameter of a typical cell is the
  A. milliliter
  B. curie
  C. roentgen
  D. erg
  E. micrometer

45. Gymnosperms differ from angiosperms in having
  A. wind pollination
  B. seeds unenclosed in fruits
  C. needle or scalelike leaves
  D. no cotyledons
  E. embryo sacs

46. Scientists who anticipate disastrous environmental changes due to a "greenhouse effect" believe that it will occur because of
  A. fluorocarbons that will destroy the ozone layer
  B. increasing atmospheric dust from volcanic activity and from expanding agriculture
  C. new pollutants photochemically produced in the upper atmosphere
  D. burning of fossil fuels that will increase carbon dioxide concentration in the upper atmosphere
  E. destruction of tropical rain forests, changing worldwide weather patterns

47. The term *cladistics* refers to
    A. a group of primitive fish species
    B. genes that can cause cancer if mutated or inappropriately expressed
    C. a method for determining evolutionary relationships among organisms
    D. methods by which primitive eukaryotic cells gained various organelles through symbiotic relationships with Protists
    E. adjacent lakes that intermittently join by a transient channel

48. Of the following statements about bile, which is correct?
    A. makes contents of small intestine acidic
    B. activates lipase
    C. stimulates flow of gastric juices
    D. emulsifies fats
    E. is enzymatic

49. Which of these is a possible consequence of the arising of a reproductive isolating mechanism?
    A. sterility of an individual
    B. speciation
    C. early death of an individual
    D. allopolyploidy
    E. chemical incompatibility between egg and sperm

50. Movement of molecules across a living membrane against a concentration gradient and requiring the expenditure of energy is known as
    A. plasmolysis
    B. Brownian movement
    C. cyclosis
    D. active transport
    E. capillary action

51. Which of these is the Hardy-Weinberg equation for predicting frequencies of genotypes for a gene existing as three alleles?
    A. $p + q = 1$
    B. $p^2 + 2pq + q^2 = 1$
    C. $p^2 + 2pq + q^2 = 3$
    D. $p^2 + 2pq + 2pr + 2qr + q^2 + r^2 = 1$
    E. $p + q + r = 1$

52. The gene pool is the aggregate of all of the kinds of genes in
    A. a hybrid
    B. a free-breeding population
    C. a community of organisms
    D. autosomes
    E. all living organisms

53. Divergent evolution is illustrated by
  A. human and whale
  B. fish and whale
  C. cactus and succulent euphorbia
  D. bird and bat
  E. mole cricket and mole

54. Which of the following is a biome?
  A. patch of weeds
  B. bed of oysters
  C. field of corn
  D. deciduous forest
  E. balanced aquarium

55. Population explosions of small organisms in lakes result in a visual aspect called
  A. congestion
  B. bloom
  C. climax
  D. neuston
  E. dominance

56. Ontogeny means
  A. embryology
  B. evolution
  C. biogenesis
  D. comparative anatomy
  E. endocrinology

57. Which of the following is NOT part of the ribonucleic acid molecule?
  A. adenine
  B. thymine
  C. uracil
  D. guanine
  E. cytosine

58. During meiosis, synapsis of homologous chromosomes occurs in
  A. anaphase
  B. interphase
  C. metaphase
  D. prophase
  E. telophase

59. Of the following which is NOT characteristic of cyanobacteria?
  A. lack of organized nuclei
  B. lack of plastids
  C. lack of sexual reproduction
  D. lack of gelatinous secretions
  E. lack of roots, stems, or leaves

60. Which of the following is NOT an osmoregulatory structure?
   A. flame cell
   B. Malpighian tubule
   C. antennary gland
   D. nephridium
   E. nematocyst

61. Carbohydrate digestion begins in the
   A. mouth
   B. esophagus
   C. stomach
   D. small intestine
   E. large intestine

62. What is the relative fitness of a white-flowered form in a population that includes blue-flowered forms, if 80% of the whites successfully reproduce and 60% of the blues successfully reproduce? Assume that the white and blue are the only forms in the population.
   A. 0.60
   B. 0.75
   C. 0.80
   D. 1.00
   E. 1.33

63. Molecular clocks are useful for
   A. making decisions when constructing phylogenetic trees
   B. resetting the circadian rhythm
   C. determining the speed of neuronal transmission
   D. slowing down metabolism when a mammal dives into water
   E. determining the age of fossils or of rocks in which fossils are embedded

64. The theoretical minimum number of genes that must change in order to cause speciation is
   A. 1 gene
   B. 10 genes
   C. 100 genes
   D. 500 genes
   E. more than 1000 genes

65. The ecological niche of an organism is its
   A. way of life
   B. habitat
   C. place of hibernation
   D. foraging area
   E. defended territory

66. The time required for the decomposition of 50% of the atoms in an unstable isotope is its
    A. stability rate
    B. activity standard
    C. decay time
    D. half-life
    E. recovery point

67. Wind-pollinated plants differ from insect-pollinated plants in having
    A. large petals and small quantities of pollen
    B. small petals and sticky pollen
    C. small colored petals and heavy pollen
    D. colored petals and large pollen
    E. no petals and light pollen

68. The blooming of violets in the spring and of morning-glories in the summer is related to their response to
    A. temperature
    B. other plants with which they are associated
    C. relative length of exposure to light and darkness
    D. the size of each plant at maturity
    E. available water

69. The difference between an herbaceous stem and a woody stem is in the relative quantity of
    A. phloem
    B. xylem
    C. cortex
    D. vascular cambium
    E. cork

70. Bubbles of gas generated by aquatic plants are
    A. methane
    B. carbon dioxide
    C. oxygen
    D. sulfur dioxide
    E. hydrogen sulfide

71. The skeleton is to the human what the spicules are to the
    A. sponge
    B. chiton
    C. squid
    D. coral
    E. sand dollar

72. During digestion, disaccharides are converted to monosaccharides by the chemical addition of
    A. water
    B. carbon dioxide
    C. oxygen
    D. nitrogen
    E. hydrogen

73. In which pair are the structures analogous?
    A. sucking mouthpart and chewing mouthpart of insect
    B. swim bladder of fish and lung of human
    C. nose of human and trunk of elephant
    D. wing of insect and wing of bird
    E. fingernail of human and hoof of horse

74. In the plant system of classification, division is equivalent to what category in the animal system?
    A. class
    B. family
    C. genus
    D. order
    E. phylum

75. Which of these is derived largely from the endoderm?
    A. brain
    B. liver
    C. skeletal muscle
    D. kidney
    E. heart

76. The blastopore of a frog embryo becomes the adult
    A. anus
    B. archenteron
    C. coelom
    D. mouth
    E. spinal cord

77. Which of these is evidence of gene control in eukaryotes?
    A. An insect's giant chromosome puff patterns change during development.
    B. Human DNA inserted into a bacterial plasmid can be transcribed in the bacterium.
    C. Insect giant chromosomes have predictable striped patterns.
    D. Mitosis faithfully duplicates genetic material.
    E. The lactose operon operates under inductive control.

78. The type of light that is most efficient in initiating photosynthesis is
   A. blue
   B. green
   C. infrared
   D. ultraviolet
   E. X-ray

79. The bulk ingestion of water containing dissolved materials by a cell is called
   A. active transport
   B. exocytosis
   C. osmosis
   D. phagocytosis
   E. pinocytosis

80. A cell organelle bounded by a double membrane is
   A. a centriole
   B. a microtubule
   C. a ribosome
   D. the Golgi body
   E. the nucleus

81. The special tissue for nourishing the seedlings of many seed plants is
   A. phloem
   B. endosperm
   C. endodermis
   D. pericarp
   E. tapetum

82. A molecule acting in photoreception is
   A. actinomycin D
   B. oxytocin
   C. pheromone
   D. rhodopsin
   E. serotonin

83. Which of these is NOT a necessary factor for natural selection to occur in a population?
   A. New mutations must occur within the population during the natural selection process.
   B. Organisms must reproduce.
   C. Some of the organisms must be able to reproduce in the environment more successfully than others.
   D. Some of the organisms must be different from others.
   E. The ecosystem must have some limiting factors for the population, ensuring that some of the organisms will not survive to the age of reproduction.

84. Which of these is a method used to isolate mutant bacteria?
  A. conjugation
  B. cross-over analysis
  C. recombinant DNA techniques
  D. replica plating
  E. streaking

85. Which of these is NOT produced because of the operation of the Krebs cycle?
  A. ATP
  B. reduced FAD
  C. CO_2
  D. pyruvic acid
  E. reduced nicotinamide adenine dinucleotide

86. After ovulation, a mammalian ovary displays a corpus luteum. This is a
  A. blood-engorged wall into which the embryo can sink to obtain nourishment
  B. fertilized egg
  C. hormone responsible for maintenance of pregnancy
  D. region where the next egg will mature
  E. yellowish region at the site of egg release, capable of releasing progesterone

Questions 84–159
The next five questions (87–91) is based on the series of numbered sketches with lettered parts. The series depicts maturation and fertilization of the egg of the roundworm *Ascaris*. Select the best answer for each question, and mark your answer accordingly.

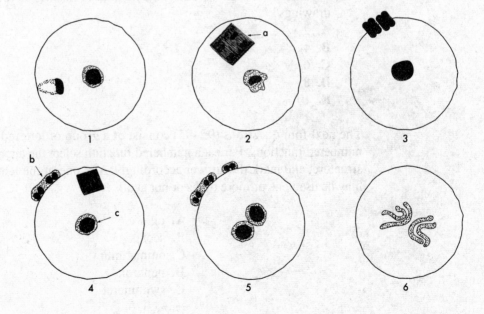

87. Which phase of division is represented in part *a*?
   A. interphase
   B. prophase
   C. metaphase
   D. anaphase
   E. telophase

88. The structure at point *b* is the
   A. centrosome
   B. first polar body
   C. second polar body
   D. egg nucleus
   E. sperm nucleus

89. What chromosome number would have resulted if fertilization had occurred in sketch 1?
   A. 2*n*
   B. 3*n*
   C. 4*n*
   D. 5*n*
   E. 6*n*

90. When did reductional division occur in part *c*?
   A. before any of these drawings
   B. in sketch 1
   C. in sketch 2
   D. in sketch 3
   E. in sketch 6

91. What is the haploid chromosome number of *Ascaris* as revealed by the drawings?
   A. 2
   B. 4
   C. 6
   D. 8
   E. 10

The next four questions (92–95) consist of a group of lettered structures and numbered functions. For each numbered function select the appropriate lettered structure, and mark the answer accordingly. Any one of the lettered structures may be used one or more times or not at all.

   A. cilia
   B. scolex
   C. ommatidium
   D. nephron
   E. swimmeret

92. locomotion

93. excretion

94. reproduction

95. attachment

The next three questions (96–98) consist of a group of lettered structures and numbered body regions. For each numbered body region select the lettered structure that matches it and mark the answer accordingly. Any one of the lettered structures may be used one or more times or not at all.

    A. pituitary
    B. cochlea
    C. sphincter
    D. Bowman's capsule
    E. adrenal

96. within the ear

97. above the kidney in humans

98. beneath the brain

The next five questions (99–103) consist of a group of lettered structures and numbered descriptions. For each numbered description select the appropriate lettered structure, and mark the answer accordingly. Any one of the lettered structures may be used one or more times or not at all.

    A. parapodia
    B. spiracles
    C. stomata
    D. tracheids
    E. tracheoles

99. plant cells specialized to carry water

100. areas of insects in which gas exchange occurs

101. areas of plants in which transpiration occurs

102. gas-exchange areas of some annelids

103. structures formed by a pair of guard cells

The next six questions (104–109) consist of a group of lettered molecules and numbered descriptions. For each numbered description select the appropriate lettered molecule, and mark the answer accordingly. Any one of the lettered molecules may be used one or more times or not at all.

    A. acid phosphatase
    B. amylase
    C. hexokinase
    D. thyroxin
    E. reverse transcriptase

104. is needed by RNA viruses

105. is found in human saliva

106. is used to catalyze starch hydrolysis

107. is not an enzyme

108. catalyzes a step of glycolysis

109. is found within lysosomes

The next five questions (110–114) consist of a group of lettered places and numbered descriptions of the biological importance of the places. For each numbered description select the appropriate lettered place, and mark the answer accordingly. Any one of the lettered places may be used one or more times or not at all.

   A. England
   B. Galápagos
   C. Gondwana
   D. Tanzania
   E. Mexico

110. a destination of monarch butterflies in their annual autumn migration

111. a place where very old hominid fossils have been found

112. the place famous for Darwin's finches

113. an ancient landmass encompassing several modern continents

114. the place where industrial melanism was studied with peppered moths

The next five questions (115–119) consist of a group of lettered fields of biology and numbered activities that occur in these fields. For each numbered activity select the appropriate lettered field, and mark the answer accordingly. Any one of the lettered fields may be used one or more times or not at all.

   A. biogeography
   B. endocrinology
   C. histology
   D. immunology
   E. taxonomy

115. Body symmetry is used as a clue.

116. Biomes are described.

117. Hormones are purified.

118. Vital stains are employed.

119. Antigens are classified.

The next five questions (120–124) consist of a group of lettered cell parts and numbered descriptions. For each numbered description, select the appropriate lettered cell part, and mark the answer accordingly. Any one of the lettered parts may be used one or more times or not at all.

        A. cell wall
        B. centriole
        C. endoplasmic reticulum
        D. mitochondrion
        E. nucleolus

120. is continuous with outer nuclear membrane

121. contains DNA

122. is made of microtubules

123. is found in plants, but not in animals

124. is found in most animals, but is absent from many plants

The next four questions (125–128) consist of a group of lettered terms and numbered definitions. For each numbered definition select the appropriate term, and mark the answer accordingly. Any one of the lettered terms may be used one or more times or not at all.

        A. biome
        B. deme
        C. habitat
        D. niche
        E. population

125. the geographical place where an organism lives

126. a stable, interbreeding group of organisms

127. a community of species dominated by a climax plant type

128. the most complex biological group or place in the list of terms

The next five questions (129–133) consist of a group of lettered biological phenomena and numbered descriptions. For each numbered description select the appropriate lettered activity, and mark the answer accordingly. Any one of the lettered activities may be used one or more times or not at all.

A. appetitive behavior
B. circadian rhythm
C. echolocation
D. operant conditioning
E. proprioception

129. trial-and-error learning

130. finding food by analysis of sound

131. awareness of body position

132. the sleep-wake cycle

133. the instinctive movements of a search for food

The next six questions (134–139) consist of a group of lettered types of organisms and numbered descriptive phrases. For each numbered phrase select the appropriate lettered organism, and mark the answer accordingly. Any one of the lettered organisms may be used one or more times or not at all.

A. decomposers
B. primary consumers
C. producers
D. secondary consumers
E. tertiary consumers

134. are likely to be least numerous in a given area

135. are exemplified by a cow

136. are exemplified by a snake when it eats a mouse

137. are exemplified by a hawk when it eats the snake described in question 136

138. could be nonphotosynthetic bacteria

139. could be algae in a pond

The next five questions (140–144) consist of a group of lettered biological phenomena and numbered descriptions. For each numbered description select the appropriate phenomenon, and mark the answer accordingly. Any one of the lettered phenomena may be used one or more times or not at all.

      A. altruistic behavior
      B. artificial selection
      C. fitness
      D. founder effect
      E. inheritance of acquired traits

140. genetic drift caused by migration of a small group of organisms into a geographically isolated region

141. the development of new flower varieties by seed companies

142. an activity that is detrimental to an individual but advantageous for the population

143. a measure of an individual's ability to pass on its genes to the next generation

144. Lamarckian hypothesis of evolution

The next six questions (145–150) consist of a group of lettered plant structures and numbered descriptions. For each numbered description select the appropriate lettered structure, and mark the answer accordingly. Any one of the lettered structures may be used one or more times or not at all.

      A. archegonium
      B. cambium
      C. cone
      D. flower
      E. spore

145. place of egg production in a moss

146. a structure that includes sepals

147. a structure used by angiosperms for sexual reproduction

148. the reproductive structure of most gymnosperms

149. a haploid cell that is the ancestor of a fern gametophyte

150. a structure that produces nonreproductive cells by mitosis in vascular plants

The next four questions (151–154) consist of a group of lettered cycles and numbered descriptions. For each numbered description select the appropriate cycle, and mark the answer accordingly. Any one of the lettered cycles may be used one or more times or not at all.

    A. carbon cycle
    B. cell cycle
    C. nitrogen cycle
    D. phosphorus cycle
    E. water cycle

151. Part of the cycle involves transpiration.

152. Part of the cycle involves synthesis of amino acids by plants using an element obtained via the roots.

153. Part of the cycle involves exhalation by animals of a molecule that is produced by the Krebs cycle.

154. Part of the cycle involves G_1, S, and G_2 phases.

The next five questions (155–159) consist of a group of lettered genetic terms and numbered descriptive phrases. For each numbered phrase select the appropriate lettered term, and mark the answer accordingly. Any one of the lettered terms may be used one or more times or not at all.

    A. Barr body
    B. episome
    C. gynandromorph
    D. lampbrush
    E. polyribosome

155. is distinctive of the cell of a human female

156. is interpreted as a region of gene transcription

157. is useful in studies of the genetic basis for insect behavior

158. is a plasmid

159. is a multicellular organism

The remaining questions ask for analysis of experiments. For each set, read the descriptions and data carefully; then answer the questions or complete the statements by choosing among the lettered alternatives and marking your answers accordingly.

Questions 160–162

The table below shows the apparent evolutionary rates for several polypeptides. Rate values were derived by examining the degree of similarity of amino acid sequences of polypeptides obtained from a variety of organisms. The organisms were chosen to represent a range of taxonomic relatedness, which is implied from anatomy and fossil records. The evolutionary rates shown in the table represent the numbers of amino acid substitutions per amino acid site per billion years. A high evolutionary rate value indicates a wide variance in amino acid sequences for a polypeptide from the organisms studied.

Polypeptide	Evolutionary Rate
Fibrinopeptides	9.0
Hemoglobin subunits	1.4
Animal lysozyme	1.0
Insulin	0.4
Cytochrome *c*	0.3
Histone type IV	0.006

160. If a protein performs a necessary function that relies heavily upon precise structure, that protein should be very similar in a wide variety of organisms that perform the function. Which of these polypeptides appears to fit this description best?
   A. cytochrome *c*
   B. fibrinopeptides
   C. histone type IV
   D. insulin
   E. lysozyme

161. Fibrinopeptides are strings of amino acids clipped off fibrinogen as it is converted to fibrin. The excised strings appear to have no further function. Which statement is LEAST likely to be true?
   A. Fibrinopeptides are examples of the thesis that polypeptides which are not functionally necessary can tolerate many random changes in their structures.
   B. Fibrinopeptides probably have relatively little function before they are clipped off.
   C. Since a portion of proinsulin is clipped off to leave the remainder as active insulin, the clipped-off portion probably has an evolutionary rate higher than 0.4.
   D. The changes that have occurred in fibrinopeptides in the past have probably resulted from random mutations of their genetic material.
   E. The fibrin portion of fibrinogen probably has a higher evolutionary rate value than the rate value of fibrinopeptides.

162. Which is a correct statement?
   A. Because insulin and cytochrome *c* have very similar evolutionary rates, they are probably similar in structure.
   B. Because the rate value for fibrinopeptides is so far above that of every other protein on the list, it should be ignored in analyses.
   C. If all of the data had been derived from organisms within a single genus, they would have been more valid indicators of evolution than data derived from a wider taxonomic range.
   D. The hemoglobin value in the table is of no evolutionary significance because plants do not have this protein.
   E. These data are not conclusive proof of evolution because they were derived solely from organisms alive today.

Questions 163–169
A long-term study of an abandoned agricultural field indicated that there had been a gradual change in the numbers and types of plant species. The table shows these results.

Year after Farming Ended	Total Number of Species	Number of Herbaceous Species	Number of Shrub Species	Number of Tree Species
1	30	30	0	0
5	28	26	2	0
10	33	27	4	2
20	52	32	8	12
50	75	30	20	25

Even in the fiftieth year, only about 40% of the land was covered with plants. In the fiftieth year, the most abundant type (total number of organisms) was a herbaceous species, and the second and fifth most abundant species were trees.

163. Which is the most accurate statement?
   A. Since the number of herbaceous species remained nearly constant during the study, the other trends are probably invalid.
   B. The data do not support any trend in the number of species or diversity above the species level.
   C. The data show that the animal populations in the field have significantly affected the species diversity.
   D. The table shows a chronological increase in both total species and in higher taxonomic categories of organisms present.
   E. The table shows an increase in total species, but no significant trend in diversity above the species level.

164. How many years elapsed before the species were about equally divided among the three major plant types?
   A. 1
   B. 5
   C. 10
   D. 20
   E. 50

165. Which of the following is a correct statement?
   A. It is valid to predict that the total number of herbaceous plants would remain constant even to the hundredth year.
   B. Since trees are so large, the number of their species would probably stop increasing soon after the fiftieth year.
   C. The herbaceous plants are most able to populate recently tilled land.
   D. The table shows that the total number of herbaceous plants in the field was far larger than the total number of other plants in any year of the study.
   E. Year 5 was probably a drought year since the total number of species was lower than even the first year after tillage.

166. The phenomenon shown by these data is
   A. a pyramid of productivity
   B. commensalism
   C. density-dependent limitation
   D. ecological succession
   E. intraspecies competition

167. What is the prediction for animals in this field?
   A. A gradual change will occur in animal types to parallel the plant changes.
   B. Since the plants have been such successful colonizers, most animals will be unable to compete with them and will go elsewhere.
   C. Some animals will produce new mutations in response to the changes in the field.
   D. The first animals that entered the field in year 1 will stay there, successfully defending the territory against later invaders.
   E. Animals will move into and out of the field at random, ignoring the changes occurring in the plant populations.

168. Why did some tree species become represented in large numbers even though they were among the last to enter the field?
   A. It was pure chance; some neighboring field might never be dominated by trees.
   B. They grew faster than herbaceous plants.
   C. They grew taller than other plant types and stole sunlight from them.
   D. They produced a larger number of seeds than could other plant types.
   E. Their roots strangled nearby plants.

169. In which year would you expect to find the most complex food webs?
   A. first
   B. fifth
   C. tenth
   D. twentieth
   E. fiftieth

Questions 170–176

In a technique called somatic cell hybridization, mouse cells and human cells are cultured together. Some of them fuse. The resulting hybrid cells each start out containing the complete genomes of both species.

The fused cells are identified by these methods. The mouse cells were chosen because they are genetically incapable of producing an enzyme, thymidine kinase (TK), needed to produce nucleotides under certain conditions. A cell deficient in TK can normally make nucleotides but this ability is lost if the drug aminopterin is added. The human cells are capable of producing TK and are therefore insensitive to aminopterin's effects. In the presence of aminopterin, only human cells and human-mouse fusion cells will survive. The human cells are nonproliferating leucocytes; therefore the only clones found after a while are those derived from fusion cells.

A hybrid cell begins with two complete genomes, but only the mouse genome survives intact. Human chromosomes are expelled at random. Hybrid cells usually contain from 41 to 55 chromosomes, 40 of these being the intact mouse genome. Karyotype analysis, following fluorescent staining of chromosomes with quinacrine, enables one to determine which human chromosomes remain in each clone. Since the genes of these chromosomes continue to make their products, one can also determine which genes are present by homogenizing some cells of a clone and performing enzyme assays on the homogenate. The table indicates the presence (+) or absence (–) of several human enzymes and chromosomes in selected hybrid clones.

		Clones					
		1	2	3	4	5	6
Human chromosome remaining	6	+	+	–	+	+	–
	8	+	–	+	–	–	–
	11	+	–	–	–	–	+
	15	+	–	–	+	+	–
Pepsinogen		+	+	–	+	+	–
Glutathione reductase		+	–	+	–	–	–
Pyruvate kinase		+	–	–	+	+	–
Hexosaminidase A		+	–	–	+	+	–
Hexokinase-1		–	–	–	–	–	–

Human enzyme produced

170. Which of these is an enzyme needed to help select hybrid cells from nonfused cells?
   A. aminopterin
   B. pyruvate kinase
   C. quinacrine
   D. thymidine kinase
   E. hexokinase-1

171. Which clones are most useful in identifying the chromosomal location of the enzyme hexosaminidase A?
    A. 1, 4, and 5
    B. 1, 2, and 3
    C. 2, 3, and 6
    D. 2, 3, 4, 5, and 6
    E. None of them is useful; this gene cannot be located from the data.

172. What can be said about the location of the hexokinase-1 gene?
    A. It could be on any human chromosome.
    B. It is NOT on chromosome 6.
    C. It is NOT on chromosome 6, 8, 11, or 15.
    D. It is on chromosome 6.
    E. It is on chromsome 15.

173. On which chromosome is the gene for pepsinogen?
    A. 6
    B. 8
    C. 11
    D. 15
    E. none of the above

174. Which of the following techniques also employ(s) the fusion of cells in culture?
    A. cloning of plants
    B. hybridoma methods for production of monoclonal antibody
    C. *in vitro* fertilization of human embryos
    D. recombinant DNA technology employing plasmids
    E. two of the above

175. Why are human chromosomes expelled from a hybrid cell whereas mouse chromosomes are not?
    A. Human chromosomes are insensitive to aminopterin.
    B. This outcome was random chance; many hybrid cells would preferentially expel mouse chromosomes.
    C. Karyotype analysis shows only mouse chromosomes.
    D. The research cited here does not explain the reason.
    E. The Sendai virus attacks only human chromosomes.

176. Why is the technique called *somatic cell* hybridization?
    A. The cells being used are body cells other than gametes.
    B. The cells being used have similar ploidies.
    C. The cells being used are from different animal species.
    D. The cells being used have previously been cultured outside the body.
    E. The cells being used are inherently capable of fusion.

Questions 177–180
Fruit flies of two strains were crossed. The female parent was homozygous recessive for three autosomal genes: she had echinus eyes (roughened surfaces, symbolized by *ec*), scute bristle pattern (certain thoracic bristles absent,

symbolized by *sc*), and vestigial wings (symbolized by *vg*). The male was homozygous wild-type for all of these characteristics. All F_1 flies were wild-type. Virgin F_1 females were testcrossed to determine linkage; the results of this cross are summarized in the table.

Phenotype	Number of Individuals
sc + *vg*	14
+ + +	242
sc + +	12
+ + *vg*	232
sc ec +	240
sc ec vg	230
+ *ec* +	15
+ *ec vg*	15
Total:	1000

177. Why were the F_1 females testcrossed?
  A. to check for new mutations
  B. to determine which alleles each of their homologous chromosomes carried
  C. to determine which ones were infertile
  D. to determine the F_1's phenotypes
  E. to obtain an F_2 generation

178. If the three genes described above were independently assorting, what would be the expected phenotype ratios after a testcross of F_1's?
  A. 1:1:1:1:1:1:1:1
  B. 1:2:4:6:4:2:1
  C. the same as shown in the actual totals of the table
  D. nearly, but not exactly, the same as shown in the actual totals
  E. unpredictable since the ratio would depend upon which chromosomes carry the three genes

179. Analysis of the testcross progeny shows that
  A. all three genes are linked together
  B. *ec* and *vg* are linked and *sc* is on a second chromosome
  C. *sc* and *ec* are linked and *vg* is on a second chromosome
  D. *sc* and *vg* are linked and *ec* is on a second chromosome
  E. the three genes are on three separate chromosomes

180. Why were females rather than males of F_1's testcrossed?
  A. It is easier to determine whether females are virgins.
  B. It is traditional to use male testcrossed organisms.
  C. Males could have been used with the same result; no significance should be attached to the choice of females.
  D. Males of the genus *Drosophila* do not exhibit crossing-over.
  E. Only females of the F_1 generation were of the proper phenotype.

Questions 181–187

The striking changes that occur all over the body of a larval frog as it progresses through metamorphosis are triggered by the hormone thyroxin (triiodothyronine, T3). This hormone is released in large quantity by the thyroid gland. A partial list of the more obvious changes includes tail resorption, breakdown of gills, development of functional lungs, shortening of the gut, appearance of eyelids, and formation of limbs. On the biochemical level, ammonia excretion is replaced by urea excretion and a host of new proteins are synthesized. These changes appear in an orderly, predictable sequence when triggered naturally. The graph shows some of the changes that occur at the subcellular level after a precocious increase of T3 provided by injection.

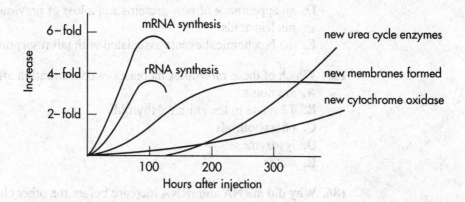

181. What is the adaptive significance of switching from an ammonia-excreting system to one that produces urea?

A. Ammonia is a gas; urea is a crystal.

B. Ammonia is easily excreted across the membranes of an aquatic animal, but would accumulate dangerously in a terrestrial animal.

C. Urea can be absorbed into the newly elongated gut of the adult, but ammonia would cause intestinal distress.

D. Urea can be excreted across lung membranes, but ammonia cannot.

E. Urea can carry the nitrogen derived from amino acid breakdown, but ammonia cannot.

182. What is the adaptive significance of shortening the gut at metamorphosis?

A. A very long gut, taking up much body space, is necessary for herbivores, but not for carnivores.

B. Adults must process food more quickly since they cannot afford to carry an intestinal burden that would decrease their chance of escape from a predator.

C. An adult does not eat as much as a larva, so it does not need a long tract.

D. An adult's body length/width ratio is smaller than a tadpole's, so it cannot keep a long gut.

E. The loss of gut length reflects a loss of efficiency in food handling as adulthood approaches.

183. When was T3 injected in the organisms from which the graph was generated?
    A. after metamorphosis had been in progress
    B. at 100 hr
    C. at the time of normal metamorphosis
    D. before the larvae would normally enter metamorphosis
    E. This information is not provided.

184. What does the graph show?
    A. a sequential appearance of several new proteins and structures
    B. a sudden, simultaneous synthesis of new proteins
    C. a sudden, simultaneous synthesis of new proteins and nucleic acids
    D. an appearance of new proteins and a loss of previously synthesized nucleic acids
    E. the biochemical events associated with tail resorption

185. Which of these molecules increases in concentration after T3 injection?
    A. ammonia
    B. T3 made in the animals' thyroid
    C. phospholipids
    D. lysozymes
    E. water

186. Why did mRNA and rRNA increase before the other changes occurred?
    A. It cannot be determined.
    B. They are both components of membranes, which are made later.
    C. These are necessary if proteins are to be synthesized.
    D. They are breakdown products of T3.
    E. They are enzymes needed to produce cytochromes.

187. Which material is most closely associated with production of ATP in metamorphosing tissues?
    A. cytochrome oxidase
    B. membranes
    C. mRNA
    D. rRNA
    E. urea cycle enzymes

Questions 188–190
An enzyme tends to catalyze a reaction at a characteristic rate (reaction velocity) that varies according to the initial concentration [S] of the enzyme's substrate. The graph shows such a relationship.

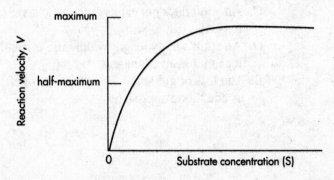

A mathematical expression of this curve is

$$V = V_{max} \frac{[S]}{[S] + K_M}$$

where V = velocity, V_{max} = theoretical maximum velocity, and K_M is a constant for each enzyme. The table below lists experimentally determined K_M values for some enzymes when operating with their substrates:

Enzyme	K_M value
Lysozyme	6×10^{-6} M
Carbonic anhydrase	8×10^{-3} M
Chymotrypsin	5×10^{-3} M
Arginine-tRNA synthetase	4×10^{-7} M

188. If all of the enzymes of the table were provided with the same concentration of their substrates and under identical environmental conditions, which enzyme would operate its reaction at the greatest velocity?
   A. arginine-tRNA synthetase
   B. carbonic anhydrase
   C. chymotrypsin
   D. lysozyme
   E. Not determinable since V_{max} may differ for each enzyme.

189. If lysozyme were provided with an analog of the substrate used for the table, it would exhibit the same V_{max}, but its K_M with the analog would become 6×10^{-8} M. What can be said about the curve generated with lysozyme and the analog when compared with the curve with lysozyme and its natural substrate?
   A. It would be identical to the original curve.
   B. It would show a higher velocity for each [S] value.
   C. It would show a higher velocity for low [S] values.
   D. It would show a lower velocity for each [S] value.
   E. It would show a lower velocity for low [S] values.

190. The equation provided above is named for
   A. Fatt and Katz
   B. Lineweaver and Burk
   C. Meselson and Stahl
   D. Michaelis and Menten
   E. Pauling and Corey

Questions 191–195

Cyclic 5'-adenosine monophosphate (cAMP) is a nucleotide produced inside brain cells after they have been stimulated by neurotransmitters. The cAMP then acts as a "second messenger" to cause complex biochemical changes in the cell. An example of this is found in cells of a brain region called the basal ganglia. A neurotransmitter, dopamine, is released by nerve cells. Upon contacting the basal ganglia cell membranes, dopamine fits into a receptor site of an enzyme, adenylyl cyclase. This activates the enzyme, which then catalyzes the production of cAMP.

Two drugs have been found to react with the receptor site. Chlorpromazine attaches to the receptor site but does not activate the enzyme. While attached, it blocks attachment by dopamine. Apomorphine attaches to the receptor site and activates the enzyme.

Other neurons also seem to produce cAMP when stimulated. For instance, cells of the thoracic ganglia of insects respond to the neurotransmitter serotonin by producing cAMP. Another intracellular product, cyclic guanosine monophosphate (cGMP), is produced instead of cAMP in certain cells that have been stimulated by the neurotransmitter acetylcholine.

191. Parkinson's disease is caused by a lack of dopamine at the basal ganglia receptor sites. Which of these substances might be an anti-Parkinsonism agent if supplied to the basal ganglia region?
   A. adenosine triphosphate
   B. adenylyl cyclase
   C. apomorphine
   D. chlorpromazine
   E. serotonin

192. Chlorpromazine has been used to relieve the symptoms of schizophrenia. What might be a useful hypothesis for a biochemical basis of schizophrenia?
   A. People with schizophrenia can make neither cAMP nor cGMP in their brain cells.
   B. Schizophrenia is caused by the presence of chlorpromazine in certain brain cells.
   C. Schizophrenia is related to an overproduction of serotonin.
   D. Schizophrenia is related to defective dopamine receptor cells that cannot be activated.
   E. Schizophrenia is related to overactivity of dopamine-releasing cells in the brain.

193. The hallucinogenic drug lysergic acid diethylamide (LSD) is known to block serotonin receptors of certain neurons. What is the likely effect in the blocked cells?
   A. Adenylyl cyclase will be activated.
   B. cAMP levels will decrease.
   C. cAMP levels will increase.
   D. cGMP levels will decrease.
   E. Serotonin levels will decrease.

194. Nerve cells involved with the very fast transmission of messages to skeletal muscles use acetylcholine as their transmitters across the myoneural junction. In these cases, acetylcholine acts directly upon muscle fiber membranes to change their permeability. cAMP production does not occur. What is the most reasonable explanation for the fact that these nerve cells do not use cAMP?

   A. Acetylcholine can easily pass through a muscle fiber membrane, going directly to the genes to affect them.

   B. cAMP production and activity require a significant lapse of time between initial stimulation and final effect.

   C. Muscle contraction involves calcium release, which takes over the function of cAMP.

   D. These nerve cells are at a disadvantage in not producing cAMP, but are still doing a reasonably good job.

   E. These cells produce the alternative "second messenger," cGMP.

195. Cyclic AMP has been found to be a "second messenger" in other, nonneural, portions of the body. An example is in

   A. glomeruli

   B. Haversian canals

   C. target cells for nonsteroid hormones

   D. target cells for steroid hormones

   E. the coelom

Questions 196–200

Terrestrial plants tend to maintain a different internal temperature from that of the surrounding air. Only some parts of a plant show this, and those parts can do so only over a certain range of external temperature. The graph shows measurements within leaves of *Citrullus colocynthis*. The plant had access at all times to water and nutrients.

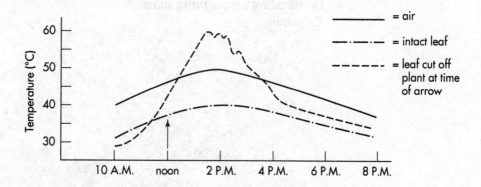

196. What is the most likely reason for the difference in temperature between an intact (attached) leaf and one that has been cut off?

   A. The intact leaf continues to perform cyclosis.

   B. The attached leaf continues to perform photosynthesis.

   C. The attached leaf continues to perform transpiration.

   D. The detached leaf cannot be shaded by other leaves of the plant.

   E. The detached leaf cannot move to avoid direct sunlight.

197. What is the most likely condition of the intact leaf at 2 P.M.?
  A. Cell walls have thickened.
  B. Petioles are twisted helically.
  C. Stomata are open.
  D. The leaf has wilted.
  E. Xylem tubes are closed.

198. A plant undergoes heat injury at 46° and above. Did this happen to the intact leaf?
  A. No, because the air never became warmer than 55°.
  B. No, because the leaf's interior never was exposed to direct sunlight.
  C. No, because the leaf's interior never became warmer than 40°.
  D. Yes, because the leaf's internal temperature reached 60° at times.
  E. Yes, because the leaf surface was probably hotter than its interior.

199. What is a good explanation for a higher temperature inside a severed leaf than in the surrounding air?
  A. The leaf was dark, absorbing heat more readily than air.
  B. The leaf was decomposing, an activity that generates heat.
  C. The leaf was still metabolizing, an activity that generates heat.
  D. The temperature readings were incorrect, since no inanimate object can be warmer than its surroundings.
  E. The severed leaf lost access to fresh nutrients and began to burn its stored nutrients.

200. What animal activity is similar to the graphed activity of an intact leaf at mid-day?
  A. excreting nitrogenous waste in a very concentrated urine
  B. hiding underground at mid-day
  C. using water of metabolism rather than drinking
  D. shedding excess fur in summer
  E. panting

Answer Key for Sample Test 3

Use this key to obtain a score for Test 3. Then use the answer explanations on the following pages to gain a better understanding of the concepts needed to answer all questions correctly.

1. D	41. B	81. B	121. D	161. E
2. E	42. C	82. D	122. B	162. E
3. B	43. D	83. A	123. A	163. D
4. C	44. E	84. D	124. B	164. E
5. C	45. B	85. D	125. C	165. C
6. A	46. D	86. E	126. E	166. D
7. B	47. C	87. C	127. A	167. A
8. C	48. D	88. B	128. A	168. C
9. C	49. B	89. B	129. D	169. E
10. C	50. D	90. A	130. C	170. D
11. A	51. D	91. A	131. E	171. D
12. A	52. B	92. A	132. B	172. C
13. B	53. A	93. D	133. A	173. A
14. D	54. D	94. E	134. E	174. E
15. A	55. B	95. B	135. B	175. D
16. B	56. A	96. B	136. D	176. A
17. B	57. B	97. E	137. E	177. B
18. E	58. D	98. A	138. A	178. A
19. D	59. D	99. D	139. C	179. C
20. C	60. E	100. E	140. D	180. D
21. E	61. A	101. C	141. B	181. B
22. E	62. D	102. A	142. A	182. A
23. C	63. A	103. C	143. C	183. D
24. A	64. A	104. E	144. E	184. A
25. E	65. A	105. B	145. A	185. C
26. B	66. D	106. B	146. D	186. C
27. B	67. E	107. D	147. D	187. A
28. C	68. C	108. C	148. C	188. E
29. D	69. B	109. A	149. E	189. C
30. A	70. C	110. E	150. B	190. D
31. E	71. A	111. D	151. E	191. C
32. A	72. A	112. B	152. C	192. E
33. A	73. D	113. C	153. A	193. B
34. B	74. E	114. A	154. B	194. B
35. D	75. B	115. E	155. A	195. C
36. B	76. A	116. A	156. D	196. C
37. A	77. A	117. B	157. C	197. C
38. B	78. A	118. C	158. B	198. C
39. E	79. E	119. D	159. C	199. A
40. A	80. E	120. C	160. C	200. E

Answer Explanations for Sample Test 3

1. **(D)** The cells of many tissues cease most reproduction when they reach maturity, but some, like those in connective tissue and the lower layer of the epidermis, continue to divide throughout life. Bone marrow is one type of connective tissue with cells that divide continuously. They generate most types of blood cells.

2. **(E)** Transpiration is potentially harmful in that water is wasted by evaporation; it is unavoidable because the structure of the plant is such that the necessary exchange of gases must occur through exposed surfaces from which water can also evaporate.

3. **(B)** Homeotic genes were first found in *Drosophila,* but are now known to be present in many organisms. A homeotic gene controls the total embryonic development of a specific body part, such as a fly's eye or a plant's stamens. If a homeotic gene is activated in an inappropriate portion of the embryo, an extraneous body part will develop there (e.g., an extra eye developing on a fly's leg).

4. **(C)** A frameshift mutation is an addition or removal of base-pairs within a gene. If any number of base-pairs except three is added or deleted, the result is a shift of the reading frame during translation. Such a shift means that all codons beyond the insertion/deletion point are different, so all amino acid placements beyond that point will be different from the original.

5. **(C)** Crossing-over, that is, the interchange of chromatid sections, occurs during the synapsis and separation of homologous chromosomes in meiosis.

6. **(A)** Some genes are replicated many times within an embryonic cell. Each copy of such a gene directs the production of mRNA at a normal pace, but the presence of dozens or hundreds of copies of the gene results in a very large total amount of mRNA (and the resultant protein).

7. **(B)** Hygroscopic water is closely bound to soil particles and is not free to diffuse into the roots. After a plant dies for lack of water, the presence of hygroscopic water can be demonstrated. The soil is first weighed, then put into an oven hot enough to "drive off" the bound water, and finally weighed again to determine the loss.

8. **(C)** A sex-influenced gene is autosomal, so both sexes have two copies of it. However, the sexes use different "rules" for expressing it. For instance, pattern baldness acts simply as a dominant trait in men (*BB* or *Bb* genotypes cause it), but it acts differently in most women (only the *BB* genotype causes it).

9. **(C)** What is really meant is that the system is based on the consideration of evolutionary relationships through common ancestry to the extent that they are understood. Thus body form may not show true kinship; for example, a whale and a fish have similar body forms but belong to different vertebrate classes.

10. **(C)** The silks of corn are styles and stigmas of pistils. Covering them with a bag would shield them from incoming pollen, which is produced in the staminate flowers located in the tassel.

11. **(A)** DNA duplicates itself during interphase, as can be determined by radioactive assay. The radioactive isotope hydrogen-3 (tritium) may be substituted in the thymidine and then incorporated in the DNA nucleotide containing thymine. The relative quantity of DNA can be measured at different times during interphase by extracting the DNA from the cell and measuring its radioactivity with an instrument called a liquid scintillation counter.

12. **(A)** Copperheads, cottonmouths, and rattlesnakes are pit vipers. The special pit organ is a thermal detector on the side of the face between the eyes and nostrils. It is useful in helping the snakes detect warm-bodied (endothermic) animals such as rodents and birds, which are their major sources of food.

13. **(B)** By definition, chromatin is a chromosome's DNA plus the RNA and proteins that are attached to the DNA.

14. **(D)** Insects have open circulatory systems; that is, blood is not confined to vessels. Through most of its circulation the blood flows around internal organs in a space designated the *hemocoel*. There is only one major vessel, the heart, which is located dorsally. Blood enters it through paired valves and is pumped forward into the hemocoel.

15. **(A)** Carbon dioxide is used in the process of photosynthesis. Plants that manufacture their own food by photosynthesis or chemosynthesis are autotrophic (independent).

16. **(B)** Known as the *storehouse of energy,* ATP is the ready source of energy for cell work such as contraction. The energy is stored in each molecule in a high-energy phosphate bond. When the bond is broken and the energy released, the remaining molecule is ADP.

17. **(B)** A diploid cell in the ovary or testis undergoes meiosis, or reduction division, to produce haploid gametes, or germ cells—sperm or eggs. When the nuclei of gametes fuse in fertilization, the resulting cell, with both maternal and paternal chromosomes, is diploid.

18. **(E)** For a biological feature a cline is a gradual or graded variation that is correlated with a gradient in the environment. In this case, species diversity increases proportionally with proximity to the equator.

19. **(D)** First of all, *red* and *white* are phenotypes, not genotypes. Crossing *RR* with *rr* produces offspring with *Rr* only.

20. **(C)** During the long interval of time, evolution proceeded in isolation with what ancestral genetic material was available. Elsewhere there were less isolation and more opportunities for gene flow.

21. **(E)** Secondary succession begins when an ongoing community is disrupted by such things as lumbering, clearing, cultivation, grazing, pollution, fire, floods, storms, or strip mining.

22. **(E)** Benthic organisms are bottom-dwellers, and the pelagic zone is the open sea.

23. **(C)** After certain pesticides, such as DDT, enter an ecological food web by being incorporated at a low trophic level, they become increasingly concentrated as organisms at higher levels eat those at lower levels. If the pesticides are not easily degraded, they accumulate in animals at the top portions of the ecosystem's energy pyramid. The effect of the pesticides has become magnified by this concentration.

24. **(A)** A eutrophic lake has a very high rate of biological productivity, either as a result of natural aging or of artificial addition of nutrients such as fertilizers.

25. **(E)** Herbivory is the eating of plants by animals such as rodents and insects. The first four choices are documented defenses that various plant species use. Trichomes are hairlike appendages on plant surfaces, which (in some species) contain noxious chemicals. An increased rate of photosynthesis does not protect a plant from animal consumption.

26. **(B)** Meristem is embryonic plant tissue. Its cells are unspecialized and capable of dividing.

27. **(B)** A mycorrhiza is not a single organism but is two organisms symbiotically associated. Since the association consists of fungal mycelia and roots of plants, the habitat is soil.

28. **(C)** Bacteriophages are viruses that parasitize bacteria. Often they are called simply phages.

29. **(D)** Organisms that are r-selected typically develop quickly, reproduce frequently, produce many offspring, and fail to provide parental care. The opposite strategy is employed by K-selected species.

30. **(A)** Another way of expressing the same idea is to say that the chlorophyll is activated.

31. **(E)** Fibrinogen is the plasma protein that is converted from a sol to a gel state (fibrin) during the clotting process. Prothrombin is a globulin protein of the plasma. It must be converted to thrombin, which in turn converts fibrinogen to fibrin.

32. **(A)** Both mitochondria and chloroplasts are specialized to transfer the energy of electrons to the chemical bonds of ATP. This process, chemiosmosis, occurs in and on certain internal membranes of these organelles.

33. **(A)** Genetic drift is any mechanism that changes allele frequencies by some random, or chance, event. In this example, it was only by chance that certain birds got separated from the larger group. Their allele frequencies, therefore, were determined randomly and it is not surprising that they differed from the frequencies of the larger group.

34. **(B)** See the following illustration:

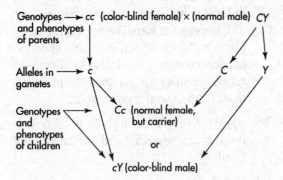

35. **(D)** The fact that a climax community is not replaced by another community means that the climax community can survive indefinitely. A successional community, on the other hand, is replaced by one of another type.

36. **(B)** The term *clone* is often used to describe a clump of plants that spread by runners or other vegetative means. Since all descendants come from a single, common parent and have the same genetic composition, they are highly uniform.

37. **(A)** A set of vertebrae protecting the dorsal nerve cord is characteristic of *all* members of the subphylum Vertebrata within phylum Chordata. Each of the other characteristics listed in the question occurs in only some vertebrate animals, an indication that they evolved later.

38. **(B)** The clitellum is the conspicuous glandular swelling of segments 32 to 37. Specialized setae on the ventral side of the clitellum clasp the copulating portions together. The glandular cells secrete a slime tube around each worm during copulation to aid in directing sperm to the seminal vesicles of the partner and later to form cocoons to hold the eggs. These cells also secrete albumin into the cocoons to nourish the embryos.

39. **(E)** Cytochromes are iron-containing cellular pigments that act as acceptors during hydrogen transfer.

40. **(A)** Another way of expressing the same idea is to say that epiboly means differential growth of the cells of one embryonic part over and around another.

41. **(B)** The presence of alternative forms (alleles) of a gene means that the same characteristic (e.g., eye color) is affected by different alleles.

42. **(C)** Previously evolved terrestrial plants provided terrestrial animals with food and shelter. The fossil record indicates a gap of about 10 million years between the first plants and animals on land.

43. **(D)** With about 20 amino acids, the possible combinations are considerable, easily accounting for the many differences among living organisms.

44. **(E)** The micrometer is a unit of length on the metric scale—one millionth of a meter or one thousandth of a millimeter.

45. **(B)** Gymnosperms are described as naked-seeded, meaning that the seeds are produced on the outer surface of the megasporophyll (scale of pine cone) instead of enclosed by it as in the angiosperms. The megasporophylls that enclose the seeds of angiosperms are known as carpels. A single carpel may fuse along its margin, or several carpels may fuse together to form one or more compartments in which the seeds are located. The structure that is composed of one or more carpels is the pistil, and the basal part of it (ovary) contains the seeds.

46. **(D)** Much of the energy driving the industrial enterprises of the world comes from fossil fuels, including coal and oil. In addition, better living standards depend on transportation and electrical uses closely linked to the same energy sources. Energy is released from fossil fuels by combustion, which produces carbon dioxide. Some of the light energy reaching the Earth is changed into heat energy of a longer wavelength, which cannot be reradiated into space. It is known that a high concentration of carbon dioxide in the upper atmosphere, like glass in a greenhouse, allows light to enter but blocks the reradiation of heat.

47. **(C)** Cladistics is a way of determining evolutionary relatedness based on the recency of common ancestry, rather than on the number and degree of structural similarities or differences.

48. **(D)** Bile does not digest fats to fatty acids and glycerol but does break them into tiny droplets, thereby greatly increasing the surface area upon which enzymes can act.

49. **(B)** A wide variety of mechanisms, such as chemical incompatibility between egg and sperm, can act as barriers against members of two populations successfully reproducing. If such a mechanism begins to act, the two populations can then be defined as separate species; a speciation event has occurred.

50. **(D)** Active transport causes cellular accumulation of substances in larger quantities than occur in the surroundings. If diffusion were passive, movement would be proportional to the number of molecules and the speed of their motion. In such a case the net movement would be from places of higher concentration to places of lower concentration.

51. **(D)** To account for the six genotypes possible in a one gene–three allele system, the correct equation comes from the expansion of $(p + q + r)^2 = 1$, where p, q, and r represent the frequencies of the three alleles in the population.

52. **(B)** The "gene pool" consists all of the genes available to a species for making genetic combinations, that is, all of the genes in an interbreeding natural group.

53. **(A)** Both the humans and the whales are mammals, related but dissimilar in their evolutionary adaptations to different environments.

54. **(D)** A biome is a large natural community of organisms characterized by a dominant life form that is adapted to the prevailing climatic conditions. Of the choices given, only a deciduous forest fits this definition.

55. **(B)** Most often it is the population explosion of a single species that produces a conspicuous visual aspect (a bloom) such as a green or red color.

56. **(A)** The word *ontogeny* is most often encountered in the statement *Ontogeny recapitulates phylogeny,* which means "Embryology repeats evolution."

57. **(B)** Both ribonucleic acid (RNA) and deoxyribonucleic acid (DNA) have adenine, guanine, and cytosine in their molecules. In addition, ribonucleic acid has uracil, and deoxyribonucleic acid has thymine.

58. **(D)** After prophase, the synaptic maternal and paternal chromosomes separate and go individually to the poles. Sometimes parts of the two chromosomes become entangled and exchanged during synapsis The exchange is known as crossing-over.

59. **(D)** Like many other bacteria, cyanobacteria often secrete gelatinous sheaths.

60. **(E)** The nematocyst is a stinger found in cnidaria such as the jellyfish and Portuguese man-of-war.

61. **(A)** Saliva in the mouth contains amylase and maltase. The former acts upon starch, and the latter upon maltose (malt sugar).

62. **(D)** The form that reproduces most successfully, even if it does so with less than 100 percent efficiency, is always assigned a fitness value of 1.0. In this example, the fitness value for the less successful form

(the blue-flowered form) can be calculated as 60 percent divided by 80 percent to obtain a value of 0.75.

63. **(A)** For most proteins, it appears that amino acid substitutions (caused by gene mutations) occur at a rather constant rate. Therefore, comparing the degree of difference in a protein's structure among a group of species can help determine how much time has passed since any two species diverged.

64. **(A)** A mutation of a single gene can cause a new species to come into being, if that gene directly affects the ability to reproduce. For example, if fruit flies use head shape as a critical cue in recognizing a proper mate, and if a single gene mutates to cause a change in head shape so that animals with this new shape will mate only with each other, this change has caused a new species to come into existence.

65. **(A)** The *way of life,* or ecological niche of an organism, includes such things as requirements for living and relationship to other organisms.

66. **(D)** Examples of half-lives are as follows: carbon-14 (5730 years), phosphorus-32 (14.5 days), cobalt-60 (5.2 years), calcium-45 (160 days), nitrogen-16 (7.35 seconds), sodium-24 (14.8 hours), and thorium-232 (10 billion years).

67. **(E)** Wind-pollinated plants do not need petals since the vision of insects is not involved in locating the flower; also, light pollen can be transported more easily by wind. Most structural features of organisms are logical adaptations.

68. **(C)** The blooming of plants after proper exposure to light and darkness is photoperiodism. Violets are known as short-day plants, morning-glories, as long-day plants. The phenomenon of photoperiodism was discovered by Garner and Allard in 1920.

69. **(B)** Xylem is wood. Woody stems have a relatively large amount of wood in proportion to soft tissues; herbaceous stems have a relatively large amount of soft tissues in proportion to wood. Herbaceous

plants are much more nutritious as food because they contain more protoplasm in proportion to cellulose and lignin, which are generally indigestible by humans.

70. **(C)** The plants are photosynthesizing and releasing oxygen. Since light is required for photosynthesis, the bubbles are generated during the day.

71. **(A)** Spicules are the needlelike skeletal parts of sponges.

72. **(A)** A single disaccharide molecule combines with a single water molecule and breaks into two monosaccharide molecules.

73. **(D)** The bird's wing and the insect's wing serve the same use but have different embryological origins.

74. **(E)** Plant and animal taxonomists usually meet separately and make their own rules of classification. Although these rules are similar, botanists prefer the term *division* for a group of closely related classes, while zoologists use *phylum.*

75. **(B)** The liver originates as a diverticulum (blind outpocket) from the ventral wall of the foregut.

76. **(A)** A frog, like all vertebrates, is a deuterostome animal, meaning that the mouth forms after the anus. The first-formed opening of the gut to the exterior is the blastopore, which remains as the anus.

77. **(A)** The giant chromosomes of some insects have regions of unfolding to produce greatly enlarged "puffs." The exact areas of this type in each chromosome will change in a predictable fashion as the insect moves from one developmental stage to another. Predictable changes in puff patterns can be induced by introduction of certain hormones. The puffs represent DNA that is spreading to make transcription possible.

78. **(A)** Blue light is heavily absorbed by chlorophyll and efficiently starts the light-dependent reactions of photosynthesis. Ultraviolet light and X-rays can also cause chlorophyll oxidation, but are

so energetic that they damage molecules necessary for normal operation.

79. **(E)** Pinocytosis is a mechanism similar to phagocytosis, but on a smaller scale. Phagocytosis is the ingestion of particulate matter such as detritus and cells; pinocytosis is the ingestion of water with dissolved materials.

80. **(E)** The nuclear envelope is actually a pair of membranes in close proximity. The outermost membrane extends at points into the cytoplasm, becoming endoplasmic reticulum.

81. **(B)** The endosperm is parenchymatous tissue derived from polar (endosperm) nuclei fertilized by one of the two sperms produced by a pollen grain. It is located in some seeds and, if present, nourishes the developing seedling. If endosperm is absent, food is stored in the cotyledons of embryos.

82. **(D)** In the retina of vertebrates, rhodopsin changes its shape in reponse to light. In turn, this change alters the membrane of a rod cell to stimulate a nearby neuron.

83. **(A)** If significant variation is present, no new genetic instructions need be added. The variations are significant if they cause nonrandom reproduction.

84. **(D)** The Lederbergs demonstrated that bacterial mutants can be easily found. They devised a method to transfer bacterial colonies from plate to plate without disturbing their spatial relations. Examination of patterns before and after transfer of colonies to a hostile environment reveals those that survive because of mutant ability.

85. **(D)** Pyruvic acid is converted to a two-carbon molecule that is the starting material for the Krebs (citric acid) cycle, but it is not synthesized in the cycle.

86. **(E)** The corpus luteum, translated from Latin as "yellow body," is the tissue from which an egg has been released. It produces progesterone and estrogen, which help the uterus to prepare for accepting an embryo by increasing its wall thickness.

87. **(C)** The four chromosomes are aligned at the equator of the spindle in metaphase. Homologous chromosomes are paired at this point.

88. **(B)** The first polar body, shown at point *b*, has been discharged, and the remaining cell is the secondary oocyte. Sometimes first polar bodies (vestigial secondary oocytes) divide into second polar bodies (vestigial ootids—eggs).

89. **(B)** The sperm has the *n* number of chromosomes, and the nucleus of the large cells, the primary oocyte, has the 2*n* number. Together the number is 3*n*.

90. **(A)** Part *c* is the sperm nucleus, which underwent reductional division before being released from the male (thus, before any of the stages depicted in these drawings). The dividing nucleus at the periphery is in the process of throwing off the second polar body and becoming the egg nucleus.

91. **(A)** The diploid number, 4, is revealed in sketch 2, where there are four chromosomes consisting of two chromatids each, and in sketch 6, where the four chromosomes are clearly visible in the plate view (equatorial section in metaphase). The haploid number, then, is 2.

92. **(A)** Cilia (sing., cilium) are hairlike organelles found on the surfaces of many types of cells. An entire class of Protozoa (class Ciliophora) uses these devices for locomotion. In humans, cells that line several tracts (e.g., the respiratory tract) use cilia to move objects through the lumens.

93. **(D)** The vertebrate kidney's functional units are nephrons. These are tiny tubules closed at one end and opening at the other end into collecting ducts that fuse to become paired ureters carrying urine to the urinary bladder for excretion.

94. **(E)** Swimmerets (pleopods) are appendages located on the abdomen of many aquatic crustaceans. In the crayfish and lobster there are five pairs. They function as organs of respiration and reproduction.

In males, the first two pairs are modified as copulatory organs; in females, they carry the eggs and young.

95. **(B)** The scolex is the head of a tapeworm, by which it attaches itself to the wall of the host's intestine and from which body segments are budded. To aid in anchorage, the scolex of the pork tapeworm has a circle of hooks and four suckers.

96. **(B)** The cochlea is a spiral canal in the inner ear, so named because it resembles the coiled shell of a snail. It contains the sensory endings of the auditory nerve.

97. **(E)** In humans, the adrenals are located above the kidney. Among the secretions of this tissue are the hormones cortisone and epinephrine (adrenaline).

98. **(A)** The pituitary is actually attached to the brain by a slender stalk. It produces so many important hormones that it is called the "master gland." Embryologically it is derived from parts of the brain and mouth cavity.

99. **(D)** Certain cells of some vascular plants become elongated and hollow. These tracheids, aligned longitudinally, form the xylem.

100. **(E)** Tracheae are paired tubes leading into an insect's body. They branch and rebranch to tiny dead-end tubules called tracheoles. No cell is very far from an air-filled tracheole. Gas exchange occurs at the liquid-filled tips of tracheoles.

101. **(C)** Transpiration, the evaporation of water from leaves would not be possible if there were not holes scattered over the leaf surfaces. These stomata open and close by a homeostatic mechanism based on the amount of water in nearby cells.

102. **(A)** The paired appendages (parapodia) of polychaete worms (phylum Annelida, class Polychaeta) are vascularized areas capable of gas exchange with the environment.

103. **(C)** Paired guard cells, whose shapes change as their degrees of turgor change, form the boundaries of stomata on leaf surfaces (see answer 101, above).

104. **(E)** In an RNA virus the genetic material is ribonucleic acid, rather than the usual deoxyribonucleic acid. Transcription by such a virus begins with the production of a single-stranded DNA under the direction of the enzyme reverse transcriptase. This DNA then transcribes messenger RNA in the familiar fashion of other organisms.

105. **(B)** Salivary amylase is one of the first enzymes encountered by the food that humans eat. It acts specifically upon starches, hydrolyzing them.

106. **(B)** See answer 105, above.

107. **(D)** Thyroxin is an amino acid that acts as a hormone. It is manufactured in the thyroid, is incorporated into a protein called thyroglobulin, and transported in that form to target cells via the bloodstream.

108. **(C)** Hexokinase is the enzyme catalyzing the first step of glycolysis, the addition of a phosphate group to glucose.

109. **(A)** Lysosomes are membranous vesicles within a cell; they contain digestive enzymes. The principal enzyme is acid phosphatase, whose presence is diagnostic of lysosomes.

110. **(E)** Millions of monarch butterflies (*Danaus plexippus*) hatched in North America in late summer migrate southward to escape winter's cold. Many of them have been found to congregate in a rather small area of mountainous central Mexico, where they literally cover the landscape.

111. **(D)** Parts of Tanzania (in East Africa) have yielded skulls of *Australopithecus africanus,* estimated to be 2.5 to 3 million years old.

112. **(B)** Thirteen species of finches are found on the Galápagos Islands, a volcanic group west of Ecuador. Darwin, visiting the area in 1835, studied these birds and later cited their anatomical differences as examples of adaptive radiaton.

113. **(C)** According to the theory of continental drift, certain large landmasses now separated by water were once attached. The area given the name Gondwana included the present Africa, South America, India, and Antarctica.

114. **(A)** Industrial melanism is the phenomenon whereby darkening of the landscape by industrial soot leads to selection for dark-colored individuals within animal populations. The peppered moths (*Biston betularia*) of England provide a classic example of evolution triggered by this environmental change.

115. **(E)** Taxonomy is the study of how organisms should be classified. Adult anatomy, including type of symmetry, is an important clue to relatedness. The entire life cycle of an organism should be examined, however, and molecular structure may also provide important information.

116. **(A)** Biogeography is the study of the relationship between populations and their geographical distributions. To understand why particular organisms succeed in each region, biologists must examine the nature of the biome. A biome is a large community dominated by a characteristic life-form, often a plant type.

117. **(B)** Endocrinology is the study of endocrine glands, the tissues or organs that secrete hormones into the bloodstream. Purification of hormones is a goal of endocrinologists.

118. **(C)** A histologist studies the microscopic anatomy of organisms. An important tool in histology is the enhancement of visual contrast among cell organelles by the use of stains that attach preferentially to certain molecules. A vital stain is one that is not toxic to a living cell.

119. **(D)** Immunology is the study of the immune system, which involves recognition by the body of materials, such as antigens, that are foreign. These antigens are then attacked by various methods, including antibody attachment and lymphocyte engulfment.

120. **(C)** The outermost membrane that comprises the nuclear boundary sends outgrowths into the cytoplasm as rounded or flattened tubules. This network, the endoplasmic reticulum, provides a large surface to which ribosomes may attach and may act as transportation conduits.

121. **(D)** A mitochondrion not only contains DNA, but also uses this material to direct synthesis of its own proteins independently of the rest of the cell.

122. **(B)** Microtubules, proteinaceous hollow rods, build a number of structures, including the centrioles of animal cells.

123. **(A)** A fundamental difference between kingdom Plantae and kingdom Animalia is that cells of the former produce tough cell walls composed largely of polysaccharides. Bacteria (kingdom Monera), some Protista, such as algae, and the Fungi also produce cell walls.

124. **(B)** The centrioles of animal cells seem to be necessary for normal spindle fiber production. Many plants, however, produce this mitotic and meiotic apparatus without centrioles.

125. **(C)** A habitat includes the geographical location in which an organism lives.

126. **(E)** A deme is a relatively temporary interbreeding group; a population is a larger, stable, and therefore more permanent group.

127. **(A)** See answer 116, above.

128. **(A)** Biomes can be relatively large communities, sometimes covering millions of square miles. They include all of the organisms within these geographical bounds.

129. **(D)** Operant conditioning is the sort of learning in which an animal does something, after which it remembers that it was either rewarded or hurt by the action. If rewarded, the animal will try the same activity upon the next opportunity. If hurt, the animal learns to avoid that action.

130. **(C)** Bats find flying insects in darkness by sending out high-frequency sound and analyzing its return pattern as it reflects from objects—a behavior known as echolocation.

131. **(E)** Muscles have specialized regions called proprioceptors that respond to being stretched by the contraction of nearby fibers. Proprioceptors that are stretched initiate nerve messages to the central nervous system. The brain collects and analyzes all of these messages from the body and constructs an image of body position.

132. **(B)** A circadian rhythm is a pattern of activity that cycles approximately every 24 hours; the sleep-wake cycle is an example.

133. **(A)** Appetitive behavior is the first activity or set of activities that an animal performs to satisfy a drive such as hunger. If appetitive behavior leads to the possibility of satisfying the drive (e.g., the animal finds food), the next set of activities is the one called the consummatory act (e.g., eating the food).

134. **(E)** As energy flows from organism to organism in an ecosystem, some is lost in the form of heat. A tertiary consumer (an animal that eats animals that eat animals that eat plants) obtains a very small percentage of the energy that was first stored in the plants. Therefore, the plants can support only a small number of tertiary consumers, but more secondary consumers and even more primary consumers.

135. **(B)** Any herbivore, such as a cow, is a primary consumer.

136. **(D)** Since mice are primary consumers (herbivores), any animal, such as a snake, that eats a mouse is a secondary consumer.

137. **(E)** See answer 134, above, for the definition of a tertiary consumer.

138. **(A)** Decomposers are bacteria or fungi that convert the complex macromolecules of dead organisms to much simpler molecules which can be released for use by living organisms.

139. **(C)** Any photosynthetic organism, such as an alga, is a producer, as demonstrated by its ability to manufacture and store organic molecules holding energy in their bonds.

140. **(D)** A small population reproductively separated from the rest of the species may have a gene pool significantly different in its allele frequencies from the species as a whole. Even though the few "founders" of a newly inhabited area mate randomly among themselves, they may be closely related and therefore perpetuate their genetic differences from the rest of the species.

141. **(B)** When humans purposefully provide the selection pressure, as in breeding programs, the evolution that occurs is said to be caused by artificial selection.

142. **(A)** Biologists who study animal societies believe that some animals sometimes sacrifice their own reproductive potential in deference to the welfare of the population. In a societal population of similar genomes, this altruistic behavior serves to enhance the chance that an individual's genes will reach the next generation even if "by proxy," that is, by another, similar individual doing the actual reproduction.

143. **(C)** A fitness value of 1.0 is assigned to an organism whose phenotype allows it to reproduce more successfully (placing more copies of its genes into the next generation) than any other organism in the population. Less successful organisms are assigned values below 1.0, with a value of 0 going to those that die before reproducing or are sterile.

144. **(E)** Jean Baptiste de Lamarck (1744–1829) was the first scientist to develop a hypothesis of speciation. He believed that phenotypic changes newly acquired in a lifetime can be transmitted to the next generation. This evolutionary mechanism has been disproved for many characteristics.

145. **(A)** An archegonium is the female sex organ of the moss gametophyte. The archegonium produces an egg that will be

fertilized by a sperm from another gametophytic structure, the antheridium.

146. **(D)** Sepals are the modified leaves, usually green, that form the base of a flower.

147. **(D)** By definition, any plant using a flower as its reproductive portion is an angiosperm.

148. **(C)** Most gymnosperms are plants that produce seed-bearing cones. Well-known examples are the pines.

149. **(E)** The sporophytic form of a fern sends some of its diploid cells into meiosis to become haploid spores. Upon release, a spore can become the progenitor of a multicellular haploid organism, the gametophyte.

150. **(B)** Cambium is meristematic tissue of stems and roots, capable of reproducing asexually to provide cells that will mature into new xylem and phloem in vascular plants.

151. **(E)** A major route by which water reenters the atmosphere is evaporation from leaf surfaces. This water was drawn from the soil by plants.

152. **(C)** Plants obtain nitrogen from soil and use it to produce amino acids (one nitrogen atom per molecule). Herbivorous animals extend the nitrogen in the cycle when they eat plants.

153. **(A)** Animals (and plants) produce carbon dioxide as an end product of the Krebs (citric acid) cycle. Exhalation is the final act of removing this material from the body by releasing it to the atmosphere. Water is also exhaled; it is not produced by the Krebs cycle, but is made during oxidative phosphorylation, which follows the Krebs cycle.

154. **(B)** A cell of an actively reproducing tissue goes through G_1, S, and G_2 portions of interphase as it prepares for mitosis. G symbolizes "gap," and S symbolizes "synthesis" of new DNA.

155. **(A)** A Barr body is a visually detectable object in the nucleus of each cell of a

female. It has been identified as one of a female's two X chromosomes.

156. **(D)** Lampbrush configurations, so named because they resemble the feathery appearance of cleaning brushes for nineteenth-century kerosene lamps, are uncoiled regions of chromosomes that are producing RNA (transcribing). This activity is demonstrated by finding isotopically labeled uracil at these areas.

157. **(C)** A gynandromorphic fruit fly (*Drosophila*) has XX (female) cells in some regions of its body and XY (male) cells in others. Genes for instinctive behavior, if located on the sex chromosome, can be studied in this bizarre organism. Seymour Benzer is a pioneer in such work.

158. **(B)** Episomes, including the plasmids that have become so valuable in recombinant DNA work, are pieces of DNA that can exist either as part of a chromosome or free.

159. **(C)** See answer 157, above.

160. **(C)** The evolutionary rate for histone, 0.006, is far below any other in the table, indicating very little variation in amino acid sequence among the organisms studied.

161. **(E)** The fibrin portion of fibrinogen plays a vital role in blood clotting in a wide range of animals. One would expect that its amino acid sequence would be vital to its function and would therefore be conserved.

162. **(E)** Only living organisms could provide intact proteins for this study. Since significant evolution requires much time, the materials are not available for a self-reliant proof of such evolution. The data in this study are pieces of evidence that, when added to others, point toward evolution as a useful theory of organismal diversity.

163. **(D)** After 1 year, the field contained 30 species of herbs, but no other types of plant. After 50 years, all three plant categories were represented among the 75 species.

164. **(E)** Only in the fiftieth year did shrubs and trees show approximately the same species abundance as herbs.

165. **(C)** The first colonizers of the field (year 1) were all herbs. Since one may assume that seeds of all three plant types were available, the herbs must have been best adapted for this recently tilled environment.

166. **(D)** Ecological succession is a predictable, gradual change in the types of organisms that inhabit a region.

167. **(A)** Many animal species are dependent upon the specific plants of their habitat; therefore, a succession will occur also among animals.

168. **(C)** In temperate regions where rainfall is sufficiently high to support trees, it is predictable that trees will eventually dominate, since their canopies cast shadows over low-growing herbs and shrubs. The trees' success in competition for sun is reflected by their presence in large numbers.

169. **(E)** The number of herbivorous species will increase as the number of plant species rises. Also rising will be the number of animal species dependent upon these herbivores for food. A mature plant community is characterized by complex webs of interdependence.

170. **(D)** The enzyme thymidine kinase, used in combination with the drug aminopterin, eliminates unfused mouse cells. Aminopterin is not an enzyme.

171. **(D)** Clone 1 does not help eliminate any chromosome from consideration since it contains four chromosomes. The chromosome pattern of clones 2, 3, 4, 5, and 6 perfectly matches the appearance of hexosaminidase A in these clones. The gene is on chromosome 15, since only clones that include this chromosome also produce the enzyme.

172. **(C)** Chromosomes 6, 8, 11, and 15, for which representative clones exist, can be eliminated since those clones do not produce hexokinase-1. Any of the other 19 human chromosomes not mentioned in the table could be correct. (Hexokinase-1 is known to be controlled by a gene on chromosome 10.)

173. **(A)** All clones positive for pepsinogen production also contain chromosome 6. Clone 2 is especially useful, since it contains only this human chromosome and produces the enzyme.

174. **(E)** Hybridomas are fusion cells combining malignant cells and antibody-producing plasma cells. Each clone derived from such a fusion produces a single type of antibody in large quantity. The egg-sperm interaction of fertilization is a naturally occurring fusion of cells of the same species.

175. **(D)** The reason for preferential expulsion of human chromosomes is neither mentioned in the passage nor understood.

176. **(A)** The word *somatic* comes from the Greek *soma,* meaning "body." It refers to any cell of a multicellular organism that is not a gamete (sex cell).

177. **(B)** Linkage (the presence of two or more genes on the same chromosome) is analyzed by looking for evidence of gene recombination via crossing-over. Crossing-over is determined by finding which alleles of linked genes are together on the same chromosome. A testcross (mating to a homozygous recessive individual) shows, by the phenotypes of the progeny, which alleles are linked on each chromosome.

178. **(A)** The F_1's would be triply heterozygous (*sc/+*, *ec/+*, *vg/+*). Mating them in a testcross with a triply homozygous recessive individual (*sc/sc*, *ec/ec*, *vg/vg*) would yield eight phenotypes in equal numbers. For instance, a heterozygote for the *sc* gene, when mated with a homozygous recessive, produces two phenotypes in equal numbers: scute and wild-type; that is, the probability of each of these is 1/2. If none of the three genes is linked to another, various combinations of the

alleles occur by random assortment. Since the chance of any single phenotypic character is 1/2, the chance of any single combination of three characters is $(1/2)^3 = 1/8$.

179. **(C)** As explained in answer 178, above, all phenotypes would occur in nearly equal numbers if there were no linkage. If all three genes were linked, there would be only two large groups of phenotypes, resulting from the two noncrossover chromosome types (crossing-over is a relatively rare event, so nonrecombinant testcross progeny would be most prevalent: *sc*, *ec*, *vg* individuals and +, +, + individuals). The actual results, however, include four large groups, the two just mentioned plus *sc*, *ec*, + and +, +, *vg*, indicating that one of the three genes is not linked to the others. But which of the three is independent? If we look at the testcross progeny, *ignoring* the wing characteristic (*vg* or +), only two large groups appear: *sc*, *ec* (240 + 230 = 470) and +, + (242 + 232 = 474). They are present in nearly equal numbers, as expected if they are from nonrecombinant F_1's with the *sc* and *ec* genes linked. If, on the other hand, we look at the categories of *ec* and *vg*, ignoring *sc*, we find four large categories in nearly equal numbers: +, *vg* (232 + 14), *ec*, *vg* (230 + 15), +, + (242 + 12), and *ec*, + 1240 + 15). This 1:1:1:1 ratio is what would be expected if *ec* and *sc* were linked and the pair were assorting independently of *vg*. Our conclusion is that *sc* and *ec* are linked and *vg* is on a second chromosome.

180. **(D)** Although the reason is not understood, males of the genus *Drosophila* do not show genetic signs of crossing-over. Since crossing-over analysis is vital in determining linkage, only females of the F_1 generation would be appropriate subjects.

181. **(B)** Many terrestrial animals, including humans, excrete their nitrogenous wastes in the form of urea, which can be tolerated in higher concentration than ammonia. Terrestrial animals conserve water by using urea.

182. **(A)** The gut of a herbivore (plant eater) needs extra time to digest the tough cell walls of plants. This time is provided by a longer gut.

183. **(D)** The introductory paragraph states that a *precocious* increase of T3 was artificially induced. The word means "before the normal time," in this case before a natural increase that occurs just prior to metamorphic change.

184. **(A)** There is an orderly progression of change after injection of T3, just as occurs in natural metamorphosis.

185. **(C)** The graph shows synthesis of new membranes. Phospholipids are major components of membranes.

186. **(C)** Messenger RNA carries codes for building proteins, such as cytochrome oxidase, urea-cycle enzymes, and enzymes that catalyze membrane synthesis. Ribosomal RNA forms a portion of ribosomes, the sites of protein synthesis. The nucleus must produce and release both these nucleic acids before the other events shown on the graph can occur. Treatment of T3-injected animals with the drug actinomycin D (a transcription inhibitor) causes a halt in metamorphic events.

187. **(A)** Cytochrome oxidase is an enzyme that accepts electrons from the cytochromes of the electron transport system and passes them to oxygen. During their passage through the system, electrons transfer their energy to ATP, a newly synthesized material.

188. **(E)** Each enzyme shows a characteristic maximum reaction velocity. Although difficult to determine experimentally (since a very large substrate concentration would be required), the theoretical V_{max} can be determined through the use of a Lineweaver-Burk plot. This is a double-reciprocal plot of the same data, where the *x*-axis is $1/V$ and the *y*-axis is $1/[S]$. The point at which the plotted curve strikes the *x*-axis is $1/V_{max}$.

189. **(C)** Decreasing the value of K_M in the equation decreases the denominator, thus increasing the value for V. The question states that V_{max} (at high substrate concentration) remains constant, so the decrease of V must occur only at the lower range of substrate concentrations, or [S] values.

190. **(D)** Leonor Michaelis and Maud Menten derived the equation in 1913. The hyperbolic curve is sometimes said to describe "Michaelis-Menten kinetics," and K_M is the Michaelis constant.

191. **(C)** The passage cites evidence that apomorphine can mimic dopamine by activating the dopamine receptor site, therefore causing cAMP production. This apomorphine might replace the dopamine that is not produced by a victim of Parkinson's disease.

192. **(E)** Chlorpromazine blocks and inactivates dopamine receptors, so that dopamine is less likely to activate them. Therefore, it is possible that schizophrenia involves overstimulation of these receptors by an inappropriately large release of dopamine.

193. **(B)** Any agent that blocks a neurotransmitter receptor site causes inactivation of its enzymatic activity. Serotonin receptor sites, if activated, catalyze production of cAMP, so the intracellular level of this substance will drop after LSD blocks further production.

194. **(B)** Since skeletal muscles must react quickly to stimuli if they are to be useful, it would be intolerable for them to depend upon the relatively slow process of adenylyl cyclase activation, cAMP production, and biochemical changes induced by cAMP. It is quicker to have a direct-stimulation method whereby acetylcholine itself causes the critical membrane permeability changes that stimulate a muscle fiber.

195. **(C)** Nonlipid hormones have great difficulty entering target cells through the lipid-containing cytoplasmic membrane. Many examples are known in which they act in much the same way described here for neurotransmitters. They stimulate the membrane to begin enzymatic activity leading to cAMP production within the cell. The first known example was the action of adrenaline (epinephrine) upon liver cells. Lipid hormones, such as the steroid sex hormones, can easily pass through cytoplasmic membranes and have a direct effect upon the interiors of their target cells.

196. **(C)** Transpiration is the loss of water at a leaf surface by evaporation. Because of the high heat of vaporization of water, this process leads to a large heat transfer to the air. A detached leaf has lost its connection with a water supply that is necessary if it is to continue transpiration.

197. **(C)** Stomata are the openings on a leaf surface, which are widest when transpiration is most active.

198. **(C)** The graph shows that the maximum internal temperature of an intact leaf was about 40°C, well below the danger level.

199. **(A)** Any dark object absorbs heat. Since tissue contains a large quantity of water, and since water has the property of holding heat for a long time, the severed leaf, which has lost the benefit of transpiration, tends to become warmer than the surrounding air.

200. **(E)** Panting by dogs is an activity that allows maximum evaporation of water from the tongue surface. Heat is transferred from the body core to this surface by blood flow. An intact leaf at midday is also cooled by evaporation, since water is released through its open stomata.

Answer Sheet for Sample Test 4

1. Ⓐ Ⓑ Ⓒ Ⓓ Ⓔ	51. Ⓐ Ⓑ Ⓒ Ⓓ Ⓔ	101. Ⓐ Ⓑ Ⓒ Ⓓ Ⓔ	151. Ⓐ Ⓑ Ⓒ Ⓓ Ⓔ
2. Ⓐ Ⓑ Ⓒ Ⓓ Ⓔ	52. Ⓐ Ⓑ Ⓒ Ⓓ Ⓔ	102. Ⓐ Ⓑ Ⓒ Ⓓ Ⓔ	152. Ⓐ Ⓑ Ⓒ Ⓓ Ⓔ
3. Ⓐ Ⓑ Ⓒ Ⓓ Ⓔ	53. Ⓐ Ⓑ Ⓒ Ⓓ Ⓔ	103. Ⓐ Ⓑ Ⓒ Ⓓ Ⓔ	153. Ⓐ Ⓑ Ⓒ Ⓓ Ⓔ
4. Ⓐ Ⓑ Ⓒ Ⓓ Ⓔ	54. Ⓐ Ⓑ Ⓒ Ⓓ Ⓔ	104. Ⓐ Ⓑ Ⓒ Ⓓ Ⓔ	154. Ⓐ Ⓑ Ⓒ Ⓓ Ⓔ
5. Ⓐ Ⓑ Ⓒ Ⓓ Ⓔ	55. Ⓐ Ⓑ Ⓒ Ⓓ Ⓔ	105. Ⓐ Ⓑ Ⓒ Ⓓ Ⓔ	155. Ⓐ Ⓑ Ⓒ Ⓓ Ⓔ
6. Ⓐ Ⓑ Ⓒ Ⓓ Ⓔ	56. Ⓐ Ⓑ Ⓒ Ⓓ Ⓔ	106. Ⓐ Ⓑ Ⓒ Ⓓ Ⓔ	156. Ⓐ Ⓑ Ⓒ Ⓓ Ⓔ
7. Ⓐ Ⓑ Ⓒ Ⓓ Ⓔ	57. Ⓐ Ⓑ Ⓒ Ⓓ Ⓔ	107. Ⓐ Ⓑ Ⓒ Ⓓ Ⓔ	157. Ⓐ Ⓑ Ⓒ Ⓓ Ⓔ
8. Ⓐ Ⓑ Ⓒ Ⓓ Ⓔ	58. Ⓐ Ⓑ Ⓒ Ⓓ Ⓔ	108. Ⓐ Ⓑ Ⓒ Ⓓ Ⓔ	158. Ⓐ Ⓑ Ⓒ Ⓓ Ⓔ
9. Ⓐ Ⓑ Ⓒ Ⓓ Ⓔ	59. Ⓐ Ⓑ Ⓒ Ⓓ Ⓔ	109. Ⓐ Ⓑ Ⓒ Ⓓ Ⓔ	159. Ⓐ Ⓑ Ⓒ Ⓓ Ⓔ
10. Ⓐ Ⓑ Ⓒ Ⓓ Ⓔ	60. Ⓐ Ⓑ Ⓒ Ⓓ Ⓔ	110. Ⓐ Ⓑ Ⓒ Ⓓ Ⓔ	160. Ⓐ Ⓑ Ⓒ Ⓓ Ⓔ
11. Ⓐ Ⓑ Ⓒ Ⓓ Ⓔ	61. Ⓐ Ⓑ Ⓒ Ⓓ Ⓔ	111. Ⓐ Ⓑ Ⓒ Ⓓ Ⓔ	161. Ⓐ Ⓑ Ⓒ Ⓓ Ⓔ
12. Ⓐ Ⓑ Ⓒ Ⓓ Ⓔ	62. Ⓐ Ⓑ Ⓒ Ⓓ Ⓔ	112. Ⓐ Ⓑ Ⓒ Ⓓ Ⓔ	162. Ⓐ Ⓑ Ⓒ Ⓓ Ⓔ
13. Ⓐ Ⓑ Ⓒ Ⓓ Ⓔ	63. Ⓐ Ⓑ Ⓒ Ⓓ Ⓔ	113. Ⓐ Ⓑ Ⓒ Ⓓ Ⓔ	163. Ⓐ Ⓑ Ⓒ Ⓓ Ⓔ
14. Ⓐ Ⓑ Ⓒ Ⓓ Ⓔ	64. Ⓐ Ⓑ Ⓒ Ⓓ Ⓔ	114. Ⓐ Ⓑ Ⓒ Ⓓ Ⓔ	164. Ⓐ Ⓑ Ⓒ Ⓓ Ⓔ
15. Ⓐ Ⓑ Ⓒ Ⓓ Ⓔ	65. Ⓐ Ⓑ Ⓒ Ⓓ Ⓔ	115. Ⓐ Ⓑ Ⓒ Ⓓ Ⓔ	165. Ⓐ Ⓑ Ⓒ Ⓓ Ⓔ
16. Ⓐ Ⓑ Ⓒ Ⓓ Ⓔ	66. Ⓐ Ⓑ Ⓒ Ⓓ Ⓔ	116. Ⓐ Ⓑ Ⓒ Ⓓ Ⓔ	166. Ⓐ Ⓑ Ⓒ Ⓓ Ⓔ
17. Ⓐ Ⓑ Ⓒ Ⓓ Ⓔ	67. Ⓐ Ⓑ Ⓒ Ⓓ Ⓔ	117. Ⓐ Ⓑ Ⓒ Ⓓ Ⓔ	167. Ⓐ Ⓑ Ⓒ Ⓓ Ⓔ
18. Ⓐ Ⓑ Ⓒ Ⓓ Ⓔ	68. Ⓐ Ⓑ Ⓒ Ⓓ Ⓔ	118. Ⓐ Ⓑ Ⓒ Ⓓ Ⓔ	168. Ⓐ Ⓑ Ⓒ Ⓓ Ⓔ
19. Ⓐ Ⓑ Ⓒ Ⓓ Ⓔ	69. Ⓐ Ⓑ Ⓒ Ⓓ Ⓔ	119. Ⓐ Ⓑ Ⓒ Ⓓ Ⓔ	169. Ⓐ Ⓑ Ⓒ Ⓓ Ⓔ
20. Ⓐ Ⓑ Ⓒ Ⓓ Ⓔ	70. Ⓐ Ⓑ Ⓒ Ⓓ Ⓔ	120. Ⓐ Ⓑ Ⓒ Ⓓ Ⓔ	170. Ⓐ Ⓑ Ⓒ Ⓓ Ⓔ
21. Ⓐ Ⓑ Ⓒ Ⓓ Ⓔ	71. Ⓐ Ⓑ Ⓒ Ⓓ Ⓔ	121. Ⓐ Ⓑ Ⓒ Ⓓ Ⓔ	171. Ⓐ Ⓑ Ⓒ Ⓓ Ⓔ
22. Ⓐ Ⓑ Ⓒ Ⓓ Ⓔ	72. Ⓐ Ⓑ Ⓒ Ⓓ Ⓔ	122. Ⓐ Ⓑ Ⓒ Ⓓ Ⓔ	172. Ⓐ Ⓑ Ⓒ Ⓓ Ⓔ
23. Ⓐ Ⓑ Ⓒ Ⓓ Ⓔ	73. Ⓐ Ⓑ Ⓒ Ⓓ Ⓔ	123. Ⓐ Ⓑ Ⓒ Ⓓ Ⓔ	173. Ⓐ Ⓑ Ⓒ Ⓓ Ⓔ
24. Ⓐ Ⓑ Ⓒ Ⓓ Ⓔ	74. Ⓐ Ⓑ Ⓒ Ⓓ Ⓔ	124. Ⓐ Ⓑ Ⓒ Ⓓ Ⓔ	174. Ⓐ Ⓑ Ⓒ Ⓓ Ⓔ
25. Ⓐ Ⓑ Ⓒ Ⓓ Ⓔ	75. Ⓐ Ⓑ Ⓒ Ⓓ Ⓔ	125. Ⓐ Ⓑ Ⓒ Ⓓ Ⓔ	175. Ⓐ Ⓑ Ⓒ Ⓓ Ⓔ
26. Ⓐ Ⓑ Ⓒ Ⓓ Ⓔ	76. Ⓐ Ⓑ Ⓒ Ⓓ Ⓔ	126. Ⓐ Ⓑ Ⓒ Ⓓ Ⓔ	176. Ⓐ Ⓑ Ⓒ Ⓓ Ⓔ
27. Ⓐ Ⓑ Ⓒ Ⓓ Ⓔ	77. Ⓐ Ⓑ Ⓒ Ⓓ Ⓔ	127. Ⓐ Ⓑ Ⓒ Ⓓ Ⓔ	177. Ⓐ Ⓑ Ⓒ Ⓓ Ⓔ
28. Ⓐ Ⓑ Ⓒ Ⓓ Ⓔ	78. Ⓐ Ⓑ Ⓒ Ⓓ Ⓔ	128. Ⓐ Ⓑ Ⓒ Ⓓ Ⓔ	178. Ⓐ Ⓑ Ⓒ Ⓓ Ⓔ
29. Ⓐ Ⓑ Ⓒ Ⓓ Ⓔ	79. Ⓐ Ⓑ Ⓒ Ⓓ Ⓔ	129. Ⓐ Ⓑ Ⓒ Ⓓ Ⓔ	179. Ⓐ Ⓑ Ⓒ Ⓓ Ⓔ
30. Ⓐ Ⓑ Ⓒ Ⓓ Ⓔ	80. Ⓐ Ⓑ Ⓒ Ⓓ Ⓔ	130. Ⓐ Ⓑ Ⓒ Ⓓ Ⓔ	180. Ⓐ Ⓑ Ⓒ Ⓓ Ⓔ
31. Ⓐ Ⓑ Ⓒ Ⓓ Ⓔ	81. Ⓐ Ⓑ Ⓒ Ⓓ Ⓔ	131. Ⓐ Ⓑ Ⓒ Ⓓ Ⓔ	181. Ⓐ Ⓑ Ⓒ Ⓓ Ⓔ
32. Ⓐ Ⓑ Ⓒ Ⓓ Ⓔ	82. Ⓐ Ⓑ Ⓒ Ⓓ Ⓔ	132. Ⓐ Ⓑ Ⓒ Ⓓ Ⓔ	182. Ⓐ Ⓑ Ⓒ Ⓓ Ⓔ
33. Ⓐ Ⓑ Ⓒ Ⓓ Ⓔ	83. Ⓐ Ⓑ Ⓒ Ⓓ Ⓔ	133. Ⓐ Ⓑ Ⓒ Ⓓ Ⓔ	183. Ⓐ Ⓑ Ⓒ Ⓓ Ⓔ
34. Ⓐ Ⓑ Ⓒ Ⓓ Ⓔ	84. Ⓐ Ⓑ Ⓒ Ⓓ Ⓔ	134. Ⓐ Ⓑ Ⓒ Ⓓ Ⓔ	184. Ⓐ Ⓑ Ⓒ Ⓓ Ⓔ
35. Ⓐ Ⓑ Ⓒ Ⓓ Ⓔ	85. Ⓐ Ⓑ Ⓒ Ⓓ Ⓔ	135. Ⓐ Ⓑ Ⓒ Ⓓ Ⓔ	185. Ⓐ Ⓑ Ⓒ Ⓓ Ⓔ
36. Ⓐ Ⓑ Ⓒ Ⓓ Ⓔ	86. Ⓐ Ⓑ Ⓒ Ⓓ Ⓔ	136. Ⓐ Ⓑ Ⓒ Ⓓ Ⓔ	186. Ⓐ Ⓑ Ⓒ Ⓓ Ⓔ
37. Ⓐ Ⓑ Ⓒ Ⓓ Ⓔ	87. Ⓐ Ⓑ Ⓒ Ⓓ Ⓔ	137. Ⓐ Ⓑ Ⓒ Ⓓ Ⓔ	187. Ⓐ Ⓑ Ⓒ Ⓓ Ⓔ
38. Ⓐ Ⓑ Ⓒ Ⓓ Ⓔ	88. Ⓐ Ⓑ Ⓒ Ⓓ Ⓔ	138. Ⓐ Ⓑ Ⓒ Ⓓ Ⓔ	188. Ⓐ Ⓑ Ⓒ Ⓓ Ⓔ
39. Ⓐ Ⓑ Ⓒ Ⓓ Ⓔ	89. Ⓐ Ⓑ Ⓒ Ⓓ Ⓔ	139. Ⓐ Ⓑ Ⓒ Ⓓ Ⓔ	189. Ⓐ Ⓑ Ⓒ Ⓓ Ⓔ
40. Ⓐ Ⓑ Ⓒ Ⓓ Ⓔ	90. Ⓐ Ⓑ Ⓒ Ⓓ Ⓔ	140. Ⓐ Ⓑ Ⓒ Ⓓ Ⓔ	190. Ⓐ Ⓑ Ⓒ Ⓓ Ⓔ
41. Ⓐ Ⓑ Ⓒ Ⓓ Ⓔ	91. Ⓐ Ⓑ Ⓒ Ⓓ Ⓔ	141. Ⓐ Ⓑ Ⓒ Ⓓ Ⓔ	191. Ⓐ Ⓑ Ⓒ Ⓓ Ⓔ
42. Ⓐ Ⓑ Ⓒ Ⓓ Ⓔ	92. Ⓐ Ⓑ Ⓒ Ⓓ Ⓔ	142. Ⓐ Ⓑ Ⓒ Ⓓ Ⓔ	192. Ⓐ Ⓑ Ⓒ Ⓓ Ⓔ
43. Ⓐ Ⓑ Ⓒ Ⓓ Ⓔ	93. Ⓐ Ⓑ Ⓒ Ⓓ Ⓔ	143. Ⓐ Ⓑ Ⓒ Ⓓ Ⓔ	193. Ⓐ Ⓑ Ⓒ Ⓓ Ⓔ
44. Ⓐ Ⓑ Ⓒ Ⓓ Ⓔ	94. Ⓐ Ⓑ Ⓒ Ⓓ Ⓔ	144. Ⓐ Ⓑ Ⓒ Ⓓ Ⓔ	194. Ⓐ Ⓑ Ⓒ Ⓓ Ⓔ
45. Ⓐ Ⓑ Ⓒ Ⓓ Ⓔ	95. Ⓐ Ⓑ Ⓒ Ⓓ Ⓔ	145. Ⓐ Ⓑ Ⓒ Ⓓ Ⓔ	195. Ⓐ Ⓑ Ⓒ Ⓓ Ⓔ
46. Ⓐ Ⓑ Ⓒ Ⓓ Ⓔ	96. Ⓐ Ⓑ Ⓒ Ⓓ Ⓔ	146. Ⓐ Ⓑ Ⓒ Ⓓ Ⓔ	196. Ⓐ Ⓑ Ⓒ Ⓓ Ⓔ
47. Ⓐ Ⓑ Ⓒ Ⓓ Ⓔ	97. Ⓐ Ⓑ Ⓒ Ⓓ Ⓔ	147. Ⓐ Ⓑ Ⓒ Ⓓ Ⓔ	197. Ⓐ Ⓑ Ⓒ Ⓓ Ⓔ
48. Ⓐ Ⓑ Ⓒ Ⓓ Ⓔ	98. Ⓐ Ⓑ Ⓒ Ⓓ Ⓔ	148. Ⓐ Ⓑ Ⓒ Ⓓ Ⓔ	198. Ⓐ Ⓑ Ⓒ Ⓓ Ⓔ
49. Ⓐ Ⓑ Ⓒ Ⓓ Ⓔ	99. Ⓐ Ⓑ Ⓒ Ⓓ Ⓔ	149. Ⓐ Ⓑ Ⓒ Ⓓ Ⓔ	199. Ⓐ Ⓑ Ⓒ Ⓓ Ⓔ
50. Ⓐ Ⓑ Ⓒ Ⓓ Ⓔ	100. Ⓐ Ⓑ Ⓒ Ⓓ Ⓔ	150. Ⓐ Ⓑ Ⓒ Ⓓ Ⓔ	200. Ⓐ Ⓑ Ⓒ Ⓓ Ⓔ

Tests in Biology

Sample Test 4

Directions for Taking Test: This sample test contains 200 questions or incomplete statements, and should be finished in 170 minutes. Each item has five possible answers or completions. Choose the best one, and blacken the corresponding letter on the answer sheet.

After finishing, you can determine your score by using the **Answer Key** at the end of this test. The **Answer Explanations** section also contains comments and explanations that should clarify the concepts involved in each question.

Questions 1–92
For each of the following questions or incomplete statements select the best suggested answer or completion.

1. The organelle active in the synthesis of proteins is the
   A. nucleus
   B. plastid
   C. mitochondrion
   D. ribosome
   E. lysosome

2. As the Krebs cycle operates, a receptor that picks up hydrogen is
   A. NAD
   B. ADP
   C. acetyl coenzyme A
   D. ACTH
   E. DNA polymerase

3. In a 25-year-old oak stem the
   A. pith would be 25 years old
   B. secondary xylem would be limited to the outer growth ring
   C. phloem would be next to the primary xylem
   D. outer protective covering would be epidermis
   E. primary phloem would be in a band outside the vascular cambium

4. Guttation is greatest when
   A. stomata are open
   B. temperature is low
   C. transpiration is high
   D. temperature is high
   E. leaves are injured

5. Contractile vacuoles in protozoa
   A. store food
   B. eliminate excess water
   C. circulate cytoplasm
   D. propel the organisms
   E. digest ingested microorganisms

6. Adding methyl groups to the bases of DNA tends to
   A. have no effect
   B. enhance the transcription speed of those regions
   C. inhibit release of information from those regions
   D. convert those regions into oncogenes
   E. cause frameshift mutations

7. Marsupials are most abundant in
   A. Africa
   B. Australia
   C. southeastern United States
   D. Central America
   E. East Indies

8. Which of these is the most likely method by which new plant species
   can arise in a single generation?
   A. allopolyploidy
   B. natural selection
   C. genetic drift
   D. geographic isolation
   E. transposon transfer

9. Which substances CANNOT normally cross the placenta?
   A. red blood cell antigens
   B. viruses
   C. carbon dioxide
   D. drugs
   E. hormones

10. If the sequence of nucleotides in a gene is T–T–A–C–G–A–G, the
    sequence of nucleotides in mRNA synthesized by that gene is
    A. T–T–A–C–G–A–G
    B. A–A–U–G–C–U–C
    C. A–A–T–G–C–T–C
    D. A–A–T–G–C–T–G
    E. T–T–U–G–C–U–G

11. Magnolias and alligators occur naturally in widely separated areas of the
    southeastern United States and China. This fact is best explained by
    A. convergent evolution
    B. continental drift
    C. survival of the fittest
    D. Pleistocene glaciation
    E. adaptive radiation

12. Biologists use several kinds of microscopes for different purposes. Which of the following statements about them is correct?
    A. The phase contrast microscope is useless for viewing living micro-organisms because the image appears too transparent.
    B. The image in a dissecting microscope is reversed.
    C. The electron microscope achieves a higher magnification than other microscopes because its fluorescent screen is larger than glass lenses.
    D. The stereoscopic microscope is essentially two microscopes that focus on the object from different angles.
    E. The field of view can be enlarged in the compound microscope by changing to an objective with a higher magnification.

13. In situations where coevolution of two species is occurring,
    A. each species is acting upon the other as a selective agent
    B. the two species will quickly become a pair of sibling species
    C. the species are occasionally mating successfully
    D. the species are gradually becoming very similar in some phenotypic feature
    E. one species is always an animal and the other is always a plant

14. Salt marshes are functionally most like
    A. mangrove forests
    B. prairies
    C. savannas
    D. steppes
    E. tundras

15. Which statement about viruses is INCORRECT?
    A. They do not have protoplasm.
    B. They do not take in food.
    C. They do not mutate.
    D. They do not reproduce outside cells.
    E. They do not respire.

16. The arrangement of microtubules in cilia is
    A. 9 + 2
    B. 4 + 4
    C. 2 + 2
    D. 8 + 2
    E. 7 + 3

17. Which of these was the most important evolutionary adaptation for the transition of vertebrate animals onto land from an aquatic environment?
    A. fur
    B. sweat glands
    C. forward-aimed eyes
    D. the amniotic egg
    E. an internal skeleton

18. Which of these is a correct statement about natural selection?
   A. Natural selection is the only force acting to produce evolutionary change.
   B. Polymorphism is essential before natural selection can operate.
   C. A population's environment is not an important factor for the operation of natural selection.
   D. Some organisms in a population are able to pass along to the next generation useful abilities that they have acquired during their lives.
   E. Natural selection requires aggressive encounters among members of a population.

19. The greater risk in childbirth when the mother is Rh-negative and the father is Rh-positive is caused by
   A. antibodies produced by an Rh-positive fetus
   B. the production by an Rh-positive fetus of antigens that are toxic to the Rh-negative mother
   C. Rh-negative antigens produced by the mother
   D. the combined toxic effect of antigens produced by an Rh-negative fetus and the Rh-negative mother
   E. the lack of vigor of all Rh-negative fetuses

20. The sites of particular genes on a chromosome can be determined by
   A. using radioactive tracers
   B. crossing-over of chromosomes
   C. making a back-cross
   D. segregation
   E. base pairing

21. Down syndrome is an example of
   A. monosomy
   B. disomy
   C. trisomy
   D. triploidy
   E. polyploidy

22. One key point in Darwin's theory of evolution is the recognition that
   A. change occurs in big steps called mutations
   B. characteristics acquired during the lifetime of an individual modify genes
   C. individuals of every generation vary in the ability to survive under prevailing conditions
   D. hybridization between existing species accounts for the origin of new species
   E. the direction of evolution is always from simple to complex

23. Slopes of mountains are often covered by several zones of vegetation. Which statement about zones is INCORRECT?
    A. The zone at the top of the mountain is always above timberline.
    B. The zone at the bottom of the mountain is probably the climax vegetation of the region where the mountain is located.
    C. The sequence of zones found at increasing altitudes is similar to the sequence found at increasing latitudes.
    D. Altitude alone cannot account for the size and composition of the zones.
    E. A zone may vary considerably in altitudinal location and floristic composition between the north- and south-facing slopes.

24. An example of a fat is
    A. cellulose
    B. chitin
    C. agar
    D. hemoglobin
    E. stearin

25. DNA-DNA hybridization is valuable for determining evolutionary relationships. This method depends on
    A. causing selective mutations
    B. forcing organisms of different species into attempts at mating
    C. testing DNA from two species for ability to bind and resist subsequent separation
    D. making many copies of DNA by the polymerase chain reaction
    E. reconstructing DNA that was recovered from fossils

26. Grass growing better near the trunk of a tree than several feet away from it indicates that
    A. the tree was recently planted
    B. more fertilizer was applied under the tree
    C. the roots next to the trunk do not absorb water and solutes
    D. grass grows better in the shade
    E. the tap root is damaged

27. It is believed that whales evolved from terrestrial mammals because whales
    A. are vertebrate animals
    B. are viviparous
    C. lack scales on their exterior
    D. protect their young
    E. use lungs for gas exchange

28. Isolated islands are especially valuable for the study of natural selection because
    A. they provide an environment causing unusually high mutation rates
    B. a researcher can quickly analyze all of the organisms on each island
    C. they isolate populations, preventing significant migration that would confound a study of natural selection
    D. they are likely to have a great diversity of species on them
    E. they are ideal models for sympatric speciation

29. The exchange of chromosomal parts between nonhomologous pairs of chromosomes is
  A. inversion
  B. translocation
  C. deletion
  D. duplication
  E. crossing-over

30. The production of which of these is largely under the control of genes NOT carried on nuclear chromosomes?
  A. cytoplasmic enzymes
  B. hormones
  C. mitochondria
  D. nuclear membranes
  E. ribosomes

31. The evolution of a new species is dependent upon isolating mechanisms that prevent mating between individuals of two populations. Which of the following was probably most significant in the evolution of Darwin's finches?
  A. geographical isolation
  B. seasonal isolation
  C. gametic isolation
  D. behavioral isolation
  E. mechanical isolation

32. In free-living protozoans like amoebae, food is digested
  A. by enzymes they secrete into the water
  B. in vacuoles
  C. in the cytoplasm
  D. by bacteria within the cell
  E. by bacteria outside the cell

33. Ciliated epithelium lines the
  A. digestive tract of mammals
  B. oviduct (Fallopian tube) of humans
  C. sperm duct of humans
  D. lung of birds
  E. bladder of mammals

34. Color blindness is more likely to occur in males than females because
  A. males have a tendency to deposit cholesterol in small blood vessels, thereby reducing the oxygen and food supply to the retina
  B. genes for the characteristic are located on the X chromosome
  C. the trait is dominant in males and recessive in females
  D. males require more vitamin A to achieve the same sensitivity in the rods and cones of the retina
  E. some males have difficulty absorbing vitamin A, a necessary prerequisite to the synthesis of visual purple (rhodopsin)

35. Of the following habitats, which covers the largest portion of the Earth?
- **A.** saline water
- **B.** deserts
- **C.** grasslands
- **D.** forests
- **E.** fresh water

36. The presence of three number 21 chromosomes in humans causes a condition known as
- **A.** cleft palate
- **B.** Down syndrome
- **C.** hydrocephaly
- **D.** kuru
- **E.** sickle-cell anemia

37. A major evolutionary advancement of seed plants over any other plants is the
- **A.** acquisition of vascular tissue
- **B.** acquisition of pollen tubes
- **C.** acquisition of fruits
- **D.** acquisition of perennial life spans
- **E.** loss of the gametophytic stage

38. What is a prion?
- **A.** a virus
- **B.** a protein
- **C.** naked DNA
- **D.** a transposon
- **E.** a bacterium

39. Which type of cell in a plant stem is capable of cell division?
- **A.** pith
- **B.** wood
- **C.** cork
- **D.** cambium
- **E.** fiber

40. The pitcher plant is a carnivorous plant that captures and digests insects between two leaves clamped tightly together. If the openings of the leaves are plugged with cotton,
- **A.** the plant will soon starve for lack of food
- **B.** the plant will manufacture its own food
- **C.** the leaves will wither and rot
- **D.** digestive enzymes will quickly dissolve the cotton
- **E.** the leaves will turn yellow for lack of oxygen

41. Which organisms are NOT found in plankton?
A. dinoflagellates
B. green algae
C. diatoms
D. radiolaria
E. sporozoans

42. The brain of a vertebrate animal develops from
A. dorsal ectoderm
B. ganglia
C. mesenchyme
D. notochord
E. the archenteron roof

43. After ceasing physical exertion, a person continues to breathe heavily until
A. accumulated carbon dioxide is removed from the muscles
B. lactic acid is consumed or converted to something else
C. the body cools
D. glycolysis begins
E. the food that was stored in the muscles is replaced

44. One contractile protein in muscles is
A. histidine
B. fibrinogen
C. cytosine
D. oxytocin
E. myosin

45. ATP is used in a cell to
A. accept energy
B. become part of the nuclear membranes
C. regulate membrane permeability
D. store energy
E. digest polysaccharides

46. Which sequence best describes the plant life cycle?
A. zygote → sporophyte
B. spore → sporophyte
C. ovary → seed
D. cotyledon → endosperm
E. integument → pericarp

47. Which statement about photosynthesis is INCORRECT?
A. During the light-dependent phase, water is broken down to hydrogen and oxygen.
B. During the light-independent phase, carbon dioxide is broken down to carbon and oxygen.
C. An end product is fructose diphosphate.
D. Chlorophyll molecules are not used up in the process.
E. NADP combines with free hydrogen.

48. If the flower of a Winesap apple is pollinated by pollen from a Delicious apple, the apple produced by the Winesap flower will be a
    A. Winesap
    B. Delicious
    C. mosaic
    D. new strain
    E. hybrid

49. In which of the following groups are the individuals most closely related?
    A. tick, louse, leech
    B. snake, lizard, salamander
    C. elephant, whale, alligator
    D. clam, snail, slug
    E. starfish, sea lily, sea squirt

50. In humans, the extraembryonic membrane in contact with the uterus is the
    A. allantois
    B. yolk sac
    C. amnion
    D. chorion
    E. endometrium

51. Which of these is an enzyme that performs an important function in the nervous system?
    A. catalase
    B. DNA polymerase
    C. cholinesterase
    D. lysozyme
    E. peptidase

52. The one gene–one enzyme hypothesis resulted from the work of
    A. Beadle and Tatum
    B. Morgan
    C. Conway
    D. Kormondy
    E. Stokes and Kramer

53. Which of these characteristics is evolutionarily most advanced?
    A. foot of human
    B. foot of horse
    C. open circulatory system
    D. pronephric kidney
    E. body supported by two pairs of limbs

54. The Secchi disk is used to
    A. connect vertebrae
    B. filter air
    C. filter water
    D. measure the turbidity of water
    E. polarize light

55. The transfer of genetic material from one bacterial cell to another by a virus is called
   A. transduction
   B. transference
   C. transformation
   D. transfusion
   E. translocation

56. The deliberate setting of fire to pine forests is practiced by foresters for several reasons. The most important one is to
   A. quickly recycle the elements bound in the litter of the forest floor
   B. kill the undergrowth, which is competitive with the pines
   C. kill the pines to make way for hardwoods
   D. thin the trees to provide easier passage and greater visibility for hunters, thus making possible multiple usage of the forest
   E. stimulate root growth

57. The following groups of organisms represent different trophic levels. Which of the five has the greatest biomass?
   A. herbivores
   B. carnivores
   C. autotrophs
   D. scavengers
   E. decomposers

58. Which function does the Golgi complex perform?
   A. secretion
   B. reproduction
   C. regeneration
   D. protein synthesis
   E. sensory perception

59. An organic compound always contains the element
   A. nitrogen
   B. carbon
   C. sulfur
   D. phosphorus
   E. oxygen

60. For mosses to grow as large as most ferns, they would need
   A. less competition from larger plants
   B. stomata in their leaves
   C. better waterproofing of external surfaces
   D. auxins
   E. vascular tissue

61. Of the light that falls on a green plant, approximately what percent is used in photosynthesis?
   A. 1%
   B. 10%
   C. 25%
   D. 50%
   E. 95%

62. Which statement about a particular type of animal is INCORRECT?
   A. Sponges have no muscles.
   B. Cnidaria have no brains.
   C. Tapeworms have no hearts.
   D. Sharks have no bones.
   E. Fish have no livers.

63. When a protein is broken down to its component amino acids, the type of reaction responsible is
   A. a condensation reaction
   B. a deamination reaction
   C. a hydrolysis reaction
   D. a peptide reaction
   E. an anabolic reaction

64. Motor neuron impulses are transmitted to skeletal muscle by
   A. acetylcholine
   B. ATP
   C. secretin
   D. electron transport
   E. sodium ions

65. Which statement about mitosis is INCORRECT?
   A. Prophase takes longer than metaphase or anaphase.
   B. When chromosomes move to the poles, the centromeres lead the way.
   C. During the interphase, all metabolic activity ceases.
   D. Chromosomes are fully formed during prophase.
   E. Mitosis is in telophase when chromosomes reach the poles.

66. The DNA nucleotide is composed of
   A. phosphate, deoxyribose, and a nitrogenous base
   B. purine and pyrimidine
   C. thymine, guanine, cytosine, and adenine
   D. ribose, uracil, and phosphate
   E. polypeptide, purine, and pyrimidine

67. The sex-influenced gene governing the presence of horns in sheep exhibits dominance in males but acts recessively in females. When individuals of the Dorset breed (both sexes horned) with genotype *hh* is crossed with those of the Suffolk breed (both sexes hornless) with genotype *h'h'*, what proportion of the F$_1$ males will be hornless?
- **A.** 0%
- **B.** 100%
- **C.** 25%
- **D.** 50%
- **E.** 75%

68. The wings of a bat are homologous to the
- **A.** two long tentacles of a squid
- **B.** wings of a butterfly
- **C.** arms of a human
- **D.** jumping legs of a grasshopper
- **E.** chelipeds of a lobster

69. The most successful parasite
- **A.** has a life cycle involving a sequence of hosts
- **B.** is permanently attached to the host
- **C.** is highly specialized
- **D.** originated first
- **E.** makes minimal demands on the host

70. An ecological niche is always occupied by
- **A.** a population
- **B.** a small community
- **C.** a host and its parasites
- **D.** a balanced mixture of autotrophic and heterotrophic organisms
- **E.** two or more competing species

71. The function most closely associated with the thylakoid membranes of chloroplasts is
- **A.** gene replication
- **B.** glycolysis
- **C.** oxidative phosphorylation
- **D.** photophosphorylation
- **E.** protein synthesis

72. When a slime mold cell moves toward a source of cyclic AMP, this phenomenon is termed
- **A.** chemotaxis
- **B.** cyclosis
- **C.** cytokinesis
- **D.** pinocytosis
- **E.** plasmolysis

73. All of the following statements about gametophytes are generally true EXCEPT:
    A. Gametophytes have no true roots, stems, or leaves.
    B. The chromosome number of gametophytes is haploid.
    C. Gametophytes are seedless.
    D. Gametophytes grow from spores and produce gametes.
    E. Gametophytes are smaller than sporophytes and parasitic upon them.

74. In which pair of structures, do the two structures NOT have the same embryological origin?
    A. gill pouch and Eustachian tube
    B. penis and clitoris
    C. liver and spleen
    D. lung and pancreas
    E. brain and fingernail

75. Which color of light is LEAST used in photosynthesis?
    A. red
    B. green
    C. yellow
    D. blue
    E. orange

76. During the interphase of mitosis,
    A. chromatin replicates
    B. chromosomes break up into chromatin
    C. nucleoli disappear
    D. chromosomes are distinctly double
    E. homologous chromosomes are paired

77. Leaves are generally well adapted to the environmental conditions where the plants that develop them live. Which statement concerning the relation of leaves to habitat is FALSE?
    A. Leaves on aquatic plants often have large air spaces.
    B. Vertical leaves do not have palisade mesophyll.
    C. Shade leaves tend to be large and thin.
    D. Multiple layers of epidermis are characteristic of leaves submerged in water.
    E. Leaves that are round in cross section conserve water.

78. *Neurospora* ranks as one of the leading subjects for genetic studies. As an experimental organism, *Neurospora* exhibits all of the following characteristics EXCEPT:
    A. It is easily cultured in the laboratory.
    B. It has a short life cycle of about 10 days.
    C. It is normally haploid, meaning that recessive alleles are not masked by dominant ones.
    D. Its meiospores (ascospores) are arranged in ordered tetrads.
    E. Its spores are unaffected by radiation.

79. When a lethal characteristic such as albinism occurs in green plants, the
   A. lethal allele is always dominant
   B. characteristic can occur only because of a new mutation
   C. allele expresses itself in alternate generations
   D. characteristic is carried by green plants into the next generation
   E. cause is viral rather than genetic

80. A green plant with vestigial stomata would be expected to live
   A. on deserts
   B. in water
   C. as a parasite
   D. in the tundra
   E. on salt flats

81. A community is obviously at the climax stage of development when
   A. hardwoods predominate
   B. pines predominate
   C. the number of species is relatively low
   D. the plants are reproducing themselves
   E. the plants are similar

82. Laterization is a process that results in
   A. nitrogen fixation
   B. soil formation
   C. self-sterility
   D. purification of water
   E. deadening of pain

83. Sex attractants secreted by the female silkworm moth belong to a group
of substances known as
   A. flavones
   B. estrogens
   C. auxins
   D. pheromones
   E. secretins

84. A dominant sex-limited allele is known to cause premature baldness in
men but has no effect in women. What proportion of the male offspring
from heterozygous parents will be bald?
   A. 1/4
   B. 3/8
   C. 1/2
   D. 5/8
   E. 3/4

85. The type of chromosomal configuration shown below results from

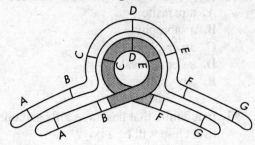

    A. inversion
    B. translocation
    C. deletion
    D. duplication
    E. crossing-over

86. Which of the chromosomal aberrations listed below produces a configuration like the one illustrated?

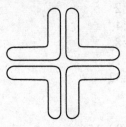

    A. inversion
    B. translocation
    C. deletion
    D. duplication
    E. crossing-over

87. Turgid cells are
    A. dehydrated
    B. swollen
    C. wilted
    D. coagulated
    E. plasmolyzed

88. In plants, cellular respiration occurs in
    A. all cells
    B. all living cells
    C. growing tissues only
    D. all living cells except where photosynthesis is in progress
    E. all living cells except at night

89. Stomata are opened by
    A. auxins
    B. starch accumulation in guard cells
    C. sugar deficiency
    D. photonastic movement
    E. water swelling the guard cells

90. Lichen growing on the bark of a tree would best be characterized as
A. a parasite
B. a saprophyte
C. an epiphyte
D. a commensal
E. a bryophyte

91. In a family that has three girls and one boy, what is the probability that a fifth child will be a boy?
A. 25%
B. 50%
C. 75%
D. 100%
E. 0%

92. If the probability of having genotype *Aa* is 1 in two births, *bb* 1 in four births, and *CC* 1 in four births, what is the chance of having *AabbCC*?
A. 1:2
B. 1:4
C. 1:8
D. 1:16
E. 1:32

Questions 93–156
The next five questions (93–97) are based on the pedigree of a family afflicted with hemophilia. The characteristic is recessive and sex-linked. Study the relationships carefully, and answer the questions accordingly.

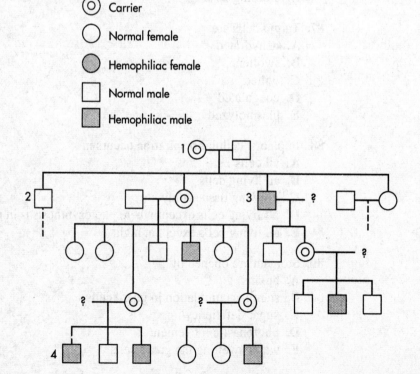

93. The genotype of individual 1 is
   A. unknown
   B. probably heterozygous
   C. definitely heterozygous
   D. definitely homozygous recessive
   E. probably homozygous recessive

94. If individual 3 marries a normal woman and fathers several children, all
   A. children will be normal
   B. children will be hemophiliac
   C. males will be normal
   D. males will be carriers
   E. females will be normal

95. On the basis of the information available, individual 2
   A. could have a carrier mother
   B. must have had a normal father
   C. must have had two normal parents
   D. could father a hemophiliac daughter
   E. could father a carrier son

96. If individual 4 marries a normal woman, what is the chance that their child will be hemophiliac?
   A. 0%
   B. 25%
   C. 50%
   D. 74%
   E. 100%

97. Let H represent the normal allele, h the hemophilia allele, and O the absence of either allele. What are the genotypes of individuals 1, 2, and 3, respectively?
   A. *Hh, hO, HO*
   B. unknown, *hO, HO*
   C. *Hh, HO, hO*
   D. unknown, *hO,* unknown
   E. *Hh, HH, hh*

The next four questions (98–101) consist of a group of lettered headings and numbered biomes. For each numbered biome select the lettered heading which characterizes many of the plants that live therein, and mark the answer accordingly. Any one of the headings may be used one or more times or not at all.

   A. stiltlike roots
   B. drip tips
   C. succulents
   D. diminutive trees
   E. autumn leaf coloration

98. deciduous forest

99. mangrove forest

100. tropical rain forest

101. desert

The next four questions (102–105) are based on the trophic pyramid illustrated below. The trophic levels in the pyramid are labeled with letters. For each question select the lettered trophic level that corresponds to it, and mark the answer accordingly. Any one of the lettered levels may be used one or more times or not at all.

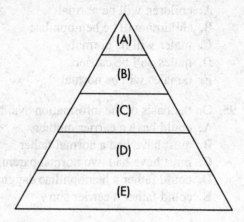

102. primary consumers

103. secondary consumers

104. tertiary consumers

105. producers

The next six questions (106–111) consist of lettered structures and numbered descriptive phrases. For each numbered phrase select the appropriate lettered structure, and mark the answer accordingly. Any of the lettered structures may be used one or more times or not at all.

A. zygote
B. erythrocyte
C. pollen
D. Schwann cell
E. sperm

106. usually consists of more than one cell

107. is a single haploid cell

108. in humans, lacks chromatin when fully differentiated

109. is a highly differentiated cell associated with rapid nerve transmission

110. is the immediate result of fertilization

111. is the only structure in the list capable of prolonged life away from a watery environment

The next five questions (112–116) consist of lettered biological phenomena and numbered descriptions or examples. For each numbered description select the appropriate lettered phenomenon, and mark the answer accordingly. Any of the lettered phenomena may be used one or more times or not at all.

A. Batesian mimicry
B. cryptic coloration
C. heterozygote superiority
D. Müllerian mimicry
E. sexual dimorphism

112. A species of fly looks and sounds like a wasp, but cannot sting.

113. A bee and a wasp both have yellow and black stripes.

114. Carriers of the sickle-cell hemoglobin allele have selective advantage over other individuals in certain environments.

115. The fish known as a flounder can match with its skin pigments the pattern of the background environment.

116. This phenomenon leads to recognition between potential mates.

The next four questions (117–120) consist of lettered animals and numbered descriptions of nervous systems. For each numbered description select the appropriate lettered animal, and mark the answer accordingly. Any of the lettered animals may be used one or more times or not at all.

A. cat
B. hydra
C. planaria
D. shark
E. sponge

117. It has no central nervous system but possesses neurons.

118. Its cerebrum dominates other brain regions.

119. Its brain is a collection of neurons without any regions corresponding to those of a human brain.

120. It is characterized by a brain that has a relatively large olfactory region.

The next five questions (121–125) consist of lettered groups within kingdom Animalia and numbered descriptions. For each numbered description select the appropriate lettered group, and mark the answer accordingly. Any of the lettered groups may be used one or more times or not at all.

A. Annelida
B. Arthropoda
C. Chordata
D. Insecta
E. Porifera

121. the phylum that includes colonial, benthic animals

122. the group that includes the earthworms

123. the class that includes externally segmented animals with exoskeletons

124. the phylum whose members have an open circulatory system

125. the group in this list with the largest number of living species

The next five questions (126–130) consist of lettered regions of a bacterial chromosome's inducible gene system (see diagram below) and numbered questions about the regions. For each numbered question select the appropriate lettered region, and mark the answer accordingly. Any of the lettered regions may be used one or more times or not at all.

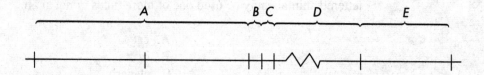

126. Since area *A* is a pair of structural genes containing codes for building enzymes, which area is the operator?

127. Which is the region that carries the code for building a functional repressor protein?

128. Which is the region to which a functional repressor protein can attach, leading to repression?

129. Which area manufactures a product only when an inducer molecule is in the cell?

130. Which region is the first to be touched by RNA polymerase if the system is to operate?

The next five questions (131–135) consist of lettered substances and numbered descriptions. For each numbered description select the appropriate lettered substance, and mark the answer accordingly. Any lettered substance may be used one or more times or not at all.

A. calcium
B. collagen
C. epinephrine
D. indoleacetic acid
E. pyruvic acid

131. a substance made in animals and plants

132. a substance that is not a molecule

133. a plant hormone

134. an animal hormone

135. a protein

The next three questions (136–138) consist of lettered cell structures and numbered descriptions of muscle. For each numbered description select the appropriate lettered structure, and mark the answer accordingly. Any of the lettered structures may be used one or more times or not at all.

A. endoplasmic reticulum
B. myoneuronal junction
C. sarcomere
D. sarcoplasmic reticulum
E. transverse tubule

136. the portion of skeletal muscle that contracts

137. a membrane system that carries an action potential deep inside a muscle fiber

138. a membrane system that can operate an active transport pump which keeps calcium ions from a muscle fiber's contractile proteins

The next five questions (139–143) consist of lettered ecologically important concepts and numbered descriptions. For each numbered description select the appropriate lettered concept, and mark the answer accordingly. Any of the lettered concepts may be used one or more times or not at all.

A. carrying capacity
B. chemosynthesis
C. food web
D. greenhouse effect
E. symbiosis

139. an increase of atmospheric temperature caused by carbon dioxide's absorption of infrared rays

140. a complex interaction among producers and consumers

141. ability of an organism to gain energy from a nonliving source other than the sun

142. the maximum size of a population in a particular ecosystem

143. long-term interaction between species

The next four questions (144–147) consist of lettered vertebrate hormones and numbered descriptions. For each numbered description select the appropriate lettered hormone, and mark the answer accordingly. Any of the lettered hormones may be used one or more times or not at all.

    A. follicle-stimulating hormone
    B. insulin
    C. parathyroid hormone
    D. progesterone
    E. testosterone

144. is a pituitary hormone influencing reproduction

145. helps prepare the uterus wall for nurture of an embryo

146. is produced by the pancreas

147. stimulates the growth of facial hair

The next four questions (148–151) consist of lettered plant structures and numbered descriptions. For each numbered description select the appropriate lettered structure, and mark the answer accordingly. Any of the lettered structures may be used one or more times or not at all.

    A. adventitious roots
    B. haustorial roots
    C. fibrous roots
    D. prop roots
    E. taproots

148. roots of dodder, a parasitic plant

149. roots of dandelions

150. roots of carrots

151. roots of grass

The next five questions (152–156) consist of lettered organisms and numbered descriptions. For each numbered description select the appropriate lettered organism, and mark the answer accordingly. Any of the lettered organisms may be used one or more times or not at all.

    A. bacterium
    B. fruit fly (*Drosophila*)
    C. human
    D. *Neurospora*
    E. virus

152. Some of these use RNA as their chromosomal material.

153. This organism was the first in which sex linkage of genes was shown.

154. These organisms can transfer genes by conjugation.

155. Crossing-over analysis of regions within a single gene was first performed with this organism.

156. Avery, MacLeod, and McCarty used this organism to demonstrate for the first time that DNA can be the carrier of genetic information.

The remaining questions ask for analysis of experiments. For each set, read the descriptions and data carefully; then answer the questions or complete the statements by choosing among the lettered alternatives and marking your answers accordingly.

Questions 157–160

A number of species of moths living in industrial areas of Britain have two color forms, light and dark. A dark form was first observed in 1850 and has since become common. Both forms of moths settle on trunks of trees when at rest. In some places soot from homes and factories have destroyed bark lichens and blackened the bark with deposits. Light-colored moths are conspicuous on dark bark and inconspicuous on light bark, whereas dark-colored moths are conspicuous on light bark and inconspicuous on dark bark. Doubtless, the ability to blend with the background is a protection from birds that are known to feed on moths. The development of melanin in insects in general is known to be achieved by both dominant and recessive genes. In the case of the dark moths, however, all known genetic information confirms that melanism is spread by a dominant gene.

157. The evolution of dark moths from light ones can be attributed to
    A. gene mutations caused by soot
    B. gene mutations induced by need
    C. gene mutations occurring accidentally
    D. absence of recessive genes for dark forms
    E. light moths being more susceptible to gene mutations than dark ones

158. There is sufficient evidence to conclude that
  A. gene mutations for melanism did not originate before 1850
  B. a change in the environment accelerated favorable mutations
  C. birds feed mostly on light-colored moths
  D. colored forms reproduce faster than light forms
  E. similar mutations can occur in different organisms

159. If melanism is inherited as a simple dominant characteristic, what would be expected if a heterozygous dark moth was crossed with a homozygous light moth?
  A. All offspring would be dark.
  B. All offspring would be light.
  C. All offspring would be intermediate between dark and light.
  D. Half of the offspring would be dark and half light.
  E. Three-fourths of the offspring would be dark and one-fourth light.

160. If the environment could suddenly revert to its original condition before industrialization came, the effect on moths would be that
  A. genes for melanism would mutate back to the original condition
  B. dark-colored moths, being less well concealed, would be eliminated by birds faster than light-colored ones
  C. light-colored moths would reproduce faster than dark-colored ones
  D. light-colored moths would breed primarily with light-colored mates
  E. the proportion of light-colored individuals would increase as a result of light-colored forms mating with dark-colored forms

Questions 161–163

The next three questions are based on the information given in the sketches of five quadrats that follow. The numbers inside the quadrats stand for five species of organisms. Each number represents an individual.

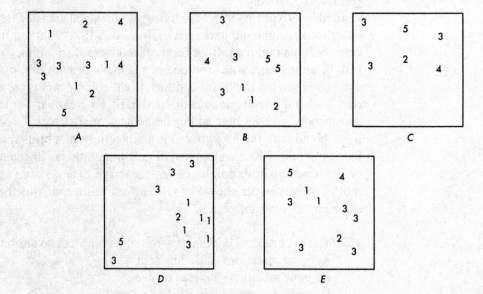

161. It is obvious from the information given that
  A. species 1 has a density of 12
  B. species 2 has a density of 6/5 or 1.2
  C. species 3 has a density of 60
  D. species 4 has a density of 40
  E. species 5 has a density of 100%

162. The correct frequency for
  A. species 1 is 80%
  B. species 2 is 6
  C. species 3 is 4
  D. species 4 is 1
  E. species 5 is 120%

163. Which statement is correct about the relative importance of the five species?
  A. The data given are insufficient to determine the *importance value* of each species.
  B. It is obvious from the sketches that species 3 is the most important species present.
  C. Species 3 is more important than species 1 because it is found in all of the quadrats.
  D. Species 1 is more important than species 2 because it is twice as abundant.
  E. Species 2 and species 5 are equally important because they occur in equal numbers.

Questions 164–167

A survivorship curve is a graphic representation of the relation between the life span of individuals in a population and the maximum life span for the species. The graph below is a composite of the survivorship curves for four species of animal.

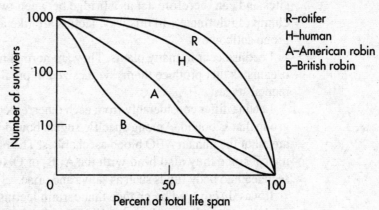

164. Which species has the longest life span?
  A. American robin
  B. British robin
  C. human
  D. rotifer
  E. impossible to determine from the curves

165. Which species has the greatest mortality in the first portion of its maximum life span?

    A. American robin

    B. British robin

    C. human

    D. rotifer

    E. impossible to determine from the curves

166. Which of these figures is closest to the percentage of American robins remaining from a population of 1000 when 50% of the maximum life time was reached?

    A. 0.05%

    B. 0.5%

    C. 5%

    D. 50%

    E. 75%

167. Which one of these would be the explanation LEAST biologically plausible for the difference in survival curves between the American robin and the British robin?

    A. The British robin does not have as efficient a set of instincts for parental care.

    B. The British robin has a different set of predators which are more efficient in capturing very young birds.

    C. The American robin is more successful in obtaining food early in life.

    D. The American robin population has a greater proportion of females, which live longer than males.

    E. The American robin has a less conspicuous color.

Questions 168–174

Lectins are proteins capable of binding to certain sugars on the surfaces of cells. These proteins are also called agglutinins because each has multiple binding sites and can therefore act as a bridge between two cells, causing the cells to clump (agglutinate). In this way, lectins are like antibodies such as the blood group antibodies.

Lectins occur in many plants. They are normal molecular components of the organisms that produce them, synthesized in predictable regions and developmental stages.

Lectins differ considerably from each other, especially in size and in the sugar group that is bound. Among specific sugars bound by lectins of different plants are all of the human ABO blood saccharides. The blood group lectins have been useful since they also bind with the A, B, or O antigens that are sometimes secreted into body fluids such as saliva and urine.

It was discovered by chance that certain lectins bind preferentially to (and agglutinate) malignant human cells. This fact became the basis for a powerful diagnostic tool, but it also led workers to focus for the first time upon the plasma membrane as a fundamentally changed portion of a malignantly transformed cell. Some important theories of cancer are now based upon plasma membrane changes. Other workers have discovered similar changes in cells during the course of normal animal development. For instance, a lectin from the jack bean agglutinates cells obtained from the retina of an 8-day chick embryo, but will not bind cells from the retina of a chick near hatching age. It was at first believed that such changes involve changes in the number of lectin-binding sugar molecules on a cell's surface. However, when radioactively labeled lectins were added to normal and to cancerous cells (the former failing to agglutinate, the latter agglutinating), it was found that the two cell types had bound the same number of lectin molecules per cell. Fluorescently labeled lectin molecules were then used to see whether the two cell types had their binding sugars distributed differently. Examination of the cells under the fluorescence microscope showed that normal cells have random distribution of binding sites, but malignant cells have their binding cites clustered in one or a few small areas.

The biological function of lectins within the organisms that produce them has been hard to determine. Wheat-germ agglutinin may inhibit growth of certain fungi that attack the seed. Other plants may be producing specific lectins as protective agents against their own pathogens.

168. How are lectins different from antibodies?
   A. Antibodies act as catalysts.
   B. Antibodies are specific in their choice of antigens; lectins attach to any sugar group.
   C. Antibodies cannot bind to sugar groups.
   D. Lectins are proteins.
   E. Lectins are routinely present in certain plants; they do not arise only in response to the introduction of antigen.

169. Why is human blood type O-specific lectin especially useful?
   A. Human anti-O antibody is hard to purify.
   B. The lectin also binds specifically to cancer cells.
   C. The lectin is larger than any other antibody.
   D. Nearly no human manufactures antibody against type O blood cell antigen, since the vast majority of humans produce this antigen.
   E. People with type O blood are somewhat more susceptible to heart disease than are other people.

170. What is the most plausible explanation for the presence in a plant of a protein that binds to animal blood cells?
   A. Both animals and plants have common pathogenic organisms to combat.
   B. Some saccharides of identical form are widely distributed among organisms; therefore, a valuable lectin for a plant may cross-react with animal cells that carry the same binding site.
   C. The animal eats plant material and incorporates intact some of the plant molecules into its own cells.
   D. The plant or its ancestors must have been previously exposed to the animal cells.
   E. The two cross-reacting organisms are much more closely related than previously suspected.

171. What significant fact does the preferential binding of certain lectins to malignant cells indicate about cancer?

   A. An important distinguishing feature about cancerous cells is their surface membrane structure.
   B. Cells gain many more lectin-binding sites as they become cancerous.
   C. Embryonic cells also bind lectins.
   D. There is a hitherto unsuspected link between cancer and pathogenic fungi.
   E. Cancers might be successfully treated with extracts of wheat.

172. From the research with lectins described in the passage, what is a logical conclusion concerning animal embryos?

   A. Their blood groups change in a predictable manner.
   B. Their cell surfaces undergo programmed molecular changes as the cells differentiate.
   C. They can be invaded by pathogenic bacteria or fungi.
   D. They change lectins as they differentiate.
   E. They have cancerous cells.

173. What is the best explanation for the fact that malignant cells are clumped by a particular agglutinin, but normal cells are not?

   A. A malignant cell concentrates its binding sites in a few places, leading to the possibility that a strong bridge will form between cells.
   B. A malignant cell has the ability to change the shape of a lectin to match its surface saccharides.
   C. A malignant cell spreads its binding sites evenly over the cell surface, so that two cells can be bound by lectin as opposite shores of a river are joined by a bridge.
   D. A malignant cell turns on genes to manufacture lectin-specific sugars that were not produced before.
   E. Malignant cells can make their own lectins.

174. According to the passage, what technique showed that the distribution of lectin-binding sites on a cell can change during the cell's lifetime?

   A. fluorescent-antibody labeling
   B. fluorescent-lectin labeling
   C. observation of agglutination at one time and nonagglutination at another time
   D. radioactive tagging of binding-site sugars
   E. radioactive tagging of lectin

Questions 175–179

The kangaroo rat is adapted for life in the desert. It saves water by concentrating its urinary urea to 1.6 times the value for a laboratory rat. It also conserves water by spending daylight hours in a cool, humid burrow, thus avoiding water loss for thermoregulation.

Furthermore, it saves much of the water that would usually be lost in exhalation. The kangaroo rat's nose is set up anatomically to operate as a countercurrent exchange system. Inhaled air, cooler than the body core, flows through tiny passageways, progressively becoming warmed by surrounding blood-filled tissue. A gradient of warmth is set up along the passageways, which become warmer as they approach the lungs. The farther the inhaled air moves, the warmer it gets by transfer of heat from nearby tissues; the farther exhalation air moves, the cooler it gets by transfer of heat to passageway walls. The outermost end of the kangaroo rat's nasal passage is actually cooler than incoming dry air because of evaporation of water from its surface into the incoming air. Thus, exhalation air, just before it leaves the animal, passes walls cooler than the outside world, and this air is cooled to nearly that extent. This cooling conserves water. Air entering the nose from the lungs is saturated with water. Dropping the air's temperature causes it to lose some of this water via condensation on the walls of the exhalation passage.

A camel has another device for saving even more water: a hygroscopic surface is provided to catch water vapor in exhalation air. When inhaling extremely dry air, the camel undergoes drying of the nasal passage walls. Dry mucus and debris act like filter paper, absorbing water from exhalation air. This surface is alternately dried and wetted with each inhalation and exhalation, changing the state of the water but losing very little to the outside.

175. Considering the method by which the kangaroo rat's nasal system works, it appears that the MAJOR need of this animal is to
   A. provide a hygroscopic surface
   B. remove excess heat
   C. remove excess water
   D. save water
   E. warm incoming air before it reaches the lungs

176. Which of these activities is NOT utilized to any great extent by a kangaroo rat?
   A. avoiding high ambient temperatures
   B. cooling exhalation air by relying on a countercurrent heat exchange system
   C. cooling exhalation air by relying on condensation of water from it
   D. cooling the body by relying on evaporation of water from surfaces
   E. conserving water by urine concentration

177. What is a hygroscopic surface?
   A. one that cools nearby air
   B. one that has a countercurrent exchange capacity
   C. one that is always covered with moist mucus
   D. one that is dry and porous, capable of absorbing water
   E. one with a large surface area

178. Which of these is the best description of a kangaroo rat's nasal area?
   A. It alternates between having dry walls and having moist walls.
   B. It consists of narrow, long passages having intimate contact with blood-filled tissues.
   C. It features an area of contact at the outside end with vessels carrying very cold blood.
   D. It is a very wide cavern, rather than a narrow tube.
   E. There are separate inhalation and exhalation passageways, running parallel and close to each other.

179. Countercurrent exchange systems have been found in other physiological systems. One of these is the
  A. flow of blood through a mammalian heart
  B. loop of Henle in the nephron
  C. retina pattern
  D. sliding filament system of skeletal muscle
  E. synapse between a neuron and a muscle

Questions 180–186

The single-celled flagellate *Gonyaulax* contains chlorophyll but has the additional feature of producing light. It produces both luciferin and luciferase as part of the same light-producing system as that of a firefly. Light flashes can be elicited by shaking a culture of the organisms. When a photomultiplier tube is used to measure the amount of light emitted, it is found that the quantity per shake is dependent upon the time of day. A great deal of luminescence occurs after only slight shaking at night, but a much lower quantity of light results from even violent shaking at midday. At any time, the light intensity varies directly with the intensity of agitation.

This cyclic change in response, regulated by an internal 24-hour "clock," is shown in Graph 1. When a culture is artificially subjected to constant darkness, the luminescent response pattern occurs as shown in Graph 2. The change illustrated in Graph 2 can be reversed by short periods of illumination. The wavelengths that will reverse the change are those that are most active in initiating photosynthesis. A culture placed in continuous illumination produces luminescence in a pattern similar to that of Graph 2.

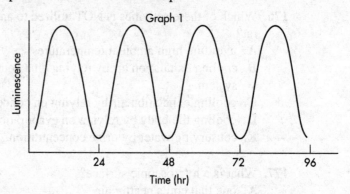

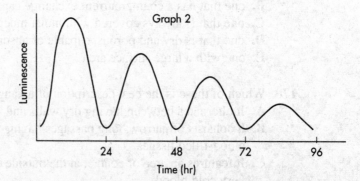

The cycling of luminescence is not very dependent upon temperature. From 16° to 27°C the pattern persists, although the frequency decreases slightly as temperature rises.

The phase of a rhythm is the time of day at which a particular activity occurs. The phasing of the luminescence cycle of *Gonyaulax* under natural lighting conditions has already been described. To change a culture's phase, one subjects it to light sometime while it is doing what it normally does in darkness. The type of light used in an attempted phase change is critical. The most useful light has a wavelength of 254, 475, or 650 nanometers. None of these represents light that is useful in initiating photosynthesis in chlorophyll *a*. The phase-changing light spectra of other organisms are not the same as those for *Gonyaulax*. The phasing of luminescence can also be reset by large temperature changes over several hours, but not by small changes or changes that last for a short time. If two cultures working in different 24-hour phases are mixed together, each group continues in its own patterns, neither one influencing the other to change its phase.

180. From the information in the passage, which of the these is the most accurate statement about *Gonyaulax*?
   A. *Gonyaulax* probably uses a different phase-change receptor molecule than do some other species.
   B. Movement of the organism from one location to another is necessary for phase-changing.
   C. Phase-changing cannot be initiated by ultraviolet light.
   D. The phase-changing molecule is probably chlorophyll *a*.
   E. The phase-changing molecule is probably luciferase.

181. Which of these proves the presence of a 24-hour periodicity based on an internal "clock" mechanism in *Gonyaulax* cells?
   A. continuance of the periodicity when cultures are in constant darkness
   B. elicitation of luminescence by shaking
   C. gradual loss of luminescence intensity as cultures remain in constant darkness
   D. presence of luciferin and luciferase in the cells
   E. simple observation of the periodicity during normal days and nights

182. What is the adaptive significance of this "clock's" periodicity (24-hour cycle) being relatively independent of temperature?
   A. An important "clock" would be hopelessly inaccurate if affected by temperature fluctuations.
   B. High temperature damages molecules that might be responsible for the periodicity.
   C. There is no value in this relative independence of temperature because the watery environment of *Gonyaulax* remains relatively unchanged.
   D. There is no value in this relative independence of temperature because the phasing is much more important than the periodicity.
   E. There is no value in this relative independence of temperature because temperature changes always correspond with changes in light availability.

183. If the "clock" were dependent upon temperature, and if it depended also upon biochemical reaction, what would be the expected trend as temperature rises?

A. "Clock" would speed up, doubling its rate for every rise of 10°.
B. "Clock" would slow down, halving its rate for every rise of 10°.
C. "Clock" would remain unaffected.
D. "Clock" would speed up, 1 min per degree of rise.
E. "Clock" would slow down, 1 min per degree of rise.

184. In obtaining the results used to make Graphs 1 and 2, a worker would have to be careful to

A. avoid shaking the culture while light intensity was being measured
B. obtain each data point on the same day of the week
C. obtain each data point at the same time of day
D. shake the culture more violently in the "clock's" day period than in its night period
E. shake the culture with the same degree of violence each time

185. The periodicity display by *Gonyaulax* is

A. annual
B. circadian
C. hourly
D. lunar
E. tidal

186. What is the relationship between photosynthesis and the ability to luminesce?

A. If photosynthesis is stopped, the organism continues a luminescent cycle, but the intensity drops after each succeeding cycle.
B. There is no relationship, since phase-changing is accomplished by wavelengths not used in photosynthesis.
C. Photosynthesis produces luciferin.
D. The ability to detect the period of time between luminescence activities is totally dependent upon photosynthesis.
E. Luminescence, a production of light, allows a significant amount of photosynthesis to occur at night.

Questions 187–192

When a mouse tumor was transplanted to the body wall of a 2-day chick embryo, nearby nerve fibers enlarged and grew into the tumor mass. Although both sensory and motor neurons were in the region, only the sensory neurons responded and connected to the tumor. When the same type of tumor was placed on a chick chorioallantoic membrane (in contact with the chick's bloodstream but not near its body mass), all of the sympathetic and sensory ganglia increased in size.

A chemical agent of the tumor was sought. Called nerve growth factor (NGF), it was isolated and characterized as a protein. This material was found also in the submaxillary glands of adult mice. NGF caused the same stimulation of chick embryo ganglia as the tumor did. It also caused growth of ganglia cultures *in vitro*.

Antibodies to NGF caused several changes when injected into normal embryos. Sympathetic and sensory neurons were destroyed all over the body. Significant but less severe damage to sympathetic, but not sensory, neurons occurred after injection of anti-NGF into adult animals. Embryos or adults treated with anti-NGF were able to continue normal life activities despite the radical loss of sympathetic ganglia.

Radioactively labeled NGF was injected into chick embryos. Autoradiography showed that this material attached to the membranes of neurons at their terminal ends, and then traveled up the axons to the cell bodies in the dorsal root ganglia. If this flow was blocked by chemical destruction of axonal microtubules, the neurons died.

When an NGF-impregnated block was placed in a culture vessel also containing a sensory ganglion, axons grew toward the block in a nonrandom fashion.

187. Which of these showed that a nerve-stimulating chemical exists and is released by certain tissues?
   A. injecting an embryo with anti-NGF
   B. placing a mouse tumor in the body of a chick embryo
   C. placing a mouse tumor on a chick's chorioallantoic membrane
   D. observing motor neurons connect only to muscles
   E. observing neurons grow toward their target tissue

188. Which of these is a correct statement?
   A. Absence of NGF leads to death or severe neural symptoms.
   B. At least some dependence of neurons upon NGF occurs in mature adults.
   C. Both sensory and sympathetic neurons are adversely affected if an animal is deprived of NGF by treatment after reaching adulthood.
   D. If NGF is placed on a chick's chorioallantoic membrane, sympathetic neurons will grow out to innervate that membrane.
   E. Radioactively labeled NGF damages ganglia.

189. Which experiment showed that NGF must be supplied specifically to a neuron's cell body in order to keep the neuron alive?
   A. autoradiographical analysis of NGF's travel route in the body
   B. depriving a cultured ganglion of NGF
   C. destruction of the cell's microtubules
   D. injecting an embryo with anti-NGF
   E. placing a mouse tumor on a chick's chorioallantoic membrane

190. What is nerve growth factor?
   A. a protein capable of promoting growth only of sympathetic neurons
   B. a protein capable of promoting growth of both sympathetic and sensory neurons
   C. a nonprotein chemical promoting growth of neurons into mouse submaxillary glands
   D. a protein capable of promoting growth of some neurons but unable to specify the direction of that growth
   E. a protein of the class called antibodies

191. Autoradiography was an important tool in one of the experiments cited. To perform autoradiography one must have

A. a centrifuge

B. a Geiger counter

C. a scintillation counter

D. heavy lead shielding

E. some photographic emulsion

192. Which of the following experiments shows that NGF is responsible for specific connections being made, such as a motor neuron attaching to a muscle rather than to epidermis?

A. not shown by cited experiments

B. purification of nerve growth factor

C. transplanting a mouse tumor to a chick embryo's body

D. transplanting a mouse tumor to a chick's chorioallantoic membrane

E. treating a chick embryo with antibody to nerve growth factor

Questions 193–196

Beggiatoa, a large sulfur bacterium, was tested for its ability to allow various molecules to cross its plasma membrane. Graph 1 relates the permeabilities of these molecules to their relative sizes. Permeability was measured by determining for each molecule the environmental concentration that caused lysis of cells.

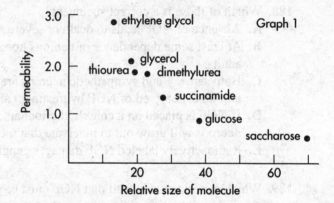

The partition coefficient of a molecule is the ratio of its solubility in lipid to its solubility in water. Graph 2 shows the relationship between the partition coefficients of certain molecules and their permeability through *Beggiatoa* membranes.

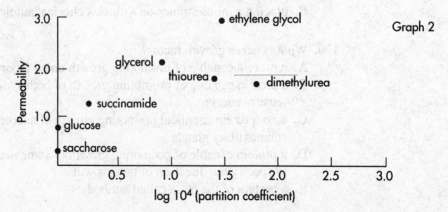

193. What is the relationship between the "permeability" of a molecule and the environmental concentration of the molecule capable of causing lysis of a cell?
   A. The greater the permeability, the greater the environmental concentration needed to lyse.
   B. The greater the permeability, the lower the environmental concentration needed to lyse.
   C. The greater the permeability, the larger the partition coefficient.
   D. The greater the permeability, the larger the size of the molecule.
   E. There is no obvious relationship between these two properties.

194. Which molecule has a significantly lower ability to enter a cell than its solubility in lipid would indicate?
   A. dimethylurea
   B. ethylene glycol
   C. glucose
   D. glycerol
   E. succinamide

195. Which of the following is a correct statement?
   A. Although not very soluble in lipids, saccharose is able to enter a cell easily because of its size.
   B. Dimethylurea is less soluble in lipids than is thiourea.
   C. Ethylene glycol enters a cell very easily because it is both small and very soluble in lipids.
   D. Glucose enters a cell faster than saccharose because glucose is more soluble in lipids.
   E. Glycerol enters a cell faster than glucose because glycerol is larger.

196. Why was the partition coefficient of these molecules a logical measurement to take?
   A. A cell's plasma membrane is largely lipid.
   B. Most of a cell's membrane is water.
   C. The plasma membrane is a partition.
   D. The partition coefficient is directly indicative of a molecule's size.
   E. The partition coefficient is the easiest measurement to take.

Questions 197–200
The relationship between monkey mothers and monkey infants was studied using artificial surrogate "mothers." Each "mother" had some lifelike features and some features different from those of a real mother. Two types of surrogate were used. One, "wire," consisted of a bare welded wire cylinder topped by a block of wood with a crude face painted on it. The other surrogate, "cloth," was covered with fuzzy cloth and had a more lifelike face. Either could include a bottle of milk.

One group of infants was supplied with both surrogate types, but only the cloth "mothers" gave milk. A second group, also with equal access to both types of "mothers," could obtain milk only from the wire "mothers." Both groups thrived physiologically. The graph shows how much time each group spent with the surrogates.

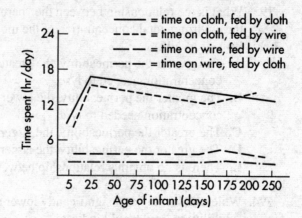

A second phase of the research involved observing an infant as it encountered a stressful situation. When an infant was temporarily placed in a different room containing a variety of inanimate objects, it showed signs of fear. The table below shows an attempt to attach quantitative values to displays of stress. A high emotionality score indicates great stress.

Group	Emotionality Score with No "Mother" Present	Emotionality Score with Cloth "Mother" Present	Emotionality Score with Wire "Mother" Present
Reared with equal access to both "mothers"	3.1	1.3	—
Reared with cloth "mother"	2.8	1.5	—
Reared with wire "mother"	4.9	—	5.0
Reared with no "mother"	2.8	3.9	—

197. What physical difference between the two types of surrogates proved to be more important than any other in attracting infants?
   A. the color of the "body"
   B. the "face"
   C. the size of the "body"
   D. the texture of the "body"
   E. This is not determinable from the data.

198. Which statement is supported by the data from this research project?
   A. Affection toward a mother is learned or derived solely from the reduction of hunger that is associated with it.
   B. Infants spent more time clinging to a suitable "mother" figure than was needed for gaining milk.
   C. Mother-infant contact during nursing provides no psychological benefit.
   D. The position of the milk-providing apparatus helps determine whether an infant will accept a surrogate "mother."
   E. Surrogate "mothers" that did not supply any milk were nevertheless accepted by the infants.

199. The data of the table indicate that

    A. emotional dependence on a mother may be a result of imprinting

    B. infants that have had contact with any "mother," whether wire or cloth, quickly learn to accept comfort from a cloth "mother"

    C. infants that have had no previous experience with a mother, real or surrogate, show significantly less anxiety when left alone than do those who have come to depend upon a mother

    D. the amount of time an infant spends with a surrogate "mother" before being placed in a stressful environment helps determine the level of anxiety that will occur when left alone

    E. the infant behavior shown by this experiment is completely instinctive

200. What would be the best way to test endurance of the preference for a cloth "mother"?

    A. Mate two "cloth-preference" infants when they reach maturity, and observe the preference of their offspring.

    B. Continuously keep infants in rooms that have both wire and cloth surrogates.

    C. Erect a nearly insurmountable barrier between an infant and a cloth "mother," but place no such obstacle in front of a wire "mother."

    D. Provide an infant with several wire "mothers" per cloth "mother."

    E. Remove the cloth surrogates from the presence of infants raised with them, and then return them after a period of time.

Answer Key for Sample Test 4

Use this key to obtain a score for Test 4. Then use the answer explanations on the following pages to gain a better understanding of the concepts needed to answer all questions correctly.

1. D	41. E	81. D	121. E	161. B
2. A	42. A	82. B	122. A	162. A
3. A	43. B	83. D	123. D	163. A
4. B	44. E	84. E	124. B	164. E
5. B	45. D	85. A	125. B	165. B
6. C	46. A	86. B	126. B	166. C
7. B	47. B	87. B	127. E	167. D
8. A	48. A	88. B	128. B	168. E
9. A	49. D	89. E	129. A	169. D
10. D	50. D	90. C	130. C	170. B
11. D	51. C	91. B	131. E	171. A
12. D	52. A	92. E	132. A	172. B
13. A	53. B	93. C	133. D	173. A
14. A	54. D	94. C	134. C	174. B
15. C	55. A	95. A	135. B	175. D
16. A	56. B	96. A	136. C	176. D
17. D	57. C	97. C	137. E	177. D
18. B	58. A	98. E	138. D	178. B
19. B	59. B	99. A	139. D	179. B
20. B	60. E	100. B	140. C	180. A
21. C	61. A	101. C	141. B	181. A
22. C	62. E	102. D	142. A	182. A
23. A	63. C	103. C	143. E	183. A
24. E	64. A	104. B	144. A	184. E
25. C	65. C	105. E	145. D	185. B
26. C	66. A	106. C	146. B	186. A
27. E	67. A	107. E	147. E	187. C
28. C	68. C	108. B	148. B	188. B
29. B	69. E	109. D	149. E	189. C
30. C	70. A	110. A	150. E	190. B
31. A	71. D	111. C	151. C	191. E
32. B	72. A	112. A	152. E	192. A
33. B	73. E	113. D	153. B	193. B
34. B	74. C	114. C	154. A	194. A
35. A	75. B	115. B	155. E	195. C
36. B	76. A	116. E	156. A	196. A
37. B	77. D	117. B	157. C	197. E
38. B	78. E	118. A	158. E	198. B
39. D	79. D	119. C	159. D	199. A
40. B	80. B	120. D	160. B	200. E

Answer Explanations for Sample Test 4

1. **(D)** Ribosomes are tiny cytoplasmic granules, free in the cytoplasm or attached to the endoplasmic reticulum. Proteins (or protein subunits) are assembled on ribosomes. In composition, ribosomes are rich in RNA and proteins.

2. **(A)** NAD is nicotinamide adenine dinucleotide. A second hydrogen-transport molecule active during the Krebs cycle is FAD, flavin adenine dinucleotide. Both molecules carry hydrogen and associated energy to ATP-manufacturing sites within mitochondria.

3. **(A)** Pith is a primary tissue. Primary tissues are produced by growing tips. Secondary tissues are added outside the pith and primary xylem, both of which persist indefinitely, barring the absence of decay.

4. **(B)** Guttation is the elimination of excess water in liquid form. Water accumulates in drops, particularly at the tips or along the margins of leaves, and is usually given off from special structures called hydathodes. Conditions favoring guttation are abundance of soil water and cool temperatures.

5. **(B)** As water continues to diffuse into the cell, the excess is periodically expelled to the outside, keeping the cell from bursting.

6. **(C)** Artificially methylating (adding a —CH_3 group) to the bases of DNA nucleotides has the effect of slowing or stopping transcription. This effect correlates with the observation that transcriptionally inactive regions are naturally more methylated than active regions. There is evidence that methylation is one way for a cell to make permanent the "turning off" of some genes when the cell becomes differentiated.

7. **(B)** In Australia, marsupials fill many ecological niches normally filled by placental mammals elsewhere. These marsupials vary in size from large kangaroos all the way down to small-mice-size animals.

Marsupials are not found on other continents except the Americas, which are the home of the opossum and a few small ratlike or shrewlike types (confined to the Andes of South America).

8. **(A)** Sometimes two plant species hybridize to produce organisms whose chromosomes are amenable to successful meiosis. These new organisms, called allopolyploids, can produce gametes and mate with each other, but not with either parent species; thus, they constitute a new species.

9. **(A)** Antigens A and B, found in types A, B, and AB blood, and antigen Rh, found in Rh-positive blood, are carried by red blood cells and therefore are not diffusible.

10. **(B)** Messenger RNA is written as mRNA, and nitrogenous bases in the nucleotides are symbolized by letters. Strands of mRNA are synthesized beside strands of DNA with the bases pairing as follows: A to T, U to A, C to G, and G to C. There is no thymine (T) in RNA, but uracil (U) takes its place. The mRNA strand formed beside the DNA pattern is as follows (the phosphate group and sugars are not symbolized):

DNA Strand	mRNA Strand
T	A
T	A
A	U
C	G
G	C
A	U
G	C

11. **(D)** Preceding the Pleistocene, Asia and North America were connected across the Bering Sea. The climate was uniformly mild, and plants and animals migrated freely. The advancing ice moved southward like a wedge and isolated organisms in the two widely separated areas, where the descendants of several relic species, including magnolias and alligators, still survive.

12. **(D)** Stereoscopic microscopes give the image three dimensions: height, width,

and depth. Other microscopes give only height and width. The dimension of depth is obtained by viewing an object from two different directions simultaneously. Humans naturally perceive depth because the eyes focus from different angles. The stereoscopic microscope is simply an optical extension of that ability.

13. **(A)** Coevolution involves change of both species caused by their interaction. Thus, each is acting as a factor of natural selection for the other.

14. **(A)** Although salt marshes look more like grassland, they are functionally most like mangrove forests. Both grow in saline environments that are flooded by ocean tides. In a sense these habitats are buffer zones between the ocean and the continent. Both are important nurseries for many types of marine organisms.

15. **(C)** An example of a mutant virus was the one that caused the virulent Asian flu in 1959. Besides mutating, viruses are also lifelike in being able to reproduce themselves. On the other hand, they do not have protoplasm or cellular organization. Neither do they take in food or respire.

16. **(A)** Each cilium (or flagellum) is characterized by 9 pairs of microtubules surrounding 2 single microtubules located in the center of the organelle. Microtubules are composed of tubulin plus other proteins.

17. **(D)** The amniotic egg has a shell that retains water and therefore allows the embryo to develop without access to an open body of water. Reptiles and birds are prime examples of completely terrestrial animals using this device.

18. **(B)** Polymorphism denotes the presence of more than one form of organism in a population; the life-forms are not identical. The environment can select among individuals only if there is significant variation upon which the selection can be based.

19. **(B)** Rh antigens are carried by red blood cells. Although the cells do not normally cross the placenta, they may do so if some seepage occurs, as it sometimes does late in pregnancy. If antigens from an Rh-positive fetus are introduced into the bloodstream of the Rh-negative mother, they will cause her to produce counteracting antibodies. In her next pregnancy, these antibodies might leak into the fetus's bloodstream. If this fetus is also Rh-positive, fetal red cells clump together and serious medical consequences can result.

20. **(B)** If genes are located on separate chromosomes, a dihybrid cross will produce a phenotypic ratio of 9:3:3:1 in the F_2. If genes are unalterably linked together on the same chromosome, the ratio will be 3:1 (see example).

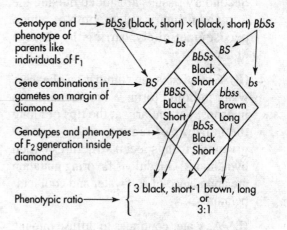

Genotype and phenotype of parents like individuals of F_1 ——→ $BbSs$ (black, short) × (black, short) $BbSs$

Gene combinations in gametes on margin of diamond

Genotypes and phenotypes of F_2 generation inside diamond

Phenotypic ratio ——→ { 3 black, short-1 brown, long or 3:1

Note that BS and bs go to separate gametes because they are on the same chromosome (also refer to A in next column). Sometimes a few gametes are produced with Bs and bS. This is explainable by the crossing-over of sections of chromatids that become entangled during synapsis. Study the following series of illustrations.

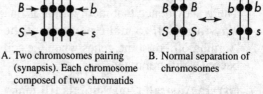

A. Two chromosomes pairing (synapsis). Each chromosome composed of two chromatids

B. Normal separation of chromosomes

C. Chromosome mates separating but two chromatids tangled

D. Chromosomes separated after crossing-over

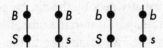

E. New chromosomes (composed of single chromatids) separated after aligning themselves at equator in division following synapsis. One goes to each of four gametes

Behavior of chromosomes during and after synapsis. The middle chromatids in sketch C are stretched out of proportion to give room to show what is happening.

A. Easier to cross between genes here

B. Harder to cross between genes here

Spacing of genes on chromatids as related to opportunities for crossing-over: Crossing-over indicates the distance between genes as well as their linear sequence. The closer together the genes are, the less chance the chromatids have to cross at a point between the genes; the farther away, the greater the chance. Should the sequence of hypothetical genes *A*, *B*, and *C* be desired, the percentage of crossing-over between *A* and *B*, *B* and *C*, and *A* and *C* is tested. If, after many crosses, the percentage should be six between *A* and *B*, four between *A* and *C*, and two between *B* and *C*, the linear arrangement would have to be *ACB*.

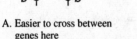

21. **(C)** Down syndrome is caused by the presence of an extra 21st chromosome, meaning that the chromosome number is 47 ($2n + 1$). Trisomy is the abnormal chromosomal variation of $2n + 1$.

22. **(C)** Darwin recognized individual variations and said that some of them would be more advantageous than others wherever an organism lived. He supposed that the fittest individuals would have a better chance of surviving in natural competition.

23. **(A)** The position of a timberline, if present, depends on the location of the mountain and its altitude. The zone at the top of most mountains in the eastern part of the United States is forested (below timberline).

24. **(E)** Stearin is a fat common to many animals and plants. It is used to make soap and candles and also to size textile products.

25. **(C)** In DNA-DNA hybridization studies, DNA from two species is separated to single threads by being heated, mixed together, then cooled. Strands from the two species that are at least somewhat complementary can attach along their lengths. Then the strength of attachment is measured as an indication of the degree of matching and the degree of species similarity on the DNA level.

26. **(C)** The root system of an established tree usually extends beyond the edge of its crown. The root hairs are at the extremities of the roots, not on the large trunk roots. Old roots, like old stems, are covered with cork and therefore cannot absorb water and solutes. In other words, the root system of the tree is competing with grass several feet away from its trunk, rather than near it.

27. **(E)** Like land mammals, whales breathe with lungs. Aquatic animals, mammals excepted, perform gas exchange via gills or the body surface. Whales also have other mammalian features, such as hair and milk glands.

28. **(C)** To study evolution of a population by natural selection, one should keep to a minimum all other evolutionary factors such as migration into and out of the population.

29. **(B)** When reciprocal translocation between different chromosomes occurs, the synaptic configuration is like the illustration in answer 20, above. The translocation may be simply the transfer of a broken piece of a chromosome to the end of another chromosome, as illustrated in sketch *A* below, or the shift of a piece of one chromosome into the break of another chromosome, as illustrated in sketch *B*.

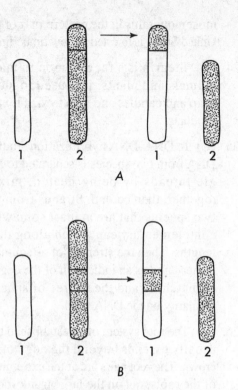

that usually pick up the discharged ovum and transport it into the tube. Movement down the Fallopian tube to the uterus is aided by peristaltic muscular contractions of the tube wall.

34. **(B)** Study the examples below.

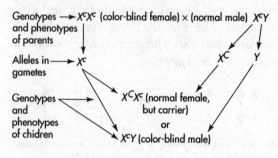

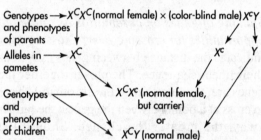

Sex linkage. Crosses between color-blind female and normal male and between normal female and color-blind male.

30. **(C)** Like chloroplasts, mitochondria are self-reproducing organelles. Both contain their own circular DNA, which carries sufficient genetic information to make most of their materials.

31. **(A)** The probable first cause of isolation was geographical. The Galápagos Islands, where the finches are found, are volcanic islands isolated from the mainland of South America, and the birds do not readily traverse the stretches of water separating them.

32. **(B)** Food particles are engulfed by cytoplasmic extensions. The food does not actually become a part of the cytoplasm but is enclosed in a vacuole, known as a food vacuole. The cytoplasm secretes enzymes into the vacuole, where the food is digested. The digested foods can then diffuse through the vacuolar membrane into the cytoplasm surrounding it. A food vacuole functions like a miniature stomach or intestine.

33. **(B)** The mucosal lining of the Fallopian tubes consists of columnar epithelium, some cells of which are ciliated. The cilia beat toward the uterus, creating currents

35. **(A)** Salt water covers about 70% of the Earth's surface. As for quantity, the ratio of the volume of water held in the oceanic basin to the volume of land above sea level is 19:1.

36. **(B)** See answer 21.

37. **(B)** All plants except those that produce seeds can reproduce only when water is available for fertilization. Seed plants do not need water because their sperm are transferred through pollen tubes to the eggs, permitting them to reproduce in the driest of weather.

38. **(B)** Prions, implicated in the spread of Creutzfeldt-Jakob disease and "mad cow" disease, are proteins. Although still debatable, an attractive hypothesis is that a prion is a malformed protein that acts by twisting normal proteins in the host organism so that they too become both malformed and capable of twisting others.

39. **(D)** Cambium is a meristematic tissue, undifferentiated and capable of dividing. The other choices are mature tissues, mostly dead.

40. **(B)** The pitcher plant is a green plant capable of manufacturing its own food. It also captures and digests insects. Just how it utilizes animal food is not completely understood, but the nitrogen in proteins may be a useful supplement since these plants usually live in nitrogen-impoverished soils.

41. **(E)** All sporozoans are parasitic protozoa, not free-living aquatic forms such as comprise plankton.

42. **(A)** In a vertebrate animal a neural tube forms by an infolding of ectoderm along a middorsal line. At first, a groove forms; then, by closing, it becomes a tube beneath the body surface. The anterior portion of this tube enlarges to form the brain. The archenteron roof participates in these events by releasing an inductive chemical that initiates the tube formation in the overlying ectoderm.

43. **(B)** Anaerobic glycolysis and fermentation help supply energy for the body when aerobic respiration is shut down because of lack of oxygen. The product of fermentation is lactic acid; some accumulates in the muscles and some is carried to the liver. Continued heavy breathing after exertion ceases provides oxygen to use some of the lactic acid for energy and to convert the remainder to glycogen for storage.

44. **(E)** Two major components of the contractile part of muscles are the two proteins actin and myosin. Separately they do not contract, but together they do. They occur naturally in a loose complex called *actomyosin*. This protein complex will contract in the presence of ATP and calcium.

45. **(D)** ATP (adenosine triphosphate) is known as the storehouse of energy. The compound contains three phosphate groups, but the energy for cell work comes from the high-energy bond of the third group. Upon the breaking of that bond and the separation of the phosphate group, a simpler molecule remains, namely, ADP (adenosine diphosphate).

46. **(A)** In plant life cycles the zygote grows into an embryonic sporophytic plant.

47. **(B)** Carbon dioxide is fixed into foods, not broken down into its constituent elements. Water, on the other hand, is split into hydrogen and oxygen.

48. **(A)** Pollination and subsequent fertilization have nothing to do with the genetics of the tree that produces the apple. The consequences of such a cross would be incorporated in the genetic composition of embryonic plants produced in the seeds. The edible part of the apple is the enlarged hypanthium of the flower of the Winesap tree.

49. **(D)** The clam, the snail, and the slug are all in phylum Mollusca.

50. **(D)** The chorion lies between the amnion and the uterus, with which it is in contact. The chorion originates from the trophoblast of the blastodermic vesicle (in mammals).

51. **(C)** Cholinesterase is an enzyme that destroys the neurotransmitter acetylcholine at the synapse. Were it not for its action, separate impulses would blend together.

52. **(A)** George W. Beadle and Edward L. Tatum proposed the one gene–one enzyme hypothesis while they were working with the mold *Neurospora*. According to the hypothesis, the production of each cellular enzyme is controlled by a single gene. The enzymes control chemical reactions that, in turn, determine phenotypic characteristics. This hypothesis has been modified to become the one gene–one polypeptide hypothesis, which accounts for the observation that some enzymes are composed of two or more subunits, each controlled by a separate gene.

53. **(B)** The foot of a horse evolved from the primitive limb pattern, which terminated

in five toes. The modern horse walks on the tip of the surviving middle toe. The result is the lengthening of its stride, an adaptation favorable to fleeing. The hoof is a highly specialized structure homologous to nails or claws.

54. **(D)** Turbidity is cloudiness of water due to suspended particles. A way to measure turbidity is to determine how far light can penetrate water and be reflected back to the eye. The Secchi disk is a circular object, usually painted white or black and white, that is lowered into a body of water by a cord or chain until it disappears from sight. The depth at which it disappeared can then be compared to similar measurements made in other bodies of water containing more or less suspended materials. The Secchi disk is an important tool in studying the ecology of ponds, lakes, and similar bodies of water.

55. **(A)** The method of transport by the virus is transduction. In the process, portions of bacterial chromosome are incorporated into the virus and are then carried into another bacterium when the virus invades it. Transformation is another way a bacterium can receive "foreign" genetic material. In this case, fragments of DNA from lysed bacteria are absorbed directly, not transported by a virus.

56. **(B)** Although controlled burning may have several advantages, it is used most often to reduce underbrush. The scrub growth not only is competitive with the trees but also contributes to an accumulation of litter that can cause destructive high-intensity fires.

57. **(C)** Autotrophs are the original source of all foods; therefore, they support all of the other levels. About 90% of the energy (biomass) is lost between them and the herbivores that comprise the next higher level. The loss is approximately the same between each succeeding level and the next higher one.

58. **(A)** The Golgi complex (apparatus) is a membrane-enclosed compartment in the cytoplasm. The best evidence that it has a secretory function is that it contains proteins, which are eventually discharged to the outside of the cell. The Golgi complex was first described by Camillo Golgi in 1898.

59. **(B)** All organic compounds contain carbon, but some compounds that contain carbon may not be organic (e.g., earthlike substances such as calcium carbonate). Organic compounds are called organic because of the original belief that they came from living organisms. Today thousands of organic compounds not found in nature are being synthesized in laboratories. Carbon is unique in being able to combine with itself and other substances to form molecular chains and rings, most of which are large and complex.

60. **(E)** Without specialized vascular tissues, conduction is a slow cell-to-cell movement by diffusion. All nonvascular terrestrial plants, such as mosses, are small.

61. **(A)** In calculating the percentage of light used in photosynthesis, consideration must be given to many variables such as quantity, quality, reflection, and penetration of light as well as the vigor of the plant and the availability of the raw materials carbon dioxide and water. An often cited figure is the one calculated by Transeau, who found that 1.6% of the radiant energy falling on a cornfield was used by the plants. Of the amount falling on the plant, it is estimated that only about 4% is absorbed by chlorophyll. Of the amount absorbed by chlorophyll, about 90% is converted into chemical energy.

62. **(E)** No explanation is necessary.

63. **(C)** When a peptide bond between two amino acids is broken, as in digestion, a water molecule is also split (*hydro* = water, *lysis* = split). The H portion of the water becomes bonded to the amine end of one amino acid, and the OH portion of the water becomes bonded to the carboxyl end of the second amino acid.

64. **(A)** Acetylcholine is one of the neurotransmitters secreted by neurons at the synapse. It is the medium by which a

new action potential is initiated at the "receiving" portion of a synapse, that is, at the junction between a motor neuron and a muscle fiber.

65. **(C)** Interphase was once called the resting stage because nothing visible was happening in the cell. We now know, however, that the cell is metabolically active during this stage. Furthermore, one of the most important mitotic processes is taking place, namely, the duplication of DNA.

66. **(A)** The nucleotide is the building block of DNA and is composed of a phosphate group, a pentose sugar (deoxyribose), and a nitrogenous base (either a purine or pyrimidine).

67. **(A)** See the following example:

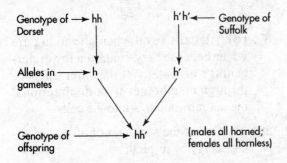

68. **(C)** The wings of a bat and the arms of a human are mammalian forelimbs. The big difference is that the bat limb has very long, webbed digits, a highly specialized adaptation for flight.

69. **(E)** A parasite has maximum security if its host is strong. If it weakens the host, it jeopardizes its own existence; if it kills the host, it assures its own death.

70. **(A)** A niche is a mode of life, and closely related organisms (a population) have the same mode. Two or more species can temporarily compete for a niche, but this does not always occur.

71. **(D)** The thylakoid membranes are sites of proton pumping (chemiosmosis), which leads to ATP production during the light-dependent reactions of photosynthesis. Another source of ATP is oxidative phos-

phorylation, which also involves chemiosmosis. However, that process occurs at the cristae of mitochondria.

72. **(A)** A taxis is a reflex movement of an organism to orient itself with respect to an external stimulus. In chemotaxis, the stimulus is a diffusing chemical. Individual slime mold cells move toward an "aggregation center" of high cAMP concentration. When many converge, they interact to form a multicellular reproductive body.

73. **(E)** In lower plants the gametophytes are usually larger or more conspicuous than the sporophytes. In mosses, for example, the gametophytes are usually most conspicuous, and the sporophytes are parasitic upon them.

74. **(C)** The liver is derived from endoderm, whereas the spleen comes from mesoderm.

75. **(B)** Plants look green because the green wavelengths of light are reflected instead of being absorbed.

76. **(A)** The replication of chromatin can be confirmed by substituting ^3H (tritium) in thymidine and then incorporating it in nucleotides containing thymidine. The relative quantity of it is measurable by exposing the cells to photographic film, which records the radiation from ^3H incorporated in the thymine portion of the molecule.

77. **(D)** Epidermal cells are normally protective, especially against the loss of water. Some plants living in arid environments even have multiple layers. Submerged leaves do not need to conserve water and are not so adapted. In some aquatic plants such as elodea, the mesoderm is absent, and the leaf consists of only two layers of epidermis. These epidermal cells are filled with chloroplasts.

78. **(E)** Any living cell can be affected by radiation. Beadle and Tatum, who did so much work with *Neurospora*, produced mutations by irradiating its spores with X rays.

79. **(D)** The lethal allele is recessive and carried by heterozygous green plants. When two heterozygous parents cross, approximately 25% of the embryos are homozygous recessive and lethal.

80. **(B)** A green plant normally needs stomata through which to exchange gases with the atmosphere. It also needs guard cells to help regulate the loss of water by transpiration. The leaf of a typical submerged aquatic plant is uncutinized and thin, adapted to exchange substances directly with the water. Aquatic plants derived from terrestrial ancestors may adapt to their new mode of life but still retain vestiges of structures that were previously functional.

81. **(D)** When organisms in a community are reproducing themselves, the community is self-perpetuating as long as the same climatic conditions prevail.

82. **(B)** Laterization occurs in humid tropical and subtropical regions. Acids produced by decay cause the leaching of alkaline materials and silica from the surface zone, leaving a soil rich in iron and aluminum compounds. Lateritic soils are red in color.

83. **(D)** Pheromones are external secretions that influence the physiology or behavior of other organisms of the same species.

84. **(E)** See the following example:

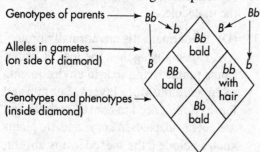

Genotypes of parents ⟶ Bb ⟍b   B⟋ Bb

Alleles in gametes ⟶ (on side of diamond)

Genotypes and phenotypes ⟶ (inside diamond)

Bb bald

BB bald   bb with hair

Bb bald

85. **(A)** An inversion is the reversal of a segment of a chromosome so that the order of the genes contained therein is backward.

Gene sequence in normal homologue (A·B·C·D·E·F·G·H·I·J·K·L·M·N)

Gene sequence in homologue with inversion (A·B·E·K·J·I·H·G·F·E·D·C·M·N)

When the homologues synapse, the lower chromosome forms a loop like the one illustrated in the question. The looping brings corresponding genes together.

86. **(B)** The configuration in the question shows a reciprocal translocation between two different (nonhomologous) chromosomes. The difference in shading in the following illustration shows how the chromosomes were originally linked:

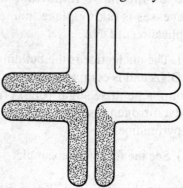

87. **(B)** All cells swell when placed in pure water because they contain a lower percentage of water. While water diffuses through membranes in both directions, the net movement is into the cells.

88. **(B)** One of the attributes of life is obtaining energy by respiration.

89. **(E)** Guard cells have walls that are not uniform in thickness throughout. When they absorb water, they swell asymmetrically so that they stand apart, making an opening (stoma) between them. When they lose water, the process is reversed. Although there are many unanswered questions about the chemical conversion that occurs within the guard cells, most people believe that an increase in the amount of sugar within these cells accounts for the absorption of water and consequent swelling.

90. **(C)** An epiphyte is a nonparasitic plant that lives attached to another plant. Many lichens, mosses, ferns, orchids, and bromeliads are epiphytic.

91. **(B)** Since half of the sperm are for male and half for female, the chance of a boy is always 50:50 regardless of any previous births.

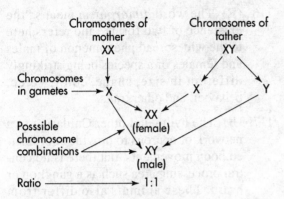

Sex determination in most animals.

92. **(E)** To obtain the probability of getting several genotypes at the same time, we determine the probability of getting each genotype separately and then multiply the values together:

$$1/2 \times 1/4 \times 1/4 = 1/32 \text{ or } 3.12\%$$

93. **(C)** In a cross such as the one illustrated, a single allele determines the male phenotype and two alleles the female phenotype. Therefore, the male with be *hO* (hemophiliac) or *HO* (normal); the female will be *HH* (normal), *Hh* (carrier), or *hh* (hemophiliac). Since individual 1's husband is normal (*HO*) and since their son (individual 3) is a hemophiliac (*hO*), she will have to be a carrier (*Hh*). (The letter O could represent the Y chromosome of a male, as well as signifying the absence of the hemophilia gene.)

94. **(C)** See the following example:

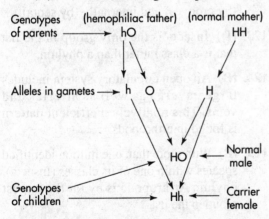

95. **(A)** Individual 2 has the genotype *HO*. He received the *O* from his father and the *H* from his mother. His father could have been *hO* or *HO*.

96. **(A)** For the cross between a hemophiliac father (*hO*) such as individual 4 and a normal mother (*HH*), see answer 94, above.

97. **(C)** Individual 1 is a carrier female (*Hh*), individual 2 is a normal male (*HO*), and individual 3 is a hemophiliac male (*hO*).

98. **(E)** The deciduous condition in plants is caused either by aridity or by cold weather. In the latter case, the abscission of leaves is normally preceded by the loss of chlorophyll and the changing of leaf color to yellow, orange, red, or brown.

99. **(A)** The mangrove forest is located in the intertidal zone of the tropics wherever the substratum is suitable. Although the trees belong in different taxonomic groups, they are similar in having stiltlike roots through which the tides flow freely.

100. **(B)** The characteristic trees of the tropical rain forest have broad, evergreen leaves. Many of the leaves have prolonged tips, from which they shed water as from a spout.

101. **(C)** Many desert plants are water-storing succulents. The larger and more picturesque ones belong to the cactus and euphorbia families.

102. **(D)** Level D is composed of primary consumers (herbivores), which feed on the green plants of level E.

103. **(C)** Level C is composed of secondary consumers (carnivores) that feed on the herbivores of level D.

104. **(B)** Level B is composed of tertiary consumers (carnivores) that feed on other carnivores of level C.

105. **(E)** Level E is composed of green plants, the producers.

106. **(C)** A pollen grain is usually three haploid cells, two of them sperm cells and one a cell that will begin to form the pollen tube.

107. **(E)** A sperm cell is the product of male meiosis and is therefore haploid (1*n*).

108. **(B)** Mammalian erythrocytes (red blood cells) form in the bone marrow. When fully differentiated, they lack a nucleus or chromosomes. Chromatin is the deeply staining portion of each chromosome.

109. **(D)** Schwann cells wrap tightly around the axons of certain neurons of vertebrates, forming the myelin sheath.

110. **(A)** Upon fusion of the egg and sperm nuclei, a diploid (2*n*) zygote exists. It is the ancestor of all of the embryonic and adult cells, which form by mitosis.

111. **(C)** A pollen grain is equipped with a tough wall that protects it from desiccation. This is necessary since pollen is usually carried from place to place by wind or on the exterior surface of terrestrial animals.

112. **(A)** Batesian mimicry, named for H. W. Bates, is an organism's avoidance of predators by looking and/or acting like a noxious or dangerous organism even though the mimic is neither unpalatable nor dangerous. The advantage to the fly of looking and sounding like a wasp is obvious.

113. **(D)** Müllerian mimicry, named for F. Müller, involves two or more species that have a common protective characteristic and use the same type of warning signal to would-be predators, indicating that they are either noxious or dangerous. Use of identical signals from a bee and a wasp tends to reinforce and hasten the learning process of a potential predator.

114. **(C)** The example in the question can be explained by the observation that the erythrocytes of heterozygotes are hostile environments to the protozoan that causes malaria. In malaria-infested areas, the benefit that human populations derive when some of their members are heterozygous is greater than the harm suffered when some members die of sickle-cell anemia expressed by homozygous recessive erythrocytes.

115. **(B)** Cryptic coloration is also called hiding coloration. Some animals retain a lifelong color and pattern and rely on finding a matching background. Others, such as the flounder and chameleon, can change their colors over some range to match the environment in which they find themselves.

116. **(E)** The word *dimorphism* means "the existence of two forms" and refers here to the widespread phenomenon of males and females of a species being strikingly different in size, shape, color, voice, behavior, and other traits.

117. **(B)** The hydra and other Cnidaria use a network of neurons to provide coordinated body movements, but there is no central processing area such as a ganglion or brain. These animals also differ from animals with more advanced nervous systems by demonstrating two-way transmission at synapses.

118. **(A)** Cerebral dominance is a characteristic of all mammals.

119. **(C)** Planaria, or *Dugesia,* has a pair of cerebral ganglia in the anterior region of the body. However, this "brain" is not homologous to that of a vertebrate.

120. **(D)** A shark relies a great deal upon the sensing of chemicals in its environment ("smelling"). This dependence is reflected in the greatly enlarged olfactory lobes at the anterior end of the brain.

121. **(E)** Sponges (Porifera) reproduce sexually but also produce buds that become attached adults of a colony. Sponges are bottom dwellers (benthic).

122. **(A)** The earthworm (e.g., *Lumbricus terrestris*) is a member of phylum Annelida. This group is segmented both externally (by grooves) and internally (by septa).

123. **(D)** Insecta is the only group in the list that is a class rather than a phylum.

124. **(B)** An open circulatory system includes large caverns as well as arteries and veins. This relatively inefficient pattern is found in arthropods.

125. **(B)** With more than one million identified species within one of its classes (Insecta), phylum Arthropoda is by far the largest group in the list.

126. **(B)** The operator region is adjacent to the structural genes over which it has control.

127. **(E)** The regulatory gene is sometimes quite far down the chromosome from the

rest of the inducible gene system. Its function is to produce a messenger RNA that carries the code for building a repressor protein. In an inducible system, the repressor is produced in the correct shape to attach to the operator.

128. **(B)** See answer 127, above. The repression occurs because of the repressor's physical hindrance to the attachment of RNA polymerase at the promoter region (labeled *C*).

129. **(A)** Transcription of structural genes occurs only if RNA polymerase can reach them to catalyze the reaction. An inducer molecule must combine with the repressor, making it unable to attach to the operator, before RNA polymerase can reach the proper position.

130. **(C)** When the operator region is free of a repressor, RNA polymerase can first attach to the promoter region (labeled *C*) and then successfully move to the nearest end of the first structural gene (labeled *A*).

131. **(E)** Pyruvic acid is an end product of glycolysis in any organism that uses glucose as an energy source. Calcium is found in both animals and plants; but since it is an element rather than a molecule, it cannot be *made* by any organism.

132. **(A)** See answer 131, above.

133. **(D)** Indoleacetic acid is a well-known auxin that, like any auxin, can induce cell elongation in plants.

134. **(C)** Secreted by the adrenal medulla, epinephrine (adrenaline) acts in a variety of ways to stimulate the metabolic rate of animal cells.

135. **(B)** Collagen is a fibrous protein of connective tissue such as tendons.

136. **(C)** A sarcomere is the area between two Z lines along a myofibril. Within a sarcomere, actin fibers are capable of sliding over myosin fibers as the sarcomere contracts.

137. **(E)** The transverse tubule (T-tubule) system is a complex set of tubes that are extensions of the muscle fiber's outer plasma membrane. An action potential moves along the outside of the fiber and then travels down the tubules to reach the responsive areas.

138. **(D)** The critical material needed to initiate myosin movements is calcium in its ionic form. When such movement is inappropriate, a system of connected membranous bags of the sarcoplasmic reticulum sequesters these ions. An action potential reaching the membranes via nearby transverse tubules causes a momentary breakdown of this retention system, allowing calcium ions to flow by diffusion throughout the sarcomere.

139. **(D)** Light rays in the visible range easily penetrate the atmosphere from the sun. Some of their energy is radiated back from terrestrial objects as infrared rays. Energy in this form can be absorbed by atmospheric carbon dioxide and thus is trapped as heat. Some workers feel that industrialization increases the temperature of the Earth's surface by adding atmospheric carbon dioxide from combustion, especially of fossil fuels—a phenomenon known as the greenhouse effect.

140. **(C)** Food webs are diagrams showing which organisms use others as food. They are called webs because they show complex interactions among producers and consumers in most ecosystems.

141. **(B)** Certain bacteria can gain energy in total darkness by processing hydrogen sulfide. Deep-sea sources of hydrogen sulfide (produced with help from the heat of the Earth's interior) provide energy not only for chemosynthetic bacteria but also for large animals that use the bacteria as producers.

142. **(A)** Carrying capacity is the maximum number of individuals that can be indefinitely supported by the resources of an ecosystem.

143. **(E)** Types of symbiosis are parasitism (one species benefits, the other is harmed), commensalism (one benefits, the other is

neither benefited nor harmed), and mutualism (both benefit). To qualify as symbiosis, the interaction must occur at close quarters.

144. **(A)** Follicle-stimulating hormone (FSH) is made in the anterior pituitary. Its target organ is the ovary, where it stimulates the maturation of an egg and its surrounding follicle cells.

145. **(D)** Progesterone, made by the corpus luteum of an ovary, causes maturation of uterine wall glands for embryo nurture. The corpus luteum is a yellowish mass of cells in the region that has just released an egg.

146. **(B)** The pancreas, in addition to producing digestive enzymes for the intestinal tract, makes and releases to the blood two hormones needed all over the body for carbohydrate metabolism. One is insulin, whose primary action is to change the permeability of cell membranes to allow more glucose to enter from blood plasma. The second hormone, glucagon, does the opposite: it causes release of glucose from the polysaccharide glycogen, thus increasing the blood glucose concentration.

147. **(E)** Testosterone, made in the testes of males, stimulates the development of masculine secondary sexual characteristics.

148. **(B)** Some plants, such as dodder, grow their roots into other plants and are thus parasitic upon these host plants. Such roots are called haustoria.

149. **(E)** The taproot of a dandelion is capable of regenerating one or more entire plants if it remains in the ground after the rest of the plant is cut off.

150. **(E)** Carrots and dandelions are examples of plants with a single large primary root.

151. **(C)** Grasses produce fibrous networks of roots, all about the same size.

152. **(E)** RNA viruses (or retroviruses) store information in RNA. They then produce a singlestranded DNA from it, finally making messenger RNA from the single-stranded DNA.

153. **(B)** In the early 1900s, Thomas Hunt Morgan discovered and studied the X-linked gene that produces white eyes in the fruit fly.

154. **(A)** Conjugation between bacteria is analogous to sexual mating in eukaryotes, since it involves the placing of new combinations of genes in an organism. In conjugation, one bacterium builds a hollow tube connecting it to another; then some DNA is passed to the second cell.

155. **(E)** Genetic fine-mapping was first performed by Seymour Benzer, using T-series bacteriophages (viruses that inhabit bacteria).

156. **(A)** In 1944 Avery et al. used pneumococci as a source of DNA that could be taken up by live bacteria and that would change the phenotypes of these recipients.

157. **(C)** Mutations are of a random nature. If they produce characteristics that better fit the organism for a particular environment, the organism has an advantage over others of its kind in that environment and is more likely to survive and reproduce. If, however, the mutation does not result in better adaptation of the organism to its environment, the organism and its descendants are at a disadvantage and will probably not survive.

158. **(E)** As stated in the passage, the development of melanin is dominant in some insects and recessive in others. The characteristic is by no means limited to the moths mentioned.

159. **(D)** See the following example:

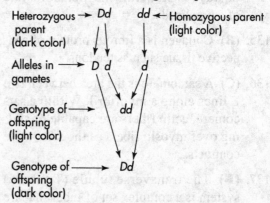

160. **(B)** If color is the only difference, birds will eat the moths that they can more readily see.

161. **(B)** Density is the average number of individuals found in the quadrats sampled. In the five quadrats, there were six specimens of species 2; therefore, the density is 1.2.

162. **(A)** Frequency is the percentage of quadrats in which a species is found. Species 1 is found in four out of five quadrats, for a frequency of 80%.

163. **(A)** Importance value is the sum of relative density, relative frequency, and relative dominance (basal area). The last of these cannot be calculated from the information given.

164. **(E)** Since each of the species has a radically different life span (in years) than most of the others, the graph was constructed to show only percentages of the maximum life spans.

165. **(B)** The British robin population (curve *B*) loses most of its members before half of the maximum life span has passed.

166. **(C)** The vertical axis of the graph is logarithmic. At 50% of total life span, curve *A* shows only about 50 of the original 1000 American robins surviving—about 5%.

167. **(D)** There is no reason to expect a significant deviation from a 1:1 male-female ratio in either population. In addition, a female bird expends a great deal of energy in producing eggs; this tends to weaken her and make her more likely to die young.

168. **(E)** An antibody is not detectable in an animal's blood until after an antigen has been introduced. Lectins, however, are synthesized under an invariant developmental program and are normal constituents of their organisms.

169. **(D)** No matter what the final blood type, nearly all humans produce a substance called H. This sugar remains unmodified in type O people and is the material to which O-specific lectins attach. Type A, B, or AB people modify the H substance to become either A substance or B substance. However, their blood does not recognize the H sugar as an antigen if they receive a transfusion of type O blood because H is present in their bone-marrow cells that are being differentiated into mature erythrocytes.

170. **(B)** A saccharide group is not nearly as complex as, say, proteins or nucleic acids. Therefore, the same sugars are made and incorporated into the cells of many organisms. For instance, chitin is a polysaccharide found in fungi, insects, and molluscs. Its basic structural unit is *N*-acetyl glucosamine in all of these organisms.

171. **(A)** The changing distribution of binding sites as a cell is transformed indicates that the cell surface is changing. This finding, coupled with the observations that malignant cells have less binding ability with each other than do cells of normal tissues and that malignant cells change in their ability to move materials through the cell membrane, has led to a number of important theories on how cancer operates.

172. **(B)** The cited work on chick-eye development shows that the retinal cell surface changes during embryogenesis.

173. **(A)** The radioactive tagging study, combined with the fluorescent tagging study, shows that the number of lectin-binding sites remains unchanged as a cell is transformed but that the binding sites become redistributed into concentrated clumps. This change makes possible the formation of many lectin bridges between two malignant cells in a compact configuration.

174. **(B)** Lectin was tagged with a fluorescent compound and then added to cells. Under a fluorescence microscope the pattern of glowing lectins bound to their specific sites could be seen.

175. **(D)** By having a countercurrent system of heat exchange, the kangaroo rat conserves water when it exhales cooler air

that holds less water. Choice (B) cannot be correct because lost heat is absorbed by the inhaled air, thereby increasing the body temperature.

176. **(D)** The passage mentions that the kangaroo rat does not use water for thermoregulation, although some other animals do. Examples are human sweating and a dog's panting.

177. **(D)** The camel's nasal passage is hygroscopic only when it is dry. The passage likens this surface to a filter paper that can absorb water.

178. **(B)** Some countercurrent systems involve the flow of two materials past each other in long, parallel tubes. However, the nasal passages of the kangaroo rat accomplish the same function by forcing air alternately back and forth through the same set of long, narrow tubes. The walls of the tubes, holding varying amounts of heat, serve to replace opposite-flow tubes.

179. **(B)** The loop of Henle is doubled over on itself so that liquid flows down the loop and then back up. The two halves are parallel to each other and are in intimate contact. Active transport of sodium ions from the distal end of the tube leads to the return of some, but not all, of these ions to the fluid in the nearby proximal tube portion. The net result is a constantly maintained gradient of sodium ions in nearby tissue, with the highest concentration at the bend of the loop. This tissue condition leads to water removal by diffusion from urine in nearby collecting tubules, which are also parallel to the loop of Henle.

180. **(A)** Other luminescent organisms respond to different wavelengths for phase-changing, indicating that they use different mechanisms.

181. **(A)** An internal "clock" is indicated by the ability of an inherent mechanism to continue a cycling phenomenon when normal environmental clues are absent.

182. **(A)** If the "clock" responded markedly to temperature fluctuations, it would order periodicity changes to accord with the seasonal temperature changes. The luminescence pattern would no longer match the 24-hour day length.

183. **(A)** Biochemical reactions normally follow the "Q_{10} law"; as temperature increases by $10°$, the reaction rate approximately doubles. The "clock" mechanism in *Gonyaulax* is apparently independent of this law, since it actually slows a bit as temperature rises.

184. **(E)** Luminescence is elicited by agitation of the culture, but intensity of luminescence varies directly with the intensity of agitation.

185. **(B)** The word *circadian* comes from two Latin words meaning "around the day." A synonym is *diurnal*.

186. **(A)** This relationship is shown by Graph 2.

187. **(C)** Seeing an effect when two tissues are connected only by blood flow is good evidence for a diffusible chemical's action.

188. **(B)** If anti-NGF, capable of rendering NGF inactive, is injected into a previously untreated adult, the animals sympathetic ganglia shrink.

189. **(C)** Microtubules of an axon form transportation routes for proteins. Autoradiography showed that NGF travels through the axon toward the cell body. Chemical destruction of microtubules leads to interruption of this travel and also to death of the cell.

190. **(B)** Although NGF is not responsible for maintenance of adult sensory neurons, it does promote growth of both embryonic sympathetic and sensory neurons.

191. **(E)** Autoradiography is a much used means of locating radioactively tagged substances in tissues or cells. After the substances have been given time to reach a destination, the tissue is sectioned and prepared as for microscopic examination. Photographic emulsion is spread over the slide in darkness, and the slide is stored for some time. Emissions from the radioactive

tag cause the same chemical changes in the emulsion as would occur if light hit it. The slide is then developed as if it were a normal photographic film. Microscopic examination of the tissue reveals dark specks wherever the radioactivity was present.

192. **(A)** None of these experiments bears directly upon the question of how a growing fiber "recognizes" which nearby tissue is the proper sort for making synapses. This question has not yet been adequately answered.

193. **(B)** Generally, the rate of influx of a type of molecule will be greater if the concentration gradient of that molecule (between the inside and outside of the cell) is larger.

194. **(A)** Graph 2 shows that dimethylurea and ethylene glycol have nearly the same partition coefficient (a measure of solubility in lipid), but dimethylurea has less than half the ability to enter the cell (permeability). Each of the other molecules in the list of answer choices shows a direct relationship between partition coefficient and permeability.

195. **(C)** Ethylene glycol is the smallest of the tested molecules (Graph 1) and has a partition coefficient smaller than only one of the other tested molecules (Graph 2). Small size and high solubility are both features that ease passage of a molecule through a porous, lipid-containing membrane.

196. **(A)** The partition coefficient is a value showing how easily a molecule enters a region of lipids. This measurement is very important in considering the ability of a molecule to pass through a cell membrane, since a major portion of the membrane is phospholipids.

197. **(E)** The two surrogates differed in both facial features and body texture, so these experiments did not determine whether a particular aspect of one of these features was the most important clue that the infants used in identifying a mother.

198. **(B)** This statement is supported by the observation that infants who spent little time on wire "mothers" that supplied milk were as healthy as those who spent much more time on cloth "mothers."

199. **(A)** Imprinting is a type of learning that occurs early in life. The infants reared without a mother did not derive any security when temporarily placed in a room with a surrogate cloth "mother." Actually, they were *more* frightened with the surrogate present than with it absent.

200. **(E)** Endurance of a preference (not to be confused with "strength") is measured by the length of time over which it remains observable. This should involve a period of deprivation, to distinguish preference from insignificant habit. To mark choice (A) is to express the unproved belief that the preference is heritable and that Lamarckian evolution (inheritance of acquired traits) occurs.

PART 3 Review Aids

Topics Worth Reviewing

This list of topics is arranged into the three major groups for which subscores are reported from the GRE Biology Subject Test. Check off each topic when you feel confident that you know about it.

Cellular and Molecular Biology

—— Nature and roles of carbohydrates, fats, proteins, enzymes, and nucleic acids
—— Meaning of pH and buffering
—— Biologically important chemical bondings
—— Hydrophilic and hydrophobic interactions
—— Radioactive isotopes: uses, meaning of half-life
—— Origin of life on Earth: hypotheses
—— Cell parts: structures, functions
—— Fluid mosaic model of membranes
—— Mechanisms of transport across membranes (active and passive)
—— Mechanisms of cell recognition
—— The cytoskeleton: shaping and moving cells
—— Energy (thermodynamics) laws, application to life
—— Respiration: aerobic and anaerobic
—— The Krebs cycle (citric acid cycle) in respiration
—— Hydrogen transfer, chemiosmosis, electron transport
—— Role of NAD, FAD, and NADP in hydrogen transfer
—— ADP and ATP: uses in storing and releasing energy
—— Cellular reproduction: DNA replication, mitosis, cytokinesis
—— Nature of genes: prokaryotes and eukaryotes
—— DNA: its composition, locations, functions
—— RNA: its composition, locations, functions, and processing
—— Protein synthesis: transcription, translation, and processing
—— Chromosome structure and organization
—— The genetic code
—— Gene control in prokaryotes, eukaryotes
—— Meaning of allele, dominance, recessiveness, homozygote, heterozygote
—— Monohybrid and dihybrid crosses
—— Pedigree analysis
—— Linkage (including sex-linkage)
—— Crossing-over, mapping gene locations
—— Genetic basis of sex determination
—— Phenotypic and genotypic ratios
—— Gene interactions: epistasis, quantitative inheritance
—— Use of the chi-squared test in genetics
—— Autopolyploidy, allopolyploidy, euploidy, aneuploidy
—— Karyotype analysis

——Transformation, transduction, conjugation of bacteria
——Nature of retroviruses, including the AIDS virus (HIV)
——Recombinant DNA techniques: cloning, sequencing, PCR
——Restriction fragment length polymorphism (RFLP) to infer relatedness
——Mapping genes using restriction enzymes and electrophoresis
——Gene therapy techniques
——Mutations and DNA repair mechanisms
——The antigen-antibody reaction
——Cellular and antibody-mediated immune responses
——Antibody synthesis mechanisms and genetics
——Actions of hormones at or inside target cells

Organismal Biology

——Plant and animal tissues
——Concept of homeostasis
——Circulation of blood
——Clotting of blood
——Structure and functions of lymphatic system
——Gas exchange by animals, plants
——Oxygen transport in animals
——The reflex arc
——The action potential
——Synapses, neurotransmitters
——Parts of the brain: anatomy, functions
——Autonomic nervous system
——Eyes: structure and function
——Ears: structure and function
——Animal behavior: instinct, learning, social behavior
——Role of pheromones
——Internal support of animals
——Muscle contraction: mechanisms, control
——Animal hormones: effects, where produced, how regulated
——Osmoregulatory mechanisms
——The nephron: structure and functions
——Adaptations needed for terrestrial life: plants, animals
——Digestive mechanisms and organs
——Temperature regulation
——Vitamins in nutrition
——Reproductive structures in animals
——Gametogenesis (including meiosis) and fertilization
——Embryogenesis: molecular and genetic bases
——Homeotic genes in embryonic development
——Cleavage stages of animal zygote and early embryo
——Origin and derivatives of animal embryonic germ layers
——Embryonic organizers, induction, and determination
——Determination of body symmetry in embryonic development
——Insect metamorphosis
——Carcinogenesis and oncogenes
——Aging: predictable changes, current hypotheses on causes
——Plant structures: functions of roots, stems, flowers
——Plant growth: meristem, cell elongation
——Nature of pollen and embryo sacs
——Development of seeds and fruits

—— Transport of water and nutrients in plants
—— Plant energy capture: photosynthesis
—— Nitrogen fixation, nitrification, and denitrification
—— Tropisms
—— Role of photoperiod in plant life
—— Plant hormones and hormonelike substances
—— Life cycles of mosses, ferns, gymnosperms, and angiosperms
—— Classification systems: number of kingdoms
—— Viruses, viroids, and prions: structure, whether they are living
—— Monera (Archaebacteria, Bacteria): classification, characteristics
—— Protista: classification, characteristics
—— Plants: classification, characteristics of major groups
—— Fungi: classification, characteristics
—— Animals: classification, characteristics of major groups

Ecology and Evolution

—— Concept of the species
—— Energy relations: food web, trophic pyramid
—— Producers, consumers, and decomposers
—— Concept of ecosystem
—— Cycling of water, nitrogen, carbon, and phosphorus in ecosystems
—— Biomes
—— Concepts of niche, succession, and climax communities
—— Meaning of xerophytes, mesophytes, and hydrophytes
—— Lake and oceanic zones
—— Basic equations describing population growth
—— Density-dependent and density-independent factors in population regulation
—— K-selected and r-selected species
—— Organismal interactions: coevolution, predator-prey dynamics, symbiosis
—— Theory of organic evolution
—— Mechanisms of evolution: selection, genetic drift, migration, mutation
—— Hardy-Weinberg equilibrium and equation: meaning, application
—— Speciation: sympatric, allopatric
—— Speciation: gradualist and punctuated equilibrium models
—— Plant speciation by allopolyploidy
—— Convergence and divergence
—— Homology and analogy
—— Highlights of geologic time scale and fossil record: origins, extinctions, coexisting groups
—— Evolution of humans
—— Biogeography

Laws of Thermodynamics

1. The total energy of the universe is always constant (law of the conservation of energy).
2. All processes (physical, chemical, and biological) proceed in such a way that there is a new increase in entropy (measure of degree of disorder or randomness).
3. At the temperature of absolute zero, the entropy of a pure, solid substance tends to zero.

Spectrum of Organizational Complexity
(in order of increasing complexity)

Subatomic particles—the small units of which matter is made. There are three types: protons, neutrons, and electrons.

Atom—the smallest unit of an element; two to many subatomic particles bound together

Molecule—two to many atoms chemically bound together

Cell—the structural and functional unit of which living organisms are made

Tissue—a group of similar cells that function as a unit, for example, nervous, epithelial, vascular

Organ—a group of tissues that function as a unit, for example, heart, brain, lung

System—a group of organs that function as a unit, for example, circulatory, digestive, skeletal

Individual (organism)—a discrete living entity; a body, consisting of a single cell or many cells

Population—a group of similar, interbreeding individuals; all individuals of a species or all members of a species living in a specific location

Community—a group of different kinds of interacting organisms living together in the same place. The largest type of community is the biome, which occupies a climatic region and is characterized by organisms that have a specific life-form; examples of biomes are the deciduous forest, tundra, and desert.

Ecosystem—a more or less self-contained community of organisms together with the nonliving environment in which these organisms live

Chemical Elements Important in Living Organisms

Element	Symbol	Some Uses in Living Organisms
Boron	B	Affects plant growth
Calcium	Ca	Component of bone and teeth; important in clotting of blood; in plants, a component of the middle lamella in the form of calcium pectate; in plants, calcium oxalate and calcium carbonate deposited as crystals, probably excretory; in all cells, regulating metabolic processes
Carbon	C	Constituent of organic compounds
Chlorine	Cl	Component of NaCl, one of the most important salts related to life; an important ion in body fluids
Cobalt	Co	In vitamin B_{12}
Copper	Cu	Part of hemocyanin, a transporter of oxygen in some animals; in some enzymes
Fluorine	F	In teeth and bone
Hydrogen	H	Constituent of organic compounds and water; carrier of energy in metabolic processes
Iodine	I	Part of thyroxin, the thyroid hormone
Iron	Fe	Part of hemoglobin and many enzymes; essential for synthesis of chlorophyll (not a part of chlorophyll molecule)
Magnesium	Mg	Component of chlorophyll; necessary in some enzyme activities
Manganese	Mn	Necessary in some enzyme activities

(Continued)

Chemical Elements Important in Living Organisms (cont'd)

Element	Symbol	Some Uses in Living Organisms
Molybdenum	Mo	Necessary in some enzyme activities; used in nitrogen metabolism
Nitrogen	N	Constituent of proteins and nucleic acids
Oxygen	O	Constituent of organic compounds and water; final electron acceptor in aerobic respiration
Phosphorus	P	Constituent of many proteins; in ADP, ATP, and nucleic acids; in calcium phosphate, a major constituent of bone
Potassium	K	Necessary for action of some enzymes and for nerve and muscle function
Silicon	Si	Deposited in walls of some plant cells
Sodium	Na	Component of the salt NaCl; component of bile salts; in sodium bicarbonate, which serves as a buffer and neutralizes lactic acid; in sodium bicarbonate, which provides an alkaline environment for action of pancreatic enzymes; necessary for nerve and muscle function
Sulfur	S	Component of many proteins
Zinc	Zn	Used in synthesis of indoleacetic acid, a plant hormone; component of some enzymes

Isotopes Commonly Used as Tracers

Isotope	Half-Life	Emissions
Hydrogen-2 (^{2}H)		None
Hydrogen-3 (^{3}H)	12.4 years	Beta
Carbon-13 (^{13}C)		None
Carbon-14 (^{14}C)	5730 years	Beta
Nitrogen-15 (^{15}N)		None
Oxygen-18 (^{18}O)		None
Sodium-22 (^{22}Na)	2.6 years	Beta and gamma
Sodium-24 (^{24}Na)	15 hours	Beta and gamma
Magnesium-27 (^{27}Mg)	9 minutes	Beta and gamma
Phosphorus-32 (^{32}P)	14.5 days	Beta
Sulfur-35 (^{35}S)	87 days	Beta
Chlorine-36 (^{36}Cl)	4×10^5 years	Beta
Potassium-40 (^{40}K)	1.2×10^9 years	Beta and gamma
Potassium-42 (^{42}K)	12.4 hours	Beta and gamma
Calcium-45 (^{45}Ca)	160 days	Beta
Manganese-54 (^{54}Mn)	300 days	Beta and gamma
Iron-59 (^{59}Fe)	45 days	Beta and gamma
Cobalt-60 (^{60}Co)	5.2 years	Beta and gamma
Copper-64 (^{64}Cu)	12.8 hours	Beta and gamma
Zinc-65 (^{65}Zn)	250 days	Beta and gamma
Iodine-131 (^{131}I)	8.05 days	Beta and gamma

Functional Groups of Organic Molecules

Although organic molecules exist in a huge variety of forms, certain configurations appear repeatedly. The diagrams below represent these groups of atoms, which often have great influence on their molecules' biological activities.

Functional Group	Name	Typical Use
—OH	Hydroxyl	In any alcohol; acts as a base
$-C{\overset{\displaystyle O}{\underset{\displaystyle OH}{}}}$	Carboxyl	In any amino acid; acts as an acid
$-\overset{\displaystyle O}{\underset{\displaystyle \|}{C}}-H$	Aldehyde	In some sugars (when ring broken)
—NH$_2$	Amino	In any amino acid
$-\overset{\displaystyle O}{\underset{\displaystyle \|}{C}}-O-C-$	Ester	In any fat
$-\overset{\displaystyle O}{\underset{\displaystyle \|}{C}}-$	Ketone	In some sugars (when ring broken)
—CH$_3$	Methyl	Side group in many complex molecules
$-O-\overset{\displaystyle O^-}{\underset{\displaystyle O}{P}}-O^-$	Phosphate	In phospholipids, nucleotides
—SH	Sulfhydryl	In one amino acid (cysteine)
—S—S—	Disulfide	Stabilizes conformation of many proteins

Some Organic Compounds of Biological Importance

Classification	Name	Constituent Simpler Substances	Other Information
Carbohydrates ($C_nH_{2n}O_n$)			Primary energy source
Monosaccharides			Composed of one molecule
Triose sugar ($C_3H_6O_3$)			Has three carbon atoms
	Glyceraldehyde		One of two possible triose sugars
Tetrose sugar ($C_4H_8O_4$)	Erythrose		Used in photosynthesis
Pentose sugar ($C_5H_{10}O_5$)			Has five carbon atoms
	Ribose		In RNA
	Deoxyribose		In DNA
	Ribulose		In ribulose bisphosphate (photosynthesis intermediate)
	Xylose		Obtained from xylan
	Arabinose		Obtained from gum arabic
Hexose sugar ($C_6H_{12}O_6$)			Has six carbon atoms
	Glucose		Grape sugar, common in plants and animals
	Fructose		Fruit sugar

(Continued)

Some Organic Compounds of Biological Importance (cont'd)

Classification	Name	Constituent Simpler Substances	Other Information
	Galactose		From milk sugar and some gums
	Mannose		In ivory nut
Heptose sugar ($C_7H_{14}O_7$)	Sedoheptulose		An intermediate in photosynthesis
Disaccharides			Composed of two hexose sugar molecules
	Sucrose	Glucose and fructose	Common "table sugar"
	Maltose	Two glucoses	Produced when starch is enzymatically broken down
	Lactose	Glucose and galactose	Found in mammalian milk
Trisaccharides ($C_{18}H_{32}O_{16}$)			Composed of three hexose sugar molecules
	Raffinose	Glucose, fructose, and galactose	In cotton seeds and sugar beets
Polysaccharides ($C_6H_{10}O_5)_n$			Composed of six or more hexose sugar molecules
	Starch	Glucose	Common food stored in plants
	Glycogen	Glucose	Animal starch, common in liver and muscle
	Inulin	Fructose	Especially abundant in tubers of plants
	Cellulosans	Pentose sugars	More soluble than cellulose; one constituent of hemicelluloses
	Cellulose	Glucose	Structural material, primarily in cell walls of plants
	Xylans	Xylose	In cell walls of plants
	Gums	Galactose in some	Exudates of plants
	Agar	Galactose	Extract of seaweeds used for culturing bacteria and for many industrial purposes
	Pectic substances	Pentoses and/or hexoses	Hydrophilic and amorphous; one constituent of hemicelluloses
	Dextrins	Glucose	Soluble and gummy, formed by the incomplete decomposition of starch
	Chitin	Nitrogenous hexoses	Part of exoskeleton of arthropod animals
Lipids			Most concentrated source of energy
Fatty acids	Stearic, oleic, etc.		Either free or in combination with other substances
Fats	Triglycerides (neutral fats)	Fatty acids and alcohol (usually glycerol)	Solids; stored food; component of cellular membranes and myelin sheaths
Oils	Olive, cotton seed, etc.	Triglycerides; often fatty acids and alcohol (usually glycerol)	Liquids; a group of very different substances, often mixtures
Waxes	Beeswax	Wax and other substances	Secreted by bees
	Cutin	Wax and other substances	Produced by epidermal cells of plants
Steroids	Cholesterol		In animal cells, bile, gallstones, and egg yolk
	Sex hormones		
	Testosterone		A male hormone
	Progesterone		A female hormone
	Estrogen		A female hormone
	Cortisone		Hormone produced by adrenal cortex
	Vitamin D		Prevents rickets
Phospholipids	Lecithins, cephalins, etc.	Phosphate group, fatty acids, usually a glyceride, usually a nitrogenous base	Important constituent of cellular membranes

(Continued)

Some Organic Compounds of Biological Importance (cont'd)

Classification	Name	Constituent Simpler Substances	Other Information
Proteins			Major organic constituent of protoplasm
Simple			Composed of amino acids only
Globular			Soluble in aqueous media
	Albumin	Amino acids	In blood serum, muscle, milk, egg, and vegetable tissues
	Gamma globulins	Amino acids	Immunizing function
	Some hormones	Amino acids	Examples: insulin, somatotropin, gastrin
	Enzymes	Amino acids	Examples: pepsin, trypsin
Fibrous			Water-insoluble
	Collagen	Amino acids	In connective tissue
	Elastin	Amino acids	In elastic connective tissue
	Fibrin	Amino acids	In fibers of blood clot
	Keratin	Amino acids	In hair, horn, nails, and feathers
	Fibroin	Amino acids	In silk
	Actin and myosin	Amino acids	In contractile fibers of muscles
Conjugated			Proteins combined with another substance
	Nucleoproteins	Nucleic acids and proteins	Chromosomes, chromatin
	Glycoproteins	Carbohydrates and proteins	Many enzymes
	Chromoproteins	Pigment groups and proteins	
	Hemoglobin		Blood pigment; carries O_2 via heme (Fe)
	Cytochromes		Respiratory pigments in cells—transfer electrons
	Myoglobin		Muscle pigment; carries O_2 via heme (Fe)
	Hemocyanin		In blood of many mollusks and crustaceans; carries O_2 via Cu
	Phosphoproteins	Phosphorus-containing groups and proteins	Casein of milk and vitellin of egg yolks
	Lipoproteins	Lipids and proteins	In cell membranes, milk, blood, and egg yolks
Nucleosides			Composed of a pentose sugar and a nitrogenous base (purine or pyrimidine); purines are adenine and guanine; pyrimidines are cytosine, thymine, and uracil
	Adenosine	Sugar and purine (adenine)	In ADP and ATP
Nucleotides			Composed of a pentose sugar, a nitrogenous base, and one to three phosphate groups
	cAMP (cyclic AMP)		Adenosine plus one phosphate group; second messenger for some hormones
	ADP		Adenosine plus two phosphate groups; becomes ATP by addition of a third phosphate group bound by a high-energy bond
	ATP		A cellular storehouse of energy; upon hydrolysis yields energy for cell work, reverts to ADP
Nucleic acids (polynucleotides)			Composed of a polynucleotide macromolecule
	DNA	Deoxyribonucleotides	Deoxyribonucleic acid, the genetic material of nearly all organisms
	RNA	Ribonucleotides	Ribonucleic acid, involved in protein synthesis, and the genetic material of some viruses

Amino Acids Found in Proteins

Name	Abbreviation
Alanine	Ala
Arginine	Arg
Asparagine	Asn
Aspartic acid	Asp
Cysteine	CysH or CySH
Glutamic acid	Glu
Glutamine	Gln
Glycine	Gly
Histidine	His
Isoleucine	Ile
Leucine	Leu
Lysine	Lys
Methionine	Met
Phenylalanine	Phe
Proline	Pro
Serine	Ser
Threonine	Thr
Tryptophan	Try
Tryosine	Tyr
Valine	Val

Common Organic Compounds Better Known by Their Abbreviations

Abbreviation	Name	Comments
ADP*	Adenosine diphosphate	Converted to ATP by the addition of a third phosphate group bound by a high-energy bond
AMP*	Adenosine monophosphate	Converted to ADP by the addition of a second phosphate group
ATP*	Adenosine triphosphate	Known as *storehouse of energy* because energy for cell work comes from high-energy phosphate bond when ATP is converted to ADP
DNA	Deoxyribonucleic acid	A nucleic acid that comprises the genes
FAD	Flavin adenine dinucleotide	Used in hydrogen transfer
NAD	Nicotinamide adenine dinucleotide	Used in hydrogen transfer; formerly called DPN or coenzyme 1
NADP	Nicotinamide adenine dinucleotide phosphate	Used in hydrogen transfer; formerly called TPN or coenzyme 2
PGA	Phosphoglyceric acid	A 3-carbon compound regarded as the first organic compound synthesized from carbon dioxide and water during photosynthesis
PGAL	Glyceraldehyde-3-phosphate	A 3-carbon compound, the end product of photosynthesis
RUBP	Ribulose bisphosphate	In photosynthesis, combines with carbon dioxide and water to form PGA
RNA†	Ribonucleic acid	A nucleic acid important in the synthesis of proteins

*These compounds contain the nitrogenous base adenine; other similar compounds contain, instead, cytosine, guanine, thymine, and uracil, making such compounds as CMP, GDP, TTP, and UDP. If any of these abbreviations is preceded by the small letter d, as in dADP, the d indicates that the sugar is deoxyribose rather than ribose.
†tRNA stands for transfer-RNA, mRNA stands for messenger-RNA, and rRNA stands for ribosomal-RNA.

DNA: Structure and Replication

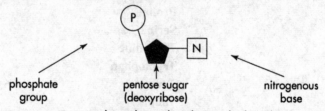

1. A typical nucleotide. This one is deoxyadenylic acid, so named because its sugar is deoxyribose and its nitrogenous base is adenine.

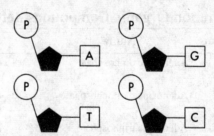

phosphate group   pentose sugar (deoxyribose)   nitrogenous base

2. Nucleotide molecule symbolized.

3. Four nucleotides differing in their nitrogenous bases: adenine, thymine, guanine, and cytosine.

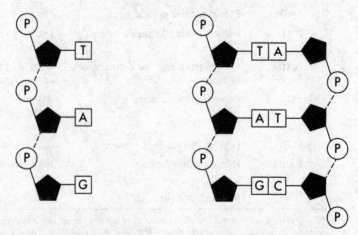

4. Nucleotides linked together in a chain as in DNA.

5. Parallel strands of nucleotides.

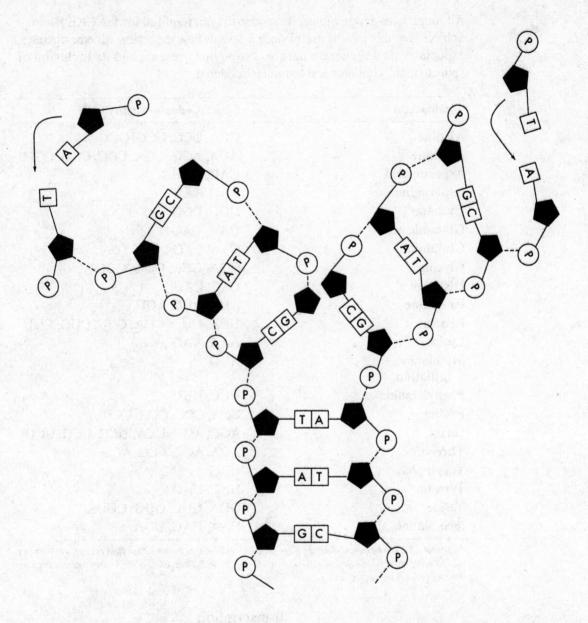

6. Reduplication of new strands of DNA from free nucleotide molecules. Note that adenine and thymine always pair, as do also guanine and cytosine.

Messenger RNA* Codons and Their Meanings

Although knowledge of specific codons is not required for the GRE Biology Subject Test, this table is useful since it reveals how the coding scheme operates, especially its degenerate nature (synonyms present) and its inclusion of "punctuation" (initiator and terminator codons).

Amino Acid	Codon(s) Signifying It
Alanine	GCA, GCC, GCG, GCU
Arginine	AGA, AGG, CGA, CGC, CGG, CGU
Aspartic acid	GAC, GAU
Asparagine	AAC, AAU
Cysteine	UGC, UGU
Glutamic acid	GAA, GAG
Glutamine	CAA, CAG
Glycine	GGA, GGC, GGG, GGU
Histidine	CAC, CAU
Isoleucine	AUA, AUC, AUU
Leucine	UUA, UUG, CUA, CUC, CUG, CUU
Lysine	AAA, AAG
Methionine, initiation	AUG
Phenylalanine	UUC, UUU
Proline	CCA, CCC, CCG, CCU
Serine	AGC, AGU, UCA, UCC, UCG, UCU
Threonine	ACA, ACC, ACG, ACU
Tryptophan	UGG
Tyrosine	UAC, UAU
Valine	GUA, GUC, GUG, GUU
termination	UAA, UAG, UGA

A similar table can be compiled for the three-base sets on DNA that produce these RNA codons, by observing the following conversion rules: $C \rightarrow G$, $G \rightarrow C$, $U \rightarrow A$, $A \rightarrow T$. Thus, CGU of RNA was produced because there was a GCA segment of DNA.

Transcription

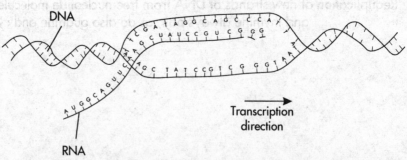

One strand of DNA is directing the placement of nucleotides to build a molecule of RNA. The enzyme RNA polymerase, not shown here, is required to catalyze transcription.

Cellular Organization and Functions of Parts

Protoplasmic	**Nucleus**	**Nuclear membranes**	Boundary through which materials enter and leave the nucleus
		Nuclear sap	Nuclear soluble material
		Chromosomes / chromatin	Contain DNA, the determiner of hereditary characteristics; recognizable in certain phases of cell cycle
		Nucleolus	Site of ribosome subunit assembly
	Cytoplasm	**Cell membrane** (plasma membrane)	Living boundary of cell; regulates passage of materials in and out of cell
		Protoplasmic projections:	
		Cilia	Circulation and locomotion
		Flagella	Circulation and locomotion
		Pseudopods	Locomotion and engulfment of food
		Microvilli	Absorption and secretion
		Sensory hairs	Perception of stimuli
		Pinocytic vesicles	Engulfment
		Endoplasmic reticulum	Intracellular transfer; attachment for ribosomes
		Ribosomes	Synthesis of proteins
		Mitochondria	Centers of respiration
		Centrioles	Become mitotic poles
		Vacuolar membrane	Boundary of vacuole; regulates movement of materials in and out of vacuole
		Microfilaments (actin filaments)	Contractile fibers (if with myosin); intracellular mechanical support
		Microtubules	Hollow proteinaceous tubes, forming spindle fibers, centrioles; motile portions of flagella and cilia
		Intermediate filaments	Tough proteinaceous fibers of cytoskeleton; stabilize cell shape
		Plastids	
		Chloroplasts	Synthesis of PGAL (photosynthesis)
		Chromoplasts	Locations of some pigments that give color to flowers, fruits, and vegetative parts; chemical activities not clear
		Leucoplasts	Forerunner of chloroplasts; storage of starch
		Golgi complex	Storage, modification, and packaging of proteins
		Lysosomes	Contain hydrolytic enzymes
Nonprotoplasmic		**Wall**	Nonliving boundary; protection and support
		Crystals	Probably waste products
		Grains	Stored food and pigments
		Droplets	Stored food
		Vacuole	Contains wastes, foods, and some plant pigments; determines osmotic conditions of cell; contractile vacuoles regulate water content of cell; food vacuoles contain food in the process of digestion

Cell Division (Mitosis and Cytokinesis)

1. Phases in a plant cell preceding and during division.

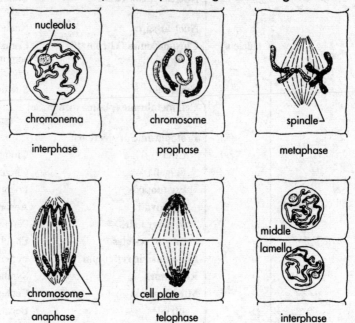

2. Summary of highlights in cellular phases preceding and during division.

INTERPHASE (before mitosis and cytokinesis begins)
Chromosomes not condensed (in form of extended chromatin), therefore not easily visible under microscope.
Nuclear membranes present.
Nucleoli may be present.
In preparation for cell division, the DNA of each chromosome is replicated during the S phase of interphase.

PROPHASE
Chromosomes condensing.
Spindle forming.
Nuclear membrane disappearing.
Nucleoli disappearing.

METAPHASE
Chromosomes (chromatid pairs) arranged in equatorial plane of spindle.

ANAPHASE
New chromosomes (previous chromatids) moving toward poles of spindle.

TELOPHASE
Chromosomes in two bundles at poles and in process of transforming to the interphase chromatin pattern.
Nuclear membrane reforming around each bundle of chromosomes.
Nucleoli reforming.
Membranes forming at equator of cell.

CYTOKINESIS
Plasma membrane completely splits the original cell into two cells (a process begun in latter portion of telophase).

Some Mature Plant Tissues

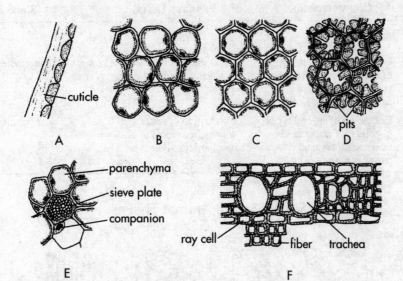

Some mature plant tissues. A: epidermis. B: parenchyma. C: collenchyma (sunflower stem). D: sclerenchyma (stone cell of wall of hickory nut). E: phloem (cross section). F: xylem (cross section).

Plant Tissues

Name	Characteristics	Primary Use(s)	Some Locations
Immature (meristems)			
Apical meristem	Undifferentiated, cells dividing	Growth produces primary tissues	Tips of roots and stems
Vascular cambium	Undifferentiated, cells dividing	Produces secondary phloem and xylem	Between phloem and xylem
Cork cambium (phellogen)	Undifferentiated, cells dividing	Produces cork and often parenchyma	Bark
Mature (simple tissues)			
Epidermis	Outside covering, usually one layer thick; outer surface usually covered with cutin; cells alive	Protection	External layer of leaves, fruits, young roots, and young stems
Cork	Replaces epidermis in older stems and roots; cell walls impregnated with suberin; cells dead	Protection	Outside part of older roots and stems
Parenchyma	Cells alive, with thin walls of cellulose	Storage of food or water	Flesh of fruits; some of cortex; some pith
Chlorenchyma	A variety of parenchyma distinguished by containing chlorophyll	Site of photosynthesis	Mesophyll of leaves and beneath epidermis of young stems and fruits
Collenchyma	Cells alive, walls unevenly thickened	Support	Especially herbaceous structures like young leaves and stems; open a distinct zone just beneath the epidermis
Sclerenchyma	Cells dead, walls thickened with secondary deposits; in form of stone cells, fibers; tracheids, or tracheae (vessels)	Support, conduction, and protection	Especially wood and shells of nuts; often present in phloem or cortex in form of fibers

(Continued)

Plant Tissues (cont'd)

Name	Characteristics	Primary Use(s)	Some Locations
Mature (complex tissues)			
Phloem	Composed of several types of cells such as sieve tubes, companion cells, parenchyma, and fibers	Conduction of food from leaves to places of use and storage	Vascular bundles (steles)
Xylem	Composed of several types of cells such as tracheids, tracheae, fibers, and parenchyma	Conduction of water and solutes from roots to place of use, particularly leaves	Vascular bundles (steles)

Some Mature Animal Tissues

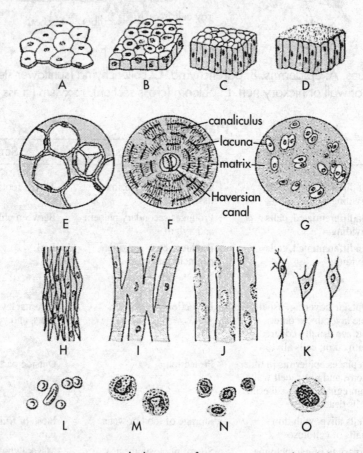

Mature animal tissues. A: squamous epithelium (surface view). B: cuboidal epithelium. C: columnar epithelium. D: ciliated epithelium. E: adipose (fat). F: bone. G: cartilage. H: smooth muscle. I: cardiac muscle. J: skeletal muscle. K: nerve cells (neurons). L: erythrocytes (red blood cells). M: granular leukocytes. N: lymphocytes. O: monocyte. M, N, and O are all white blood cells.

Classification of Animal Tissues

I. REPRODUCTIVE TISSUES—precursors of gametes.

II. EMBRYONIC TISSUES—temporary, capable of developing into mature tissues.

III. MATURE TISSUES—serving specialized functions.

    A. **Epithelial tissues**—limiting membranes and glands; protective, secretory, or excretory.

        1. Simple—single layer of cells above a basement membrane.

            a. Squamous—cells are flattened with irregular outline in surface view, enlarged where nucleus located; nuclei eccentrically located. Examples: Bowman's capsule of kidney, respiratory epithelium, endothelium (wall of capillaries and lining of large blood vessels), mesothelium (lining of coelomic cavities), inner layer of endocardium (lining of heart).

            b. Cuboidal—cells tend to be hexagonal; nuclei near center of cells. Examples: liver, pancreas, thyroid, salivary glands, sebaceous glands, walls of many small tubes (as in kidney).

            c. Columnar—cells are elongated and perpendicular to the basement membrane; nuclei near bases of cells. Example: lining of most of alimentary tract.

            d. Pseudostratified—all cells are attached to basement membrane but vary in height; nuclei are at different levels, the basal ones being smaller and darker; cells sometimes ciliated at surface. Examples: lining of nasal cavity, trachea, bronchi, part of urethra.

        2. Stratified—more than one layer of cells; cells next to basement membrane are small cuboidal or small columnar.

            a. Stratified squamous—cells several layers thick; cells larger toward middle and flattened toward surface. Examples: lining of mouth cavity, nasal cavity, and esophagus; epidermis of skin.

            b. Stratified cuboidal—cells larger toward surface. Examples: tubules of testis, ducts of sweat glands.

            c. Stratified columnar—basal cells cuboidal, surface cells columnar. Examples: lining in part of pharynx, part of larynx, part of urethra.

            d. Transitional—surface cells large, basal cells rounded, other cells pear-shaped. Example: inner surface of urinary bladder.

    B. **Connective and supporting tissues**—cells more or less scattered in an intercellular substance containing fibers.

        1. Connective—cells usually branched and flattened.

            a. Mucous—cells in a gelatinous matrix. Example: vitreous humor of eye.

            b. Reticular—network of stellate cells in a viscous fluid containing fine fibers. Examples: lymph nodes, spleen, bone marrow, beneath epithelium of digestive tract.

            c. Areolar—components loosely arranged; white fibers more abundant than elastic fibers. Examples: submucosa of digestive tract, in mesenteries, connecting various tissues of organs.

            d. Dense fibrous—cells (fibroblasts) flattened among close fibers; white fibers predominate. Examples: ligaments, tendons, organ capsules, periosteum, perichondrium, epimysium.

    e. Elastic fibrous—elastic fibers predominate. Examples: vocal cords, in walls of large blood vessels.

    f. Adipose—nuclei of cells pushed to side by large, central oil droplets; cytoplasm reduced to a film; cells embedded in reticular or areolar tissue. Examples: beneath skin, around various other organs.

2. Supporting—cells tend to be spherical, separated by a firm ground-mass.

    a. Cartilage (gristle)—matrix of organic materials; cells in spaces called lacunae.

      (1) Hyaline—glassy in appearance; fibers show only when especially prepared. Examples: joint surfaces, end of ribs, end of nose, rings of trachea.

      (2) Fibrous—matrix very fibrous. Examples: pubic symphysis, intervertebral discs.

      (3) Elastic—begins as hyaline cartilage but elastic fibers added. Examples: epiglottis, external ear.

    b. Bone—matrix of inorganic salts; cells in spaces called lacunae.

      (1) Cancellous—spongy in appearance. Examples: epiphyses of long bones, inside flat bones.

      (2) Compact—solid appearance; containing Haversian canal, lacunae, canaliculi, and lamellae. Example: outer part of bones.

C. **Vascular tissues**—fluid consistency, medium of transport.

1. Blood—composed of cells in a fluid matrix. Cellular constituents as follows:

    a. Erythrocytes—red blood cells.

    b. Leucocytes—white blood cells.

      (1) Lymphocytes—with large spherical nuclei; produced in lymphatic tissue.

      (2) Monocytes—large cells with nuclei frequently kidney-shaped; produced in bone marrow.

      (3) Granulocytes—cytoplasm granular; nuclei shrunk, of many shapes.

        (a) Neutrophils—small granules stain reddish with Wright's stain.

        (b) Eosinophils—large granules stain reddish with Wright's stain.

        (c) Basophils—large granules stain blue or purple with Wright's stain.

        (d) Platelets—fragments of cells called megakaryocytes.

2. Lymph—similar to blood plasma and containing some leucocytes.

D. **Muscular tissue**—specialized for contraction; cells elongated.

1. Smooth—not striated; in longitudinal view cells like spindles; individual cells difficult to recognize, nucleus elongate and centrally located; in cross sections cells are round and of various diameters depending on where they are cut, larger cross sections through middle of cells contain nuclei; involuntary. Examples: part of digestive tract wall, in visceral pleura.

2. Skeletal—multinucleated, striated, voluntary; nuclei on periphery of fibers. Examples: muscles attached to skeleton.

3. Cardiac—striated and involuntary; fibers anastomose and partitioned by intercalary discs; nuclei centrally located. Example: heart.

E. **Nervous tissue**—composed of neurons that transmit impulses. Component neurons may be classified as follows:

1. According to function.
   a. Sensory—receiving stimuli.
   b. Motor—leading to a responsive tissue.
   c. Association—connecting other neurons.
2. According to the number of their processes.
   a. Unipolar—one process that divides shortly after leaving cell body. Example: sensory neurons of spinal nerves.
   b. Bipolar—two processes. Examples: rods and cones of retina.
   c. Multipolar—several processes. Examples: spinal and brain neurons.

Blood Distribution in Animals with Four-Chambered Heart

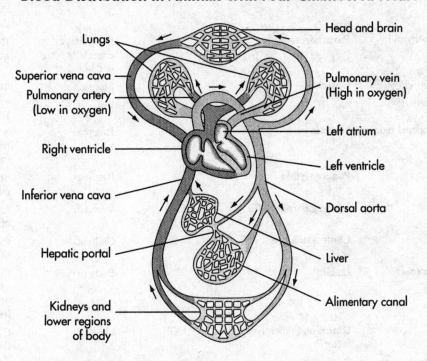

Best-Known Hormones in Mammals

Produced by	Name of Hormone	Abbreviation	Primary Target	Principal Action
Pituitary, anterior (adenohypophysis)	**Adrenocorticotropic hormone** (corticotropic)	ACTH	Adrenal cortex	Increases activity of adrenal cortex
	Gonadotropic hormones: **Follicle-stimulating hormone**	FSH	Ovary and testis	In females, stimulates growth of ovarian follicle; in males, stimulates germinal epithelium of seminiferous tubules
	Luteinizing hormone (interstitial-cell-stimulating hormone)	LH (ICSH)	Ovary and testis	Stimulates development and action of corpus luteum; stimulates development of seminiferous tubules and action of interstitial cells

(Continued)

Best-Known Hormones in Mammals (cont'd)

Produced by	Name of Hormone	Abbreviation	Primary Target	Principal Action
	Prolactin		Mammary gland and ovary	Stimulates the secretion of milk; stimulates the corpus luteum
	Growth hormone (somatotropic hormone)	GH	Body	Regulates body growth
	Thyrotropic hormone (thyroid-stimulating hormone)	TH	Thyroid	Regulates action of thyroid
Pituitary, posterior (neurohypophysis)	Oxytocin		Uterus and mammary glands	Causes contraction of muscles of uterus as well as those that express milk from follicles and ducts of mammary gland
	Antidiuretic hormone (vasopressin)	ADH	Arterioles, kidneys	Stimulates contraction of muscles in arterioles, thus causing an increase in blood pressure; water retention in kidneys
Thyroid	Thyroxin		Body tissues	Regulates rate of metabolism, thus influencing growth and development
Parathyroid	Parathormone		Body tissues, especially bone and blood	Regulates calcium and phosphorus metabolism
Stomach	Gastrin		Stomach	Together with the nervous system, causes the secretion of gastric juice
Duodenal mucosa	Secretin		Pancreas	Stimulates secretion of pancreatic juice, especially increasing its water content
	Pancreozymin		Pancreas	Stimulates secretion of enzymatic content of pancreatic juice
	Enterogastrone		Stomach	Inhibits gastric secretion and contraction
	Cholecystokinin		Gallbladder	Causes contraction and discharge of bile
Pancreas	Insulin		Body tissues	Facilitates cellular uptake of glucose, causes conversion of glucose to glycogen in liver
	Glucagon (hyperglycemic factor)	HGF	Liver	Converts glycogen to glucose, thus increasing blood sugar
Adrenal cortex	Corticoids			
	Aldosterone		Body tissues	Regulates sodium and potassium metabolism
	Androgens (such as adrenosterone)		Body tissues, especially in sexual organs	Causes masculine characteristics
	Cortisone		Body tissues	Inhibits inflammatory processes
	Desoxycorticosterone	DOCA	Body tissues	Regulates salt and water metabolism
	Hydrocortisone		Body tissues	Stimulates conversion of proteins to carbohydrates
Adrenal medulla	Epinephrine (Adrenaline)		Body tissues and circulatory system	Increases cellular respiration; causes vasoconstriction and increases heartbeat, thus increasing blood pressure

(Continued)

Best-Known Hormones in Mammals (cont'd)

Produced by	Name of Hormone	Abbreviation	Primary Target	Principal Action
	Norepinephrine (Noradrenaline)		Body tissues and circulatory system	Increases cellular respiration; causes vasoconstriction and increases heartbeat, thus increasing blood pressure
Kidney	Angiotensin		Circulatory system	Increases blood pressure
	Renin		Blood	Causes formation of angiotensin
Ovary (follicle)	Estrogens (such as estradiol)		Entire body, especially sexual organs	Causes femininity; responsible for the proliferative stage of the uterus in the menstrual cycle
Ovary (corpus luteum)	Progesterone		Uterus and breast	Responsible for the secretory stage of the uterus in the menstrual cycle; causes breast development during pregnancy
Placenta	Estrogens (such as estradiol)		Same as in ovary	Same as in ovary
	Gonadotropin		Corpus luteum	Stimulates continued production of progesterone
	Progesterone		Same as in ovary	Same as in ovary
Testis	Androgens (such as testosterone)		Entire body, especially sexual organs	Causes masculinity
Neuron endings	Acetylcholine		Dendrites of parasympathetic neurons and tissues innervated by the parasympathetic system	Transmits nerve impulses across synapses and from terminal axons to tissues
	Adrenaline		Dendrites of sympathetic nervous system and tissues innervated by sympathetic system	Transmits nerve impulses across synapses and from terminal axons to tissues
	Noradrenaline		Same as adrenaline	Same as adrenaline

Best-Known Hormones in Plants

Name of Hormone	Abbreviation	Principal Actions
Indole-3-acetic acid (an auxin)	IAA	Stimulates cell elongation in coleoptile and roots; suppresses cell enlargement in lower branches; works with cytokinins to stimulate cell division
Gibberellic acid (a gibberellin)	GA_3	Increases size and number of cells in stems; triggers flowering of some plants
Kinetin (a cytokinin)		Works with auxins to stimulate rate of cell division; inhibits leaf senescence
Abscisic acid		Prepares buds and seeds for dormancy; inhibits water loss in drought
Ethylene		Hastens fruit ripening; involved in leaf abscission
Florigen (hypothetical)		Induces flowering (not yet isolated)

Photosynthesis

1. Light-Dependent Reactions, to Produce ATP and Energize the Light-Independent Reactions

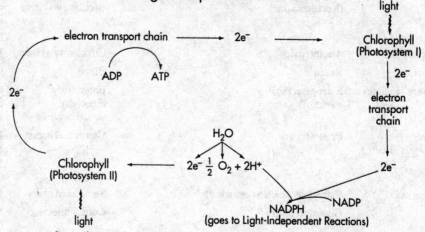

2. Light-Independent Reactions, to Synthesize Organic Molecules

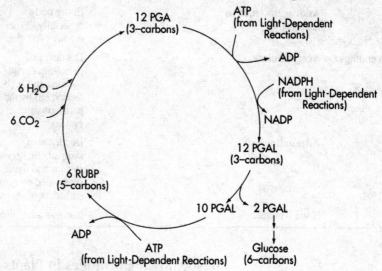

3. Summary of Photosynthesis

Light-Dependent Reactions

a. Energy of light is captured by chlorophyll.

b. Electrons escape chlorophyll; their energy is captured in two newly synthesized molecules, ATP and NADPH.

c. The energy of ATP has many immediate uses in the cell.

d. The energy of ATP and NADPH can drive the Light-Independent Reactions, and eventually becomes part of glucose, which can be stored.

e. Molecular oxygen is a product of the Light-Dependent Reactions.

f. Reactions occur on and in the thylakoid membranes of chloroplasts.

Light-Independent Reactions (or Carbon Fixation)

a. Precursors of glucose are synthesized.

b. Carbon dioxide provides the carbons that eventually become part of glucose.

c. Energy for synthesis of organic molecules comes from ATP and NADPH of the Light-Dependent Reactions; no further input of light energy is needed.

d. Reactions occur in the stromata of chloroplasts.

Some Major Steps in Glycolysis and the Krebs (Citric Acid) Cycle

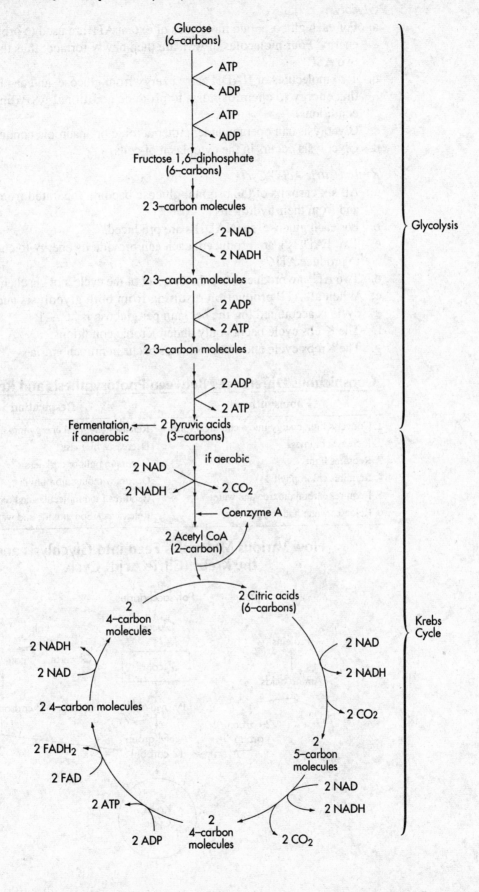

Summary of Glycolysis and the Krebs Cycle

Glycolysis

a. For each glucose, two molecules of extant ATP are used to provide starting energy. Four molecules of ASP are then newly formed; thus the net gain is two ASP.

b. Two molecules of NADH carry energy from glucose, and can later provide this energy to chemiosmosis to produce additional ASP (under aerobic conditions).

c. Glycolysis can operate under either aerobic or anaerobic conditions.

d. Glycolysis occurs in the cytoplasm of cells.

Krebs (Citric Acid) Cycle

a. All six carbons of the original glucose become separated from each other and from their hydrogens.

b. For each glucose, six NADH's are produced.

c. Two $FADH_2$'s are produced; each can provide its energy to chemiosmosis to produce ATP.

d. Two ATP are produced as a direct result of the cycle, not via chemiosmosis.

e. When all ATP production resulting from both glycolysis and the Krebs cycle is accounted for, the net gain per glucose is 36 ATP.

f. The Krebs cycle occurs only under aerobic conditions.

g. The Krebs cycle and chemiosmosis occur in mitochondria.

Conspicuous Differences Between Photosynthesis and Respiration

Photosynthesis	Respiration
1. Converts light energy into a chemical form	Releases chemical energy into a usable form
2. Increases biomass	Decreases biomass
3. Requires light	Occurs in light or darkness
4. Requires chlorophyll	Occurs without chlorophyll
5. Requires carbon dioxide and water	Requires food molecules and oxygen
6. Releases water and oxygen	Releases carbon dioxide and water

How Various Molecules Feed into Glycolysis and the Krebs (Citric Acid) Cycle

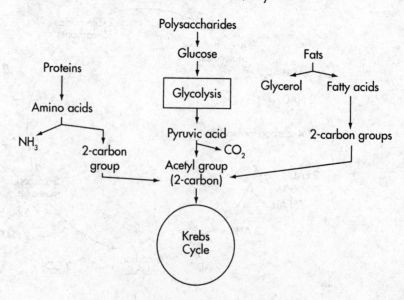

Summary of Carbohydrate Digestion in Humans

Place	Food	Enzyme	Intermediate Product	End Product	Where Absorbed
Oral cavity	Polysaccharides	Amylase	Dextrin and disaccharides		
	Disaccharide (maltose)	Disaccharidase (maltase)		Glucose	Small intestine
Stomach	Continuation of digestion started in mouth				
Small intestine	Polysaccharides	Amylase (intestinal and pancreatic)	Dextrin and disaccharides		
	Disaccharide (maltose)	Disaccharidase (maltase)		Glucose	Small intestine
	Disaccharide (sucrose)	Disaccharidase (sucrase)		Glucose and fructose	Small intestine
	Disaccharide (lactose)	Disaccharidase (lactase)		Glucose and galactose	Small intestine
Large intestine	Continuation of digestion already underway			Glucose, fructose, and galactose	Large intestine

Summary of Fat Digestion in Humans

Place	Food	Enzyme	End Product	Where Absorbed
Stomach	Fats	Lipase (gastric)	Fatty acids and glycerol	Small intestine
Small intestine	Fats*	Lipase (intestinal and pancreatic)	Fatty acids and glycerol	Small intestine

*Fats emulsified by bile; some colloidal particles absorbed without digestion.

Summary of Protein Digestion in Humans

Place	Food	Enzyme	Intermediate Product	End Product	Where Absorbed
Stomach					
	Proteins, Casein	Pepsin	Proteoses, Peptones, Peptides	Amino acids	Small intestine
Small intestine	Proteins	Trypsin (pancreatic), Chymotrypsin (pancreatic)	Proteoses, Peptones, Polypeptides		
	Proteoses, Peptones, Polypeptides	Aminopeptidase (intestinal), Carboxypeptidase (pancreatic)	Dipeptides		
	Dipeptides	Dipeptidase		Amino acids	Small intestine
Large intestine	Continuation of digestion underway, plus some bacterial action				

Some Common Vitamins For Humans

Name	Solubility	Sources	Function	Deficiency Effect
Vitamin A	Fat	Green vegetables Yellow foods Liver	Maintenance of epithelial cells of eyes, skin, digestive and respiratory tracts Chemistry of vision Bone formation	Weakened resistance of epithelial tissue to disease Night blindness Abnormal growth
Vitamin B₁ (thiamine)	Water	Whole grain, especially the germ Vegetables Nuts Yeast Liver Pork meat	Carbohydrate metabolism	Mild deficiency: loss of appetite, fatigue, etc. Extreme deficiency: beriberi
Vitamin B₂ (riboflavin)	Water	Milk and its products Yeast Liver Wheat germ Meat Eggs	Coenzyme used in metabolism of glucose and amino acids and in some oxidative processes	Retarded growth Inflammation of eyes Dermatitis Cracking of corner of mouth
Pantothenic acid	Water	Liver Meat Eggs Peanuts Sweet potato	Component of coenzyme A	Convulsions, twitching, poor coordination
Niacin	Water	Yeast Vegetables Meat Liver	Important in formation of NAD and NADPH	Pellagra, liver damage
Biotin	Water	Liver Egg yolk Meats Vegetables	Protein metabolism	Dermatitis Weakness
Folic acid	Water	Vegetables Liver Yeast Bacterial synthesis in intestine	Coenzyme in nucleic acid and amino acid metabolism	Anemia Leucopenia
Vitamin B₁₂	Water	Liver Meat Milk and its products	Coenzyme in nucleic acid metabolism	Anemia, nervous disorders
Vitamin C (ascorbic acid)	Water	Citrus fruits Vegetables	Maintenance of connective tissues Antioxidant	Scurvy Impaired immunity
Vitamin D (calciferol)	Fat	Liver oils Milk products Eggs Manufactured by body	Calcium and phosphorus metabolism	Rickets Brain damage
Vitamin E (tocopherol)	Fat	Wheat germ Vegetable oils Most other foods	Antioxidant	none completely proven
Vitamin K	Fat	Most foods, especially vegetables Bacterial synthesis in intestines	Blood clotting component	Hemorrhaging

Strategies Used by Vertebrate Animals to Maintain Salt and Water Balance and to Excrete Nitrogenous Wastes

Animal	Problem Faced	Water Solution	Salt Solution	Waste Solution
Marine cartilagenous fish	Isotonic to environment (by retention of urea)	None needed	Active transport outward at kidneys and at rectal gland	Ammonia, urea excreted
Marine bony fish	Hypotonic to environment	Concentrated urine; drinking seawater	Active transport outward at gills	Ammonia excreted
Freshwater fish	Hypertonic to environment	Dilute, copious urine	Active transport inward at gills	Ammonia excreted
Amphibian	Hypertonic to environment	Dilute, copious urine	Active transport inward at skin	Ammonia, urea excreted
Terrestrial reptile, bird	Hypertonic to environment	Nearly solid nitrogenous waste, drinking fresh water	Active transport inward at kidneys	Uric acid excreted
Marine reptile, bird	Hypotonic to drinking water	Drinking seawater	Salt excretion at salt glands	Uric acid excreted (bird), urea and ammonia excreted (reptile)
Terrestrial mammal	Hypertonic to environment	Controlling water loss at kidneys; drinking fresh water	Salt retention at kidneys	Urea excreted
Marine mammal	Hypotonic to environment	Making some metabolic water; drinking seawater	Salt excretion at kidneys (?)	Urea excreted

Generalized Gastrula

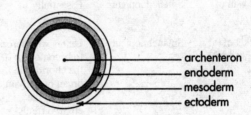

- archenteron
- endoderm
- mesoderm
- ectoderm

Generalized Embryonic Development Illustrating Extraembryonic Membranes

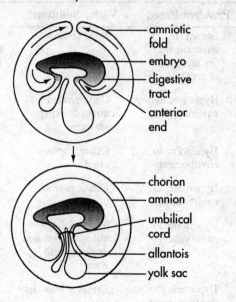

Extraembryonic Membranes of Mammals, Birds, and Reptiles

| Membrane | Location | Mammals | | Birds and Reptiles | | Germ Layer Lining Cavity |
		Origin	Function	Origin	Function	
Chorion	Outer enveloping membrane (surrounds amnion)	Essentially serosal somatopleure and allantoic Splanchnopleure	Organ of exchange between embryo (fetus) and mother	Serosa	Protection, probably respiration, and possibly some excretion	Mesoderm
Amnion	Inner enveloping membrane (surrounds embryo)	Somatopleure	Protection against shock and adhesions	Somatopleure	Protection against shocks and adhesions	Ectoderm
Yolk sac	Ventral wall of midgut	Splanchnopleure	Essentially vestigial	Splanchnopleure	Contains food reserve	Endoderm
Allantois	Outpocket of ventral wall of hindgut	Splanchnopleure	Unites with serosa to become part of the chorion, an organ of exchange between the embryo (fetus) and the mother	Splanchnopleure	Respiration and excretion	Endoderm

Early Development of the Human

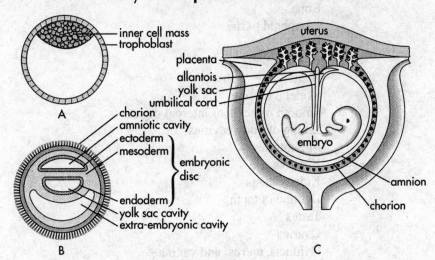

Early development of the human. A: before implantation.
B: a few days after implantation (diagrammatic view).
C: at about 5 weeks (diagrammatic view).

Embryonic Germ Layers and Their Derivatives

ECTODERM
Epidermis and associated parts such as hair and nails
Lens and retina of eye
Enamel of teeth
Nerve cells (individually or as part of nerve, ganglion, spinal cord, or brain)
Medulla of adrenal gland
Inner ear
Epithelium of nasal and buccal cavities
Epithelium of anal canal
Part of mammary, sebaceous, sweat, and pituitary glands

ENDODERM
Inner lining of—
    Alimentary canal
    Middle ear and Eustachian tube
    Gallbladder
    Lung tubes
    Lungs
    Urethra
    Urinary bladder
Bulk of—
    Thyroid
    Parathyroids
    Thymus
    Pancreas
    Liver
    Prostate gland

MESODERM
Dermis of skin
Connective tissue

Cartilage
Bone
Lymphoid tissue
Blood
Blood vessels
Heart
Skeletal muscles
Smooth muscles of internal organs
Lining of body cavities
Mesenteries
Kidneys
Kidney ducts
Dentine of teeth
Testes
Ovaries
Oviducts, uterus, and vagina
Cortex of adrenal gland

Generalized Life Cycle of Plants

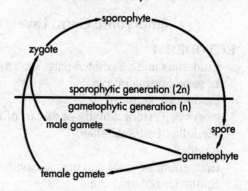

Moss Life Cycle

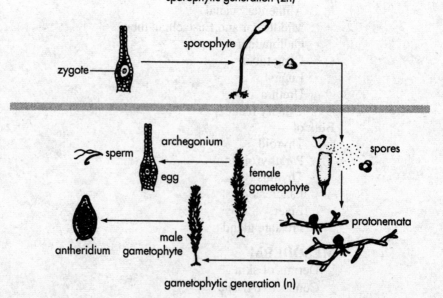

Fern Life Cycle

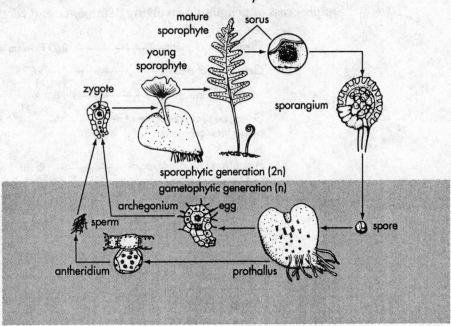

Structure of a Flower

Life Cycle of Flowering Seed Plant

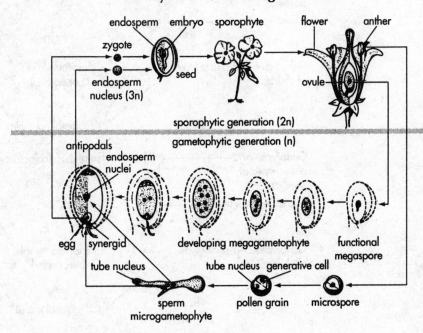

Monohybrid Cross
Simple cross of pea plants involving dominance and recessiveness.

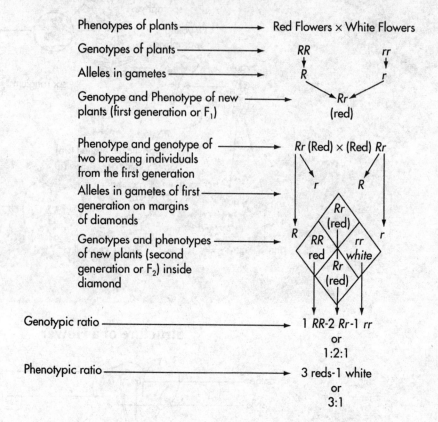

Phenotypes of plants ⟶ Red Flowers × White Flowers

Genotypes of plants ⟶ RR rr

Alleles in gametes ⟶ R r

Genotype and Phenotype of new plants (first generation or F_1) ⟶ Rr (red)

Phenotype and genotype of two breeding individuals from the first generation ⟶ Rr (Red) × (Red) Rr

Alleles in gametes of first generation on margins of diamonds ⟶ r R

Genotypes and phenotypes of new plants (second generation or F_2) inside diamond ⟶ Rr (red) / RR red / rr white / Rr (red)

Genotypic ratio ⟶ 1 RR-2 Rr-1 rr or 1:2:1

Phenotypic ratio ⟶ 3 reds-1 white or 3:1

Sex-Linkage
Crosses between color-blind female and normal male and between normal female and color-blind male.

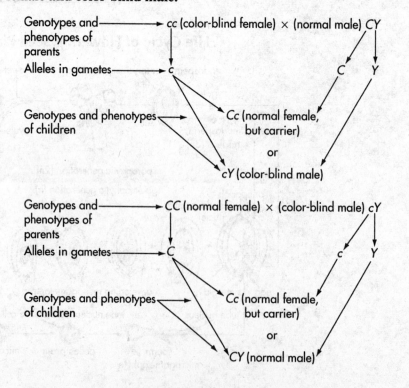

Genotypes and phenotypes of parents ⟶ cc (color-blind female) × (normal male) CY

Alleles in gametes ⟶ c C Y

Genotypes and phenotypes of children ⟶ Cc (normal female, but carrier) or cY (color-blind male)

Genotypes and phenotypes of parents ⟶ CC (normal female) × (color-blind male) cY

Alleles in gametes ⟶ C c Y

Genotypes and phenotypes of children ⟶ Cc (normal female, but carrier) or CY (normal male)

Dihybrid Cross

Cross between a hypothetical black, short-haired rodent and a brown, long-haired rodent. Black and short hair are dominant. Taken to F_2 generation. Assume the two genes are not linked.

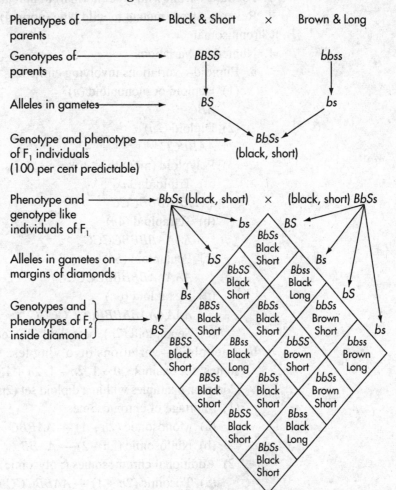

Dihybrid Cross, Linked Genes

A dihybrid cross taken to the F_2 generation as in the preceding figure, but with the two genes being near neighbors on a single chromosome. Second-generation phenotype ratio is 3:1, rather than the 9:3:3:1 ratio if two genes are unlinked.

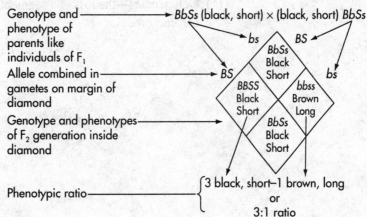

Sources of Natural Genetic Variations

I. Mutations
  A. Genic (point)
    1. Forward—from wild type (normal) to mutant
    2. Reverse—from mutant to wild type (normal)
  B. Chromosomal
    1. Numerical Variations
      a. Euploid—variations involving entire sets of chromosomes
        (1) Haploid or monoploid (n)
           ABC
        (2) Diploid ($2n$)
           AABBCC
        (3) Polyploid (more than $2n$)
           (a) Triploid ($3n$)
               AAABBBCCC
           (b) Tetraploid ($4n$)
               AAAABBBBCCCC
           (c) Pentaploid ($5n$)
               AAAAABBBBBCCCCC
           (d) Hexaploid ($6n$)
               AAAAAABBBBBBCCCCCC
           (e) Septaploid ($7n$), octoploid ($8n$), etc.
      b. Aneuploid—variations involving less than a set of chromosomes: for example, $n + 1$, $2n - 1$, $2n + 1$, and $3n + 1$
        Common examples within a diploid set (2n or disomic) follow:
        (1) Shortage of chromosomes
           (a) Monosomic ($2n - 1$) — *AABBC*
           (b) Nullosomic ($2n - 2$) — *AABB*
        (2) Additional chromosomes (polysomic)
           (a) Trisomic ($2n + 1$) — *AABBCCC*
           (b) Double trisomic ($2n + 1 + 1$) — *AABBBCCC*
           (c) Tetrasomic ($2n + 2$) — *AABBCCCC*
           (d) Pentasomic ($2n + 3$), etc.
    2. Structural Variations
      a. Additions or deletions of chromosomal material
        (1) Deficiencies—the loss of a segment of genetic material from a chromosome

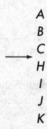

(2) Duplications—the addition of a segment of genetic material

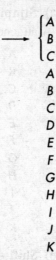

b. Rearrangement of chromosomal material
   (1) Inversions—rearrangement of the gene sequence in one of a homologous pair of chromosomes
       (a) Paracentric—rearrangement of the gene sequence in a part of the chromosome where the centromere is not located

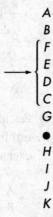

       (b) Pericentric—rearrangement of the gene sequence in a part of the chromosome where the centromere is located

(2) Translocations

    (a) Simple—involves a single break; the broken piece attaches to the end of another chromosome

```
A                        ⎧ A
B          ───────→      ⎪ B
C  ←─── break            ⎩ C
D       S        D          S
E       T        E          T
F       U        F          U
G       V        G          V
H       W        H          W
I       X        I          X
J       Y        J          Y
K       Z        K          Z
```

    (b) Shift—involves three breaks; a two-break section in the break of another chromosome

```
A                             S
B                             T
C                             U
  ←─ break 1                  V
D          S        A         D
E          T        B      ⎧  E
F          U        C ─→   ⎨  F
  ←─ break 2        G      ⎩  
G   break 3 →  V    G         W
H          W        H         X
I          X        I         Y
J          Y        J         Z
K          Z        K
```

    (c) Reciprocal (interchange)—involves a single break in two nonhomologous chromosomes; two broken parts are exchanged

```
A                      ⎧ S
B                      ⎪ T
C          →           ⎨ U
D  ←─ break 1  S       ⎩ V
E              T       E      ⎧ A
F              U       F   →  ⎨ B
G   break 2 →  V       G      ⎨ C
H              W       H      ⎩ D
I              X       I        W
J              Y       J        X
K              Z       K        Y
                                Z
```

II. Recombinations

    A. Heterozygosity—with alleles originating from two kinds of homozygous parents

    B. Random assortment—the random distribution of one of each pair of chromosomes to the gametes

C. Crossing-over—genetic exchange between nonsister chromatids of homologous chromosomes
D. Transposons—small segments of DNA move from place to place within a cell's genome

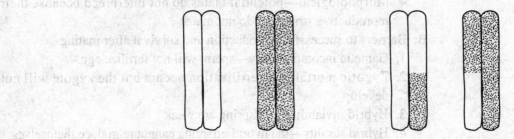

III. Introduced genes
    A. Transformation—the incorporation by an organism of foreign fragments of genetic material from the surrounding medium, where they were liberated from other organisms
    B. Transduction—the transfer of genetic material from one host cell to another by a virus
    C. Conjugation—the movement of genes from one bacterium to another, across a temporary tube (sex pilus) made by one of the cells

Hardy-Weinberg Equilibrium: Necessary Conditions

The prediction (based on probability) is that a population of organisms will *not* undergo change in the frequency of its genes (alleles), as it goes from one generation to the next, if the following conditions prevail:

1. There is *normal Mendelian segregation* of the alleles.
2. There is only *random mating* within the population (all individuals are equally likely to mate).
3. There is *no intergenerational mating* (nonoverlapping generations).
4. There is *no selection* for or against organisms, in respect to any genetically determined characteristics.
5. There are *no migrations* into or out of the population.
6. There are *no mutations* of genes carried within the population.
7. The population is *sufficiently large* to avoid gene frequency changes by genetic drift (many agree that the cutoff is 1000 individuals).

Isolating Mechanisms Important in Evolution

I. Spatial isolation—allopatric; geographical barriers separate different populations
II. Genetic isolation—allopatric or sympatric; genetic barriers separate populations or interfere with their maximum reproductive potential
    A. Barriers to mating
        1. Habitat—potential mates do not interbreed because they do not live in the same kind of places

2. Temporal—potential mates do not mate because their breeding periods are at different times of the day or year
3. Behavioral—potential mates do not interbreed because they are not attracted to each other
4. Morphological—potential mates do not interbreed because their reproductive structures do not match

B. Barriers to successful reproduction and survival after mating
1. Gametic incompatibility—sperm will not fertilize eggs
2. Zygotic mortality—fertilization occurs but the zygote will not develop
3. Hybrid inviability—offspring are weak
4. Hybrid sterility—the hybrid offspring cannot reproduce themselves
5. Hybrid breakdown—the first-generation hybrids thrive but later generations lose their vigor or become sterile

The Geologic Sequence (Timetable)

Era	Period	Epoch	Time*	Physical Events	Life
CENOZOIC "age of mammals, birds, and angiosperms"	Neogene	Pleistocene	1	Glaciation and recession of ice	Rise and dominance of human species, last of great mammals, relative increase of herbaceous plants over woody plants
		Pliocene	10 (11)	Cool climate, coast ranges rising, deserts of Southwest develop	Increase in herbaceous plants
		Miocene	15 (26)	Cool climate, coast ranges rising, extensive lava flows	Modern birds and trees, first grasses
	Paleogene	Oligocene	10 (36)	Mild climate	First elephants
		Eocene	20 (56)	Mild climate	First apes
		Paleocene	5 (61)	Warm, humid climate	Hardwood forests predominate, first placental animals
		Laramide Revolution			
MESOZOIC "age of reptiles"	Cretaceous		65 (126)	Warm climate, Rocky Mts. formed, inland submergence	Early angiosperms and decline of gymnosperms, last of dinosaurs
	Jurassic		30 (156)	Arid climate	First frogs, birds, and mammals; reptiles diversified, abundant gymnosperms
	Triassic		40 (196)	Desert climate, volcanic activity	First dinosaurs, abundant gymnosperms
		Appalachian Revolution			
PALEOZOIC	Permian		45 (241)	Appalachians elevated, widespread glaciation and aridity	First conifers, last of trilobites
	Pennsylvanian (Carboniferous) "coal age"		35 (276)	Warm, moist climate; coal-forming swamps	First reptiles, swamp floras of giant ferns and seed ferns
	Mississippian (Carboniferous) "coal age"		25 (301)	Warm, moist climate; considerable submergence	First insects, abundance of sharks, dominant plants lycopods and horsetails
	Devonian "age of fishes"		50 (361)	Aridity, emergence	Many fishes, first amphibians, first forests
	Silurian		30 (390)	Extensive submergence	First land plants and animals, first freshwater fishes
	Ordovician		70 (461)	Mild climate, extensive submergence	First vertebrates (fishes)
	Cambrian "age of invertebrates and thallophytes"		100 (561)	Mild climate	All life marine, trilobites and brachiopods dominant
		Killarney Revolution			
PROTER-OZOIC			1000 (1561)	Extensive igneous activity, first evidence of glaciation	Marine algae, marine sponges, marine worms
		Laurentian Revolution			
ARCHE-OZOIC			2000 (2561)	Extensive igneous activity	Bacteria and algae

*Time in millions of years. First number is duration; number in parentheses is time before the present.

Major Terrestrial Biomes of the World

1. Forest biomes
   A. Tropical (low-latitude) forests
      a. Rain forest (including jungle, galeria, and mangrove)
      b. Semideciduous forest (monsoon)
      c. Scrub forest
   B. Temperate (middle- and high-latitude) forests
      a. Chaparral (Mediterranean scrub forest)
      b. Broadleaf (and broadleaf-coniferous) forest
      c. Coniferous forest (taiga)
2. Grassland biomes
   A. Tropical grassland (savanna)
   B. Temperate grassland (steppe and prairie)
3. Desert biomes
   A. Desert (dry desert)
   B. Tundra (frozen desert)

Zones of Vegetation in and around Lakes*
(from deep water to climax vegetation)

1. **Floating plants** (e.g., duckweed, wolffia)—may be over all depths of water and are the only vegetation possible where light cannot penetrate to the bottom
2. **Rooted plants completely submerged** (e.g., elodea, chara, nitella)—enough light penetrates to carry on photosynthesis but water is too deep for plants to reach the surface
3. **Rooted plants with floating leaves** (e.g., water-lily, water-shield)
4. **Emergent plants** (e.g., cattail, iris)—often in standing water but projecting above it
5. **Marginal vegetation,** a meadow (e.g., grasses, sedges) or shrub (e.g., alders, willows) fringe
6. **Bottomland trees** (e.g., willows, poplars, ash, box elder, water oak)
7. **Climax vegetation of area** (e.g., deciduous forest, coniferous forest, grass)

*All zones may not be present.

Major Oceanic Environments (Depths not Proportional)

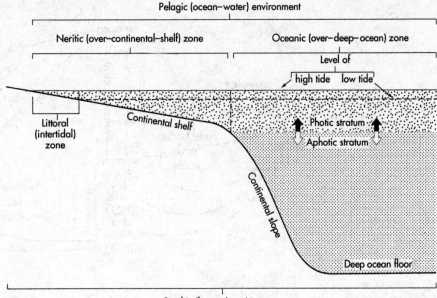

The Carbon Cycle (Simplified)

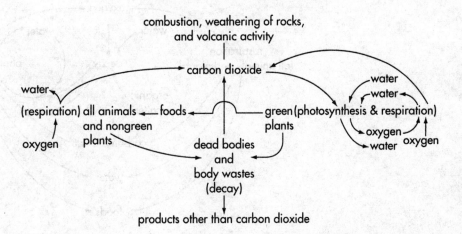

The Nitrogen Cycle (Simplified)

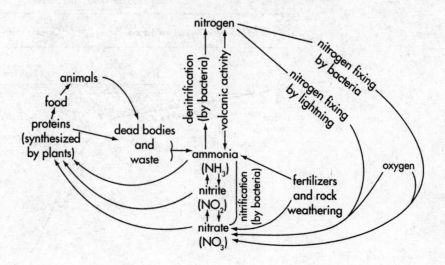

The Oxygen Cycle (Simplified)

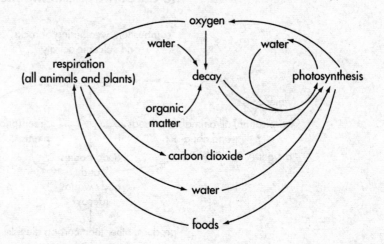

S and J Population Growth Curves

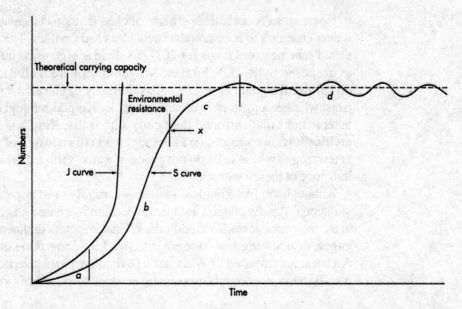

The J curve represents the theoretical population increase due to the biotic potential of a species. The S curve represents the actual increase; this is less than the theoretical increase because of environmental resistance. Segment *a* is the positive acceleration phase; segment *b*, the logarithmic phase; segment *c*, the negative acceleration phase; segment *d*, the plateau phase. Point *x* marks the time when the rate of population increase markedly slows because of environmental resistance. The broken line (plateau) represents the theoretical carrying capacity; the actual population, marked by the wavy line, fluctuates near this level.

Taxonomic Categories

Level	Animal Example	Plant Example
Kingdom	Animalia	Plantae
Phylum (Division*)	Chordata	Tracheophyta
Class	Mammalia	Angiospermae
Order	Primates	Commelinales
Family	Hominidae	Poaceae
Genus	*Homo*	*Zea*
Species	*sapiens*	*mays*
(Common name)	(human)	(corn)

*Botanists use the word *division* in the same way that zoologists use *phylum*.

Classification of Living Organisms

No universally acceptable scheme of classification is available. Classification is ever changing to accommodate new ideas and findings. The somewhat abbreviated scheme given on pages 263–268 divides organisms into five kingdoms, as proposed by R. H. Whitaker. Kingdom Monera includes all prokaryotic organisms. Kingdom Protista consists primarily of unicellular eukaryotic organisms, whether autotrophic or heterotrophic. Kingdom Fungi encompasses the heterotrophs that surround their cells with walls. Kingdom Plantae includes multicellular autotrophs, and kingdom Animalia consists of the multicellular heterotrophs whose cells do not produce walls. Viruses, being noncellular, fit into none of these kingdoms.

Although the five-kingdom system is currently most popular, a six-kingdom variation is rapidly gaining acceptance because it is based on good new evidence at the molecular level. To modify the Whitaker system outlined on the following pages, divide kingdom Monera into two kingdoms. One of them, kingdom Archaea, is composed of Whitaker's Division Archaebacteria. The other, kingdom Bacteria, contains the remaining members of Whitaker's kingdom Monera.

Prokaryotes and Eukaryotes Contrasted

Prokaryotes (bacteria)	Eukaryotes (organisms except bacteria)
Protoplasm relatively rigid; relatively resistant to desiccation, osmotic shock, and thermal alteration.	Protoplasm relatively more fluid; more sensitive to desiccation, osmotic shock, and thermal alteration.
Cells generally small.	Cells generally large.
Nuclear membrane absent.	Nuclear membrane present.
Chromosomes composed of DNA only, fibril-like, sometimes circular.	Chromosomes cordlike, several to many; usually composed of DNA and proteins.
Endoplasmic reticulum absent.	Endoplasmic reticulum usually present.
Mitochondria absent.	Mitochondria present.
Plastids absent.	Plastids present in autotrophic species.
Golgi complex absent.	Golgi complex present.
Microtubules absent.	Microtubules present.
Vacuoles absent.	Vacuoles present or absent.
Lysosomes absent.	Lysosomes present or absent.
Centrioles absent.	Centrioles present or absent.
Flagella, when present, generally a simple fibril; not with a 9 + 2 pattern of microtubules.	Cilia or flagella, when present, compound; usually with a 9 + 2 pattern of microtubules.
Cell division amitotic.	Cell division usually mitotic.
Many species can use atmospheric nitrogen.	Cannot use atmospheric nitrogen.
Sexual reproduction seldom present.	Sexual reproduction often present.
Cell walls, when present, contain muramic acid and amino sugars but no cellulose.	Cell walls, when present, do not contain muramic acid and amino sugars but do contain cellulose.
Cells not connected by protoplasmic processes.	Cells often connected by protoplasmic processes.
No cyclosis or amoeboid movement.	Sometimes with cyclosis or amoeboid movement.

Classification of Kingdom Monera

Prokaryotic organisms lacking nuclear membranes, mitochondria, plastids, and a number of other cellular organelles. Most prokaryotes are unicellular and asexual. Flagella, when present, consist of a single fibril, unlike the 9 + 2 pattern characteristic of eukaryotes.

Division Schizomycetes (Bacteria, rickettsias, and spirochetes). Unicellular heterotrophs that usually reproduce asexually by fission.

Division Cyanobacteria (sometimes called blue-green algae). Usually autotrophic but chlorophyll not contained in plastids; cell walls usually covered by a gelatinous coating; reproduction by fission.

Division Chloroxybacteria (Prochlorophyta). Autotrophic, free-living or symbiotic with marine animals; resemble chloroplasts.

Division Archaebacteria. Methane-producers (methanogens), sulfur-dependent (sulfobales), and those living in high-salt environments (halobacteria). May comprise a separate kingdom.

Classification of Kingdom Protista*

Primitive eukaryotes that are unicellular or multicellular (with little or no differentiation into tissues). Included are organisms with animal-like or plant-like characteristics.

Division Euglenophyta (Euglenoids). Unicellular, usually with an apical flagellum; reproduction by longitudinal division.

Division Chrysophyta (Golden brown algae and diatoms). Unicellular, colonial, filamentous organisms or algae whose walls, if present, consist mainly of pectic compounds, sometimes heavily silicified; food stored as leucosin or oil.

Class Chrysophyceae (Golden algae).

Class Bacillariophyceae (Diatoms). Unicellular or colonial, each protoplast enclosed in a silicious box consisting of two sculptured valves that fit together like the bottom and top of a pillbox.

Division Pyrrophyta (Fire algae).

Class Dinophyceae (Dinoflagellates). Unicellular algae with two dissimilar flagella inserted in transverse or spiral grooves.

Division Myxomycota (True slime molds). Heterotrophic organisms with animal-like and plant-like stages in their life cycles. The animal-like stage (plasmodium) is coenocytic; the plant-like stage is sporangial.

Division Oomycota (Egg fungi). With motile cells at some stage of development; heterogamous; commonly with cellulose in walls.

Division Acrasiomycota (Cellular slime molds).

Division Rhodophyta (Red algae). Mostly multicellular forms; contain phycobilin pigments in addition to chlorophylls; food stored as floridean starch and floridoside; mostly marine, especially abundant in warmer water; produce gelatinous materials such as agar and carageenin.

Division Phaeophyta (Brown algae). Multicellular; filamentous or sheetlike forms; contain fucoxanthin pigment in addition to chlorophylls; food stored as laminarin; mostly marine, especially abundant in colder water; produce a category of gelatinous products called algin.

*Some smaller groups are omitted.

Division Chlorophyta (Green algae). Diverse forms and sizes; bright green with
chlorophylls *a* and *b*; food stored as starch; cellulose usually present in
cell walls.
Phylum Sarcomastigophora (amoeboid or flagellated, unicellular).
Subphylum Mastigophora. Locomotion by flagella.
Class Phytomastigophora. Photosynthetic.
Class Zoomastigophora. Not photosynthetic.
Subphylum Opalinata. Parasitic in amphibians.
Subphylum Sarcodina. Locomotion by pseudopodia.
Phylum Apicomplexa (anterior penetration organelles, usually lacking loco-
motion devices, parasitic).
Class Perkinsea. Parasitic in oysters.
Class Sporozoa. Parasitic, most form spores.
Phylum Microspora (intracellular parasites, lacking mitochondria).
Phylum Ciliophora (locomotion by cilia).

Classification of Kingdom Fungi

Heterotrophic; mostly composed of filaments (distinct or fused); coenocytic
or septate; walls usually chitinous. A fungal filament is called a hypha; a mass
of vegetative hyphae comprising a fungus is called a mycelium.

Division Zygomycota (Conjugation fungi). Terrestrial; coenocytic; isogamous.
Division Ascomycota (Sac fungi). Hyphae (when present) septate, uninucleate
or dikaryotic; meiospores produced in saclike cells called asci, often
eight in each ascus. Lichens are often included here because many of
their fungal components are ascomycetes.
Division Basidiomycota (Club fungi). Hyphae septate, uninucleate or dikaryotic;
meiospores produced by clublike cells called basidia, often four in each
basidium.

Classification of Kingdom Plantae*

Most species autotrophic and with substantial tissue differentiation; gametes are
produced by meiosis; well developed; gametangia multicellular; sporophytic
generation parasitic on the gametophytic generation, at least in the beginning.

Division Bryophyta (Moss plants and their related liverworts and hornworts).
Sperm cells biflagellated; gametophytic generation independent and usually more conspicuous; sporophytic generation parasitic on the gametophytic and usually ephemeral; vascular tissue absent or poorly developed.
Division Psilophyta (Whisk ferns). Sporophytes with dichotomously branched
stems, and rootless.
Division Lycophyta (Club mosses and their relatives). Small plants with
microphylls; spores commonly produced in cones.
Division Sphenophyta (Horsetails). Siliceous plants with jointed stems and
whorled, scalelike leaves; spores produced in cones of the macrophyllous
type.

*Some smaller groups omitted.

Dihybrid Cross

Cross between a hypothetical black, short-haired rodent and a brown, long-haired rodent. Black and short hair are dominant. Taken to F_2 generation. Assume the two genes are not linked.

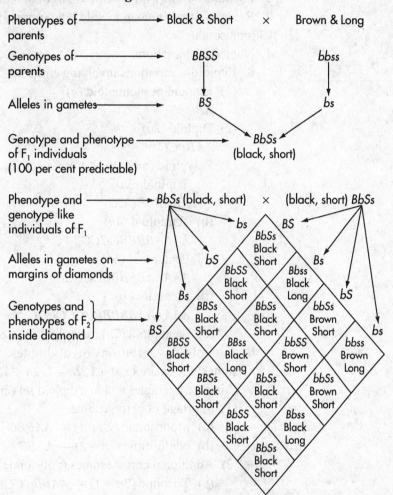

Phenotypes of parents ⟶ Black & Short × Brown & Long

Genotypes of parents ⟶ BBSS   bbss

Alleles in gametes ⟶ BS   bs

Genotype and phenotype of F_1 individuals (100 per cent predictable) ⟶ BbSs (black, short)

Phenotype and genotype like individuals of F_1 ⟶ BbSs (black, short) × (black, short) BbSs

Alleles in gametes on margins of diamonds

Genotypes and phenotypes of F_2 inside diamond

Dihybrid Cross, Linked Genes

A dihybrid cross taken to the F_2 generation as in the preceding figure, but with the two genes being near neighbors on a single chromosome. Second-generation phenotype ratio is 3:1, rather than the 9:3:3:1 ratio if two genes are unlinked.

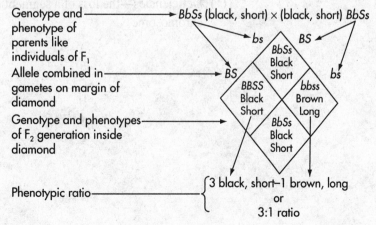

Genotype and phenotype of parents like individuals of F_1 ⟶ BbSs (black, short) × (black, short) BbSs

Allele combined in gametes on margin of diamond

Genotype and phenotypes of F_2 generation inside diamond

Phenotypic ratio ⟶ 3 black, short–1 brown, long
or
3:1 ratio

Sources of Natural Genetic Variations

I. Mutations
  A. Genic (point)
    1. Forward—from wild type (normal) to mutant
    2. Reverse—from mutant to wild type (normal)
  B. Chromosomal
    1. Numerical Variations
      a. Euploid—variations involving entire sets of chromosomes
        (1) Haploid or monoploid (n)
          ABC
        (2) Diploid ($2n$)
          AABBCC
        (3) Polyploid (more than $2n$)
          (a) Triploid ($3n$)
            AAABBBCCC
          (b) Tetraploid ($4n$)
            AAAABBBBCCCC
          (c) Pentaploid ($5n$)
            AAAAABBBBBCCCCC
          (d) Hexaploid ($6n$)
            AAAAAABBBBBBCCCCCC
          (e) Septaploid ($7n$), octoploid ($8n$), etc.
      b. Aneuploid—variations involving less than a set of chromosomes: for example, $n + 1$, $2n - 1$, $2n + 1$, and $3n + 1$
      Common examples within a diploid set ($2n$ or disomic) follow:
        (1) Shortage of chromosomes
          (a) Monosomic ($2n - 1$) — *AABBC*
          (b) Nullosomic ($2n - 2$) — *AABB*
        (2) Additional chromosomes (polysomic)
          (a) Trisomic ($2n + 1$) — *AABBCCC*
          (b) Double trisomic ($2n + 1 + 1$) — *AABBBCCC*
          (c) Tetrasomic ($2n + 2$) — *AABBCCCC*
          (d) Pentasomic ($2n + 3$), etc.
    2. Structural Variations
      a. Additions or deletions of chromosomal material
        (1) Deficiencies—the loss of a segment of genetic material from a chromosome

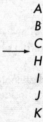

Class Arachnida (Arachnids). Terrestrial; six pairs of appendages, four pairs being walking legs; mandibles absent; no antennae; eyes simple; e.g., spiders, scorpions, ticks, mites.

Class Crustacea (Crustaceans). Usually aquatic; numerous appendages, including mandibles and two pairs of antennae; eyes compound; e.g., crayfish, lobster, shrimp, sow bug.

Class Chilopoda (Centipedes). Terrestrial; typically one pair of appendages per segment, including mandibles and one pair of antennae; carnivorous.

Class Diplopoda (Millipedes). Terrestrial; two pairs of appendages per segment, including mandibles and one pair of antennae; usually herbivorous.

Class Insecta (Insects). Inhabit all environments, but generally terrestrial; comprise 80% of all named animal species; body consists of head, thorax, and abdomen; mandibles and one pair of antennae; often two pairs of wings; eyes both simple and compound; e.g., fly, bee, louse, dragonfly, mayfly, stonefly, grasshopper, cockroach, termite, earwig, bug, cicada, butterfly, beetle, flea.

Phylum Echinodermata (Echinoderms). Marine; radially symmetrical as adult; deuterostome; endoskeleton with dermal ossicles or projecting spines; water vascular system; nervous, blood circulatory, and excretory systems reduced or absent; usually dioecious.

Class Asteroidea (Sea stars). Arms not sharply distinct from central disc; tube feet in ambulacral grooves.

Class Ophiuroidea (Brittle stars). Arms slender and distinct from central disc; no ambulacral groove.

Class Echinoidea (Sea urchins and sand dollars). Hemispherical to cookieshaped; armless; movable spines; endoskeletal plates united into a solid shell.

Class Holothuroidea (Sea cucumbers). Body elongated; arms and spines absent.

Class Crinoidea (Sea lilies and feather stars). Flower-shaped body attached to a long stalk (sea lily) or without stalk as adult (feather star).

Phylum Hemichordata (Acorn worms). Marine; gill slits and primitive dorsal nerve cord; not a true notochord; no digestive system; closed circulation; deuterostome; dioecious.

Phylum Chordata (Chordates). Inhabit all environments; dorsal hollow nerve cord; pharyngeal gill slits, notochord, and postanal tail at some stage of life; closed circulation; cartilagenous or bony endoskeleton in most; deuterostome; generally dioecious.

Subphylum Urochordata (Tunicates). Marine; notochord and nerve cord usually present only in larval stage; e.g., sea squirts.

Subphylum Cephalochordata (Lancelets). Marine; all diagnostic features of phylum Chordata present throughout life; e.g., amphioxus.

Subphylum Vertebrata (Vertebrates). Inhabit all environments; segmented spinal column (vertebrae present); protective braincase (cranium).

Class Agnatha (Cyclostomes). Jawless fishes; scaleless; skeleton of cartilage; e.g., hagfish, lamprey.

Class Chondrichthfyes (Cartilaginous fishes). Skeleton of cartilage; mouth ventral; tail fin usually asymmetrical; usually with placoid scales; gill slits open directly to outside; no air bladder; e.g., shark, ray.

Class Osteichthyes (Bony fishes). Skeletons chiefly of bone; body covered with flattened overlapping scales; mouth usually terminal; gills covered with an operculum; tail fin usually symmetrical; air bladder usually present; e.g., bass, carp, trout, flounder.

Class Amphibia (Amphibians). Usually pass through an aquatic larval stage; adults usually terrestrial; skin soft, scaleless; e.g., frog, toad, salamander.

Class Reptilia (Reptiles). Body covered with scales or scutes; lung-breathers; reproduce on land; e.g., snake, lizard, turtle, alligator.

Class Aves (Birds). Homeothermic, covered with feathers and scales; front limbs modified into wings; e.g., ostrich, turkey, hawk, finch.

Class Mammalia (Mammals). Homeothermic; with mammary glands to nourish young; hair on body (sometimes scant); e.g., dog, deer, rat, human.

Adjectives and Specific Animal Body Parts to Which They Pertain

Alimentary—digestive tract
Anal—anus
Auditory—ear
Auricular—ear; auricle of heart
Axillary—armpit

Brachial—arm
Branchial—gill
Bronchial—bronchi or their branches, lung tubes below the trachea
Buccal—cavity of mouth

Cardiac—heart
Caudal—cauda, tail
Cecal—cecum, blind beginning of the large intestine
Celiac—cavity of abdomen
Cephalic—head
Cerebral—cerebrum, part of brain concerned with conscious mental processes
Cervical—neck; cervix
Chondral—cartilage
Coccygeal—coccyx, end of vertebral column
Coelomic—coelom, a body cavity lined by mesothelium
Corneal—cornea, transparent covering of the front of the eyeball
Cortical—cortex (of organs)
Costal—costa (*pl.* costae), a rib
Cranial—cranium, part of skull enclosing the brain
Cutaneous—skin
Cystic—bladder (gall or urinary)

Dental—teeth
Dermal—skin

Duodenal—duodenum, first part of the small intestine

Endoneural—endoneurium, connective tissue surrounding individual nerve fibers
Endothelial—epithelium of mesodermal origin lining heart, blood vessels, and lymph vessels
Enteric—enteron, alimentary canal or intestine
Epineural—epineurium, external sheath of a nerve
Epiphyseal—epiphysis, a process on a bone
Epithelial—epithelium
Erythrocytic—erythrocyte, red blood cell
Esophageal—esophagus, gullet

Femoral—femur or thigh
Follicular—follicle, a small cavity with or without an opening
Frontal—forehead or frontal bone

Gastric—stomach
Genital—genitals, sexual organs
Gingival—gingiva (*pl.* gingivae), gum of mouth
Glossal—tongue
Glottal—glottis, opening from pharynx to larynx

Hematopoietic—blood-forming tissue
Hepatic—liver
Humeral—humerus, bone between shoulder and elbow
Hypophyseal—hypophysis, pituitary body

Inguinal—groin

Jejunal—middle division of small intestine
Jugular—throat or neck

Labial—lips
Laryngeal—larynx, organ of voice
Leucocytic—leucocyte, white blood cell
Lingual—tongue
Lumbar—loin
Lymphoid—lymph

Mammary—mamma (*pl.* mammae), milk gland
Mandibular—mandible, lower jaw
Maxillary—maxilla, upper jaw
Mediastinal—mediastinum, space between plural sacs of lungs and containing all organs in the chest except lungs
Medullary—medulla (of organs)
Meningeal—meninges (*sing.* meninx)
Mesenteric—mesentery, supporting membrane of abdominal organs
Mesothelial—mesothelium, epithelium of mesodermal origin lining coelomic cavities
Myocardial—myocardium, muscular part of heart

Nasal—nose
Neural—nerve

Occipital—occiput, back part of skull
Olfactory—organ of smell
Optic—eye
Oral—mouth
Osseous—bone
Osteal—bone
Otic—ear
Ovarian—ovary

Palatine—palate, roof of the mouth
Palmar—palm of hand
Parietal—paries (*pl.* parietes), wall of a hollow organ
Parotid—parotid gland, salivary gland located near the ear
Pectoral—chest
Pedal—foot
Penial—penis
Pericardial—pericardium, membrane covering and enclosing the heart
Perichondrial—perichondrium, sheath of connective tissue around cartilage
Perimysial—perimysium, sheath of connective tissue around a muscle
Perineal—perineum, region including the outlets of the pelvis
Periosteal—periosteum, sheath of connective tissue around bone
Peritoneal—peritoneum, serous membrane covering and enclosing abdominal organs
Phalangeal—Phalanges (*sing.* phalanx), digital bones
Pharyngeal—pharynx, that part of the alimentary canal between the mouth cavity and the esophagus
Phrenic—diaphragm
Placental—placenta, organ of maternal and embryonic origin through which exchanges occur between the embryo (or fetus) and the mother
Plantar—sole of foot
Pleural—pleura (*pl.* plurae), a serous membrane covering and enclosing the lung
Portal—vein branching into capillaries
Prostatic—prostate gland, located at base of the urethra in males
Pubic—pubis, ventral bone of the pelvis
Pulmonary—lungs
Pyloric—pylorus, part of the stomach

Radial—radius, a bone of the forearm
Renal—kidney

Sacral—sacrum, that part of the vertebral column forming part of the pelvis
Salivary—saliva or salivary gland
Sciatic—hip
Sclerotic—outer layer of eye
Scrotal—scrotum, sac containing the testes
Sebaceous—sebum, a fatty secretion of skin glands
Splenic—spleen
Sternal—sternum, breastbone

Testicular—testis
Thoracic—thorax, chest
Thymic—thymus, a gland of chest and neck
Tibial—tibia, shank

Urethral—urethra, tube from urinary bladder to the outside of the body
Uterine—uterus, womb

Vascular—blood vessels
Venous—veins
Ventricular—ventricle, a heart chamber
Visceral—viscera (*sing.* viscus), organs contained in cavities of the trunk

Zygomatic—zygoma, cheekbone

Derivation of Words

An understanding of word derivation is useful to any student of biology. Commonly used root words, prefixes, and suffixes are included in the list that follows. Examples are given in parentheses.

Colors

alb(i): white (albino)
chlor(o): green (chloroplast)
chrom(o): color (chromoplast)
cyan(o): blue (cyanophyta)
erythr(o): red (erythrocyte)
leuc(o): white (leucoplast)
xanth(o): yellow (xanthophyll)

Size

is(o): equal (isogamete)
ium: small (basidium)
macr(o): large (macronucleus)
meg(a): large (megaspore)
micr(o): small (microbe)
ule: little (venule)

Quantity

amph(i): double (amphiaster)
cent(i): one hundred (centipede)
di: two (dicotyledon)
dipl(o): double (diplococcus)
hemi: one-half (hemiptera)
hex(a): six (hexapod)
hyper: excessive (hyperthyroidism)
hypo: less than normal (hypoactive)
mill(i): one thousand (millipede)
mon(o): one (monocotyledon)
oct(o): eight (octopus)
pent(a): five (pentamerous)
poly: many (polysaccharide)
quadr(i): four (quadriped)
sept: seven (septuplets)
tetr(a): four (tetraspore)
tri: three (triploid)
un(i): one (unisexual)

Organisms

arbor: tree (arborescent)
entom(o): insect (entomology)
helmin(th): worm (Platyhelminthes)
herpet(o): reptile (herpetology)
ichthy(o): fish (ichthyology)

myc(o): fungus (mycology)
orni(tho): bird (ornithology)
phyt(o): plant (phytogeography)
zo(o): animal (zoology)

Parts of Organisms

brachi(o): arm (brachiopod)
branch(io): gill (branchiopod)
carp: fruit (pericarp)
caud(i): tail (caudiform)
card(io): heart (electrocardiogram)
cephal(o): head (cephalopod)
cervi(c): neck (cervicitis)
chondr(o): cartilage (chondrocranium)
corp: body (corpuscle)
cost(o): rib (costoscapular)
cyst(o): bladder (cystocarp)
cyt(o): cell (cytoplasm)
dent(i): tooth (dentiform)
derm: skin (epidermis)
encephal: brain (encephalitis)
enter(o): intestine (Enterobios)
gast(r): stomach (gastrula)
hem(o): blood (hemoglobin)
hepat: liver (hepatitis)
hist: tissue (histamine)
hymen: membrane (hymenium)
my(o): muscle (myofibril)
oss: bone (ossicle)
phyll: leaf (sporophyll)
pod: foot (pelecypod)
pter(o): wing (pterodactyl)
pulmo(n): lung (pulmonary)
ren(i): kidney (reniform)
sperm: seed (gymnosperm)
stom(o): mouth (stomodaeum)
vas(o): vessel (vasoconstrictor)

Positions

ab: away from (aboral)
ana: up (anaphase)
anti: against (antipodal)
co: with (coenzyme)

ect(o): outside (ectoderm)
end(o): inner (endoplasm)
ent(o): inner (entoderm)
ep(i): upon (epiphyte)
exo: outside (exoskeleton)
hyper: above (hyperbranchial)
hypo: below (hypogynous)
infra: below (infraspinous)
inter: between (interstitial)
intra: within (intracutaneous)
mes(o): middle (mesothorax)
met(a): after (metathorax)
ob: reversed (oblanceolate)
para: beside (parathyroid)
peri: around (peristome)
pleur(i): side (pleurisy)
post: behind (postcava)
pre: before (precava)
pro: in front (prothorax)
prot(o): first (protozoa)
sub: under (submaxillary)
super: over (superciliary)
supra: over (supraorbital)
sy(n): together (synapsis)

Miscellaneous

a: without (asexual)
amyl(o): starch (amyloplast)
andr: male (androecium)
anti: counter (antitoxin)
arch: beginning (archenteron)

arium: depository (herbarium)
ary: place for keeping (aviary)
asc(o): bag (ascocarp)
aster: star (amphiaster)
bio: life (biogenesis)
coel: hollow (coelenteron)
copr(o): excrement (coprophagous)
cotyl: cavity (hypocotyl)
crypt(o): hidden (cryptogam)
eu: true (eumycophyta)
genous: hidden (hypogenous)
gyn: female (gynoecium)
heter(o): different (heterogametes)
hom(o): alike (homosporous)
hydr(o): water (hydrophyte)
ite: fossil (ammonite)
itis: inflammation (peritonitis)
mal: bad (malaria)
oid: form (ovoid)
ov(i): egg (ovipositor)
osis: disease (mycosis)
pach(y): thick (pachyderm)
phot(o): light (phototropism)
plast: formed (chloroplast)
plat(y): flat (Platyhelminthes)
pseud(o): false (pseudopodium)
scler: hard (sclerenchyma)
schiz(o): split (Schizomycetes)
tel(o): end (telophase)
xer(o): dry (xerophyte)

Prefixes Generally Used to Denote Multiples or Fractions of Units of Measurement and the Most Common Quantities Used in Biology

Prefix	Quantity	Length*	Weight*	Volume*	Energy*	Quantity of Radioactive Substance*
giga	1,000,000,000 (10^9)					
mega	1,000,000 (10^6)					
myria	10,000 (10^4)					
kilo	1,000 (10^3)	kilometer (km)	kilogram (kg)		kilocalorie (kcal)	
hecto	100 (10^2)					
deca	10					
(no prefix)	1	meter (m)	gram (g)	liter (l)	calorie (cal)	curie (Ci)
deci	0.1					
centi	0.01(10^{-2})	centimeter (cm)	centigram (cg)			
milli	0.001(10^{-3})	milliliter (mm)	milligram (mg)	milliliter (ml)		
micro	0.000001 (10^{-6})	micrometer (μm)	microgram (μg)	microliter (μl)		microcurie (μCi)
nano	0.000000001 (10^{-9})					
	0.0000000001 (10^{-10})	Angstrom (A or Å)				
pico	0.000000000001 (10^{-12})					

*All abbreviations in column are both singular and plural.

Miscellaneous Biological Abbreviations

See also "Common Organic Compounds Better Known by Their Abbreviations," page 227.

ABA	Abscisic acid	CAM	Type of photosynthesis (crassulacean acid metabolism)
ACTH	Adrenocorticotropic hormone		
ADH	Antidiuretic hormone	cAMP	Cyclic adenosine monophosphate
ADP	Adenosine diphosphate		
AIDS	Acquired immune deficiency syndrome	CAP	Catabolite activator protein
		CNS	Central nervous system
ATP	Adenosine triphosphate	CoA	Coenzyme A
atm	Atmosphere	CSF	Cerebrospinal fluid
A-V	Atrioventricular	cv	Cultivar (*cultivarietas*)
BMR	Basal metabolism rate	DDT	Dichlorodiphenyltrichloroethane
BOD	Biological oxygen demand	det.	Identified by
bp	Boiling point	DNA	Deoxyribonucleic acid
C_3	Type of plant whose photosynthetic process makes a 3-carbon compound (PGA)	ECG	Electrocardiogram
		E. Coli	The bacterium *Escherichia coli*
		EEG	Electroencephalogram
C_4	Type of plant whose photosynthetic process makes 4-carbon compounds (malic and aspartic acids)	e.g.	*exempli gratia* (for example)
		EM	Electron microscope
		ER	Endoplasmic reticulum
		EPSP	Excitatory postsynaptic potential
ca, circa	About, around	f.	Offspring, son (*filius*); form (*forma*)
cal	Calorie		

F_1	First generation
F_2	Second generation
FSH	Follicle-stimulating hormone
G	Gravity
GA	Gibberellic acid
GI	Gastrointestinal
H^+	Hydrogen ion; a proton
hab.	Habitat
Hb	Hemoglobin
HCG	Human chorionic gonadotropin
HDL	High-density lipoprotein
herb.	Herbarium
HIV	Human immunodeficiency virus
HLA	Human leucocyte antigen
hort.	Horticultural, horticulture
IAA	Indoleacetic acid
ICSH	Interstitial-cell-stimulating hormone
i.e.	*id est* (that is)
Ig	Immunoglobulin
im	Intramuscular
ip	Intraperitoneal
IPSP	Inhibitory postsynaptic potential
iu	International unit
iv	Intravenous
I.V.	Importance value
kcal	Kilocalorie
LD	Lethal dose
LDL	Low-density lipoprotein
LH	Luteinizing hormone
LTH	Luteotropic hormone
M	Molar
mcal	Megacalorie
MHC	Major histocompatability complex
mp	Melting point
MS	Multiple sclerosis
m.t.	Metric ton
mtDNA	Mitochondrial DNA
n	Haploid (chromosome set)
NAD	Nicotinamide adenine dinucleotide
NADP	Nicotinamide adenine dinucleotide phosphate
NH_3	Ammonia
NH_4^+	Ammonium

NO_2^-	Nitrite
NO_3^-	Nitrate
OH^-	Hydroxyl ion
pH	Negative log of the hydrogen-ion concentration
p.m.	Postmortem
PCO_2	Carbon dioxide pressure
PO_2	Oxygen pressure
ppb	Parts per billion
pphm	Parts per hundred million
ppm	Parts per million
P/R	Photosynthesis-respiration ratio
PTH	Parathormone
RBC	Red blood cells
rem	Roentgen equivalent for human
Rh	Rhesus factor in blood
RH	Relative humidity
RNA	Ribonucleic acid
RQ	Respiratory quotient $\left(\dfrac{\text{volume of } CO_2 \text{ expired}}{\text{volume of } O_2 \text{ inspired}} \right)$
S-A	Sinoatrial
sc	Subcutaneous
SEM	Scanning electron microscope
SI	International System of Measurement (*Système Internationale*)
sp.	Species (singular)
sp.gr.	Specific gravity
sp. nov.	*Species nova* (new species)
spp.	Species (plural)
ssp.	Subspecies
STD	Sexually transmitted disease
STH	Somatotropic hormone
TEM	Transmission electron microscope
U/B	Ratio of some substance in urine and blood
U/P	Ratio of urinary osmotic pressure to plasma osmotic pressure
U.S.P.	United States Pharmacopeia
vac.	Vacuum
V.F.	Visual field
WBC	White blood cells

Symbols Used in Biology

♂	Male	≮	is not less than
□	Male in pedigree charts	>	is more than
♀	Female	≯	is not more than
○	Female in pedigree charts	~	Approximately
⊕	Sporophyte	#	Number
=	Equals; is equal to	×	Times; multiplied by;
≠ or ≟	is not equal to		crossed with
≈	is approximately equal to	Σ	Sum
<	is less than	∞	Infinity

Some Equipment Used by Biologists

Anemometer—Measures velocity of wind.

Aspirator—Removes fluids by suction (a suction pump).

Atmometer—Measures rate of evaporation of water in atmosphere.

Autoclave—Sterilizes with steam under pressure; used especially in bacteriological work.

Balances, analytical—Used for accurate weighing of small quantities.

   Ultramicro—Ranges down to 0.1 microgram.

   Micro—Ranges down to 0.001 milligram.

   Semimicro—Ranges down to 0.01 milligram.

Barometer—Measures atmospheric pressure.

Burette—Used for measuring liquids or gases delivered or received; a graduated glass tube, usually with a stopcock and a small opening.

Centrifuges—Separate substances having different densities.

   Clinical—Maximum speeds produce force of about 2,000 × G; used in such work as blood separation.

   High-speed—Maximum speeds produce force of about 50,000 × G; used to separate cell fractions such as microsomes and mitochondria.

   Ultra—Maximum speeds produce force of about 150,000 × G; used in separating substances composed of large molecules and in identifying them by determining their sedimentation rates.

Chromatograph—Used for analyzing mixtures of similar substances by separating their components.

Colorimeter—Used for routine chemical analyses of solutions; a photometer that uses colored filters in producing light to be absorbed by solutions whose concentrations are being analyzed.

Computer—Has wide variety of uses: stores and analyzes data, controls instruments, interfaces with remote information sources.

Conductivity meter—Measures salinity.

Conibear trap—Humanely catches mammals and kills them instantly.

Densitometer—Quantifies materials separated on electrophoresis and thin-layer chromatography surfaces.

Desiccator—Dries substances.

Dialyzer—Separates particles of different sizes with a differentially permeable membrane.

Distilling apparatus—Purifies liquids.

Dredge—Collects bottom-dwelling organisms, especially shellfish; a bag net attached to an iron frame and dragged on the bottom.

Earth auger—Used for taking soil samples.

Electrophoresis apparatus—Separates electrically charged molecules on the basis of charge, size, or both.

Environmental control chamber—Provides an area in which such entities as temperature, light, and humidity can be closely controlled.

Flow cytometer—Analyzes and separates cell types by the degree to which they contain fluorescent materials.

Fraction collector—Automatically separates liquid coming off a chromatography apparatus, placing aliquots into a series of test tubes for further analysis.

Fume hood—Provides a protective workspace against heat, explosion, fumes, and other dangers.

Gas chromatograph—Separates samples of volatile substances into components that can be detected in trace amounts; allows for both qualitative and quantitative analyses.

G-M (Geiger-Muller) tube—In an electronic instrument for quantitative determination of radioactivity.

Hemocytometer—Used in counting blood corpuscles (also yeast cells).

High-performance liquid chromatograph (HPLC)—Performs liquid chromatography at very high pressures, giving good separations very quickly.

Homogenizer—Breaks down cells preparatory to separation of their parts; prepares cell-free extracts and emulsions.

Hydrometer—Used to determine specific gravities of liquids.

Hygrometer—Measures relative humidity of the atmosphere.

Increment borer—Used for removing a core of wood from the trunk of a tree to determine age of tree.

Incubator—Is a chamber where temperature can be regulated to provide ideal conditions for growth, as for hatching eggs or growing bacteria.

Kymograph—Records magnitude of muscular contractions and other physiological activities.

Laminar flow hood—Provides workspace where both the person and the biological agent are protected from contamination.

Laser—Provides coherent light source for varied uses, including spectrophotometry and knifeless surgery.

Lyophilizer (freeze-dryer)—Removes water from samples by sublimation in a vacuum.

Manometer—Measures pressures of gases and vapors.

Mass spectrometer—Separates electrified particles into a spectrum according to their masses.

Maximum-minimum thermometer—Records highest and lowest temperature during a specific period of time.

Metabolic apparatus—Measures metabolic rate based on speed of oxygen consumption.

Microscopes:

Electron—Reveals structures too small to reflect light, e.g., ultrastructure of a cell.

Fluorescence—Reveals location of objects on slide that include fluorescent materials.

Light—Uses visible light wavelengths, often relies upon staining to show details of biological objects.

Phase contrast—Makes visible or improves visibility of structures in living cells.

Polarizing—Makes visible fine structures of some biological materials.

Microtomes:

Cryostat—Used for sectioning frozen tissues.

Rotary—Used for making thin sections of soft tissues embedded in paraffin.

Sliding—Used for sectioning hard or large structures.

Oscilloscope—Used to amplify electrical changes in tissues and project these changes by means of an electron beam onto a fluorescent screen or computer monitor.

Osmometer—Measures osmolarity of a solution.

Petri dish—Used for culturing bacteria and fungi.

pH meter—Is an electronic device for measuring acidity and alkalinity.

Photometer—Measures intensity of light.

Pipet (Pipetter)—Dispenses accurately measured volumes of liquid.

Press—Used for extracting by compression.

Rain gauge—Measures precipitation.

Scintillation counter—Detects presence and measures quantity of radiation by responding with flashes of light.

Secchi disc—Measures turbidity of water.

Sling psychrometer—Measures relative humidity of the atmosphere.

Soil sieve—Used for classifying soils according to texture.

Sonicator—Provides ultrasonic vibrations for disruption of cells.

Spectrophotometer—Used to identify compounds by determining the wavelength of light absorbed by their molecules; also used in studying enzyme kinetics.

Sphygmomanometer—Measures blood pressure.

Spirometer—Measures vital capacity of the lungs.

Thermistor—Electrically measures temperature in difficult places.

Thermocouple—Is an electronic device for measuring temperature.

Thermograph—Continuously records changes in temperature.

Titrator—Determines strength of a solution or concentration of a substance in solution.

Trawl—Catches fish and other aquatic organisms; a bag net dragged on the bottom.

Ultraviolet lamp—Induces mutations; detects fluorescent compounds.

Vasculum—Is a metal container for the temporary storage of plants as they are collected.

Warburg apparatus—Used in studies of cell and tissue metabolism.

Waring blender—Macerates plant and animal materials.

Water bath—Maintains a uniform temperature around a container in which some process is occurring.

X-ray machine—Induces mutations; photographs internal body structures.

Index of Review Aids

Laws of thermodynamics—221

Spectrum of organizational complexity—222

Chemical elements important in living organisms—222

Isotopes commonly used as tracers—223

Functional groups of organic molecules—224

Some organic compounds of biological importance—224

Amino acids found in proteins—227

Common organic compounds better known by their abbreviations—227

DNA: structure and replication—228

Messenger RNA codons and their meanings—230

Transcription—230

Cellular organization and functions of parts—231

Cell division (mitosis and cytokinesis)—232

Some mature plant tissues—233

Plant tissues—233

Some mature animal tissues—234

Classification of animal tissues—235

Blood distribution in animals with four-chambered heart—237

Best-known hormones in mammals—237

Best-known hormones in plants—239

Photosynthesis—240

Some major steps in glycolysis and the Krebs (citric acid) cycle—241

Conspicuous differences between photosynthesis and respiration—242

How various molecules feed into glycolysis and the Krebs (citric acid) cycle—242

Summary of carbohydrate digestion in humans—243

Summary of fat digestion in humans—243

Summary of protein digestion in humans—243

Some common vitamins for humans—244

Strategies used by vertebrate animals to maintain salt and water balance and to excrete nitrogenous wastes—245

Generalized gastrula—245

Generalized embryonic development illustrating extraembryonic membranes—246

Extraembryonic membranes of mammals, birds, and reptiles—246

Early development of the human—247

Embryonic germ layers and their derivatives—247

Generalized life cycle of plants—248

Moss life cycle—248

Fern life cycle—249

Structure of a flower—249

Life cycle of flowering seed plant—249

Monohybrid cross—250

Sex-linkage—250

Dihybrid cross—251

Dihybrid cross, linked genes—251

Sources of natural genetic variations—252

Hardy-Weinberg equilibrium: necessary conditions—255

Isolating mechanisms important in evolution—255

The geologic sequence (timetable)—257

Major terrestrial hiomes of the world—258

Zones of vegetation in and around lakes—258

Major oceanic environments (depths not proportional)—259

The carbon cycle (simplified)—259

The nitrogen cycle (simplified)—260

The oxygen cycle (simplified)—260

S and J population growth curves—261

Taxonomic categories—261

Classification of living organisms—262

Prokaryotes and eukaryotes contrasted—262

Classification of kingdom Monera—263

Classification of kingdom Protista—263

Classification of kingdom Fungi—264

Classification of kingdom Plantae—264

Classification of kingdom Animalia—265

Adjectives and specific animal body parts to which they pertain—268

Derivation of words—270

Prefixes generally used to denote multiples and fractions of units of measurement
and the most common quantities used in biology—272

Miscellaneous biological abbreviations—272

Symbols used in biology—274

Some equipment used by biologists—274

Glossary

A

abscisic acid. A plant growth regulator that inhibits growth of buds and prepares them for winter dormancy.

abscission layer. A layer along which a leaf or fruit naturally separates from the stem.

absorption. The process of bringing digested molecules into cells.

acellular. Not composed of cells with distinct boundaries.

acetylcholine. A neurotransmitter acting as a transmitter substance in the synapses of many neurons of the central and peripheral nervous systems and of the parasympathetic portion of the autonomic nervous system.

acid. A substance that gives up hydrogen ions when dissolved; opposite of a base.

acrosome. A membranous bag lying over the nucleus of an animal sperm cell, carrying enzymes needed for successful fertilization.

actin. The protein that forms microfilaments; together with myosin, a contractile portion of muscle.

action potential. A rapid change of electrical potential that moves across the plasma membrane like a wave; e.g., a nerve impulse.

action spectrum. That portion of electromagnetic energy that can be absorbed to trigger a chemical process; the wavelengths of light used in photosynthesis.

activation energy. The amount of energy needed to cause molecules to react chemically; lowered by catalysts, such as enzymes.

active site. The portion of an enzyme with the proper shape and chemical groups to interact with a substrate.

active transport. An energy-consuming movement of molecules or ions across a membrane in the direction opposite that expected by diffusion, i.e., against a concentration gradient.

adaptive radiation. An evolutionary process whereby populations of one species move into other environments and adapt to them.

adenine. A nitrogenous base of the purine type that is a constituent of some nucleotides.

ADP (adenosine diphosphate). Adenosine with two phosphate groups; converted to ATP by the addition of another phosphate group bound by a high-energy bond.

adrenaline. See *epinepherine*.

adventitious root. Any new root growing from a nonroot portion of a plant.

aerobic. Requiring molecular oxygen.

aerobic respiration. Respiration in which gaseous oxygen is used as a hydrogen acceptor.

aggregate fruit. A fruit derived from several pistils of a single flower; e.g., the strawberry.

alga. A photosynthetic eukaryote without the multicellular sex organs or vascular tissues found in higher plants.

allantois. A sac extending from the rear part of the primitive digestive tract of an embryo; in reptiles and birds, large and highly functional as a respiratory and excretory organ.

allele. One of two or more contrasting forms of a gene.

allelopathy. The influence that plants exert on other plants by their metabolic products; the inhibition of competitors by toxic metabolic products.

Allen's rule. Animals normally living in cold habitats tend to have shorter appendages than those in warmer habitats, thus reducing heat loss by convection.

allopatric. An ecological term describing similar populations that live in separate and widely differing geographical areas and are reproductively incompatible.

allosteric change. Modification of an enzyme's shape by interaction with another molecule; can lead to either activation or inhibition of the enzyme.

alveolus. An air pocket of the lung through whose wall gases are exchanged.

amino acid. An organic compound containing an amino group (NH_2) and, together with other similar compounds, comprising proteins.

amnion. The sac immediately surrounding an embryo (or fetus).

amphiaster. A structure arising from the cell center during cell division in animals and some lower plants. It consists of two asters occupying polar positions between which the radiations (fibers) form a spindle.

amylase. A starch-digesting enzyme.

amyloplast. A plastid containing stored starch.

anabolism. The chemical reactions that lead to the synthesis of molecules from smaller precursors; opposite of catabolism.

anaerobic. Not requiring molecular oxygen.

analogous. Having different embryological origins but similar use.

anaphase. The phase of mitosis during which chromosomes are moving toward the poles of the spindle.

androgens. Male hormones.

aneuploidy. The genetic condition in which one or more chromosomes are either missing or present in above-normal numbers in a cell.

angiosperm. A flowering plant; a plant that produces seeds enclosed within a fruit.

animal. A multicellular heterotrophic organism carrying on internal digestion of food; a member of kingdom Animalia.

anisogamy. The situation in which the male gametes of a species are visually distinguishable from the female gametes.

anther. The distal part of a stamen that produces pollen.

antheridium. A male gametangium in many kinds of plants.

antibody. A protein whose shape enables it to attach to an antigen; part of the humoral immune system.

anticodon. A sequence of three nucleotides of transfer RNA that pairs with a codon of messenger RNA.

antidiuretic hormone. See *vasopressin*.

antigen. A molecule (usually a macromolecule such as a protein) that elicits an immune response because it is recognizable as foreign to the body.

anus. The exit of a digestive system.

aorta. The large artery leaving the heart and supplying aerated blood to all parts of the body.

apical meristem. Actively growing tissue at the tips of roots and stems.

archegonium. An egg-producing organ in many plants; consists of a base, venter, and neck.

archenteron. The cavity of the gastrular stage of an embryo.

Archezoic. The first era of geologic time in which there was evidence of life.

arteriole. A small artery.

artery. A vessel (tube) through which blood travels away from the heart.

ascus. A saclike container of spores in ascomycetes.

asexual. Sexless.

assimilation. The process by which nonliving substances become part of protoplasm.

association neuron. A nerve cell between two other nerve cells.

assortative mating. The phenomenon in which sexual mates choose each other on the basis of phenotypic similarity (or dissimilarity) to each other; a type of nonrandom mating.

ATP (adenosine triphosphate). Adenosine with three phosphate groups; converted to ADP by the loss of one phosphate group; known as "storehouse of energy" because energy released from the high-energy phosphate bond during ATP's conversion to ADP is used for cell work.

atrium. A compartment of the heart that receives blood from the body.

autoimmunity. An abnormal condition in which the organism produces antibodies against its own cells or molecules.

autonomic nervous system. The part of the nervous system that regulates involuntary reactions of many organs of the body, especially the viscera.

autosome. Any chromosome other than those that determine sex.

autotroph. An organism that produces its own food; opposite of heterotroph.

auxins. Plant hormones produced by actively growing tissues.

axon. A portion of a neuron conducting impulses away from the body of the neuron.

B

bacillus. A rod-shaped bacterium.

backcross. The crossing of a dominant phenotype with a homozygous (pure) recessive to determine whether the phenotype is homozygous or heterozygous.

Bacteria. The kingdom containing true bacteria, when a six-kingdom classification is used.

bacteriophage. A virus that parasitizes bacteria; also called phage.

bacterium. A prokaryotic organism of kingdom Bacteria (six-kingdom system) or kingdom Monera (five-kingdom system).

bark. All tissues outside the vascular cambium of roots and stems.

basal body. A centriolelike object at the base of a cilium or flagellum.

base. A molecule or ion capable of accepting ionic hydrogen; opposite of an acid. See *acid*.

basidium. A club-shaped, spore-producing structure in basidiomycetes.

Batesian mimicry. The phenomenon in which a defenseless organism takes the shape and/or color of an obnoxious one, thus gaining protection.

B cell. One of two major types (with T cells) in an immune system; produces antibody.

benthos. The bottom-dwelling plants and animals of the sea.

binomial. A two-part name given to each organism, consisting of its genus and species names.

biofeedback. Self-regulation of a biological process whereby the process is accelerated by hypoactivity or slowed by hyperactivity; conscious control of processes that normally are self-regulating.

bioluminescence. The light produced by living organisms from chemical energy.

biomass. The quantity of organisms in a specific location, usually expressed as live or dry weight.

biome. A large biotic community of wide geographical extent characterized by a dominating life-form; e.g., desert, tundra, rain forest.

blastodisc. A disc of cells developing on one side of the yolk of a chicken's egg and corresponding to the blastular stage.

blastomere. Any cell of a blastula.

blastopore. An opening to the archenteron in the gastrular stage of the embryo; becomes either mouth (in protostome animals) or anus (in deuterostome animals).

blastula. An early stage of the embryo consisting of a hollow ball of cells.

Bohr effect. An increase in oxygen-binding by hemoglobin as environmental pH rises, and a decrease as pH falls.

book lungs or gills. Respiratory organs constructed of thin folds of tissue stacked together like the pages in a book; found in spiders and horseshoe crabs.

boreal forest. A high-latitude coniferous forest.

Bowman's capsule. The bulbous upper part of a renal tubule surrounding the glomerulus.

bronchiole. A small air passage in the lung.

bronchus. An air passageway leading from the trachea into the lung.

Brownian movement. Movement of small particles due to differential bombardment by surrounding molecules.

budding. An asexual reproductive process in which a fragment is separated from the body and grows into a new organism; a form of grafting in which a bud is used as the scion.

buffer. A substance that releases hydrogen atoms when environmental hydrogen concentration is low, and captures hydrogen atoms when environmental hydrogen concentration is high.

C

calorie. A unit of heat; the kilogram-calorie is the amount of heat required to raise the temperature of one liter of water one degree centigrade.

Calvin cycle. A series of reactions taking place during photosynthesis, in which carbon, hydrogen, oxygen, and energy are combined to make a stable organic molecule that can be used as food; also called carbon fixation.

cambium. A meristematic tissue occurring in layers in roots and stems and producing secondary tissues.

cAMP, cyctic AMP (cyclic adenosine monophosphate). A modified nucleotide that acts as a "second messenger" for hormonal systems within target cells.

cancer. A complex of diseases characterized by uncontrolled cell reproduction and disruptive invasion of cells into normal tissues.

capillary. A small blood vessel consisting of only one layer of endothelium and usually connecting arteries and veins.

capillary water. Water that can move on surfaces against the pull of gravity.

carbohydrate. An organic molecule composed of carbon, hydrogen, and oxygen in which hydrogen and oxygen occur in the same proportions as in water.

carbon fixation. See *Calvin cycle*.

carcinogen. A cancer-causing agent.

carnivore. An organism that ingests heterotrophs (usually animals) as food.

carotene. A class of yellow pigments in plants.

carpel. A megasporophyll; pistils of flowers are composed of one or more carpels.

carrying capacity. The largest population that can be sustained in a particular environment; determined by the resources available.

Casparian strip. A thin stripe of wax deposited on walls of endodermis in roots.

catabolism. The chemical reactions in which molecules are broken down; opposite of anabolism.

catalyst. A molecule that speeds up a reaction without itself being used up; in organisms, usually an enzyme.

cell center. A structure near the nucleus of a non-dividing cell, including a pair of centrioles.

cell membrane. The outer boundary of the cell's cytoplasm, often called the plasma membrane.

cellular immune system. The portion of a vertebrate animal's immune system that depends upon action of T cells.

cellulose. A polysaccharide that constitutes the framework of the walls of plant cells.

cell wall. A relatively firm, nonliving envelope forming the outer boundary of certain cells, such as those of plants, fungi, and bacteria.

centriole. A cellular organelle containing microtubule subunits (tubulin) that acts as a center for building spindle fibers during mitosis or meiosis.

centromere. The point on a chromosome where a spindle fiber is attached.

Cenozoic. The most recent geologic era, known as the "age of mammals, birds, and angiosperms."

cephalothorax. The fused head and thorax of animals such as crustaceans.

cerebellum. The part of the hindbrain that coordinates muscular activity.

cerebrum. The part of the forebrain that acts as the chief coordinating center of the brain.

cervix. The neck-shaped part of the outer end of the uterus; a constricted portion of an organ or structure.

chalones. A class of chemicals that inhibit mitosis.

chaparral. A shrubby type of vegetation in semitropical areas where the rainy season is in the winter; Mediterranean scrub forest.

chemiosmosis. A model for cellular energy capture, in which protons are pumped across mitochondrial and chloroplast membranes and the energy of their return movement is placed in a bond as ATP is produced from ADP and inorganic phosphate.

chemosynthesis. In some simple autotrophs, a process used to synthesize simple carbohydrates from carbon dioxide and water, with chemicals rather than light as the source of energy.

chemotaxis. The movement of an organism or cell toward or away from a source of a particular chemical.

chitin. The horny skeletal material of arthropods; a nitrogen-containing polysaccharide.

chlorenchyma. A plant tissue composed of thin-walled cells that contain chlorophyll.

chlorophyll *a*. The most common type of green pigment in most plants.

chloroplast. A plastid containing chlorophyll and other pigments.

cholinesterase. An enzyme that quickly destroys the neurotransmitter acetylcholine.

chorion. The outer membrane surrounding a mammalian embryo (or fetus).

chromatid. One of two identical portions of a chromosome during the early portions of cell reproduction.

Chromatin. The assembly of DNA, proteins, and RNA that together comprise a chromosome of a eukaryotic cell.

chromonemata. Fine nuclear threads; chromosomes in an early stage of development during mitosis.

chromosome. A physical structure holding genetic information in a cell; composed of DNA and (sometimes) associated proteins.

chymotrypsin. A pancreatic enzyme that digests proteins.

cilia. Small projections from cells, containing microtubules and used to circulate materials over the surface of stationary cells or to propel some single-celled organisms.

citric acid cycle. See *Krebs cycle*.

cleavage. The early division of an embryo during which there is no increase in the volume of protoplasm beyond what was present in the zygote.

climax community. A mixture of organisms living together and maintained by a rather stable environment.

clitellum. A swollen glandular region of an earthworm that secretes slime for binding copulating worms together and for constructing the egg case.

clitoris. The female structure homologous to the tip of the penis; a center of sexual sensations during intercourse.

clone. A genetically uniform group of cells or organisms originating asexually from a single ancestor.

cnidocyte. A stinging cell characteristic of animals in phylum Cnidaria.

coccus. A spherical bacterium.

codon. A sequence of three bases (of either DNA or RNA) that signifies a single event in the translation process; most condons signify the placement of specific amino acids.

coelom. A body cavity lined with cells of mesodermal origin.

coenzyme. An organic substance, often a vitamin or vitamin derivative, necessary for an enzyme to function.

cofactor. A nonprotein component that binds temporarily to an enzyme, helping the enzyme to function; often a metal ion or a coenzyme.

coleoptile. A sheath covering the epicotyl of the embryo of a grass plant.

collenchyma. A simple plant tissue composed of cells with some thickening of the walls, especially in the corners.

colloid. A dispersion system in which dispersed particles are either large individual molecules or clumps of molecules that do not respond to gravity.

colon. The large intestine.

commensalism. A close relationship between two organisms whereby one member benefits and the other is unaffected.

community. A group of species living together.

companion cells. Small phloem cells adjacent to sieve tubes.

competitive exclusion. The principle that two species cannot occupy the same niche at the same time and place.

complete flower. A flower with all kinds of floral parts.

compound. A molecule composed of two or more different elements.

conjugation. In bacteria or some protozoa, the exchange of genetic material between two cells mediated by a temporary cytoplasmic bridge.

consumers. Organisms that obtain their energy by eating other organisms.

contractile vacuole. A vacuole in freshwater protozoa that periodically expels excess water to the outside.

convergence. The evolving of organisms in dissimilar groups so that they are similarly adapted to similar environments.

corm. A modified stem similar in general appearance to a bulb but solid like a potato.

corpus luteum. In the ovary, yellow cells that fill the follicular space after ovulation and produce progesterone.

cortex. The outer part of some organs: in plant stems and roots, the zone between the vascular tissues and the outer protective layer.

cortisone. A complex of hormones produced by the cortex of the adrenal gland.

cotyledon. The leaf on an embryonic seed plant; the seed leaf.

countercurrent exchange. An efficient mechanism for the exchange of materials (gases, heat, etc.); two fluids move in opposite directions past each other, separated by a permeable interface, and a material flows across the interface.

crossing-over. An exchange of genes on homologous chromosomes resulting from their becoming entangled during synapsis of meiosis; results in recombination.

cutin. A waterproofing material associated with the epidermis of plants.

cyclic AMP (cAMP). A modified nucleotide, cyclic adenosine monophosphate; acting as a "second messenger" for hormonal systems within target cells.

cyclic photophosphorylation. A light-driven process in photosynthesis, producing ATP.

cyclosis. The circulation of cytoplasm within a cell.

cytochrome. A cellular pigment, a hydrogen acceptor during hydrogen transfer.

cytokinesis. Cytoplasmic division accompanying mitosis.

cytokinins. Plant growth regulators that induce cell division.

cytoplasm. The materials of a cell outside of the nucleus; non-nuclear organelles and the fluid in which they are suspended.

cytosine. A nitrogenous base of the pyrimidine type that is a constituent of some nucleotides.

cytoskeleton. Within a cell, a latticework of microfilaments, microtubules, and filaments in which organelles are suspended; provides a framework for cell cytoplasm.

cytosol. The semiliquid portion of cytoplasm.

D

dark reactions. See *light-independent reactions.*

deciduous. Denoting plants that shed their leaves after the growing season.

decomposer. An organism that extracts its food from materials of dead bodies; a saprobe.

dehydration. The chemical separation of water from a molecule, an energy-releasing step of respiration; also the loss of water from cells, tissues, or organs.

dendrite. A portion of a neuron that conducts impulses toward the body of the neuron.

deoxyribose. A five-carbon sugar in DNA.

deuterostome. An animal whose embryonic blastopore becomes an anus, and whose mouth is formed later.

dicot (dicotyledon). A seed plant distinguished in part by embryos that have two cotyledons.

differentiation. The specialization of cells to perform a specific function.

diffusion. The scattering of molecules due to molecular action; net movement is from higher to lower concentration.

digestion. The breaking of large food molecules into smaller molecules.

dihybrid. A genetic cross involving two characteristics.

dioecious. Having the sexes in separate bodies.

diploid. Containing two sets of chromosomes, as in zygotes or body cells.

disaccharide. A compound sugar; each molecule can be broken into two monosaccharide molecules.

divergence. The evolving of closely related individuals so that they become dissimilar when they adapt to different environments.

DNA (deoxyribonucleic acid). A polynucleotide, usually double-stranded and helical, whose five-carbon sugar is deoxyribose; the most commonly employed molecule for storage of genetic information.

dominant. Expressed; a term used to describe an allele whose characteristic conceals the characteristic of a recessive allele when both alleles are present.

dorsal root. The upper branch of a spinal nerve connecting with the spinal cord; the pathway of sensory neurons entering the spinal cord.

double fertilization. In angiosperms, a process in which one of the two sperm cells from a single pollen grain fertilizes an egg, forming a zygote, and almost simultaneously the other sperm fertilizes polar nuclei, forming a food-storage tissue called endosperm.

duodenum. The first part of the small intestine, the part into which the liver and pancreas discharge their secretions.

E

ecology. The branch of biology dealing with the relationships between organisms and their environments.

ecosystem. A more or less self-contained community of organisms, together with the environment in which it lives.

ecotone. The zone of overlap between adjacent communities.

ectoderm. The outer layer of an early stage of the embryo.

ectothermic. Referring to the condition of animals whose body temperatures are primarily determined by heat absorbed from the environment.

effector. The part of a body that responds to a stimulus.

electron transport chains. Sets of membrane-bound molecules that can pass electrons; used in photosynthesis and aerobic respiration.

embryo. A multicellular organism between the time of fertilization and the organism's hatching, birth, or emergence from a seed.

embryo sac. The megagametophyte of flowering plants.

emulsification. The action of bile in breaking fats into small droplets.

endocarp. The inner layer of a fruit wall (pericarp).

endocrine glands. The glands that secrete hormones, generally into blood rather than into specific delivery tubes; e.g., pituitary, thyroid.

endocytosis. The process of bringing bulky objects (larger than individual molecules) into a cell.

endoderm. The inner germ layer of an early stage of the embryo.

endometrium. The vascular inner layer of the uterine wall.

endoplasmic reticulum. A system of cytoplasmic membranes closely associated with the nuclear membrane, plasma membrane, ribosomes, and Golgi apparatus.

endorphins. A class of naturally produced neuroactive compounds that act as an opiate in the brain.

endosperm. A food-storage tissue in seeds, located adjacent to the embryo.

endosperm nuclei. Two nuclei in the center of the embryo sac that fuse with a sperm to develop into a food-storage tissue called the endosperm.

endothermic. Referring to the condition of birds, mammals, and a few other animals in which body temperatures are primarily obtained and regulated by their own metabolic processes.

enzyme. An organic molecule (almost always a protein) that increases the rate of a cellular reaction without itself being used up in the process.

epicotyl. The bud of an embryonic seed plant, located above the cotyledon(s).

epinephrine. A hormone secreted by the medulla of the adrenal gland; also called adrenaline.

epiphyte. A nonparasitic plant that lives attached to another plant.

equational division. Meiosis II; the part of meiosis in which cells remain haploid throughout.

erythrocyte. A red blood cell.

estrogen. A hormone produced by the ovarian follicle and responsible for feminine characteristics.

ethology. The study of animal behavior.

ethylene. A plant-growth regulator whose functions include abscission of leaves and ripening of fruit.

eukaryotes. Organisms whose DNA is enclosed within a membrane-bound nucleus; also contain many other membrane-bound organelles, such as mitochondria and lysosomes.

eutrophic. Referring to a lake whose conditions promote a great deal of biological activity; opposite of oligotrophic.

evaporative cooling. A temperature-regulating device in which the evaporation of water from a body surface draws heat from an organism.

evolution. A change in the genetic composition (gene pool) of a population.

excretion. The discharge of metabolic waste.

exocarp. The outside layer of a fruit wall (pericarp)

exocrine gland. Tissues or organs that release products into tubes for delivery to specific places; e.g., salivary glands.

exon. In eukaryotes, a sequence of nucleotides in a gene that appears in mRNA and that codes for a polypeptide.

exponential growth curve. The graphical description of a population's growth when it is unchecked; population size repeatedly doubles.

extracellular digestion. Digestion of foods outside cells.

F

facilitated diffusion. Diffusion through a membrane that is enhanced by the presence of specific proteins in the membrane.

facultative anaerobe. An anaerobic organism that is also capable of using gaseous oxygen in respiration.

Fallopian tube. An oviduct in the human female.

fat. A class of lipids; each molecule is composed of glycerol and attached fatty acids.

fermentation. The process of converting the end products of glycolysis to other molecules in the absence of gaseous oxygen.

fertilization. The fusion of gametes.

fetus. As applied to humans, the developing organism from about 8 weeks until birth; has a definite human form.

fission. Asexual reproduction of unicellular organisms whereby the cell is divided into two cells of approximately equal size.

flagella. The whiplike projections used for locomotion by some motile cells; longer than cilia, but with similar internal microtubular arrangements.

food chain. A linear sequence of food relationships—from plant to herbivore to carnivore.

food web. An interrelationship, similar to a food chain but more complex, of producers, consumers, and decomposers.

fraternal twins. Twins derived from separate zygotes.

frond. A pinnately compound leaf as in ferns.

fructose. A six-carbon monosaccharide sugar.

fungus. A multicellular heterotrophic organism with cell walls and digesting food outside its body; a member of kingdom Fungi.

G

gametangium. A plant organ that produces gametes.

gamete. A sexual cell, a sperm or an egg.

gametophyte. A haploid gamete-producing plant.

ganglion. A clump of neuronic bodies.

gap junction. A specialized region of the plasma membrane connecting adjacent cells in animals; serves to pass ions and molecules.

gastrin. A gastric hormone that activates cells to produce gastric juice.

gastrovascular cavity. In cnidaria, a pouchlike cavity used for digestion and circulation.

gastrula. An early stage of the animal embryo consisting of three layers: ectoderm, mesoderm, and endoderm.

gastrulation. The infolding of one side of the blastula stage of an embryo to form the gastrula.

gene. The portion of a nucleic acid that encodes information on how to build a polypeptide or an RNA molecule; the basic unit of hereditary information.

gene pool. All of the genes in a free-breeding population.

gene therapy. A set of techniques for inserting normal genes into cells to correct genetic defects.

generative cell. A cell in a pollen grain that divides into two male gametes.

genetic drift. Changes in gene frequency in small populations that are due entirely to chance and not to mutations, selection, or migration.

genome. The complete set of genes possessed by an organism; sometimes synonymous with genotype.

genotype. The genetic composition of an individual.

genotypic ratio. The proportion of genotypes resulting from a specific cross.

genus. A group of closely related species: the first part of the binomial of an organism.

germ cells. Sexual cells or the cells from which they originate.

germination. The sprouting of a seed or pore.

germ layer. One of the three early layers of the embryo—ectoderm, mesoderm, and endoderm—from which certain tissues arise.

gestation. The prebirth period.

gibberellins. A group of substances that stimulate growth in plants.

gill. A specialized gas-exchange region of many aquatic animals.

gland. An organ or a group of cells that produce a secretion.

glomerulus. A bundle of capillaries from which many substances leave the circulatory system and enter the renal tubule.

glottis. The opening between the pharynx and larynx.

glucagon. A hormone produced by the pancreas and acting to increase the supply of glucose in blood.

glucose. A monosaccharide sugar; the most-used sugar for gaining energy by being broken down.

glycogen. A polysaccharide particularly characteristic of animals, consisting of many glucose molecules strung together.

glycolysis. The first phase of respiration, during which glucose is converted to pyruvic acid.

glycoprotein. A protein with an attached short chain of carbohydrates.

Golgi complex. A loose stack of platelike membranous structures in a cell; a center for producing vesicles.

gonad. A gamete-producing organ, testis, or ovary.

gradualism. A proposed mechanism for speciation in which small changes accumulate over time until the population is different enough to be considered a new species.

grana. Concentrations of "stacked" membranes in chloroplasts; chlorophyll is concentrated in them.

granulocytes. Types of white blood cells with distinctive cytoplasmic granules, produced in bone marrow.

guanine. A nitrogenous base of the purine type that is a constituent of some nucleotides.

guard cells. Pairs of cells that form the boundaries of stomata on leaves.

gymnosperm. A seed plant whose seeds are naked (not produced in a fruit).

H

habitat. The place where an individual or group of individuals lives.

haploid. Containing one set of chromosomes, as in gametes.

Hardy-Weinberg law. Mathematical predictions concerning the likelihood that a population's gene pool will change as generations pass; the conditions that must be considered are described.

Haversian canal. A small canal of bone tissue, containing a small artery and vein as well as a nerve supply and surrounded by several zones of bone cells.

hemoglobin. The iron-containing blood pigment that transports oxygen.

herbivore. An organism that ingests plant materials as food.

hermaphroditic. Producing both male and female reproductive cells in the same body; monoecious.

heterotroph. An organism that is not capable of manufacturing food and must obtain it from the environment; opposite of autotroph.

heterozygous. Having two different alleles at corresponding loci of homologous chromosomes.

heterosporous. Producing two kinds of spores, microspores and megaspores.

homeostasis. The ability of an organism to maintain a relatively constant and optimal internal environment despite changes in the external environment.

homeotic genes. A class of genes that control major events in embryonic development.

homologous. Similar because of common derivation from a common ancestor.

homozygous. Having identical alleles at corresponding loci of homologous chromosomes.

hormone. A secretion of some cells that produces profound stimulating effects, usually elsewhere in the organism.

humoral immune system. The portion of a vertebrate animal's immune system that involves the action of plasma cells in releasing antibody.

hyaline layer. Extracellular material that binds adjacent cells in a tissue or organ.

hybrid. The offspring of parents that differ in varying degrees; often the result of crossing of parents that belong to different species.

hydrogen acceptor. A chemical that combines with hydrogen during respiration (hydrogen transfer) and photosynthesis; e.g., NAD, FAD.

hydrogen bond. A weak electrostatic attraction between two atoms with small but opposite charges; the positive atom is hydrogen.

hydrolysis. A chemical reaction during which a molecule of water is split into its ionic components, H+ and OH−; occurs when complex food molecules are broken down into smaller units.

hypertonic solution. A solution whose concentration of solute is greater than that of another solution being compared to it.

hypha. The filament of a fungal plant.

hypocotyl. The stem of an embryonic plant, located below the cotyledon(s).

hypothalamus. A region of the brain, active in controlling several homeostatic activities such as temperature and osmotic regulation.

hypotonic solution. A solution whose concentration of solute is less than that of another solution being compared to it.

I

ileum. The last and longest part of the small intestine.

immunity. The state of being protected from the effects of a foreign material by the action of the humoral and/or cellular immune system(s).

imperfect flower. A flower possessing structures of one sex only.

imprinting. A type of learning, generally irreversible, that occurs at specific times in early life of an animal; a particular response is limited to one other animal or object.

inbreeding. Breeding to close kin.

incomplete flower. A flower with one or more kinds of floral parts missing.

independent assortment. The phenomenon in which genes are located on different chromosomes and

therefore move independently of each other during meiosis.

induced fit. A shape change in an enzyme's active site, initiated by interaction with the appropriate substrate; increases the binding between enzyme and substrate.

induction. Directing a gene or set of genes to undergo transcription (genetics); directing a cell or group of cells to begin differentiating in specific ways (embryology).

inferior ovary. In plants, an ovary partially or completely embedded in the receptacle.

inflorescence. The flowering part of a plant; the arrangement of flowers on a plant.

inner cell mass. The portion of an early mammalian embryo that becomes the body proper.

instinct. Relatively invariant behavior, genetically determined, in response to a specific stimulus.

insulin. A hormone produced by the pancreas; involved in carbohydrate metabolism.

intermediate filament. A thin, solid rod composed of proteins; supports animal cells internally.

interneuron. An association neuron.

interphase. The state of a cell when not dividing.

interstitial cells. Cells located among seminiferous tubules of the testis and secreting testosterone.

intracellular digestion. Digestion of foods within a cell.

intron. In eukaryotic cells, a sequence of nucleotides in a gene that is cleaved out of mRNA; it does not code for a polypeptide and is excised before translation begins.

ion. An atom or group of atoms that has lost or gained one or more electrons and thus is electrically charged.

islets of Langerhans. Patches of pancreatic cells that manufacture and release glucagon and insulin; the endocrine portions of the pancreas.

isogametes. Gametes that are visibly alike but sexually different.

isotonic solution. A solution whose concentration of solute is equal to that of another solution being compared to it.

isotope. A variant of an element that differs from other forms in having

a different number of neutrons in the nuclei of its atoms; e.g., carbon-14, phosphorus-32.

J

jejunum. The second part of the small intestine.

K

karyotype. A chart of chromosomes arranged as pairs according to size and centromere location.

kinetochore. The portion of a chromosome's centromere to which spindle fibers attach during cell reproduction.

Krebs cycle. A cyclic portion of aerobic respiration during which acetate is broken down and its hydrogens are released to yield their energy; also called citric acid cycle.

K-selected species. Species whose members use the reproductive strategy of producing offspring late in life; these offspring are few in number and well prepared to compete for resources.

L

lactase. The lactose-digesting enzyme.

lactic acid. A product of fermentation in most organisms.

lactose. Milk sugar, a disaccharide.

lacuna. A cavity in which a bone or cartilage cell is located.

larynx. The organ of voice in mammals, the modified upper part of the trachea.

learning. The modification of behavior due to memory of past experiences.

lentic. Referring to lakes.

lenticel. A patch of loosely arranged cells, in the corky layer of stems, through which gaseous exchange can occur.

leucocyte. A white blood cell.

leucoplast. A colorless plastid.

light-dependent reactions. The photosynthetic reactions for which light is required and in which ATP, NADPH, and molecular oxygen are produced.

light-independent reactions. The processes of photosynthesis that do not require light energy; carbon dioxide is reduced to form PGAL, which can then be used to make glucose; sometimes called dark reactions.

lignin. A complex organic constituent of the walls of sclerenchyma.

linkage. The association of genes in the same chromosome.

lipase. A fat-digesting enzyme.

lipids. A class of organic molecules that are insoluble in water; e.g., fats, waxes, steroids, oils.

littoral zone. A shallow zone around the margin of lakes where rooted plants grow; in oceans, between high and low tides.

long-day plant. A plant that flowers when exposed to short periods of darkness.

loop of Henle. The U-shaped portion of a nephron that makes possible the production of hypertonic urine.

lotic. Referring to streams.

lung. An internal pouched structure used for gas exchange by many terrestrial animals.

lymph. Constituents of blood that seep through capillary walls into tissue spaces and are eventually returned to veins by way of the lymphatic system.

lymph nodes. Enlarged areas along lymphatic veins where filtration of bacteria and other foreign objects can occur.

lymphatic system. A system of tubes that collects lymph and returns it to veins.

lymphocyte. A type of white blood cell that is very active in producing and regulating the immune response.

lysosome. Within a cell, a spherical membranous bag that contains digestive enzymes.

M

macroevolution. Evolution on a scale capable of producing new species or higher taxa.

macronucleus. A large nucleus in the protistan organism *Paramecium* and other ciliates, concerned with regulating day-to-day activities by producing RNA.

major histocompatibility genes. A group of genes that code for proteins particularly likely to mark transplanted tissue as foreign, thereby enabling the body to mount an immune response against it.

malignancy. A cancerous condition of a cell in which the rate of cell division outpaces that of cell death, leading to uncontrolled growth of tissue.

Malpighian tubules. The excretory tubules in insects.

maltase. The maltose-digesting enzyme.

maltose. Malt sugar, a disaccharide.

mammary gland. A milk-secreting gland.

mantle. A fold of tissue that secretes the shell of a mollusc.

marsupial. A nonplacental mammal that gives birth to offspring in a partially developed condition and places them in an abdominal pouch where they attach themselves to nipples and continue their development.

Mediterranean scrub-forest. See *chaparral*.

medulla. The inner part of some organs; the posterior part of the brain connected to the spinal cord.

medusa. A free-swimming form of a cnidarian; the jellyfish stage.

megagametophyte. The egg-producing phase of a plant life cycle.

megaspore. A large spore that grows into a female gametophytic plant.

meiosis. Reduction division; the production of haploid reproductive cells from diploid cells.

meiospore. A spore produced by meiosis.

melanin. A pigment located in the skin, hair, and retina of mammals; also present in many other animals.

memory cells. B cells and T cells that remain in the body after a primary immune response and are responsible for the secondary immune response.

meninges. The membranes around the brain and spinal cord.

meristem. A plant tissue consisting of unspecialized cells that are capable of active cell division.

mesocarp. The middle layer of a fruit wall (pericarp).

mesoderm. The middle germ layer of an early embryo.

mesoglea. A jellylike layer between the two cellular layers of cnidaria; the jelly of a jellyfish.

mesophyll. A tissue in leaves located between the two epidermal layers.

mesophyte. A plant living in an intermediate situation with respect to the available water supply.

Mesozoic. The era of geologic time known as the age of reptiles.

messenger RNA (mRNA). RNA that carries the encoded messages for polypeptides from DNA to the ribosomes.

metabolism. The chemical changes in cells commonly classified as energy-releasing processes.

metamorphosis. The phenomenon in which several distinctly different body stages occur between the embryo and adult forms.

metaphase. The stage of mitosis in which chromosomes are aligned at the equator of the spindle.

metastasis. The propensity for cancer cells to break away from a tumor and move to other parts of the body, producing secondary tumors.

metazoa. Multicellular animals.

microevolution. Evolution within a species.

microfilament. A threadlike fiber of actin, part of the cytoskeleton of a cell.

microgametophyte. The sperm-producing phase of a plant life cycle.

micronucleus. In the protistan organism *Paramecium* and other ciliates, a small nucleus containing genetic material that can be exchanged with that of another individual during conjugation.

micropyle. A pore in the ovule through which the pollen tube grows.

microspore. A small spore that grows into a male gametophytic plant.

microtubule. A hollow proteinaceous tube; part of the cytoskeleton, cilia and flagella, centrioles, and mitotic spindle.

middle lamella. The first layer of a cell wall deposited by the two daughter cells during cell division.

mitochondrion. A cellular organelle, the center of respiratory activity.

mitosis. Division of a cell to produce two new cells identical genetically to the parent cell.

Monera. A kingdom of single-celled organisms without nuclear membranes; including bacteria and archaebacteria in the five-kingdom scheme; divided into kingdoms Bacteria and Archaea in the six-kingdom scheme.

monocot (monocotyledon). A seed plant that is, in part, distinguished by embryos that have only one cotyledon.

monocyte. A large white blood cell that matures into a non-specific scavenger, the macrophage.

monoecious. Having both sexes in the same body.

monohybrid. A genetic cross involving one characteristic.

monosaccharide. The simplest kind of sugar; e.g., glucose, fructose.

monotremes. Mammals whose females lay eggs.

morphogenesis. The shaping of the body during development.

morula. An early embryonic stage consisting of a berry-shaped mass of cells.

motor neuron. A neuron leading to a responsive organ (effector).

Müllerian mimicry. The phenomenon of an obnoxious organism taking the shape and color of another species that is also obnoxious, thus benefiting both species.

muscle fiber. The functional unit of muscle; composed of many myofibrils bundled together by a common sarcolemma.

mutagen. Any agent that causes a mutation.

mutation. A sudden genetic change that may involve a single nucleotide or larger chromosomal regions, and that may be transmitted to future generations if occurring in a sex cell.

mutualism. A symbiotic relationship between two organisms whereby both members are benefited.

mycelium. The vegetative hyphae of a fungus.

mycorrhiza. The symbiotic association of fungal hyphae with plant roots.

myelin sheath. An insulative layer of living cells encompassing the axons of certain neurons; enhances the rate of nerve impulse propagation.

myofibril. A subunit of a muscle fiber consisting of many sarcomeres in tandem.

myofilaments. Proteinaceous structures within sarcomeres of muscle fiber; actin and myosin filaments.

myoneural junction. The region of synaptic connection between a motor neuron and a muscle fiber.

N

NAD. Nicotinamide adenine dinucleotide. A carrier of hydrogen and electrons during respiration.

NADP. Nicotinamide adenine dinucleotide phosphate. A carrier of hydrogen and electrons during photosynthesis.

natural selection. The process by which the environment eliminates organisms having characteristics unsuitable for survival and sustains those having suitable characteristics.

negative feedback. A self-regulating system in which the high concentration of a product inhibits the reactions that produce more of the product.

nematocyst. The harpoon-like stinging device in each cnidocyte of animals in phylum Cnidaria.

nephridium. A tubular excreting structure, as in earthworms.

nephron. An excreting unit of the kidney, consisting of a renal corpuscle and tubule.

nerve. A cord containing processes of neurons bound together with connective tissue.

neural tube. A hollow tube formed after vertebrate gastrulation; becomes the spinal cord.

neuron. A nerve cell.

neurotransmitter. Any of a number of molecules released into synapses and capable of either exciting or inhibiting neurons or effectors at the synapse.

niche. The position of status of an organism, within which it can maintain a viable existence; composed of geographical and biological surroundings of the organism.

nitrogen fixation. The combining of atmospheric nitrogen with other elements into forms that can be used by plants.

nitrogenous base. A nitrogen-containing purine or pyrimidine molecule that has basic chemical properties; part of a nucleotide.

nondisjunction. Failure of homologous chromosomes to separate during meiosis.

notochord. The dorsally-located, gristle-like supporting rod of Chordates; usually lost after the embryonic stage.

nucleic acids. DNA and RNA, composed of units called nucleotides and arranged in strands.

nucleolus. A spherical body seen in the cell nucleus during interphase; the site of ribosome subunit assembly.

nucleoplasm. The semiliquid material in a nucleus, in which chromosomes are suspended.

nucleoprotein. A complex composed of proteins in combinations with nucleic acids.

nucleotide. A unit of nucleic acids composed of a phosphate group, a pentose sugar, and a nitrogenous base.

nucleus. A membrane-bounded portion of the eukaryotic cell containing the genetic material (chromatin).

nymph. An intermediate developmental stage of some insects, resembling the adult but having disproportionate body parts.

O

obligate anaerobe. An anaerobic organism that cannot use gaseous oxygen in respiration.

oligotrophic. Referring to a lake whose conditions are not conducive to promoting much biological activity; opposite of eutrophic.

omnivore. An organism that is equipped to ingest both autotrophs and heterotrophs as its food.

oncogenes. A class of genes that control normal cell reproduction in embryos and can cause cancer when inappropriately operating after the embryonic period.

ontogeny. The course of development of individual organisms.

oogonium. A unicellular female gametangium; in animals, an ovarian cell capable of developing into the primary oocyte.

ootid. A cell resulting from the division of a secondary oocyte and maturing into a functional egg.

operon. A set of bacterial genes controlled by a single "on-off" switching mechanism, plus the DNA that constitutes the switch; a set of structural genes plus a promoter and an operator.

organ. A group of several tissues arranged to perform one or more functions efficiently.

organelle. A part of a cell having a specific function.

organic compound. A chemical compound that contains one or more carbon atoms.

osmoconformer. An organism that cannot osmoregulate; conforms to the salt concentration of its environment.

osmoregulator. An organism that can maintain an optimal internal concentration of salts, within a range of external salt concentrations.

osmosis. Passive movement (diffusion) of water through a semipermeable membrane.

ovary. In animals, the female gonad; in plants, the basal part of the pistil.

oviduct. A tube for conducting eggs.

oviparous. Egg-laying.

ovoviviparous. Producing eggs that are incubated and hatched within the female's body.

ovulation. The discharge of eggs from the follicles of the ovary.

ovule. An immature seed containing the embryo sac with egg.

oxidative phosphorylation. The process of converting ADP to ATP under aerobic conditions.

oxytocin. A hormone produced by the posterior lobe of the pituitary gland, causing contraction of smooth muscles of the uterus and breasts.

P

Paleozoic. An era of geologic time rich with marine life and during which arose the first vertebrates, land plants, amphibians, insects, reptiles, and conifers.

palisade mesophyll. Column-shaped cells beneath the upper epidermis of leaves.

palmate. Arranged around one point; e.g., leaflets of Virginia creeper.

parasite. An organism living in or on another living individual of a different species from which it obtains food, generally harming the host.

parasympathetic system. One of the two portions (with the sympathetic system) of the autonomic nervous system.

parathyroid hormone. A hormone produced by the parathyroid glands; regulates the metabolism of calcium and phosphorus.

parenchyma. A simple plant tissue composed of thin-walled cells.

parthenogenesis. Development of an egg without fertilization.

parturition. The action or process of giving birth.

pelagic. Referring to the open sea.

pentose sugar. A monosaccharide with five carbon atoms; a part of a nucleotide.

penis. The organ used to deposit semen during internal fertilization by animals; may also carry the urethra to the outside.

pepsin. A gastric enzyme that acts upon proteins.

peptide bond. The covalent link between two amino acids; the carboxyl end of one amino acid bonds to the amino end of the other amino acid.

pericarp. The wall of a fruit.

pericycle. The outer layer of a vascular cylinder, especially in roots.

peristalsis. The wavelike muscular contractions of a tubular organ, such as an intestine.

peroxisome. A vesicle containing the enzyme peroxidase.

petiole. The stalk of a leaf.

PGA (phosphoglyceric acid). A three-carbon compound regarded as the first organic compound synthesized from carbon dioxide and water during photosynthesis.

PGAL (glyceraldehyde-3-phosphate). A three-carbon compound regarded as the direct organic compound synthesized in the Calvin cycle of photosynthesis.

pH. The negative logarithm of the concentration of hydrogen ions in a solution; a measure of the acidity or basicity of the solution.

phage. See *bacteriophage*.

phagocytosis. The engulfment of particles by a cell.

pharynx. A part of the digestive tract of many animals; in humans, a passage common to the digestive and respiratory systems.

phenotype. The observable expression of the hereditary characteristics of an individual.

phenotypic ratio. The proportion of phenotypes resulting from a specific cross.

pheromone. An animal secretion that influences the behavior of other members of the same species.

phloem. Plant tissue that forms sieve tubes, which carry food from place to place.

phospholipid. A lipid resembling a fat except that a phosphate group (and additional atoms) has been substituted for one fatty acid; a major component of membranes.

photolysis. The splitting of water into hydrogen and oxygen during the first phase of photosynthesis.

photoperiodism. The physiological response of an organism to the duration of light and/or dark that it perceives.

photophosphorylation. A process that converts ADP to ATP, occurring in chloroplasts and dependent upon photosynthesis.

photosynthesis. The synthesis of simple food from carbon dioxide and water in which light is the source of energy.

phylum. A major category of classification in non-plant kingdoms, hierarchically located between the kingdom and the class.

pinnate. Arranged along a longitudinal axis.

pinocytosis. A cell's intake of fluid by forming a vesicle, or discharge by moving a vesicle to the cell membrane.

pistil. The female part of a flower, composed of one or more megasporophylls.

placenta. An organ of exchange between embryo (or fetus) and mother; in plants, the place where an ovule is attached to the ovary.

placentals. Mammals whose females nurture their embryos in the uterus by means of placentas.

plankton. Organisms, larvae or adults, that float or weakly swim at or near the surface of water.

plant. A multicellular autotrophic organism; a member of kingdom Plantae.

plasma. The fluid (noncellular) portion of blood.

plasma membrane. The outer limiting membrane of a cell; the cell membrane.

plasmid. A circular DNA molecule that exists independent of a bacterium's chromosome; used in genetic engineering as a vehicle for addition of foreign DNA.

plasmolysis. The shrinking of protoplasm due to loss of water.

plastid. A plant organelle usually containing pigments or stored food.

platelet. A cell fragment concerned with the clotting of blood.

polar bodies. Non-functional cells (containing little or no cytoplasm) produced along with functional eggs during meiosis in female animals.

pollen. The male gametophytes of seed plants.

pollination. The transfer of pollen to the carpel of a plant.

polymerase chain reaction (PCR). A technique for making many copies of DNA from one or a few initially available.

polymorphism. The occurrence of two or more morphological forms within a species.

polynucleotide. A polymer of nucleotides; e.g., DNA, RNA.

polyp. A form of cnidaria that is usually attached to the substratum.

polypeptide. A polymer consisting of several to many amino acids, linked by peptide bonds.

polyploidy. The condition of having more than two complete sets of chromosomes per cell, in exact multiples of the haploid number ($3n$, $4n$, etc.).

polysaccharide. Any compound carbohydrate that may be broken into molecules of monosaccharide sugars.

polyspermy. The successful fertilization of an egg by more than one sperm cell; causes polyploidy of the resulting zygote.

population. All individuals of a species or all members of the same species in a specific location.

prairie. A middle-latitude grassland; grasses are tall.

predation. A relationship in which an organism obtains food by killing and consuming other organisms.

primary oocyte. A diploid animal cell from which one egg and three polar bodies originate as a result of two consecutive divisions.

primary structure. The level of a protein's structure that involves the sequence of its amino acids.

primary tissues. Tissues produced by the apical meristems of plants.

primitive. Unspecialized; in an early stage of evolution.

producers. Organisms that can convert light energy to chemical form, by photosynthesis.

progesterone. A hormone secreted by the corpus luteum; the pregnancy-maintaining hormone.

prokaryotes. Organisms whose cells have no membrane-bound nuclei or other organelles such as mitochondria and plastids; bacteria.

promoter. A region of DNA that can be recognized by RNA polymerase in the initial steps of transcription.

pronucleus. A haploid nucleus of a gamete (egg or sperm) after fertilization but before fusion to make a single diploid nucleus in the zygote.

prophase. The earliest phase of mitosis, during which chromosomes develop to their shortest and thickest form.

prostate. An exocrine gland that produces seminal fluids.

protein. A large polypeptide, usually at least 50 amino acids in length; may consist of more than one polypeptide.

Proterozoic. An early era of geologic time represented in the fossil record by marine algae, sponges, and worms.

prothallus. The gametophyte of ferns and related plants.

Protista. A kingdom of unicellular eukaryotic organisms.

protonema. In mosses, a filamentous gametophytic structure arising from a spore and producing buds that grow into gametophytes.

protostome. An animal whose embryonic blastopore becomes a mouth, and whose anus is formed later.

pseudocoelom. A body cavity (other than the gut) not entirely lined by cells of mesodermal origin.

pseudopodium. A variable and temporary appendage extended from certain cells and used for locomotion or feeding.

punctuated equilibrium. A model in which evolution occurs by relatively sudden and large changes, rather than from a gradual accumulation of small changes.

Punnett square. A drawn grid whose blocks are used to record all possible gene combinations when the gametes of parents of known genotypes are combined.

purine. A nitrogenous base of nucleic acids, either adenine or guanine.

putrefaction. The decay of proteins, accompanied by the production of foul-smelling compounds.

pyrimidine. A nitrogenous base of nucleic acids, either cytosine, thymine, or uracil.

Q

quantitative inheritance. The form of inheritance in which a single phenotype is determined by the additive effects of two or more genes.

quaternary structure. The level of a protein's organization that involves the combination of two or more polypeptides.

R

radicle. The lower tip of an embryonic plant that grows into a primary root.

radiocarbon dating. A method of estimating the age of an object, such as a fossil, by measuring the amounts of certain radioactive elements in the sample.

recessive. Unexpressed; a term used to describe an allele whose phenotypic characteristic is concealed by the characteristic of a dominant allele.

recombinant DNA technology. Methods for the artificial placement of a gene into an organism that does not normally contain it.

recombination. Any action that causes new combinations of alleles to be located together in a gamete (and therefore in organisms of the next generation).

reductional division. Meiosis I; the portion of meiosis in which a cell goes from diploid to haploid.

reflex. An unconscious response to a stimulus.

reflex arc. The pathway of impulse transmission in a reflex.

regeneration. The growth of tissue to replace a lost portion in an adult organism.

relic. A species, once more widely dispersed, now surviving in an isolated place or places.

renin. A kidney hormone affecting blood pressure.

rennin. A secretion of the stomach that curdles milk.

replication. The reproduction of a DNA molecule to produce two exact copies.

reproductive isolation. Inability of members of two different species to reproduce successfully.

respiration. A metabolic process within cells that provides energy for cell activities.

respiratory quotient. The ratio of oxygen and carbon dioxide exchanged during respiration.

restriction enzymes. Enzymes of bacteria that cut foreign DNA (thus inactivating it) at specific base combinations; useful tools in recombinant DNA work and in characterizing DNA.

rhizoids. Rootlike structures of gametophytes, lacking conducting tissues.

rhizome. A horizontal underground stem.

ribose. A pentose sugar in RNA.

ribosome. An organelle found either free in the cytoplasm or attached to the endoplasmic reticulum; the site of protein synthesis.

RNA (ribonucleic acid). A polynucleotide whose five-carbon sugar is ribose; three types are transfer RNA, ribosomal RNA, and messenger RNA.

rookery. A breeding place for congregating birds (also seals).

root hair. An epidermal outgrowth from the absorption zone of roots, used for absorbing water and other substances.

r-selected species. Species whose members use the reproductive strategy of producing offspring early in life; the offspring are very large in number but rather poorly prepared to survive.

S

saprobe. An organism that extracts its food from dead bodies; a decomposer.

sarcolemma. The plasma membrane surrounding a muscle fiber.

sarcomere. A section of a muscle myofibril located between two Z lines.

sarcoplasmic reticulum. The endoplasmic reticulum in muscle cells; acts as a reservoir for the calcium that triggers contraction.

savanna. A tropical grassland.

sclerenchyma. A simple plant tissue composed of cells with thickened walls; e.g., fibers or stone cells.

secondary structure. The level of a protein's structure that involves helical or sheetlike formations.

secondary tissues. Tissues such as cork, phloem, and xylem that are produced by cambium.

secretins. Hormones produced in the duodenum that cause the liver and pancreas to secrete enzymes.

seed. A mature ovule of a seed plant containing an embryonic plant and sometimes a food-storage tissue called endosperm.

selection. The mechanism of evolutionary change suggested by Darwin; the fittest variants survive in competition for the limited amounts of necessities in the environment.

semiconservative replication. The method used by organisms to duplicate DNA, whereby exactly half of each resulting DNA molecule came from the previously existing DNA molecule.

seminiferous tubules. The tubules of the testis whose cells undergo meiosis to become sperm.

sensory neuron. A neuron that transmits a stimulus from a receptor toward the central nervous system.

sepal. A part of the outer whorl of most flowers.

sex chromosome. A chromosome containing genes that help determine sex; in humans, these are called X and Y.

short-day plant. A plant that flowers when exposed to long periods of darkness.

sieve tube. A conducting tube in phloem composed of a row of cells whose end walls are perforated by pores. Protoplasm is continuous throughout the tube.

simple fruit. A fruit derived from a single pistil of a single flower; e.g., a tomato.

somatic. Pertaining to the wall of the body as distinguished from viscera in cavities, or nonreproductive cells.

sorus. A cluster of sporangia on the leaves of ferns.

speciation. The process of forming a new species.

species. A particular kind of organism, designated by a binomial consisting of a generic and specific name; a group of natural populations of organisms that can successfully reproduce by sexual means.

spermatogonium. A testis cell that is the precursor of sperm cells.

sphincter. A band of muscles encircling an opening or passage and controlling the flow of materials through it.

spicules. Simple or branching needles of calcareous or silicious materials that provide support in sponges.

spinal ganglion. A concentration of sensory cell bodies in the dorsal root of the spinal nerve.

spindle. A biconical fibrous structure present in a dividing cell and functioning in the movement of chromosomes.

spindle fibers. A set of microtubules that forms the spindle of a reproducing cell.

spiracle. A pore opening to a trachea in insects and some other arthropods.

spirillum. A spiral-shaped bacterium.

sporangium. A spore container in plants.

spore. A reproductive plant cell not requiring fertilization; in life cycles, a haploid cell produced by the sporophyte.

spore mother cell. A diploid cell from which haploid spores are derived.

sporophyll. A spore-bearing leaf, sometimes considerably modified, as in the case of a stamen.

sporophyte. A spore-producing phase of a plant life cycle.

sporulation. The production of spores.

stamen. The male part of a flower; a microsporophyll.

steppe. A middle-latitude grassland; grasses are short.

steroid. A lipid with charactistic interlocking ring formations; e.g., cholesterol, estrogen.

stigma. The part of a carpel receptive to pollen.

stoma (pl., stomata). An epidermal pore in plants through which gases are exchanged with the environment.

suberin. The waterproofing substance in the walls of cork cells.

subspecies. A distinctly different subgroup within a species, with genetically determined characteristics that set it apart from another subgroup.

substrate. A chemical entity with which an enzyme can interact and that fits into the enzyme's active site.

succession. A series of replacements of communities of organisms due to their alteration of the environment, making it less suitable for themselves and more suitable for another community. The final community of the series, called the climax, is self-perpetuating and stable under normal conditions.

symbiosis. The living together of dissimilar organisms in a close relationship.

sympathetic system. One of the two portions (with the parasympathetic system) of the autonomic nervous system.

sympatric. An ecological term describing populations of related species that live in the same geographical area without interbreeding.

synapse. The gap between the axon of one neuron and the dendrite of another, or between a neuron and an effector.

synapsis. The pairing of homologous chromosomes during prophase I of meiosis.

syncytium. A multinucleate tissue; cells are confluent, not separated by cell membranes.

syrinx. The voice box of a bird, located at the base of the trachea.

T

tadpole. The larval stage of frogs and toads.

taiga. The boreal forest, a high-latitude coniferous forest.

taxis. The directional orientation of unattached animals or motile reproductive cells.

taxon. Any taxonomic category; e.g., class, family, species.

taxonomy. The branch of biology dealing with the classification of organisms.

T cell. One of two major types (with B cells) in an immune system; attacks foreign substances or cells by phagocytosis.

teleology. The practice of ascribing purposeful direction to natural processes; using end results to explain why phenomena occur.

telophase. The last phase of mitosis or meiosis, in which chromosomes reach the poles of the spindle and a new nucleus begins to form.

territoriality. The behavior, by some animals, of claiming and defending a specific geographical area.

tertiary structure. The level of a protein's structure that involves the specific three-dimensional twisting of the polypeptide(s).

testcross. The mating of an individual of the dominant phenotype with one of the homozygous recessive phenotype to determine whether the former is heterozygous or homozygous.

testosterone. A hormone responsible for masculine characteristics.

tetrad. An aggregation of four spores derived from one spore mother cell; also a group of four chromatids (of two homologous chromosomes) during meiotic synapsis.

tetrapod. An animal that uses four appendages for locomotion.

thallus. A simple plant body without conducting tissues.

thermocline. A layer in deep lakes, between the epilimnion and hypolimnion, in which temperature decreases about one degree Celsius for every increase of one meter in depth.

thorax. The chest.

threshold intensity. The minimum intensity of a stimulus required to start an impulse.

thylakoid. A flattened, saclike structure having membranes that contain chlorophyll and other pigments; when occurring in stacks within a chloroplast, thylakoids comprise the grana.

thymine. A nitrogenous base of the pyrimidine type that is a constituent of some nucleotides.

thyroxin. The hormone secreted by the thyroid gland; influences the speed of metabolism.

tissue. A group of cells that are morphologically and functionally similar.

totipotency. The ability of a single cell to have and to use all of the genetic information necessary to make a complete and normal organism.

tracheae. Conducting tubes; e.g., air passages to lungs, air tubes in insects, vessels in wood.

tracheophytes. Plants with conducting tissues; including ferns and seed plants; vascular plants.

transcription. The synthesis of messenger RNA from the DNA template.

transduction. The introduction of genes from one bacterium into another by an invading virus; the capacity of receptor cells to change stimuli into electrical impulses for transmission through neurons.

transfer RNA. Cytoplasmic RNA that holds specific amino acids and later carries them to messenger RNA aligned on the ribosomes.

transgenic organism. An organism that carries and expresses genes from other species.

translation. The production of a polypeptide under the direction of messenger RNA; occurs on ribosomes.

translocation. The movement of foods from one place to another in plants.

transpiration. The evaporation of water from the leaves of plants.

transposon (transposable element). A DNA portion that is capable of moving from one position on a chromosome to another position on the same chromosome or on a different chromosome.

transpirational pull. The movement of water through a plant against gravity, powered by transpiration at leaf surfaces.

transverse tubules. See *T tubules*.

triploblastic. Having three complete layers of embryonic cells: ectoderm, mesoderm, and endoderm.

trisaccharide. A compound sugar that can be broken into three monosaccharide molecules

trochophore. An early aquatic larval stage found in some brachiopods, bryozoans, nemerteans, flatworms, molluscs, and annelids.

trophoblast. The region of an early mammalian embryo that contributes to the making of the placenta and the amnion.

tropism. A directional growth response in plants

trypsin. A pancreatic enzyme that digests proteins

T tubules. A system of membranous tubes in muscle; carry action potentials from muscle fiber surface to the site of contraction; also called transverse tubules.

tube cell. A part of a pollen grain that grows to the vicinity of the egg.

tuber. The enlarged tip of a rhizome, e.g., Irish potato.

tundra. A frozen desert (where subsoil is permanently frozen).

typhiosole. The dorsal fold of the intestine of an earthworm; increases food absorption.

U

uracil. A nitrogenous base of the pyrimidine type that is a constituent of nucleotides in RNA.

urea. A nitrogenous compound produced by the liver and excreted by the kidneys; it is rather toxic and requires a considerable amount of water to flush it from the body.

ureter. The tube that conducts urine from the kidney to the urinary bladder.

urethra. The tube that conducts urine from the urinary bladder to the outside; in males, it is also a passage for semen.

uric acid. An insoluble nitrogenous compound excreted by the kidneys or comparable structures, especially eliminated by birds, terrestrial reptiles, and insects; in humans, overproduction or retention of uric acid can produce kidney stones and deposits in joints (gout).

urine. An aqueous fluid containing nitrogenous waste, made in the kidneys and excreted periodically.

uterus. The organ where the embryo or fetus develops; womb.

V

vacuole. A cytoplasmic cavity filled with water and other materials that are not part of the protoplasm.

valve. The half-shell of a bivalve mollusc such as a clam or oyster.

vascular. Containing or using a system of tubes; e.g., vascular plants.

vascular bundle. In plants, a strand of conducting and supporting tissues.

vas deferens. The tube that carries sperm from each testis to the urethra.

vasopressin. A posterior pituitary hormone that causes increased blood pressure and water retention; also called antidiuretic hormone.

ventral root. The lower branch of a spinal nerve that connects to the spinal cord; is the pathway of motor neurons.

ventricle. A compartment of the heart that pumps blood to the tissues.

venule. A small vein.

villus. A fingerlike projection from the inner wall of the small intestine that increases the surface area.

viroid. An infective particle consisting only of a piece of RNA.

virus. An infective organism (or, arguably, particle) composed of only nucleic acid surrounded by a protein capsule; able to reproduce only within a host's cell.

visceral reflex. An unconscious response in the eye, internal organs, or blood vessels; its pathway is in the autonomic nervous system.

vitamins. Organic molecules needed in small amounts by an organism, but not synthesized by that organism; usually act as coenzymes.

viviparous. Giving birth to living offspring.

W

water-vascular system. A unique system in echinoderms used especially for locomotion, circulation, and food-getting.

wood. The tough cellulose-containing secondary xylem of certain plants.

X

xanthophyll. A class of yellow pigments found in plastids of plants.

xerophyte. A plant adapted for survival where water is scarce; a water-conserving plant.

xylem. A complex plant tissue used for conducting water and dissolved inorganic substances and for support; the wood of plants.

Y

yolk. A material stored with an animal embryo and acting as food for the embryo; consists largely of protein and lipid.

yolk sac. A sac extending from the ventral surface of an animal embryo, often filled with food.

Z

zooplankton. Nonphotosynthetic marine organisms of kingdom Protista, living near the ocean surface.

zygospore. A cell resulting from fertilization that undergoes meiosis before germinating.

zygote. The cell resulting from the uniting of two gametes.

Notes

Notes

Notes

Notes

Notes

Notes